D1600777

DISCLAIMER

BOND'S TOP 100 FRANCHISES is based on data submitted by the franchisors themselves. Every effort has been made to obtain up-to-date and reliable information. As the information returned has not been independently verified, we assume no responsibility for errors or omissions and reserve the right to include or eliminate listings and otherwise edit and present the data at our discretion and based on our judgment as to what is useful to the readers of this directory. Inclusion in the publication does not imply endorsement by the editors or the publisher. Errors brought to the attention of the publisher and verified to the satisfaction of the publisher will be corrected in future editions. The publisher specifically disclaims all warranties, including the implied warranties of merchantability and fitness for a specific purpose.

This publication is designed to provide its readers with accurate and authoritative information with regard to the subject matter covered. It is sold with the understanding that neither the author nor the publisher is engaged in rendering legal, accounting or other professional services. If legal advice or other expert assistance is required, the services of a competent professional should be sought.

From a Declaration of Principles jointly adopted by a Committee of the American Bar Association and a Committee of Publishers.

Cover Design by Chris Buenaventura.

ISBN-10: 1-887137-76-9
ISBN-13: 978-1-887137-76-8
Printed in the United States of America.

10 9 8 7 6 5 4 3 2 1

BOND'S TOP 100 FRANCHISES is available at special discounts for bulk purchase. Special editions or book excerpts can also be created to specifications. For details, contact Source Book Publications, 1814 Franklin Street, Suite 603, Oakland, CA 94612. Phone: (800) 841-0873; (510) 839-5471; Fax: (510) 839-2104.

Dedication

After many years of picking what I thought were the top franchises, I thought it was about time that I acknowledged the top (i.e. truly exceptional) people I have had the great honor to work with over the past 20 years. In chronological order, they include:

Susan Moulton
Nikki Thompson
Alex Wedemeyer
Stephanie Woo
Kimberly Tsau
Annabelle Louie
Tina Tong
Jenny Huang
Joan Lee
Angie Hinh
Blair Cavagrotti
Katie Voronkova

Without their collective efforts and hard work, Source Book Publications and the World Franchising Network would never have flourished. I am deeply indebted to their many talents and their willingness to assume responsibility, take initiative, and work in an unstructured environment. Most importantly, however, I would like to thank them for being wonderful, thoughtful, and solid citizens in their own right. I have been exceptionally lucky indeed.

Preface

At its best, purchasing a franchise is a time-tested, paint-by-the-numbers method of starting a new business. Many of the myriad pitfalls normally encountered by someone starting a new business are avoided and the odds of success are vastly improved. Franchising represents an exceptional blend of operating independence with a proven system that includes a detailed blueprint for starting and managing the business, as well as the critical on-going support. However, purchasing a franchise is clearly not a fool-proof investment that somehow guarantees the investor financial independence.

At its worst, if the evaluation and investment decision is sloppy or haphazard, franchising can be a nightmare. If things don't work out, for whatever reason, you can't simply walk away. You are still responsible for the long-term lease on your retail space, the large bank loan that underwrote your entry into the business and/or the binding, long-term financial obligation to the franchisor. While it is easy to sell a profitable business, an unprofitable business will most likely result in a significant financial loss. If that loss is all equity, that might be an acceptable risk. If, however, you still have obligations to the bank, landlord and others, your hardship is greatly compounded. This says nothing about the inevitable stress on one's personal life, relationships and self-esteem.

Your ultimate success as a franchisee will be determined by two factors:

> 1. The homework you do at the front-end to ensure that you are selecting the optimal franchise for your particular needs, experience and financial resources.

> 2. Your commitment to work hard and play by the rules once you have signed a binding, long-term franchise agreement. For most new franchisees, this involves working 60+ hours per week until you can justify delegating some of the day-to-day responsibilities. It also requires being a team player — not acting as an entrepreneur

who does his or her own thing without regard for the system as a whole. A franchise system is only as good as the franchisees make it. This means following the script.

Another harsh reality, unfortunately, is that there is no such thing as the "Top 100 franchises." Similarly, there isn't a list of the "Top 10 colleges," the "Top 5 professional basketball players," or the "Top 3 sports cars." Like everything else in life, the beauty is in the eye of the beholder. Picking the optimal franchise is a good example. What appeals to me, even after exhaustive and, hopefully, well-thought-out research, may not appeal to you or be appropriate for you. Whereas I might be prepared to work 70-hour weeks for the first year my new business is open, you might not. Whereas I might be willing to invest $500,000 in a specific franchise concept, you might feel that the projected rewards do not outweigh the inherent risks. Whereas you might be exceptional at working with minimum wage personnel, I might be unable to communicate effectively with younger, less-educated staff. These are just a few examples of the literally hundreds of weighty considerations that you will have to consider and evaluate before deciding to invest in a specific franchise system.

In short, one prospective franchisee will clearly not have the same life experiences, talents, abilities, and financial wherewithal as the next. Therefore, it is critical that you take what we say only as a best effort on our part to go through literally hundreds of concepts before arriving at those which, we feel, best address our collective needs and experiences as professionals within the franchising industry.

My strong suggestion is that you take the time to carefully read the first two chapters of this book to better understand the industry and the variables you will have to consider in making a long-term investment decision. Even though you may already have a sense as to what type of franchise you want to purchase, maybe even a specific franchise, keep an open mind to the other options available to you. Request marketing information on all of the competing systems and rigorously evaluate each. Be sure to visit the various websites for each franchise. You may be pleasantly surprised to learn that one system offers a range of benefits that better complements your experience and capabilities. Also keep in mind that how successful you will be, in the final analysis, is up to you — not the franchisor.

Remember, this is not a game. I cannot overemphasize the fact that, in most cases, you will be making a once-in-a-lifetime investment decision.

It is incumbent on you to do it correctly at the outset. This can only be done by taking your time, properly researching all the options, realistically addressing both the "best case" and "worst case" scenarios, seeking the advice of friends and professionals, and, in general, doing the due diligence required. You want to invest in a system that will take advantage of your unique talents and experiences and not take advantage of you in the process! Don't take short-cuts. Listen carefully to what the franchisor and your advisors tell you. Don't think you are so clever or independent that you can't benefit from the advice of outside professionals. Don't assume that the franchisor's required guidelines regarding the amount of investment, experience, temperament, etc., somehow don't apply to you. Don't accept any promises or "understandings" from the franchisor that are not committed in writing in the franchise agreement. Invest the additional time to talk to and/or meet with as many franchisees in the system as you can. The additional front-end investment you make, both in time and money, will pay off handsomely if it saves you from making a marginal, or poor, investment decision. This is one of the few times in business when second chances are rare. Make the extra effort to do it right the first time.

Good luck, and Godspeed.

Rob Bond

Table of Contents

Introduction

Determining which franchises should be in the Top 100 (and, equally importantly, which ones should not) was a daunting task. It was difficult to choose only 100. Since franchises are so diverse, it was our intention to include at least one franchise from each industry category. Based on our comprehensive research, the 100 in this book are, in our opinion, among the best in the franchising industry.

The franchising industry is a large and sometimes confusing one. There are several industry categories, each with its own characteristics and subcategories. While we will try to provide you with as meaningful an overview as we can, it is your responsibility to aggressively research every aspect of any company you're interested in. Buy a franchise much like you would buy a house. Whereas you can always sell a house for roughly what you bought it for, you may not be so lucky liquidating a poorly-researched franchise investment. It's a big investment and it takes time.

Methodology

How did we arrive at our choices? There were several criteria that were taken into consideration. Primary among these were name recognition, product quality, litigation, total investment, on-going expenses, training programs, on-going support, and the exclusive territory awarded to new franchisees. Many of the criteria to take into consideration are personal choices. Is the franchise something you're interested in? Will you have the time and passion to manage it like you want to? These are questions that you'll have to answer for yourself. The information in this book will help you once you've decided what you want to do.

We chose both companies that have already established a strong brand name identity as well as those that are in the process of establishing a recognizable identity. ServiceMaster Clean, for example, is known the world over by millions of people. Conversely, companies like Spring-Green Lawn Care and More Space Place are less well-known now, but as their concepts become more and more popular, they will undoubtedly increase their name recognition in the near future.

Litigation was a silent factor in determining the Top 100 franchises. We don't have a litigation section in each profile, but while reviewing each franchisor's FDD/UFOC (Franchise Disclosure Document/Uniform Franchise Operating Circular — a required document containing 23 categories of information that must be provided by the franchisor to the prospective franchisee at the first face-to-face meeting or at least 14 days prior to the execution of the franchise agreement, whichever is sooner), we certainly took into account Item 3, which lists any relevant court cases, past and present, involving the company and tells us volumes about franchisor-franchisee relations. If a franchisor had no legal problems or a few court cases inconsequential to the reputation and operation of the company, then it was certainly a viable candidate for the Top 100.

The total investment is usually a significant determining factor in choosing a franchise. After all, money talks. Initially, investing in a franchise takes considerable patience. You are faced with numerous questions such as "Which items do I finance and which do I purchase?", "Are real estate costs included?", "Will the company help me with financing?", etc. We don't attempt to explore these questions in depth, but we do give you a brief overview of what you will be expected to invest. A Top 100 company may have a low total investment cost, financing assistance and a detailed account of what each item costs. We looked at all the franchisors and chose the ones which exemplified the best combination of these factors.

Before you open a franchise, one of the most critical steps is the initial training program, during which you will learn the basics about the franchise you choose. Training is usually held at the franchisor's headquarters and can last anywhere from five days to 12 weeks. The companies in this book all have strong, comprehensive training courses that include hours of both classroom and on-site training.

On-going expenses are made up of two fees: a royalty fee and an advertising fee. The royalty fee is a portion of your sales (usually four to eight percent) that you give to the franchisor in exchange for its expertise, on-going support and brand name. The advertising payment (three to five percent of sales) is also paid to the franchisor, and in return you receive advertising, marketing and promotional assistance. If these fees were within an acceptable range, then a company was a good candidate for the Top 100.

Most companies listed give exceptional on-going support to their franchisees: continual managerial aid, advertising assistance, access to the operations manual, etc. The basic tenet of franchising is, as Ray Kroc, the founder of McDonald's, said, "to be in business for yourself, not by yourself." Make sure the franchisor is going to support you over the long-term.

Another very important aspect of franchising that often gets overlooked is the franchisor's exclusive territory policy. An exclusive territory awarded by the franchisor describes the specific area or market in which you can operate your business. Why is this so important? By giving you an exclusive territory of, say, a three-mile radius surrounding your location, the franchisor is agreeing that it will not establish another location within that three-mile radius. So, logically, your business will have less competition. Most of the companies in the Top 100 have some sort of exclusive area policy.

All of these factors are important by themselves. Many companies exhibit some of them. But it's the rare few that combine the majority of these characteristics into one fluid franchising system. From those companies, we chose the Top 100.

Additional Factors to Consider

Three additional areas that clearly require serious examination before investing are 1) outstanding legal/litigation issues; 2) the current financial status of the franchisor; and 3) issues regarding renewal, termination, transfer, and dispute resolution. Because the first two areas can change on a daily basis, coupled with the fact that we lack the necessary expertise to comment authoritatively on either, we have intentionally left these important responsibilities to the investor.

If there is any reason to think that an outstanding legal issue may impact the company's ability to prosper or support the franchise system, you will most likely require the interpretation of a qualified and experienced franchise attorney. Prior to signing a franchise agreement, be confident that no new or potential litigation has come up since the publication of the FDD/UFOC. The franchisor is obligated to give you an accurate status report.

Similarly, the franchisor's financial health is critical to your own success. How to determine that health? Each franchisor is required to include detailed financial statements in its FDD/UFOC. Depending upon the date of the FDD/UFOC, the information may be very current.

Most likely, however, it will be outdated by 6 – 12 months. If this is the case, request current financials from the franchisor. If the company is publicly traded, there are numerous sources of detailed information. Go to the firm's website. If you don't have the expertise to judge the financial information, seek the advice of an accountant or financial consultant. As all of the companies included in the Top 100 have in excess of 50 operating units, they most likely are enjoying a positive cash flow from operations and, therefore, are in a much stronger financial position than smaller franchisors. However, this is not an excuse to avoid an investigation.

Item 17 of the FDD/UFOC covers "Renewal, Termination, Transfer and Dispute Resolution." These are critical areas that should be fully understood before you find out that, after you have developed a profitable business, the franchisor has the unilateral right to terminate your franchise or capriciously deny a sale to a qualified buyer. Don't get blind-sided because you were too lazy or frugal to get a legal interpretation. Again, this is the province of a qualified attorney.

The Food-Service Industry

The franchising industry contains over 3,500 different concepts. Food-service constitutes roughly one-third of the entire industry -- by far the largest. Within the food-service industry, there are several different themes: bakery/coffee, fast-food or quick-service, ice cream, sit-down, subs and sandwiches and other miscellaneous categories. Frequently, concepts are further subdivided. For example, in the fast-food industry, there are various different segments such as pizza, hamburger, chicken, Asian, seafood and Mexican, to name a few. What does all of this mean? Simply that food-service is a large, dominant and sometimes confusing industry that has to be fully researched before settling in on a specific franchise concept.

The following table lists the 19 food-service franchises featured in Chapter 3.

Company Name	Franchise Fee	Total Investment	Royalty	Total Units
Applebee's International	$35,000	$1.7 – $3.1 million	4%	1,168
Arby's	$37,500	$336,500 – $2.47 million	4%	3,704
Auntie Anne's Hand-Rolled Soft Pretzels	$30,000	$198,000 – $444,000	7%	951
Big Apple Bagels	$25,000	$254,300 – $379,600	5%	104
Church's Chicken	$25,000	$154,300 – $833,100	5%	1,691
Cousins Subs	$25,000	$101,700 – $295,800	6%	149
Denny's	$40,000	$1.178 – $2.4 million	4%	1,680
El Pollo Loco	$40,000	$502,000 – $1.1 million	4%	306
Famous Famiglia Pizzeria	$35,000	$250,000 – $550,000	6%	95
Great Wraps	$22,500	$225,000 – $350,000	5.5%	99
Little Caesars	$15,000 – $20,000	$193,000 – $619,500	6%	undis-closed
Manhattan Bagel Company	$25,000	$482,000 – $848,000	5%	69
Maui Wowi Hawaiian Coffees & Smoothies	$29,500 – $59,500	$65,000 – $395,000	0%	501

Company Name	Franchise Fee	Total Investment	Royalty	Total Units
Papa Murphy's Take 'N' Bake Pizza	$25,000	$180,000 – $275,000	5%	1,301
Rita's Italian Ice	$35,000	$199,400 – $378,400	6.5%	551
Schlotzsky's Deli	$30,000	$473,600 – $715,300	6%	358
Sonic Drive-In Restaurants	$45,000	$1,100 – $3,046	1 – 5%	3,555
Tasti D-Lite	$30,000	$240,000 – $425,000	5%	52
Togo's Eatery	$25,000/ $40,000	$257,000 – $417,000	5%	246

The Lodging Industry

Although this group represents less than five percent of the 3,500 different franchisors, lodging franchises are by far the most capital intensive. Only well-financed groups should consider investing in the lodging industry.

The following table lists the 3 lodging franchises featured in Chapter 4.

Company Name	Franchise Fee	Total Investment	Royalty	Total Units
Comfort Inn (Choice)	$10,000 – $60,000	$2.3 million – $14.6 million	4.25 – 5.65%	6,035
Hilton	$85,000	$53.4 million – $90.1 million	5%	524
InterContinental Hotels Group	$50,000	$2 million – $20 million	5%	4,520

The Retail Industry

Of the 3,500 different franchise concepts, over 400 are retail franchises. There are several different types of retail companies: specialty retailers, clothing, athletic wear, art supplies, convenience stores, home improvement, pet products, photographic products and electronics/computer products. Like the food-service and service-based franchises, the retail industry is large and needs to be fully researched before settling in on a specific franchise concept.

The following table lists the 9 retail franchises featured in Chapter 5.

Company Name	Franchise Fee	Total Investment	Royalty	Total Units
7-Eleven	Varies	Varies	Gross Profit Split	40,068
Fast-Fix Jewelry & Watch Repairs	$40,000	$188,800 – $381,800	6%	166
Floor Coverings International	$16,000	$150,000	5% / $325	72
Foot Solutions	$32,500 / $29,500	$225,000 – $250,000	5%	194
Merkinstock	$20,000	$150,000	5%	59
Miracle-Ear	$20,000	$127,500 – $450,000	$48.80	1,339
More Space Place	$22,000 – $29,500	$133,000 – $203,000	4.5%	42
RadioShack	$39,900	$150,000 – $350,000	7%	7,260
Wild Birds Unlimited	$18,000	$99,000 – $157,000	4%	275

The Service-Based Industry

Service-based franchises make up the remaining chunk of the franchising industry. There are several different types of service-based companies: automotive services, child development, real estate, travel, etc. The industry is large and needs to be fully researched before settling in on a specific franchise concept.

The following table lists the 69 service-based franchises featured in Chapter 6.

Company Name	Franchise Fee	Total Investment	Royalty	Total Units
AAMCO	$39,500	$232,000 – $299,000	7.5%	898
AdviCoach – A Division Business Advisors International	$45,000	$67,000 – $77,000	5 – 15%	70
Always Best Care Senior Services	$39,500	$50,700 – $150,000	6%	175
Anytime Fitness	$20,000	$44,000 – $300,000	0%	1,846
Bonus Building Care	$7,500	$9,000 – $41,900	22% Support Fee	1,315
BrightStar	$47,500	$95,000 – $162,000	5%	232
Caring Transitions	$27,900	$38,300 – $66,600	6% or $300	77
CMIT Solutions	$49,500	$124,000 – $150,000	5%	130
Coldwell Banker Real Estate – Realogy	$25,000	$37,300 – $502,000	6%	3,378

Company Name	Franchise Fee	Total Investment	Royalty	Total Units
Color Glo International	$25,000	$44,500 – $50,000	4% or $300	123
ComForcare	$39,500	$105,000 – $155,000	3 – 5%	161
Comfort Keepers	$42,000	$61,400 – $88,500	5/4/3%	712
Compound Profit	$34,000	$50,000 – $100,000	8%	71
Coverall Health-Based Cleaning System	$9,100 – $30,600	$12,600 – $37,100	5%	9,265
CruiseOne	$9,800	$7,800 – $9,800	3%	624
Decor&You	$25,000	$54,000 – $62,000	10%	70
Entrepreneur's Source, The	$45,000	$67,000 – $77,000	5 – 15%	215
ERA Franchise Systems – Realogy	$25,000	$47,000 – $210,000	NR	6,588
Estrella Insurance	$25,000	$50,000 – $80,000	1 – 1.5%	52
Express Employment Professionals	$35,000	$95,500 – $134,500	8 – 9%	565
Express Oil Change	$35,000	$950,000 – $1.6 million	5%	185
Fantastic Sams	$25,000 – $40,000	$115,000 – $228,600	Fixed Fee	1,218
FASTSIGNS	$34,500	$169,700	6%	529

Company Name	Franchise Fee	Total Investment	Royalty	Total Units
Fibrenew International	$67,000	$82,000 – $105,000	$550	198
Fiesta Auto Insurance and Tax Service	$10,000	$35,000 – $55,000	10 – 25%	153
Furniture Medic	$29,900	$51,000 – $66,000	7% / $250 min	361
Goddard School, The	$135,000	$550,000	7%	371
Granite Transformations	$25,000 – $75,000	$131,500 – $346,000	2%	170
Great Clips	$20,000	$109,400 – $202,500	6%	2,801
Griswold Home Care	$39,500	$75,000 – $95,000	3 – 5%	164
Growth Coach, The	$36,900	$47,200 – $76,400	Varies	134
Hometeam Inspection Service, The	$27,900 – $39,800	$40,000 – $80,000	6%	201
Huntington Learning Center	$24,000	$162,000 – $258,000	9% / $1,800 min	279
i9 Sports	$28,400 – $39,900	$44,900 – $69,900	7.5%	142

Company Name	Franchise Fee	Total Investment	Royalty	Total Units
Interface Financial Group, The	$39,000	$88,300 – $139,300	8%	192
Jani-King International	$8,000 – $33,000	$8,000 – $74,000	10%	13,022
Jan-Pro Cleaning Systems	$1,000 – $30,000	$125,000 – $1.5 million	10%	10,092
Kiddie Academy	$20,000	$351,700 – $620,000	7%	98
Kinderdance	$12,000 – $40,000	$15,000 – $46,000	6 – 15%	127
Kumon North America	$1,000, $1,000	$67,800 – $145,300	$32-36 / subj / month	25,199
Learning Express	$35,000	$199,500 – $345,000	5%	145
Liberty Tax Service	$40,000	$56,800 – $69,900	Varies	3,828
Liquid Capital of America	$50,000	$150,000 – $10 million	8%	62
Little Gym, The	$39,500 – $69,500	$147,500 – $294,000	8%	220
Maaco Collision Repair and Auto Painting	$40,000	$297,000	9%	458
Maids, The	$10,000 + $.95 per QHH	$93,545 – $121,295	3.9 – 6.9%	1,120

Company Name	Franchise Fee	Total Investment	Royalty	Total Units
Meineke Car Care Centers	$30,000	$149,000 – $416,000	9%	944
Mighty Distributing System of America	$5,000 + $.035Vcl	$150,000 – $250,000	5%	107
Mosquito Squad	$22,500	$30,000 – $60,000	$400 – $1,900	97
NaturaLawn Of America	$29,500	$108,000 – $155,000	7 – 9%	68
Padgett Business Services	$38,000 + $18,000 Training	$106,000	4.5 – 9%	400
Pop-A-Lock	$29,000 + $66 / 1,000 of population	$100,000 – $350,000	6%	182
Postal Annex+	$29,950	$138,800 – $200,100	5%	335
Postal Connections of America	$21,000	$115,900 – $152,900	4%	83
PostNet	$30,000	$172,000 – $198,000	5%	900
Pridestaff	$12,500	$80,400 – $126,900	65% Gross Margin	32
Pronto Auto Insurance	$20,000	$60,000 – $100,000	3%	131

Company Name	Franchise Fee	Total Investment	Royalty	Total Units
Re-Bath	$16,000 – $80,000	$62,000 – $344,000	Average $15	231
ServiceMaster Clean	$24,900 – $65,000	$41,000 – $104,700	4 – 10%	4,450
SERVPRO	$42,000	$132,050 – $180,450	3 – 10%	1,571
ShelfGenie	$45,000	$80,000 – $128,000	4%	128
Snap-on Tools	$7,500 – $15,000	$17,900 – $289,000	$102	4,766
Spherion Staffing Services	$25,000	$98,000 – $164,000	3 – 6% / 25%	397
Sport Clips	$25,000 – $49,500	$153,000 – $277,000	NR	841
Spring-Green	$30,000	$99,000 – $212,000	8 – 10%	116
TGA – Premier Junior Golf	$5,000 – $40,000	$13,000 – $57,000	8%	49
Tradebank International	$35,000 – $50,000	$10,000 – $50,000	30 – 40%	73
TSS Photography	$11,100 – $39,050	$30,250 – $75,150	0	214
Vanguard Cleaning Systems	$7,000 – $35,000	$7,500 – $35,000	5%	2,152

In closing, I'd like to emphasize that the 100 companies included in this book are here as the result of many months of intensive research and independent evaluation. We did not draw names out of a hat. We did not necessarily choose the industry "heavyweights." We did, however, pore over countless FDDs/UFOCs, confer with many franchise directors and staff members, visit actual operating units, and view numerous websites. In addition to studying each company's FDD/UFOC and marketing materials, we took full advantage of recent articles about each company we evaluated. We sought the opinion of friends, industry experts and existing franchisees. As we do not allow advertising in any of our publications, we do not have a built-in bias toward any of the companies selected. Nor do we have any financial or other hidden agendas.

It is our hope that, as a potential franchisee, you will benefit from these efforts. In designing the format, we decided the best way to present the information would be to ask the same questions you would: "How much?", "Why are they better than their competitors?", and "What do I get out of it?" These questions and more are answered as we present what we feel are among the 100 best franchises.

30-Minute Overview 1

In presenting this data, we have made some unilateral assumptions about our readers. The first is that you purchased the book because of the depth and accuracy of the data provided — not as a how-to manual. Clearly, dedication to hard work, adequate financing, commitment, good business sense and access to trusted professional counsel will determine your ultimate success as a franchisee. A strong working knowledge of the industry, however, will help ensure that you have made the best choice of franchise opportunities. I advise you to acquaint yourself with the dynamics of the industry before you initiate the evaluation and negotiation phases of selecting a franchise.

The second assumption is that you have already devoted the time necessary to conduct a detailed personal inventory. This self-assessment should result in a clear understanding of your skills, aptitudes, weaknesses, long-term personal goals, commitment to succeed and financial capabilities.

ຂຕ

There are three primary stages to the franchise selection process: 1) the investigation stage, 2) the evaluation stage and 3) the negotiation stage. This book is intended primarily to assist the reader in the investigation stage by providing a thorough list of the options available. Chapters One and Two include various observations based on our 20 or so years of involvement with the franchising industry. Hopefully, they will provide some insights that you will find of value.

Understand at the outset that the entire process will take many months and involve a great deal of frustration. I suggest that you set up a realistic timeline for signing a franchise agreement and that you stick with that

23

schedule. There will be a lot of pressure on you to prematurely complete the selection and negotiation phases. Resist that temptation. The penalties are too severe for a seat-of-the-pants attitude. A decision of this magnitude clearly deserves your full attention. Do your homework!

Before starting the selection process, you would be well advised to briefly review the areas that follow.

Franchise Industry Structure

The franchising industry is made up of two distinct types of franchises. The first, and by far the larger, encompasses product and trade name franchising. Automotive and truck dealers, soft drink bottlers and gasoline service stations are included in this group. For the most part, these are essentially distributorships.

The second group encompasses business format franchisors. This book only includes information on this latter category.

Layman's Definition of Franchising

Business format franchising is a method of market expansion by which one business entity expands the distribution of its products and/ or services through independent, third-party operators. Franchising occurs when the operator of a concept or system (the **franchisor**) grants an independent businessperson (the **franchisee**) the right to duplicate its entire business format at a particular location and for a specified time period, under terms and conditions set forth in a contract **(the franchise agreement)**. The franchisee has full access to all of the trademarks, logos, marketing techniques, controls and systems that have made the franchisor successful. In effect, the franchisee acts as a surrogate for a company-owned store in the distribution of the franchisor's goods and/or services. It is important to keep in mind that the franchisor and the franchisee are separate legal entities.

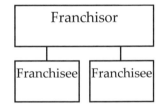

Classic Business Format Model

In return for a front-end **franchise fee** — which usually ranges from $15,000 to 35,000 — the franchisor is obligated to "set up" the franchisee in business. This generally includes assistance in selecting a location, negotiating a lease, obtaining financing, building and equipping a site and providing the necessary training, operating manuals, etc. Once the training is completed and the store is open, the new franchisee should have a carbon copy of other units in the system and enjoy the same benefits they do, whether they are company-owned or not.

Business format franchising is unique because it is a long-term relationship characterized by an on-going, mutually beneficial partnership. On-going services include research and development, marketing strategies, advertising campaigns, group buying, periodic field visits, training updates and whatever else is required to make the franchisee competitive and profitable. In effect, the franchisor acts as the franchisee's "back office" support organization. To reimburse the franchisor for this support, the franchisee pays the franchisor an on-going **royalty fee**, generally four to eight percent of gross sales or income. In many cases, franchisees also contribute an **advertising fee** to reimburse the franchisor for expenses incurred in maintaining a national or regional advertising campaign.

For the maximum advantage, both the franchisor and the franchisees should share common objectives and goals. Both parties must accept the premise that their fortunes are mutually intertwined and that they are each better off working in a co-operative effort, rather than toward any self-serving goals. Unlike the parent/child relationship that has dominated franchising over much of the past 30 years, franchising is now becoming a true and productive relationship of partners.

Legal Definition of Franchising

The Federal Trade Commission (FTC) has its own definition of franchising. So do each of the 15 states that have separate franchise registration statutes. The State of California's definition, which is the model for the FTC's definition, follows:

> *Franchise means a contract or agreement, express or implied, whether oral or written, between two or more persons by which:*

> *A franchisee is granted the right to engage in the business of offering, selling, or distributing goods or services under a marketing plan or system prescribed in substantial part by a franchisor;*

The operation of the franchisee's business pursuant to that plan or system as substantially associated with the franchisor's trademark, service mark, trade name, logotype, advertising, or other commercial symbol designating the franchisor or its affiliates; and

The franchisee is required to pay, directly or indirectly, a franchise fee.

Multi-Level Franchising

With franchisors continually exploring new ways to expand their distribution, the classic business format model shown above has evolved over the years. Modifications have allowed franchisors to grow more rapidly and at less cost than might have otherwise been possible.

If a franchisor wishes to expand at a faster rate than its financial resources or staff levels allow, it might choose to sell development rights in an area (state, national or international) and let the new entity do the development work. No matter which development method is chosen, the franchisee should still receive the same benefits and support provided under the standard model. The major difference is that the entity providing the training and on-going support and receiving the franchise and royalty fees changes.

Three variations of the master franchising model include: 1) master (or regional) franchising, 2) sub-franchising and 3) area development franchising.

In **master (or regional) franchising**, the franchisor sells the development rights in a particular market to a master franchisee who, in turn, sells individual franchises within the territory. In return for a front-end master franchise fee, the master franchisee has sole responsibility for developing that area under a mutually agreed upon schedule. This includes attracting, screening, signing and training all new franchisees within the ter-

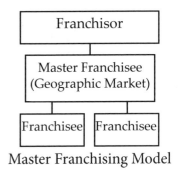

Master Franchising Model

ritory. Once established, on-going support is generally provided by the parent franchisor.

The master franchisee is rewarded by sharing in the franchise fees and the on-going royalties paid to the parent franchisor by the franchisees within the territory.

Sub-franchising is similar to master franchising in that the franchisor grants development rights in a specified territory to a sub-franchisor. After the agreement is signed, however, the parent franchisor has no on-going involvement with the individual franchisees in the territory. Instead, the sub-franchisor becomes the focal point. All fees and royalties are paid directly to the sub-franchisor, who is solely responsible for all recruiting, training and on-going support. An agreed upon percentage of all incoming fees and royalties is passed on to the parent franchisor.

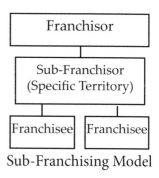

Sub-Franchising Model

In a sub-franchising relationship, the potential franchisee has to be doubly careful in his or her investigation. He or she must first make sure that the sub-franchisor has the necessary financial, managerial and marketing skills to make the program work. Secondarily, the potential franchisee has to feel comfortable that the parent franchisor can be relied upon to come to his or her rescue if the sub-franchisor should fail.

The third variation is an **area development agreement**. Here again, the franchisor grants exclusive development rights for a particular geographic area to an area development investment group. Within its territory, the area developer may either develop individual franchise units for its own account or find independent franchisees to develop units. In

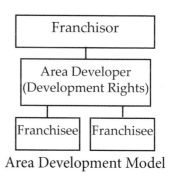

Area Development Model

the latter case, the area developer has a residual equity position in the profits of its "area franchisees."

In return for the rights to an exclusive territory, the area developer pays the franchisor a front-end development fee and commits to develop a certain number of units within a specified time period. (The front-end fee is generally significantly less than the sum of the individual unit fees.) Individual franchisees within the territory pay all contractual franchise, royalty and advertising fees directly to the parent franchisor. The area developer shares in neither the franchise fee nor in on-going royalty or advertising fees. Instead, the area developer shares only in the profitability of the individual franchises that it "owns." In essence, the area developer is buying multiple locations over time at a discount, since the franchise fee and (frequently) the royalty fee are less than the per unit rate.

Franchising's Role in the Economy

The IFA's Educational Foundation recently released *Volume 2* of the *Economic Impact of Franchised Businesses*. This report, which was prepared by PricewaterhouseCoopers for the IFA's Educational Foundation, documents the important role the franchising industry continues to play in the U.S. economy.

In 2005, more than 900,000 franchised establishments generated over $880 billion of direct economic output, or over 4.4 percent of the private sector economy in the United States. The franchising industry provided jobs for more than 11 million American workers, or just over 8 percent of all U.S. private sector employment. Including the additional economic activity that occurs outside of franchised businesses because of franchising activities, the overall economic contribution of franchised businesses was $2.3 trillion in 2005, or 11 percent of the U.S. economy.

These economic activities provided more than 20 million jobs for American workers, over 15 percent of all U.S. private sector employment. From 2001 to 2005, the franchising sector of the economy grew at a faster pace than many other sectors of the economy. Franchising now provides more jobs than many other sectors of the U.S. economy. For example, franchising provides more jobs than the durable goods manufacturing sector or the financial activities sector of the economy. The franchising sector expanded by over 18 percent from 2001 to 2005, adding more than 140,000 new establishments and creating more than 1.2 million new jobs. Direct economic output increased by more than 40 percent from 2001 to 2005, from $624.6 billion to $880.9 billion. Including the impact of additional economic activity that occurs outside of franchised businesses because of franchising activities, the franchising industry added nearly 3 million jobs and over $780 billion of economic output to the U.S. economy. Much more detailed information can be found in the full 600-plus page report, published on the IFA website at www.franchise.org.

The Players

Franchisors

After extensive research, we have selected 100 of what we think are among the best franchises the industry has to offer.

Selecting the most appropriate franchisor for your needs is crucial to becoming a successful franchisee. By providing general information, in addition to a detailed analysis of each company's identity, financial requirements, training, support and territory offering, we hope to aid the prospective franchisee in making the right choice.

The Regulatory Agencies

The offer and sale of franchises are regulated at both the federal and state levels. Federal requirements cover all 50 states. In addition, certain states have adopted their own requirements.

In 1979, after many years of debate, the Federal Trade Commission (FTC) implemented Rule 436. The Rule requires that franchisors provide prospective franchisees with a disclosure statement (called an offering circular) containing specific information about a company's franchise offering. The Rule has two objectives: to ensure that the potential franchisee has sufficient background information to make an educated investment decision and to provide him or her with adequate time to do so.

The Franchise Rule was substantially updated (and improved) on July 1, 2008 as the FTC tried to make the disclosure document more consistent with various state regulations. Among other things, the Uniform Franchise Offering Circular (UFOC) became the Franchise Disclosure Document (FDD) and Item 19 of the new FDD morphed from an Earnings Claims Statement to a Financial Performance Representation. Overall the revisions were positive and resulted in considerably more and better information being available to the prospective franchisee. Unfortunately, the revisions did not *require* all franchisors to provide a Financial Performance Representation from which potential franchisees could better determine the overall profitability of their potential investments.

Certain "registration states" require additional safeguards to protect potential franchisees. Their requirements are generally more stringent than the FTC's requirements. These states include California, Florida, Illinois, Indiana, Maryland, Michigan, Minnesota, New York, North Dakota, Oregon, Rhode Island, South Dakota, Virginia, Washington and Wisconsin. Separate registration is also required in the provinces of Alberta, Ontario and Prince Edward Island, Canada.

The regulations require that the franchisor provide a prospective franchisee with the required information at their first face-to-face meeting or at least 14 days prior to the signing of the franchise agreement, whichever is earlier. Required information includes:

1. The franchisor and any predecessors.
2. Identity and business experience of persons affiliated with the franchisor.
3. Litigation.
4. Bankruptcy.
5. Franchisee's initial fee or other payments.
6. Other fees.
7. Franchisee's estimated initial investment.
8. Obligations of franchisee to purchase or lease from designated sources
9. Obligations of franchisee to purchase or lease in accordance with specifications or from approved suppliers.
10. Financing arrangements.
11. Obligations of franchisor; other supervision, assistance or services.
12. Exclusive area or territory.
13. Trademarks, service marks, trade names, logotypes and commercial symbols.
14. Patents and copyrights
15. Obligations of the participant in the actual operation of the franchise business.
16. Restrictions on goods and services offered by franchisee.

17.   Renewal, termination, repurchase, modification and assignment of the franchise agreement and related information.
18.   Arrangements with public figures
19.   Actual, average, projected or forecasted franchise sales, profits or earnings.
20.   Information regarding franchises of the franchisor.
21.   Financial statements.
22.   Contracts.
23.   Acknowledgement of receipt by respective franchisee.

If you live in a registration state, make sure that the franchisor you are evaluating is, in fact, registered to sell franchises there. If not, and the franchisor has no near-term plans to register in your state, you should consider other options.

Keep in mind that neither the FTC nor any of the states has reviewed the FDD/UFOC to determine whether the information submitted is true or not. They merely require that the franchisor make representations based upon a prescribed format. If the information provided is false, franchisors are subject to civil penalties. However, this may not help a franchisee who cannot undo a very expensive mistake.

It is up to you to read thoroughly and fully understand all elements of the FDD/UFOC. There is no question that it is tedious reading. Know exactly what you can expect from the franchisor and what your own obligations are. Ask yourself: under what circumstances can the relationship be unilaterally terminated by the franchisor? What is your protected territory? Specifically, what front-end assistance will the franchisor provide? You should have a professional review the FDD/UFOC. It would be a shame not to take full advantage of the documentation that is available to you.

The Trade Associations

The **International Franchise Association** (IFA) was established as a non-profit trade association to promote franchising as a responsible method of doing business. The IFA currently represents over 1,200 franchisors in the U.S. and around the world. It is recognized as the leading spokesperson for responsible franchising. For most of its 50+ years, the IFA has represented the interests of franchisors only. In recent years, however, it has initiated an aggressive campaign to recruit franchisees into its membership and represent their interests as well. The IFA's address is 1501 K Street, NW, Suite

350, Washington, DC 20005. TEL (202) 628-8000; FAX (202) 628-0812, www. Franchise.org.

The **Canadian Franchise Association** (CFA), which has some 250+ members, is the Canadian equivalent of the IFA. Information on the CFA can be obtained from its offices at 5399 Eglinton Avenue W, Suite 116, Toronto, ON M9C 5K6 Canada. TEL (416) 695-2896; (800) 665-4232; FAX (416) 695-1950, www. CFA.ca.

The **American Association of Franchisees and Dealers** (AAFD) represents the rights and interests of franchisees and independent dealers. Formed in 1992 with the mission of "Bringing Fairness to Franchising," the AAFD represents thousands of franchised businesses, representing over 250 different franchise systems. It provides a broad range of services designed to help franchisees build market power, create legislative support, provide legal and financial support and provide a wide range of general member benefits. P.O. Box 81887, San Diego, CA 92138. TEL (619) 209-3775; FAX: (619) 209-3777, www.AAFD.org.

Additional Resources

During your due diligence effort, there are several other sources of information that are invaluable.

1. www.BlueMauMau.com – the industry's premier community of franchise research, news, blogs and management insights. This website is the most open-ended site for in-depth information about franchising in general and individual franchise systems in particular. Through both in-house investigative reporting and third-party blogs, the site provides an excellent snapshot of the industry at any point in time.

2. www.WorldFranchising.com – the industry's pre-eminent source of current, up-to-date and detailed information about individual franchises. The site has detailed profiles on over 900 individual franchises and over 100 suppliers. Updates on the franchisor profiles in this book can be found on the site.

3. www.UFOCs.com – the site provides access to both historical UFOCs and current FDDs and has over 10,000 current and archived FDDs/ UFOCs in inventory. In addition to industry packages of historical Item 19s, the site also provides individual Item 19s for the majority of companies that produce them. To the extent that you wish to streamline

the investigative process, it might make sense to purchase a company's FDD well before you spend a great deal of time researching a franchisor. Having access to a company's litigation history and information about their financial strength before you make a significant time commitment could save you many hours of effort.

4. www.FRANdata.com – unquestionably the leader in third-party research on the franchising industry. Their president, Darrell Johnson, is the most widely-quoted independent spokesman for the industry.

5. www.Franchise.org – the website for the International Franchising Association and the voice of the industry in representing the interests of franchising to the public.

An invaluable gauge on historical franchisee success has to do with how various franchise systems have performed in connection with SBA (Small Business Administration) loans. Although the report is not made available to the general public, one can nevertheless gain access to the report through www.BlueMauMau.com. The report is called the SBA Failure Rates by Franchise Brand and can be found at http://www.bluemaumau. org/sba_loan_failure_rates_franchise_brand_2011.

The report lists all the franchise systems that have received SBA 7(a) and 504 loans between 10/1/2001 and 9/30/2010. It lists the number of loans that were disbursed to that franchisor, the total dollar amount of the loans, the percentage failure rate (number of loans in liquidation or charged off divided by the number of loans disbursed) and, most importantly, the percentage rate that the SBA had to charge off as bad debt (dollar amount charged off divided by the dollar amount disbursed). You can download the report and sort it both alphabetically and by the amount of the charge off percentage. If a company has an above-average charge off percentage, that should certainly raise some red flags. What is not shown, however, is what has happened during the eight-year period. If the franchisor can demonstrate to your satisfaction that the problems occurred years ago and are no longer relevant, that is a good sign. If the franchisor avoids the question, that may well mean that the poor franchisee problems are still prevalent.

Franchise Survival/Failure Rate

In order to promote the industry's attractiveness, most literature on franchising includes the same often-quoted, but very misleading, statistics that leave the impression that franchising is a near risk-free investment.

In the 1970s, the Small Business Administration produced a poorly documented report that 38% of all small businesses fail within their first year of operation and 77% fail within their first five years. With franchising, however, comparative failure rates miraculously drop to only three percent after the first year and eight percent after five years. No effort was made to define failure. Instead, "success" was defined as an operating unit still in business under the same name at the same location.

While most people would agree that the failure rates for franchised businesses are substantially lower than those of independent businesses, this assumption is not substantiated by reliable statistics. Part of the problem is definitional. Part is the fact that the industry has a vested interest in perpetuating the myth rather than debunking it.

FRANdata, the industry's pre-eminent research firm, conducted a review several years ago of franchise terminations and renewals It found that 4.4% of all franchisees left their franchise system each year for a variety of reasons, excluding sales to third parties (to be fully meaningful, the data should include sales to third parties and the reasons behind a sale).

The critical issue is to properly define failure and success, and then require franchisors to report changes in ownership based on these universally accepted definitions. A logical starting point in defining success should be whether the franchisee can "make an honest living" as a franchisee. A "success" would occur when the franchisee prefers to continue as a franchisee rather than sell the business. A "failure" would occur when the franchisee is forced to sell his or her business at a loss.

A reasonable measure of franchise success would be to ask franchisees "would you do it again?" If a legitimate survey were conducted of all franchisees of all systems, my guess is that the answer to this question would indicate a "success rate" well under 70% after a five-year period. Alternatively, one could ask the question "has the franchise investment met your expectations?" I estimate that fewer than 50% would say "yes" after a five-year period. These are just educated guesses.

The failure rate is unquestionably lower for larger, more mature compa-nies in the industry that have proven their systems and carefully chosen their franchisees. It is substantially higher for smaller, newer companies that have unproven products and are less demanding in whom they accept as a franchisee.

As it now stands, the Franchise Disclosure Document (FDD) only requires the franchisor to provide the potential franchisee with the names of owners who have left the system within the past 12 months. In my opinion, this is a severe shortcoming of the regulatory process. Unless required, franchi-sors will not willingly provide information about failures to prospective franchisees. There is no question in my mind, however, that franchisors are fully aware of when and why past failures have occurred.

It is patently unfair that a potential investor should not have access to this critical information. To ensure its availability, I propose that the FDD/UFOC be amended to require that franchisors provide franchisee turn-over information for the most recent five-year period. Underlying reasons for a change in ownership would be provided by a departing franchisee on a universal, industry-approved questionnaire filled out during an "exit" interview. The questionnaire would then be returned to some central clear-ing house.

The only way to make up for this lack of information is to aggressively seek out as many previous and current franchisees as possible. Request past FDDs/UFOCs to get the names of previous owners, and then contact them. Whether successful or not, these owners are an invaluable resource. Try to determine the reason for their failure and/or disenchantment. Most failures are the result of poor management or inadequate finances on the part of the departing franchisee. But people do give up franchises for other reasons.

Current franchisees are even better sources of meaningful information. For systems with under 25 units, I strongly encourage you to contact all fran-chisees. For those having between 25 and 100 units, I recommend talking to at least half. For all others, interview a minimum of 50.

What Makes a Winning Franchise

Virtually every writer on the subject of franchising has his or her own idea of what determines a winning franchise. I maintain that there are five primary factors:

1. A product or service with a clear advantage over the competition. The advantage may be in brand recognition, a unique, proprietary product or 30 years of proven experience.

2. A standardized franchise system that has been time-tested. Look for a company in which most of the bugs in the system have been worked out through the cumulative experience of both company-owned and franchised units. By the time a system has 30 or more operating units, it should be thoroughly tested.

3. Exceptional franchisee support. This includes not only the initial training program, but the on-going support (research and development, refresher training, [800] help-lines, field representatives and on-site training, annual meetings, advertising and promotion, central purchasing, etc.).

4. The financial wherewithal and management experience to carry out any announced growth plans without short-changing its franchisees. Sufficient depth of management is often lacking in high-growth franchises.

5. A strong mutuality of interest between a franchisor and its franchisees. Unless both parties realize that their relationship is one of long-term partners, it is unlikely that the system will ever achieve its full potential. Whether they have the necessary rapport is easily determined by a few telephone calls to existing franchisees.

Financial Projections

The single most important factor in buying a franchise — or any business for that matter — is having a realistic projection of sales, expenses and profits. Specifically, how much can you expect to make after working 65 hours a week for 52 weeks a year? No one is in a better position to supply accurate information (subject to caveats) about a franchise opportunity than the franchisor itself. A potential franchisee often does not have the experience to sit down and project what his or her sales and profits will be over the next five years. This is especially true if he or she has no applied experience in that particular field.

Financial performance representations/earnings claims statements (Item 19 of the FDD/UFOC) present franchisor-supplied sales, expense and/or profit summaries based on actual operating results for company-owned and/or franchised units. Since no format is prescribed, however, the data may be cursory or detailed. The only constraint is that the franchisor must be able to substantiate the data presented. Further complicating the process is the fact that providing an financial performance representation/earnings claims statement is strictly optional. Accordingly, only around 18-22% of franchisors provide one.

Virtually everyone agrees that the information included in a financial performance representation/earnings claim statement can be exceedingly helpful to a potential franchisee. Unfortunately, there are many reasons why franchisors might not willingly choose to make their actual results available to the public. Many franchisors feel that a prospective investor would be turned off if he or she had access to actual operating results. Others may not want to go to the trouble and expense of collecting the data.

Some franchisors are legitimately afraid of being sued for "misrepresentation." There is considerable risk to a franchisor if a published financial performance representation/earnings claim statement is interpreted in any way as a "guarantee" of sales or income for new units. Given today's highly litigious society, and the propensity of courts to award large settlements to the underdog, it's not surprising that so few franchisors provide this information.

As an assist to prospective franchisees, Source Book Publications has recently published the ninth edition of *"How Much Can I Make?"* It includes 87 financial performance representations/earnings claims statements covering a diverse group of industries. It is the only publication that contains current earnings claim statements submitted by the franchisors. Given the scarcity of industry projections, this is an invaluable resource for potential franchisees and investors in determining what he or she might make by investing in a franchise or similar business. The book is $34.95, plus $8.50 shipping. See the inside rear cover of this book for additional details on *"How Much Can I Make?"* and the companies included. The book can be obtained from Source Book Publications, 1814 Franklin Street, Suite 603, Oakland, CA 94612, by calling (800) 841-0873 or (510) 839-5471, faxing a request to (510) 839-2104, or visiting our online bookstore at www.source-bookpublications.com.

New vs. Used

As a potential franchisee, you have the option of becoming a franchisee in a new facility at a new location or purchasing an existing franchise. This is not an easy decision. Your success in making this choice will depend upon your business acumen and your insight into people.

Purchasing a new franchise unit will mean that everything is current, clean and under warranty. Purchasing an existing franchise may involve a smaller investment and allow greater financial leverage. However, you will have to assess the seller's reason for selling. Is the business not performing to expectations because of poor management, poor location, poor support from the franchisor, an indifferent staff, obsolete equipment and/or facilities, etc.? The decision is further clouded because you may be working through a business broker who may or may not be giving you good information. Regardless of the obstacles, considering a "used" franchise merits your consideration. Apply the same analytical tools you would to a new franchise. Do your homework. Be thorough. Be unrelenting.

The Negotiation Process

Once you have narrowed your options down to your top two or three choices, you must negotiate the best deal you can with the franchisor. In most cases, the franchisor will tell you that the franchise agreement cannot be changed. Do not accept this explanation. Notwithstanding the legal requirement that all of a franchisor's agreements be substantially the same at any point in time, there are usually a number of variables in the equation. If the franchisor truly wants you as a franchisee, it may be willing to make concessions not available to the next applicant.

Will the franchisor take a short-term note for all or part of the franchise fee? Can you expand from your initial unit after you have proven yourself? If so, can the franchise fee be eliminated or reduced on a second unit? Can you get a right of first refusal on adjacent territories? Can the term of the agreement be extended from ten to fifteen years? Can you include a franchise cancellation right if the training and/or initial support don't meet your expectations or the franchisor's promises? The list goes on ad infinitum.

To successfully negotiate, you must have a thorough knowledge of the industry, the franchise agreement you are negotiating (and agreements of competitive franchise opportunities) and access to experienced professional advice. This can be a lawyer, an accountant or a franchise consultant. Above all else, they should have proven experience in negotiating franchise agreements. Franchising is a unique method of doing business. Don't pay someone $300+ per hour to learn the industry. Make them demonstrate that they have been through the process several times before. Negotiating a long-term agreement of this type is extremely tricky and fraught with pitfalls. The risks are extremely high. Don't be so smug as to think that you can handle the negotiations yourself. Don't be so frugal as to think you can't afford outside counsel. In point of fact, you can't afford not to employ an experienced professional advisor.

The Four Rs of Franchising

We are told as children that the three Rs of reading, 'riting, and 'rithmetic are critical to our scholastic success. Success in franchising depends on four Rs — realism, research, reserves and resolve.

Realism

At the outset of your investigation, it is important that you be realistic about your strengths and weaknesses, your goals and your capabilities. I strongly recommend that you take the time necessary to do a personal audit — possibly with the help of outside professionals — before investing your life's savings in a franchise.

Franchising is not a money machine. It involves hard work, dedication, set-backs and long hours. Be realistic about the nature of the business you are buying. What traits will ultimately determine your success? Do you possess them? If it is a service-oriented business, will you be able to keep smiling when you know the client is a fool? If it is a fast-food business, will you be able to properly manage a minimum-wage staff? How well will you handle the uncertainties that will inevitably arise? Can you make day-to-day decisions based on imperfect information? Can you count on the support of loved ones after you have gone through all of your working capital reserves, and the future looks cloudy and uncertain?

Be equally realistic about your franchise selection process. Have you thoroughly evaluated all of the alternatives? Have you talked with everyone

39

you can to ensure that you have left no stone unturned? Have you carefully and realistically assessed the advantages and disadvantages of the system offered, the unique demographics of your territory, near-term market trends, the financial projections, etc.? The selection process can be tiring. It is easy to convince yourself that the franchise opportunity in your hand is really the best one for you. The penalties for doing so, however, are extreme.

Research

There is no substitute for exhaustive research!

It is up to you to spend the time required to come up with an optimal selection. At a minimum, you will probably be in that business for five years. More likely, you will be in it ten years or more. Given the long-term commitment, allow yourself the necessary time to ensure you don't regret having made a hasty decision. Research can be a tedious, boring process. But doing it carefully and thoroughly can greatly reduce your risk and exposure. The benefits are considerable.

Based on personal experience, you may feel you already know the best franchise. Step back. Assume there is a competing franchise out there with a comparable product or service, comparable management, etc., that charges a royalty fee two percent of sales less than your intuitive choice. Over a ten-year period, that could add up to a great deal of money. It certainly justifies your requesting initial information.

A thorough analysis of the literature you receive should allow you to reduce the list of prime candidates down to six to eight companies. Aggressively evaluate each firm. Talking with current and former franchisees is the single best source of information you can get. When possible, site visits are invaluable. My experience is that franchisees tend to be candid in their level of satisfaction with the franchisor. However, since they don't know you, they may be less upfront about their sales, expenses and income. Go to the library and review studies that forecast industry growth, market saturation, industry problems, technical break-throughs, etc. Don't find out a year after becoming a franchisee of a coffee company that earlier reports suggested that the coffee market was over-saturated or that coffee was linked to some form of terminal disease.

Reserves

As a new business, franchising is replete with uncertainty, uneven cash flows and unforeseen problems. It is an imperfect world that might not bear any relation to the clean pro formas you prepared to justify getting into the business. Any one of these unforeseen contingencies could cause a severe drain on your cash reserves. At the same time, you will have fixed and/or contractual payments that must be met on a current basis regardless of sales: rent, employee salaries, insurance, etc. Adequate back-up reserves may be in the form of savings, commitments from relatives, bank loans, etc. Just make certain that the funds are available when, and if, you need them. To be absolutely safe, I suggest you double the level of reserves recommended by the franchisor.

Keep in mind that the most common cause of business failure is inadequate working capital. Plan properly so you don't become a statistic.

Resolve

Let's assume for the time being that you have demonstrated exceptional levels of realism, research and reserves. You have picked an optimal franchise that takes full advantage of your strengths. You are in business and bringing in enough money to achieve a positive cash flow. The future looks bright. Now the fourth R — resolve — comes into play. Remember why you chose franchising in the first place: to take full advantage of a system that has been time-tested in the marketplace. Remember what makes franchising work so well: the franchisor and franchisees maximize their respective success by working within the system for the common good. Invariably, two obstacles arise-

The first is the physical pain associated with writing that monthly royalty check. Annual sales of $250,000 and a six percent royalty fee result in a monthly royalty check of $1,250 that must be sent to the franchisor. Every month. As a franchisee, you may look for any justification to reduce this sizable monthly outflow. Resist the temptation. Accept the fact that royalty fees are simply another cost of doing business in the franchising industry. They are also a legal obligation that you willingly agreed to pay when you signed the franchise agreement. Look at them as the dues you agreed to pay when you joined the club.

Although there may be an incentive, don't look for loopholes in the contract that might allow you to sue the franchisor or get out of the relationship. Don't report lower sales than actual in an effort to reduce royalties. If you have received the support that you were promised, continue to play by the rules. Honor your commitment. Let the franchisor enjoy the rewards it has earned as a result of your success.

The second obstacle is the desire to change the system. You need to honor your commitment to be a "franchisee" and to live within the franchise system. What makes franchising successful as far as your customers are concerned is uniformity and consistency of appearance, product/service quality and corporate image. The most damaging thing an individual franchisee can do is to suddenly and unilaterally introduce changes to the proven system. While these modifications may work in one market, they also serve to diminish the value of the system as a whole. Imagine what would happen to the national perception of your franchise if every franchisee had the latitude to make unilateral changes in his or her operations. Accordingly, any ideas you have on improving the system should be submitted directly to the franchisor for evaluation. Accept the franchisor's decision on whether or not to pursue an idea.

If you suspect that you may be a closet entrepreneur, prone to unrestrained experimenting and tinkering, you are probably not cut out to be a franchisee. Seriously consider this before you get into such a relationship, instead of waiting until you are locked into an untenable situation.

Summary

I hope that I have been clear in suggesting that the selection of an optimal franchise is both time- and energy-consuming. If done properly, the process may take six to nine months and involve the expenditure of several thousand dollars. The difference between a hasty, gut-feel investigation and an exhaustive, well-thought out investigation may mean the difference between finding a poorly-conceived, or even fraudulent, franchise and an exceptional one.

My sense is that there is a strong correlation between the effort you put into the investigative process and the ultimate degree of success you enjoy as a franchisee. The process is to investigate, evaluate and negotiate. Don't try to bypass any one of these critical elements.

How to Use the Data 2

The data at the beginning of each company profile is the result of a 42-point questionnaire that we send out annually to the franchising community. This information is intended as a brief overview of the company; the text that follows provides a more in-depth analysis of the company's requirements and advantages.

In some cases, an answer has been abbreviated to conserve room and to make the profiles more directly comparable. All of the data is displayed with the objective of providing as much background data as possible. In cases where no answer was provided to a particular question, an "NR" is used to signify "No Response."

Please take 20 minutes to acquaint yourself with the composition of the sample questionnaire data. Supplementary comments have been added where some interpretation of the franchisor's response is required.

๛

FASTSIGNS has been selected to illustrate how this book uses the collected data.

 More than fast. More than signs.™	Email: mark.jameson@fastsigns.com Website: www.franchise.fastsigns.com Mark Jameson, Senior Vice President Franchise Support & Development
2542 Highlander Way Carrollton, TX 75006 Tel: 800-827-7446; (214) 346-5679 Fax: (866) 422-4927	Signage has never been more important. Right now, businesses are looking for new and better ways to compete. Industries are revamping to meet compliance standards. And advertisers are expanding their reach into new media, like digital signage, QR codes

and mobile websites. Join the franchise that's leading the next generation of business communication. Now more than ever, businesses look to FASTSIGNS® for innovative ways to connect with customers in a highly competitive marketplace. Our high standards for quality and customer service have made FAST-SIGNS the most recognized brand in the industry, driving significantly more traffic to the Web than any other sign company. We also lead in these important areas: #1 Sign Franchise in Entrepreneur magazine Franchise 500, 2011; Franchise Business Review Best in Category 2006-2010; World Class Franchisee Satisfaction Recognition, 2011 Franchise Research Institute; Franchisees' Choice Designation, 2011 Canadian Franchise Association. FASTSIGNS is one of only a handful of franchises approved for the Franchise America Finance Program, with 6 million dollars in financing for approved franchise owners.

BACKGROUND: IFA MEMBER
Established: 1985; 1st Franchised: 1986
Franchised Units: 529
Company-Owned Units 0
Total Units: 529
Dist.: US-451; CAN-22; O'seas-56
North America: 45 States,6 Provinces
Density: 58 in TX, 45 in CA, 35 in FL
Projected New Units (12 Months): 25
Qualifications: 5, 5, 1, 3, 4, 5

FINANCIAL/TERMS:
Cash Investment: $75K
Total Investment: $169.7K
Minimum Net Worth: $250K
Fees: Franchise — $34.5K
Royalty — 6%; Ad. — 2%
Earnings Claim Statement: Yes
Term of Contract (Years): 20/10
Avg. # Of Employees: 2-3 FT, 0 PT
Passive Ownership: Allowed
Encourage Conversions: Yes
Area Develop. Agreements: Yes, for 2 years
Sub-Franchising Contracts: No
Expand In Territory: Yes
Space Needs: 1,200-1,500 SF

SUPPORT & TRAINING:
Financial Assistance Provided: Yes (I)
Site Selection Assistance: Yes
Lease Negotiation Assistance: Yes
Co-Operative Advertising: No
Franchisee Assoc./Member: Yes/Member
Size Of Corporate Staff: 100+
On-Going Support: NA,NA,C,D,E,NA,G,H,I
Training: 2 Weeks in Dallas, TX;
1 Week On-Site

SPECIFIC EXPANSION PLANS:
US: All United States
Canada: All Except Quebec
Overseas: UK, New Zealand, and Australia

Address/Contact

1. Company name, address, telephone and fax numbers.

Comment: All of the data published in this book were current at the time the completed questionnaire was received or upon subsequent verification by phone. Over the period between annual publications, 10–15% of the addresses and/or telephone numbers become obsolete for various reasons. If you are unable to contact a franchisor at the address/telephone number listed, please call Source Book Publications at (510) 839-5471 or fax us at (510) 839-2104 and we will provide you with the current address and/or telephone number.

2. **(800) 827-7446 (214) 346-5679.** In many cases, you may find that you cannot

access the (800) number from your area. Do not conclude that the company has gone out of business. Simply call the local number.

Comment: An (800) number serves two important functions. The first is to provide an efficient, no-cost way for potential franchisees to contact the franchisor. Making the prospective franchisee foot the bill artificially limits the number of people who might otherwise make the initial contact. The second function is to demonstrate to existing franchisees that the franchisor is doing everything it can to efficiently respond to problems in the field as they occur. Many companies have a restricted (800) line for their franchisees that the general public cannot access. Since you will undoubtedly be talking with the franchisor's staff on a periodic basis, determine whether an (800) line is available to franchisees.

3. **Contact.** You should honor the wishes of the franchisor and address all initial correspondence to the contact listed. It would be counter-productive to try to reach the president directly if the designated contact is the director of franchising.

Comment: The president is the designated contact in many of the company profiles in this book. The reason for this varies among franchisors. The president is the best spokesperson for his or her operation, and no doubt it flatters the franchisee to talk directly with the president, or perhaps there is no one else around. Regardless of the justification, it is important to determine if the operation is a one-man show in which the president does everything or if the president merely feels that having an open line to potential franchisees is the best way for him or her to sense the "pulse" of the company and the market. Convinced that the president can only do so many things effectively, I would want assurances that, by taking all incoming calls, he or she is not neglecting the day-to-day responsibilities of managing the business.

Description of Business

4. **Description of Business:** The questionnaire provides franchisors with adequate room to differentiate their franchise from the competition. In a minor number of cases, some editing was required for length.

Comment: In instances where franchisors show no initiative or imagination in describing their operations, you must decide whether this is

45

symptomatic of the company or simply a reflection on the individual who responded to the questionnaire.

Background

5. **IFA.** There are two primary affinity groups associated with the franchising industry — the International Franchise Association (IFA) and the Canadian Franchise Association (CFA). Both the IFA and the CFA are described in Chapter One.

6. **Established: 1985.** FASTSIGNS was founded in 1985, and, accordingly, has 27 years of experience in its primary business. It should be intuitively obvious that a firm that has been in existence for over 27 years has a greater likelihood of being around five years from now than a firm that was founded only last year.

7. **1st Franchised: 1986.** 1986 was the year that FASTSIGNS' first franchised unit(s) were established.

Comment: Over ten years of continuous operation, both as an operator and as a franchisor, is compelling evidence that a firm has staying power. The number of years a franchisor has been in business is one of the key variables to consider in choosing a franchise. This is not to say that a new franchise should not receive your full attention. Every company has to start from scratch. Ultimately, a prospective franchisee has to be convinced that the franchise has 1) been in operation long enough, or 2) its key management personnel have adequate industry experience to have worked out the bugs normally associated with a new business. In most cases, this experience can only be gained through on-the-job training. Don't be the guinea pig that provides the franchisor with the experience it needs to develop a smoothly running operation.

8. **Franchised Units: 529.** As of 4/1/12, FASTSIGNS had 529 franchisee-owned and operated units.

9. **Company-Owned Units: 0.** As of 4/1/12, FASTSIGNS had no company-owned or operated units.

Comment: A younger franchise should prove that its concept has worked successfully in several company-owned units before it markets its "system" to an inexperienced franchisee. Without company-owned prototype stores, the new franchisee may well end up being the "testing kitchen" for the franchise concept itself.

If a franchise concept is truly exceptional, why doesn't the franchisor commit some of its resources to take advantage of the investment opportunity? Clearly, a financial decision on the part of the franchisor, the absence of company-owned units should not be a negative in and of itself. This is especially true of proven franchises, which may have previously sold their company-owned operations to franchisees.

Try to determine if there is a noticeable trend in the percentage of company-owned units. If the franchisor is buying back units from franchisees, it may be doing so to preclude litigation. Some firms also "churn" their operating units with some regularity. If the sales pitch is compelling, but the follow-through is not competitive, a franchisor may sell a unit to a new franchisee, wait for him or her to fail, buy it back for $0.60 cents on the dollar, and then sell that same unit to the next unsuspecting franchisee. Each time the unit is resold, the franchisor collects a franchise fee, plus the negotiated discount from the previous franchisee.

Alternatively, an increasing or high percentage of company-owned units may well mean the company is convinced of the long-term profitability of such an approach. The key is to determine whether a franchisor is building new units from scratch or buying them from failing and/or unhappy franchisees.

10. **Total Units: 529.** As of 4/1/12, FASTSIGNS had a total of 529 operating units.

Comment: Like a franchisor's longevity, its experience in operating multiple units offers considerable comfort. Those franchisors with over 15–25 operating units have proven that their system works and have probably encountered and overcome most of the problems that plague a new operation. Alternatively, the management of franchises with less than 15 operating units may have gained considerable industry experience before joining the current franchise. It is up to the franchisor to convince you that it is providing you with as risk-free an operation as possible. You don't want to be the first to provide a company with basic experience in the business.

11. **Distribution: US-451; CAN-22; O'seas-56.** As of 4/1/12, FASTSIGNS had 451 operating units in the U.S., 22 in Canada, and 56 overseas.

12. **Distribution: North America: 45 States, 6 Provinces.** As of 4/1/12, FASTSIGNS had operations in 45 states and 6 Canadian provinces.

Comment: It should go without saying that the wider the geographic distribution, the greater the franchisor's level of success. For the most part, such distribution can only come from a large number of operating units. If, however, the franchisor has operations in 15 states, but only 18 total operating units, it is unlikely that it can efficiently service these accounts because of geographic constraints. Other things being equal, a prospective franchisee should vastly prefer a franchisor with 15 units in New York to one with 15 units scattered throughout the U.S., Canada and overseas.

13. **Distribution: Density: TX, CA, FL.** The franchisor was asked which three states/provinces have the largest number of operating units. As of 4/1/12, FASTSIGNS had the largest number of units in Texas, California and Florida.

Comment: For smaller, regional franchises, geographic distribution could be a key variable in deciding whether or not to buy. If the franchisor has a concentration of units in your immediate geographic area, it is likely you will be well-served.

For those far removed geographically from the franchisor's current areas of operation, however, there can be problems. It is both time consuming and expensive to support a franchisee 2,000 miles away from company headquarters. To the extent that a franchisor can visit four franchisees in one area on one trip, there is no problem. If, however, your operation is the only one west of the Mississippi, you may not receive the on-site assistance you would like. Don't be a missionary who has to rely on his or her own devices to survive. Don't accept a franchisor's idle promises of support. If on-site assistance is important to your ultimate success, get assurances in writing that the necessary support will be forthcoming. Remember, you are buying into a system, and the availability of day-to-day support is one of the key ingredients of any successful franchise system.

14. **Projected New Units (12 Months): 25.** FASTSIGNS plans to establish 25 new units over the course of the next 12 months.

Comment: In business, growth has become a highly visible symbol of success. Rapid growth is generally perceived as preferable to slower, more controlled growth. I maintain, however, that the opposite is frequently the case. For a company of FASTSIGNS' size, adding 25 new units over a

12-month period is both reasonable and achievable. It is highly unlikely, however, that a new franchise with only five operating units can success-fully attract, screen, train and bring multiple new units on-stream in a 12-month period. If it suggests that it can, or even wants to, be properly wary. You must be confident a company has the financial and manage-ment resources necessary to pull off such a Herculean feat. If management is already thin, concentrating on attracting new units will clearly diminish the time it can and should spend supporting you. It takes many months, if not years, to develop and train a second level of management. You don't want to depend upon new hires teaching you systems and procedures they themselves know little or nothing about.

15. **Qualifications: 5, 5, 1, 3, 4, 5.** This question was posed to determine which specific evaluation criteria were important to the franchisor. The franchisor was asked the following: "In qualifying a potential franchisee, please rank the following criteria from Unimportant (1) to Very Important (5)." The responses should be self-explanatory:

Financial Net Worth (Rank from 1–5)
General Business Experience (Rank from 1–5)
Specific Industry Experience (Rank from 1–5)
Formal Education (Rank from 1–5)
Psychological Profile (Rank from 1–5)
Personal Interview(s) (Rank from 1–5)

Capital Requirements/Rights

16. **Cash Investment: $75K.** On average, a FASTSIGNS franchisee will have made a cash investment of $75,000 by the time he or she finally opens the initial operating unit.

Comment: It is important that you be realistic about the amount of cash you can comfortably invest in a business. Stretching beyond your means can have grave and far-reaching consequences. Assume that you will encoun-ter periodic set-backs and that you will have to draw on your reserves. The demands of starting a new business are harsh enough without the added pressures of uncertainties associated with inadequate working capital. Trust the franchisor's recommendations regarding the suggested minimum cash investment. If anything, there is an incentive for setting the recommended level of investment too low, rather than too high. The franchisor will want to qualify you to the extent that you have adequate financing. No legitimate franchisor wants you to invest if there is a chance that you might fail due to a shortage of funds.

Keep in mind that you will probably not achieve a positive cash flow before you've been in business more than six months. In your discussions with the franchisor, be absolutely certain that its calculations include an adequate working capital reserve.

17. **Total Investment: $169.7K.** On average, FASTSIGNS franchisees will invest a total of $169,700, including both cash and debt, by the time the franchise opens its doors.

Comment: The total investment should be the cash investment noted above plus any debt that you will incur in starting up the new business. Debt could be a note to the franchisor for all or part of the franchise fee, an equipment lease, building and facilities leases, etc. Make sure that the total includes all of the obligations that you assume, especially any long-term lease obligations.

Be conservative in assessing what your real exposure is. If you are leasing highly specialized equipment or if you are leasing a single-purpose build-ing, it is naive to think that you will recoup your investment if you have to sell or sub-lease those assets in a buyer's market. If there is any specialized equipment that may have been manufactured to the franchisor's specifica-tions, determine if the franchisor has any form of buy-back provision.

18. **Minimum Net Worth: $250K.** In this case, FASTSIGNS feels that a poten-tial franchisee should have a minimum net worth of $250,000. Although net worth can be defined in vastly different ways, the franchisor's response should suggest a minimum level of equity that the prospective franchisee should possess. Net worth is the combination of both liquid and illiquid assets. Again, don't think that franchisor-determined guidelines somehow don't apply to you.

19. **Fees (Franchise): $34.5K.** FASTSIGNS requires a front-end, one-time-only payment of $34,500 to grant a franchise for a single location. As noted in Chapter One, the franchise fee is a payment to reimburse the franchi-sor for the incurred costs of setting the franchisee up in business — from recruiting through training and manuals. The fee usually ranges from $15,000–30,000. It is a function of competitive franchise fees and the actual out-of-pocket costs incurred by the franchisor.

Depending upon the franchisee's particular circumstances and how well

the franchisor thinks he or she might fit into the system, the franchisor may finance all or part of the franchise fee. (See Section 32 below to see if a franchisor provides any direct or indirect financial assistance.)
The franchise fee is one area in which the franchisor frequently provides either direct or indirect financial support.

Comment: Ideally, the franchisor should do no more than recover its costs on the initial franchise fee. Profits come later in the form of royalty fees, which are a function of the franchisee's sales. Whether the franchise fee is $5,000 or $35,000, the total should be carefully evaluated. What are competitive fees and are they financed? How much training will you actually receive? Are the fees reflective of the franchisor's expenses? If the fees appear to be non-competitive, address your concerns with the franchisor.

Realize that a $5,000 differential in the one-time franchise fee is a secondary consideration in the overall scheme of things. You are in this relationship for the long-term.

By the same token, don't get suckered in by an extremely low fee if there is any doubt about the franchisor's ability to follow through. Franchisors need to collect reasonable fees to cover their actual costs. If they don't recoup these costs, they cannot recruit and train new franchisees on whom your own future success partially depends.

20. **Fees (Royalty): 6%** means that six percent of gross sales (or other measure, as defined in the franchise agreement) must be periodically paid directly to the franchisor in the form of royalties. This ongoing expense is your cost for being part of the larger franchise system and for all of the "back-office" support you receive. In a few cases, the amount of the royalty fee is fixed rather than variable. In others, the fee decreases as the volume of sales (or other measure) increases (i.e., 8% on the first $200,000 of sales, 7% on the next $100,000 and so on). In others, the fee is held at artificially low levels during the start-up phase of the franchisee's business, then increases once the franchisee is better able to afford it.

Comment: Royalty fees represent the mechanism by which the franchisor finally recoups the costs it has incurred in developing its business. It may take many years and many operating units before the franchisor is able to make a true operating profit.

Consider a typical franchisor who might have been in business for three years. With a staff of five, rent, travel, operating expenses, etc., assume it has annual operating costs of $300,000 (including reasonable owner's salaries). Assume also that there are 25 franchised units with average annual sales of $250,000. Each franchise is required to pay a 6% royalty fee. Total annual royalties under this scenario would total only $375,000. The franchisor is making a $75,000 profit. Then consider the personal risk the franchisor took in developing a new business and the initial years of negative cash flows. Alternatively, evaluate what it would cost you, as a sole proprietor, to provide the myriad services included in the royalty payment.

In assessing various alternative investments, the amount of the royalty percentage is a major on-going expense. Assuming average annual sales of $250,000 per annum over a 15 year period, the total royalties at 5% would be $187,500. At 6%, the cumulative fees would be $225,000. You have to be fully convinced that the $37,500 differential is justified. While this is clearly a meaningful number, what you are really evaluating is the quality of management and the competitive advantages of the goods and/or services offered by the franchisor.

21. **Fees (Advertising): 2%.** Most national or regional franchisors require their franchisees to contribute a certain percentage of their sales (or other measure, as determined in the franchise agreement) into a corporate advertising fund. These individual advertising fees are pooled to develop a corporate advertising/marketing effort that produces great economies of scale. The end result is a national or regional advertising program that promotes the franchisor's products and services. Depending upon the nature of the business, this percentage usually ranges from 2–6% and is in addition to the royalty fee.

Comment: One of the greatest advantages of a franchised system is its ability to promote, on a national or regional basis, its products and services. The promotions may be through television, radio, print medias or direct mail. The objective is name recognition and, over time, the assumption that the product and/or service has been "time-tested." An individual business owner could never justify the expense of mounting a major advertising program at the local level. For a smaller franchise that may not yet have an advertising program or fee, it is important to know when an advertising program will start, how it will be monitored and its expected cost.

22. **Earnings Claims Statement: Yes.** This means FASTSIGNS provides a financial performance representation/earnings claims statement to potential franchisees. Unfortunately, only approximately 18-22% of franchisors provide a financial performance representation/earnings claims statement

in their Franchise Disclosure Document (FDD). The franchising industry's failure to require financial performance representations/earnings claims statements does a serious disservice to the potential franchisee. See Chapter One for comments on the financial performance representations/earnings claims statement.

23. **Term of Contract (Years): 20/10.** FASTSIGNS' initial franchise period runs for twenty years. The first renewal period runs for an additional ten years. Assuming that the franchisee operates within the terms of the franchise agreement, he or she has thirty years within which to develop and, ultimately, sell the business.

Comment: The potential (discounted) value of any business (or investment) is the sum of the operating income that is generated each year plus its value upon liquidation. Given this truth, the length of the franchise agreement and any renewals are extremely important to the franchisee. It is essential that he or she has adequate time to develop the business to its full potential. At that time, he or she will have maximized the value of the business as an on-going concern. The value of the business to a potential buyer, however, is largely a function of how long the franchise agreement runs. If there are only two years remaining before the agreement expires, or if the terms of an extension(s) are vague, the business will be worth only a fraction of the value assigned to a business with 15 years to go. For the most part, the longer the agreement and the subsequent extension, the better. (The same logic applies to a lease. If your sales are largely a function of your location and traffic count, then it is important that you have options to extend the lease under known terms. Your lease should never be longer than the remaining term of your franchise agreement, however.)

Assuming the length of the agreement is acceptable, be clear on the circumstances under which renewals might not be granted. Similarly, know the circumstances under which a franchise agreement might be prematurely and unilaterally canceled by the franchisor. I strongly recommend you have an experienced lawyer review this section of the franchise agreement. It would be devastating if, after spending years developing your business, there was a loophole in the contract that allowed the franchisor to arbitrarily cancel the relationship.

24. **Avg. # of Employees: 2-3 FT.** The questionnaire asked, "Including the owner/operator, how many employees are recommended to properly staff the average franchised unit?" In FASTSIGNS' case, two to three full-time employees are required.

Comment: Most entrepreneurs start a new business based on their intuition feel that it will be "fun" and that their talents and experience will be put to good use. They will be doing what they enjoy as well as something they are good at. Times change. Your business prospers. The number of employees increases. You are spending an increasing percentage of your time taking care of personnel problems and less and less on the fun parts of the business. In Chapter One, the importance of conducting a realistic self-appraisal was stressed. If you found that you really are not good at managing people, or you don't have the patience to manage a large minimum wage staff, cut your losses before you are locked into doing just that.

25. **Passive Ownership: Allowed.** Depending on the nature of the business, many franchisors are indifferent as to whether you manage the business directly or hire a full-time manager. Others are insistent that, at least for the initial franchise, the franchisee be a full-time owner/operator. FAST-SIGNS does not allow franchisees to hire full-time managers to run their outlets.

Comment: Unless you have a great deal of experience in the business you have chosen or in managing similar businesses, I feel strongly that you should initially commit your personal time and energies to make the system work. After you have developed a full understanding of the business and have competent, trusted staff members who can assume day-to-day operations, then consider delegating these responsibilities. Running the business through a manager can be fraught with peril unless you have mastered all aspects of the business and there are strong economic incentives and sufficient safeguards to ensure the manager will perform as desired.

26. **Conversions Encouraged: Yes.** This section pertains primarily to sole proprietorships or "mom and pop" operations. To the extent that there truly are centralized operating savings associated with the franchise, the most logical people to join a franchise system are sole practitioners who are working hard but only eking out a living. The implementation of proven systems and marketing clout could significantly reduce operating costs and increase profits.

Comment: The franchisor has the option of 1) actively encouraging such independent operators to become members of the franchise team, 2) seeking out franchisees with limited or no applied experience or 3) going after both groups. Concerned that it will be very difficult to break independent operators of the bad habits they have picked up over the years, many only choose course two. "They will continue to do things their way. They won't, or can't, accept corporate direction," they might say to themselves. Others are simply selective in the conversions they allow. In many cases, the franchise fee is reduced or eliminated for conversions.

27. **Area Development Agreements: Yes, for 2 years** means that FAST-SIGNS offers an area development agreement for two years. Area development agreements are more fully described in Chapter 1. Essentially, area development agreements allow an investor or investment group to develop an entire area or region. The schedule for development is clearly spelled out in the area development agreement. (Note: "Var." means varies and "Neg." means negotiable.) Why not spell these out in the company profile? e.g., "Varies" and "Negotiable"

Comment: Area development agreements represent an opportunity for the franchisor to choose a single franchisee or investment group to develop an entire area. The franchisee's qualifications should be strong and include proven business experience and the financial depth to pull it off. An area development agreement represents a great opportunity for an investor to tie up a large geographical area and develop a concept that may not have proven itself on a national basis. Keep in mind that this is a quantum leap from making an investment in a single franchise and is relevant only to those with development experience and deep pockets.

28. **Sub-Franchising Contracts: No.** FASTSIGNS does not grant sub-franchising agreements. (See Chapter One for a more thorough explanation.) Like area development agreements, sub-franchising allows an investor or investment group to develop an entire area or region. The difference is that the sub-franchisor becomes a self-contained business, responsible for all relations with franchisees within its area, from initial training to on-going support. Franchisees pay their royalties to the sub-franchisor, who in turn pays a portion to the master franchisor.

Comment: Sub-franchising is used primarily by smaller franchisors who have a relatively easy concept and who are prepared to sell a portion of the future growth of their business to someone for some front-end cash and a percentage of the future royalties they receive from their franchisees.

29. **Expand in Territory: Yes.** Under conditions spelled out in the franchise agreement, FASTSIGNS will allow its franchisees to expand within their exclusive territory.

Comment: Some franchisors define the franchisee's exclusive territory so tightly that there would never be room to open additional outlets within an area. Others provide a larger area in the hopes that the franchisee will do well and have the incentive to open additional units. There are clearly economic benefits to both parties from having franchisees with multiple units. There is no question that it is in your best interest to have the option to expand once you have proven to both yourself and the franchisor that you can manage the business successfully. Many would concur that the real profits in franchising come from managing multiple units rather than being locked into a single franchise in a single location. Additional fees may or may not be required with these additional units.

30. **Space Needs: 1,200-1,500 SF.** The average FASTSIGNS retail outlet will require 1,200-1,500 square feet.

Comment: Armed with the rough space requirements, you can better project your annual occupancy costs. It should be relatively easy to get comparable rental rates for the type of space required. As annual rent and related expenses can be as high as 15% of your annual sales, be as accurate as possible in your projections.

Franchisor Support and Training Provided

31. **Financial Assistance Provided: Yes (I)** indicates that FASTSIGNS provides indirect financial assistance. Indirect (I) assistance might include making introductions to the franchisor's financial contacts, providing financial templates for preparing a business plan or actually assisting in the loan application process. In some cases, the franchisor becomes a co-signer on a financial obligation (such as equipment or space lease). Other franchisors are directly (D) involved in the process. In this case, the assistance may include a lease or loan made directly by the franchisor. Any loan would generally be secured by some form of collateral. A very common form of assistance is a note for all or part of the initial franchise fee. The level of assistance will generally depend upon the relative strengths of the franchisee.

Comment: The best of all possible worlds is one in which the franchisor has enough confidence in the business and in you to co-sign notes on the building and equipment leases and allow you to pay off the franchise fee over a specified period of time. Depending upon your qualifications, this could happen. Most likely, however, the franchisor will only give you some assistance in raising the necessary capital to start the business. Increasingly, franchisors are testing a franchisee's business acumen by letting him or her assume an increasing level of personal responsibility in securing financing. The objective is to find out early on how competent a franchisee really is.

32. Site Selection Assistance: Yes. This means that FASTSIGNS will assist the franchisee in selecting a site location. While the phrase "location, location, location" may be hackneyed, its importance should not be discounted, especially when a business depends upon retail traffic counts and accessibility. If a business is home- or warehouse-based, assistance in this area is of negligible or minor importance.

Comment: Since you will be locked into a lease for a minimum of three, and probably five, years, optimal site selection is absolutely essential. Even if you were somehow able to sub-lease and extricate yourself from a bad lease or bad location, the franchise agreement may not allow you to move to another location. Accordingly, it is imperative that you get it right the first time.

If a franchisor is truly interested in your success, it should treat your choice of a site with the same care it would use in choosing a company-owned site. Keep in mind that many firms provide excellent demographic data on existing locations at a very reasonable cost.

33. Lease Negotiations Assistance: Yes. Once a site is selected, FASTSIGNS will be actively involved in negotiating the terms of the lease.

Comment: Given the complexity of negotiating a lease, an increasing number of franchisors are taking an active role in lease negotiations. There are far too many trade-offs that must be considered — terms, percentage rents, tenant improvements, pass-throughs, kick-out clauses, etc. This responsibility is best left to the professionals. If the franchisor doesn't have the capacity to support you directly, enlist the help of a well-recommended broker. The penalties for signing a bad long-term lease are very severe.

34. Co-operative Advertising: No. This refers to the existence of a joint advertising program in which the franchisor and franchisees each contribute to promote the company's products and/or services (usually within the franchisee's specific territory).

Comment: Co-op advertising is a common and mutually-beneficial effort. By agreeing to split part of the advertising costs, whether for television, radio or direct mail, the franchisor is not only supporting the franchisee, but guaranteeing itself royalties from the incremental sales. A franchisor that is not intimately involved with the advertising campaign — particularly when it is an important part of the business — may not be fully committed to your overall success.

35. Franchisee Assoc./Member: Yes, Member. This response notes that the FASTSIGNS system includes an active association made up of FASTSIGNS franchisees and that, consequently, the franchisor is a member of such franchisee association.

Comment: The empowerment of franchisees has become a major rallying cry within the industry over the past three years. Various states have recently passed laws favoring franchisee rights, and the subject has been widely discussed in congressional staff hearings. Political groups even represent franchisee rights on a national basis. Similarly, the IFA is now actively courting franchisees to become active members. Whether they are equal members remains to be seen.

Franchisees have also significantly increased their clout with respect with the franchisor. If a franchise is to grow and be successful in the long term, it is critical that the franchisor and its franchisees mutually agree they are partners rather than adversaries.

36. Size of Corporate Staff: 100+. FASTSIGNS has over 100 full-time employees on its staff to support its 529 operating units.

Comment: There are no magic ratios that tell you whether the franchisor has enough staff to provide the proper level of support. It would appear, however, that FASTSIGNS' staff of 100+ is adequate to support 529 operating units. Less clear is whether a staff of three, including the company president and his wife, can adequately support 15 fledgling franchisees in the field.

Many younger franchises may be managed by a skeleton staff, assisted by outside consultants who perform various management functions during the start-up phase. From the perspective of the franchisee, it is essential that the franchisor have actual in-house franchising experience, and that the franchisee not be forced to rely on outside consultants to make the system work. Whereas a full-time, salaried employee will probably have the franchisee's objectives in mind, an outside consultant may easily not have the same priorities. Franchising is a unique form of business that requires specific skills and experience — skills and experience that are markedly different from those required to manage a non-franchised business. If you are thinking about establishing a long-term relationship with a firm just starting out in franchising, you should insist that the franchisor prove that it has an experienced, professional team on board and in place to provide the necessary levels of support to all concerned.

37. **On-Going Support: NA,NA,C,D,E,NA,G,H,I.** Like initial training, the on-going support services provided by the franchisor are of paramount importance. Having a solid and responsive team behind you can certainly make your life much easier and allow you to concentrate your energies on other areas. As is noted below, the franchisors were asked to indicate their support for nine separate on-going services:

Service Provided	Included in Fees	At Add'l. Cost	NA
Central Data Processing	A	a	NA
Central Purchasing	B	b	NA
Field Operations Evaluation	C	c	NA
Field Training	D	d	NA
Initial Store Opening	E	e	NA
Inventory Control	F	f	NA
Franchisee Newsletter	G	g	NA
Regional or National Meetings	H	h	NA
800 Telephone Hotline	I	i	NA

If the franchisor provides the service at no additional cost to the franchisee (as indicated by letters A–I), a capital letter was used to indicate this. If the service is provided, but only at an additional cost, a lower case letter was used. If the franchisor responded with a NA, or failed to note an answer for a particular service, the corresponding letter was omitted from the data sheet.

38. **Training: 2 Weeks Dallas, TX; 1 Week On-Site.**

Comment: Assuming that the underlying business concept is sound and competitive, adequate training and on-going support are among the most important determinants of your success as a franchisee. The initial training should be as lengthy and as "hands-on" as necessary to allow the franchisee to operate alone and with confidence. Obviously, every potential situation cannot be covered in any training program, but the franchisee should come away with at least a basic understanding of how the business operates and where to go to resolve problems when they come up. Depending on the business, there should be operating manuals, procedural manuals, company policies, training videos, (800) help-lines, etc. It may be helpful at the outset to establish how satisfied recent franchisees are with a company's training. I would also have a clear understanding about how often the company updates its manuals and training programs, the cost of sending additional employees through training, etc.

Remember, you are part of an organization that you are paying (in the form of a franchise fee and on-going royalties) to support you. Training is the first step. On-going support is the second step.

Specific Expansion Plans

39. **U.S.: All United States.** FASTSIGNS is currently focusing its growth on the entire United States. Alternatively, the franchisor could have listed particular states or regions into which it wished to expand.

40. **Canada: All Canada Except Quebec.** FASTSIGNS is currently seeking additional franchisees in all Canadian provinces except for Quebec. Specific markets or provinces could have also been indicated.

41. **Overseas: UK, New Zealand, Australia.** FASTSIGNS is currently expanding overseas with a focus on United Kingdom, New Zealand and Australia.

Comment: You will note that many smaller companies with less than 15 operating units suggest that they will concurrently expand throughout the U.S., Canada and internationally. In many cases, these are the same companies that foresee a 50+ percent growth rate in operating units over the next 12 months. The chances of this happening are negligible. As a prospective franchisee, you should be wary of any company that thinks it can expand throughout the world without a solid base of experience, staff and financial resources. Even if adequate financing is available, the demands on existing management will be extreme. New management cannot adequately fill the void until they are able to fully understand the system and absorb the corporate culture. If management's end objective is expansion for its own sake rather than by design, the existing franchisees will suffer.

Note: The statistics noted in the profiles preceding each company's analysis are the result of data provided by the franchisors themselves by way of a detailed questionnaire. Similarly, the data in the summary comparisons in the Introduction Chapter were taken from the company profile data. The figures used throughout each company's analysis, however, were generally taken from the franchisor's FDD/UFOC filed in 2010. In some cases, the data was taken from an FDD/UFOC filed in 2009. The FDDs/UFOCs, which are only printed annually, may in some cases contain information that is somewhat out of date. This is especially true with regard to the number of operating units and the current level of investment. A visit to our website at www.worldfranchising.com should provide current data.

You will note that several of the companies listed in this book have the "World-Class Franchise®" seal, along with the franchisees' ratings of their franchisors in several categories. The degree of satisfaction existing franchisees experience with their franchisor should be a fundamental consideration in making an optimal franchise investment decision. The World Franchising Network is collaborating with FranSurvey.com to determine which franchisors excel in several areas critical to the franchise selection process. FranSurvey.com confidentially contacts every existing franchisee within various franchise systems to determine their general level of happiness with their investment decision. Please visit www.fransurvey.com for additional information on this highly beneficial program, and for detailed reports on certified "World-Class" franchisors.

ॐ

If you have not already done so, please invest some modest time to read Chapter 1, 30-Minute Overview.

The Franchise Bookstore
Order Form

Call (800) 841-0873 or (510) 839-5471; or Fax (510) 839-2104

Item #	Title	Price	Qty.	Total

Basic postage (1 book)	**$8.50**
Each additional book add $4.00	
California tax @ 9.75% (if CA resident)	
Total due in U.S. dollars	
Deduct 15% if total due is over $100.00	
Net amount due in U.S. dollars	

Please include credit card number, expiration date and security code for all charge card orders! Checks should be made payable to Source Book Publications. All prices are in U.S. dollars.

Mailing Information: All books are shipped by USPS Priority Mail (2nd Day Air). Please print clearly and include your phone number in case we need to contact you. Postage and handling rates are for shipping within the U.S. For international rates, please call (800) 841-0873.

☐ **Check enclosed or**

Charge my:

☐ American Express ☐ MasterCard ☐ VISA

Card #:

Expiration Date:

Security Code:

Signature:

Name:_____

Company:_____

Address:_____

City: _____

Title: _____

Telephone No.: (_____)_____

State/Prov.:_____ Zip:_____

Special Offer — Save 15%

If your total order above exceeds $100.00, deduct 15% from your bill.

Please send order to:
Source Book Publications
1814 Franklin St., Ste. 603, Oakland, CA 94612
Satisfaction Guaranteed. If not fully satisfied, return for a prompt, 100% refund.

Food Service 3

Applebee's International

11201 Renner Blvd.
Lenexa, KS 66219
Tel: (888) 59-APPLE, (913) 967-4000
Fax: (913) 967-4135
Email: info@applebees.com
Website: www.applebees.com
Andrea Gladson, VP Franchising Development

Everyone's favorite neighbor is definitely Applebee's neighborhood grill and bar. This distinguished casual-dining restaurant has a comfortable individuality which reflects the neighborhood in which it is located, making the Applebee's concept appealing wherever it is built.

BACKGROUND: IFA Member
Established:1980; First Franchised: 1983
Franchised Units: 906
Company-Owned Units: 262
Total Units: 1,168
Dist.: US-1,155; CAN-5; O'seas-8
 North America: 47 States, 3 Provinces
 Density: 48 in OH, 62 in FL, 54 in CA

Projected New Units (12 Months): 125
Qualifications: 5, 5, 5, NA , NA, 5

FINANCIAL/TERMS:
Cash Investment: $1M-50% Liq.
Total Investment: $1.7-3.1M
Minimum Net Worth:
Fees: Franchise - $35K/Unit
 Royalty - 4%; Ad. - 3%
Earnings Claims Statement: No
Term of Contract (Years): 20
Avg. # of Employees: 75-100 FT, 0 PT
Passive Ownership: Not Allowed
Encourage Conversions: No
Area Develop. Agreements: Yes
Sub-Franchising Contracts: No
Expand in Territory: Yes
Space Needs: 5,000-5,400 SF

SUPPORT & TRAINING:
Financial Assistance Provided: No
Site Selection Assistance: Yes
Lease Negotiation Assistance: Yes
Co-operative Advertising: No
Franchisee Assoc./Member: Yes/Yes
Size of Corporate Staff: 300
On-going Support: A,B,C,D,E,NA,G,H,I
Training: 8-12 weeks certified training unit;
 3 days headquarters

SPECIFIC EXPANSION PLANS:
US: NY, LA, HI, AK
Canada: All Canada
Overseas: All Countries

63

Founded nearly three decades ago on the principles of exceptional value and family fun, Applebee's Services, Inc., operates what is today the largest casual-dining chain in the world. This prominent eatery draws people of all ages and lifestyles with its fun, family-friendly atmosphere and signature bar and grill menu. Applebee's differentiates itself with innovative attractions, like the popular Carside. To-go service available at many of its restaurants, and its successful Weight Watchers agreement, enabling it to cater to those preferring less-caloric alternatives.

Operating Units	12/31/2008	12/31/2009	12/31/2010
Franchised	1,470	1,470	1,553
% Change	--	0%	5.6%
Company-Owned	405	398	309
% Change	--	-1.7%	-22.4%
Total	1,875	1,868	1,862
% Change	--	-0.4%	-0.3%
Franchised as % of Total	78.4%	78.7 %	83.4 %

Investment Required
The franchise fee for an Applebee's franchise is $35,000.

Applebee's provides the following range of investments required to open your initial franchise. The range assumes that all items are paid for in cash. To the extent that you choose to finance any of these expense items, your front-end investment could be substantially reduced.

Item	Established Low Range	Established High Range
Franchise Fee	$35,000	$35,000
Initial Organizational and Training Expenses	$75,000	$120,000
Purchase of Land	$450,000	$1,500,000

Building Costs	$1,100,000	$1,350,000
Site Work	$72,000	$390,000
Professional Services	$65,000	$85,000
Permits/Fees	$50,000	$250,000
Furniture, Fixtures, Equipment and Signage	$550,000	$740,000
POS System	$38,000	$38,000
Smallwares	$25,000	$30,000
Initial Inventory	$25,500	$47,300
Pre-Opening Expenses	$55,000	$100,000
Initial Advertising Expense	$5,000	$40,000
Liquor License(s)	$500	$400,000
Apple Supply Chain Co-op Stock Purchase	$100	$100
Additional Funds (3 Months)	$405,000	$655,000
Total Investment	$2,951,100	$5,780,400

On-going Expenses

Applebee's franchisees pay ongoing fees equal to 4% of gross sales and advertising fees equal to 2.75%. Additional fees payable by franchisees include ongoing royalties to Weight Watchers and a cooperative advertising fund.

What You Get—Training and Support

From kitchen and service operations to marketing and business procedures, Applebee's provides franchisees with a thorough and intensive training program before opening. Ongoing refresher course are available for every level of restaurant operations.

Franchisees can tap into Applebee's well-established social media advertising campaign as well as Applebee's One-to-One email marketing campaign. Ongoing support also includes access to Applebee's Help Desk from the Restaurant Solution Center for any problems arising in the day-to-day operations of the restaurant.

Territory
Applebee's grants exclusive territories.

Arby's

1155 Perimeter Ctr. W.
Atlanta, GA 30338
Tel: (800) 487-2729 (678) 514-4100
Fax: (678) 514-5346
Email: tlinderman@arbys.com
Website: www.arbys.com
Tim Linderman, Director Franchise Development

Arby's serves slow roasted, freshly sliced roast beef, Market Fresh sandwiches, wraps, and salads, as well as Arby's Chicken Naturals.

BACKGROUND:	
Established: 1964;	First Franchised: 1965
Franchised Units:	2,542
Company-Owned Units:	1,162
Total Units:	3,704
Dist.:	US-3,577; CAN-118; O'seas-9
North America:	48 States, 8 Provinces
Density:	288 in OH, 191 in MI, 175 in FL
Projected New Units (12 Months):	132
Qualifications:	5, 5, 4, 3, 3, 5

FINANCIAL/TERMS:
Cash Investment:	$180.7-544.4K
Total Investment:	$336.5K-2.47M
Minimum Net Worth:	NA
Fees: Franchise -	$37.5K
Royalty - 4%;	Ad. - 4.2% (mkts may vary)
Earnings Claims Statement:	Yes
Term of Contract (Years):	20/Varies
Avg. # of Employees:	FT, 30 PT
Passive Ownership:	Allowed
Encourage Conversions:	Yes
Area Develop. Agreements:	Yes
Sub-Franchising Contracts:	No
Expand in Territory:	Yes
Space Needs:	2,500-3,500 SF

SUPPORT & TRAINING:
Financial Assistance Provided:	No
Site Selection Assistance:	Yes
Lease Negotiation Assistance:	No
Co-operative Advertising:	Yes
Franchisee Assoc./Member:	Yes/Yes
Size of Corporate Staff:	400
On-going Support:	NA,B,C,D,E,NA,G,H,I
Training:	7 weeks MTP-certified training locations

SPECIFIC EXPANSION PLANS:
US:	Yes
Canada:	Yes
Overseas:	Yes

Since 1964, Arby's has provided customers with high quality, unique products not typically found in fast food. Serving one-of-a-kind menu items, Arby's is well known for slow-roasted and freshly sliced roast beef sandwiches and famous Market Fresh sandwiches, wraps and salads, made with wholesome ingredients and served with the convenience of a drive-thru.

With thousands of locations nation-wide, Arby's boasts wide brand recognition alongside its enormous growth potential. Franchisees can pick from several options for their restaurant ranging from a free-standing unit to a nontraditional unit in a mall, university campus, or stadium. Arby's franchisees tap into the $500 billion food-service industry in serving innovative products that capitalize on current trends.

Operating Units	12/31/2008	12/31/2009	12/31/2010
Franchised	2,448	2,417	2,367
% Change	--	-1.3%	-2.1%
Company-Owned	1,176	1,169	1,144
% Change	--	-0.6%	-2.1%
Total	3,624	3,586	3,511
% Change	--	-1.0%	-2.1%
Franchised as % of Total	67.6%	67.4%	67.4%

Investment Required
The franchise fee for an Arby's ranges from $15,000 to $37,500.

Arby's provides the following range of investments required to open your initial franchise. The range assumes that all items are paid for in cash. To the extent that you choose to finance any of these expense items, your front-end investment could be substantially reduced.

Item	Established Low Range	Established High Range
Initial Franchise Fee	$15,000.00	$37,500.00
Expenses While Training	$4,000.00	$19,000.00
Site Development Costs	$10,000.00	$265,000.00
Misc. Opening Costs	$5,000.00	$25,000.00
Opening Inventory	$10,000.00	$20,000.00
Management Pre-Opening Salary	$10,000.00	$20,000.00
Additional Funds (3 Months)	$104,000.00	$158,000.00
Equipment, Décor and Sign Package	$200,000.00	$325,000.00
Leased Land and Building Costs (up to 5 Months)	$21,000.00	$59,000.00
Total Initial Investment	$379,000.00	$928,500.00

Ongoing Expenses
Arby's franchisees pay ongoing royalty fees that range from 4% to 7% of gross sales plus advertising fees equal to 4.2% of gross sales depending on the type of restaurant.

Training and Support
Training is a key component of the Arby's franchise system. As soon as franchisees sign their development agreement, they begin a one-day orientation program. The orientation is held at the Support Center in Atlanta, GA and is typically held once per quarter. The orientation program provides a brief overview of the Arby's system and gives franchisees the opportunity to meet with senior management.

In addition to helping with opening stores, Arby's offers ongoing workshops to help franchisees manage their businesses, as well as an annual franchise convention that facilitates feedback from franchisees and suppliers, recognizes franchisees for sales achievement and provides franchisees the opportunity to network and share best practices among each other.

Territory

Arby's grants exclusive territories.

Auntie Anne's Hand-Rolled Soft Pretzels

AuntieAnne's

P R E T Z E L   P E R F E C T

48-50 W. Chestnut St., # 200
Lancaster, PA 17603
Tel: (877) PRTZ-LUV, (717) 435-1479
Fax: (717) 442-1471
Email: lindae@auntieannesinc.com
Website: www.auntieannes.com
Linda Engels, Franchise Support Representative

Auntie Anne's, Inc. is a franchise organization with a commitment to exceeding our customers' expectations. We've built our company on the quality of our products and strong support for our franchisees, nurturing relationships for the long-term growth of the franchise system. That approach continues to drive our growth. We provide our customers with pretzels, dips, and drinks which are mixed, twisted, and baked to a golden brown in full view of our customers. Each and every one of our pretzels comes with the Pretzel Perfect Guarantee - we guarantee you'll love your pretzel or we'll replace it with one that you do.

BACKGROUND: IFA Member
Established: 1988;	First Franchised: 1991
Franchised Units:	942
Company-Owned Units:	9
Total Units:	951
Dist.:	US-745; CAN-3; O'seas-203
North America:	43 States, 2 Provinces
Density:	56 in CA, 53 in NY, 82 in PA
Projected New Units (12 Months):	50
Qualifications:	4, 2, 2, 2, 3, 5

FINANCIAL/TERMS:
Cash Investment:	$198-441K
Total Investment:	$198-444K
Minimum Net Worth:	$400K
Fees: Franchise -	$30K
Royalty - 7%;	Ad. - 1%
Earnings Claims Statement:	Yes
Term of Contract (Years):	20/Variable
Avg. # of Employees:	4 FT, 4 PT
Passive Ownership:	Allowed
Encourage Conversions:	NA
Area Develop. Agreements:	Yes
Sub-Franchising Contracts:	No
Expand in Territory:	No
Space Needs:	400-600 SF

SUPPORT & TRAINING:
Financial Assistance Provided:	Yes (I)
Site Selection Assistance:	Yes
Lease Negotiation Assistance:	Yes
Co-operative Advertising:	Yes

Franchisee Assoc./Member:	Yes/Yes	SPECIFIC EXPANSION PLANS:	
Size of Corporate Staff:	150	US:	All US
On-going Support:	NA,NA,C,D,E,NA,G,H,I	Canada:	Yes
Training:	3 weeks Lancaster, PA	Overseas:	All Countries

Since its franchising start in 1989, Auntie Anne's has provided consumers with a delicious lineup of pretzels and more from its more than 1,150 locations worldwide. Auntie Anne's franchise success leads back to a three-pronged philosophy: to provide premium products and friendly, courteous service in a sparkling clean store.

One of the most popular franchises in the industry, Auntie Anne's provides franchisees with all the necessary tools and support to develop the Auntie Anne's concept, including training for franchisees and staff at Auntie Anne's Pretzel University, ongoing field support and access to Auntie Anne's confidential manuals, training videos, and marketing materials.

Operating Units	12/31/2008	12/31/2009	12/31/2010
Franchised	702	728	761
% Change	--	3.7%	4.5%
Company-Owned	12	13	13
% Change	--	8.3 %	0%
Total	714	741	774
% Change	--	3.8%	4.5%
Franchised as % of Total	98.3 %	98.3 %	98.3 %

Investment Required
The franchise fee for an Auntie Anne's franchise is $30,000.

Auntie Anne's provides the following range of investments required to open your initial franchise. The range assumes that all items are paid for in cash. To the extent that you choose to finance any of these expense items, your front-end investment could be substantially reduced.

Item	Established Low Range	Established High Range
Franchise Fee	$30,000	$30,000
Lease, Utility and Security Deposits	$4,000	$7,000
Leasehold Improvements, Furniture and Fixtures	$90,000	$175,000
Equipment	$31,500	$34,500
Licenses and Permits	$175	$600
Initial Inventory	$3,300	$4,000
Insurance	$400	$2,500
Training Expenses	$1,000	$7,500
Opening Advertising	$500	$5,000
Signage	$4,000	$12,000
POS Equipment	$8,000	$15,000
Office Equipment and Supplies	$5,000	$10,000
Professional Fees	$5,000	$10,000
Additional Funds (3 months)	$15,000	$51,000
Total Investment	$197,875	$364,100

On-going Expenses

Auntie Anne's franchisees pay royalty fees equal to 7% of gross sales and an advertising and marketing fund contribution equal to 1% of gross sales.

Franchisee Satisfaction

A critical component of the due diligence process is that you, as a prospective franchisee, have a strong sense of existing franchisee satisfaction. Please review the franchisor's ratings below for this extremely important information.

**World-Class
Franchise®**

How do you rate Auntie Anne's in terms of:	Rating*
Overall quality of franchisor	98%
Recommend to prospective franchisees	97%
Initial training supplied by franchisor	99%

* Independent Audit of Existing Franchisees Who Rated Auntie Anne's as Excellent, Very Good, or Good

What You Get—Training and Support
All franchisees go through five days of complete store operations training, with three days in a classroom setting and two days in a store setting. Franchisees can also take advantage of an additional five-day supplemental training program that covers everything from managing to marketing. Up to six days of on-site training are available once a store opens. Auntie Anne's continually provides ongoing training and support for franchisees and their employees, boasting approximately one corporate employee for every three franchisees.

Territory
Auntie Anne's does not grant exclusive territories.

Big Apple Bagels

500 Lake Cook Rd., # 475
Deerfield, IL 60015
Tel: (800) 251-6101 (847) 948-7520
Fax: (847) 405-8140
Email: tcervini@babcorp.com
Website: www.babcorp.com
Anthony S. Cervini, Director of Development

Bakery-cafe featuring three brands: fresh-from-scratch Big Apple Bagels, My Favorite Muffin, and freshly roasted Brewster's specialty coffee. Our product offering covers many day parts with a delicious assortment of made-to-order gourmet sandwiches, salads, soups, espresso beverages, and fruit smoothies. Franchisees can develop beyond their stores with corporate catering and gift basket opportunities, as well as wholesaling opportunities within their market area.

BACKGROUND: IFA Member
Established: 1992; First Franchised: 1993
Franchised Units: 103
Company-Owned Units: 1
Total Units: 104
Dist.: US-103; CAN-0; O'seas-1
North America: 21 States
Density: 19 in WI, 37 in MI, 8 in IL

Projected New Units (12 Months): 10
Qualifications: 3, 4, 3, 3, 3, 5

FINANCIAL/TERMS:
Cash Investment: $60K
Total Investment: $254.3-379.6K
Minimum Net Worth: $250K
Fees: Franchise - $25K
 Royalty - 5%; Ad. - 1%
Earnings Claims Statement: No
Term of Contract (Years): 10/10
Avg. # of Employees: 3 FT, 11 PT
Passive Ownership: Allowed
Encourage Conversions: Yes
Area Develop. Agreements: Yes
Sub-Franchising Contracts: No
Expand in Territory: Yes
Space Needs: 1,600-1,900 SF

SUPPORT & TRAINING:
Financial Assistance Provided: No
Site Selection Assistance: Yes
Lease Negotiation Assistance: Yes
Co-operative Advertising: No
Franchisee Assoc./Member: No
Size of Corporate Staff: 20
On-going Support: NA,NA,C,D,E,F,G,H,I
Training: 2 weeks Milwaukee, WI

SPECIFIC EXPANSION PLANS:
US: All
Canada: All
Overseas: All Countries

BAB, Inc. offers customers a wide range of high quality foods through its three brands, My Favorite Muffin, Brewsters Coffee, and Big Apple Bagels. Each of the restaurants offers a casual yet comfortable atmosphere in which customers can order to-go or linger in the dining area with the wide assortment of breakfast and lunch items, treats, and beverages. On the menu, BAB restaurants offer freshly baked bagels, fresh deli sandwiches, cake-like muffins prepared with soybean oil, as well as salads, soups, and specialty drinks made to order. BAB recognizes that today's consumer wants to make informed choices about the foods they eat, and BAB restaurants serve a wide range meal options that can easily fit into a healthy, balanced diet.

Each restaurant doubles as a bakery-café. Additionally, the restaurant is not only a retail destination, but also a wholesale distributorship from which franchisees' baked-from-scratch bagels and muffins can be sold in bulk to corporate clients, restaurants, convenience stores, and other businesses for resale.

Operating Units	12/31/2008	12/31/2009	12/31/2010
Franchised	111	103	100
% Change	--	-7.2%	-2.9%
Company-Owned	1	1	1
% Change	--	0%	0%
Total	112	104	101
% Change	--	-7.1%	-2.9%
Franchised as % of Total	99.1%	99%	99%

Investment Required

The franchise fee for a BAB Production Store is $25,000.

BAB, Inc. provides the following range of investments required to open a BAB Production Store franchise. The range assumes that all items are paid for in cash. To the extent that you choose to finance any of these expense items, your front-end investment could be substantially reduced.

Item	Established Low Range	Established High Range
Franchise Fee	$25,000	$25,000
Training	$1,600	$3,000
Leasehold Improvements	$87,000	$135,000

Furniture, Fixtures, Equipment, Signage and Display	$98,000	$128,028
Opening Inventory and Supplies	$10,000	$11,300
First Month's Rent and Security Deposit	$4,000	$10,500
Marketing Deposit	$7,500	$7,500
Insurance	$5,200	$7,200
Prepaid Expenses, Deposits	$500	$2,000
Professional Fees	$2,500	$7,000
Additional Funds (3 Months)	$7,500	$22,100
Total Investment	$248,800	$358,628

On-going Expenses

BAB franchisees pay a royalty fee equal to 5% of gross revenues plus a marketing fund contribution equal to 3% of gross revenues, which is subject to increase by BAB but not to exceed 5% of gross revenues.

What You Get—Training and Support

Pre-opening support for BAB franchisees includes site selection assistance, restaurant layout and design, Grand Opening marketing campaign, full seasonal marketing strategies, and a password-protected BAB Franchisee Intranet featuring a download center, online sales reporting, resource center, and trading post.

Additionally, franchisees undergo BAB Inc.'s initial training program comprised of hands-on learning in our company-owned location and classroom instruction. This training details day-to-day restaurant operations, hiring training and retaining good employees, and maintaining financial controls.

Territory

BAB, Inc. does not grant exclusive territories.

Church's Chicken

980 Hammond Dr., Bldg. # 2, # 1100
Atlanta, GA 30328-6161
Tel: (800) 639-3495 (770) 350-3800
Fax: (770) 512-3924
Email: pperry@churchs.com
Website: www.churchsfranchise.com
Patricia Perry, Sr. Mgr. Franchise Sales & Dev.

Founded in San Antonio, Texas in 1952, Church's Chicken is a highly recognized brand name in the QSR sector and is one of the largest quick-service chicken concepts in the world. Church's Chicken serves freshly prepared, high quality, flavorful chicken and tenders with signature sides and hand-made from scratch biscuits at low prices. Church's differentiates from its competitors in care and attention given in preparation of food, and is positioned as the Value Leader in the Chicken QSR category. As of April 2010, the Church's system had 1,650+ locations worldwide in 23 countries, with system sales exceeding $1 billion.

BACKGROUND: IFA Member
Established: 1952;   First Franchised: 1967
Franchised Units: 1412
Company-Owned Units: 279
Total Units: 1,691
Dist.:   US-1,255; CAN-19; O'seas-417

North America:	33 States, 1 Province
Density:	488 in TX, 90 in GA, 73 in CA
Projected New Units (12 Months):	120
Qualifications:	5, 5, 4, 3, 3, 5

FINANCIAL/TERMS:
Cash Investment:	$300K
Total Investment:	$154.3-833.1K
Minimum Net Worth:	$1M
Fees: Franchise -	$25K
Royalty - 5%;	Ad. - 5%
Earnings Claims Statement:	Yes
Term of Contract (Years):	20/10
Avg. # of Employees:	15 FT, 6 PT
Passive Ownership:	Allowed, But Discouraged
Encourage Conversions:	Yes
Area Develop. Agreements:	Yes
Sub-Franchising Contracts:	Yes
Expand in Territory:	Yes
Space Needs:	168-1,850 SF

SUPPORT & TRAINING:
Financial Assistance Provided:	No
Site Selection Assistance:	Yes
Lease Negotiation Assistance:	No
Co-operative Advertising:	Yes
Franchisee Assoc./Member:	Yes/Yes
Size of Corporate Staff:	151
On-going Support:	NA,NA,C,D,E,NA,G,H,I
Training:	5 weeks regional

SPECIFIC EXPANSION PLANS:
US:	All US
Canada:	Selected provinces
Overseas:	Asia, ME, Russia, C America, Mexico, L. America, Caribbean, India

As one of the largest quick-service chicken concepts in the world, Church's Chicken has been serving freshly cooked original and spicy fried chicken since 1952. Church's Chicken is an international brand with over $1.2 billion in sales per year that serves three million customers per week. Church's menu appeals to a diverse audience. While the famous chicken franchise is best known for its fried chicken, both original and spicy, Church's also serves other specialties including fried okra, cole slaw, mashed potatoes, jalapeno peppers, french fries, corn on the cob, and Church's unique Honey Butter Biscuits. Church's Chicken provides remarkable franchisee support via its purchasing and supply chain as well as strategic marketing campaigns and product development.

Operating Units (includes Dual Concept Restaurants)	1/29/2008	1/28/2009	1/26/2010
Franchised	1,080	1,081	1,094
% Change	--	0.1%	1.2%
Company-Owned	232	285	268
% Change	--	22.8%	-6.0%
Total	1,312	1,366	1,362
% Change	--	4.1%	-0.3%
Franchised as % of Total	82.3%	79.1%	80.3%

Investment Required
The initial fee for a Church's franchise is $15,000 with a $30,000 development fee.

Church's provides the following range of investments required to open your initial franchise. The range assumes that all items are paid for in cash. To the extent that you choose to finance any of these expense items, your front-end investment could be substantially reduced.

Item	Established Low Range	Established High Range
Franchise Fee	$15,000	$15,000
Development Fee	$20,000	$20,000
Site Work	$90,000	$185,000
Building and Improvements	$273,000	$390,000
Equipment and Signs	$100,000	$260,000
Fees, Misc., A&E Services, Deposits	$45,000	$150,000

Initial Training	$0	$6,500
Opening Supplies	$4,500	$10,000
Insurance	$7,500	$10,000
Utility Deposits	$2,000	$3,000
Business Licenses	$300	$600
Additional Funds (3 Months)	$10,000	$20,000
Total Initial Investment (Excluding Real Estate)	$567,300	$1,070,100

On-going Expenses

Franchisees pay ongoing royalty fees equal to 5% of gross sales plus an advertising fund contribution equal to 5% of gross sales.

What You Get—Training and Support

Franchisees are partnered with a Development Director and are provided with access to quantifying tools that provide valuable market analysis. Church's Architecture & Engineering (A&E) group shares resources with franchisees that include brand standards, sample floor plans, and equipment specifications. Franchise restaurant managers attend a structured five-week, in-depth management training program that is designed to ensure optimum effectiveness and preparedness for Church's restaurant systems and operations. Ongoing training support is provided including training procedures for new product rollouts.

Franchisees are also assigned a dedicated Regional Franchise Director/ Manager who provides essential ongoing support to aid in all day-to-day restaurant operations. Church's field operations team has extensive experience in working through business strategies and challenges and is always available to share that knowledge.

Territory

Church's Chicken offers exclusive territories through its Exclusive Development Agreement.

Cousins Subs

N83 W13400 Leon Rd.
Menomonee Falls, WI 53051
Tel: (800) 238-9736
Fax: (262) 364-2984
Email: mcairns@cousinssubs.com
Website: www.cousinsfranchise.com
Mark Cairns, Director of Franchise Sales

Over 33 years of excellence describes our Eastern-Style submarine sandwich concept. Our Cousins Subs niche is offering a quality submarine sandwich 25% larger than most of our competitors. Hot and cold subs are highlighted by our freshly baked bread, delicious soups, and garden salads made to order! The value and portability of our products promote leveraging outside sales to bottom line profitability. We have high expectations for 2012 and invite you to learn more about our exciting franchise opportunities. We offer single unit and multi-unit franchises.

BACKGROUND:

	IFA Member
Established: 1972;	First Franchised: 1985
Franchised Units:	133
Company-Owned Units:	16
Total Units:	149
Dist.:	US-149; CAN-0; O'seas-0
North America:	6 States

Density:	128 in WI, 6 in MN, 11 in AZ
Projected New Units (12 Months):	15
Qualifications:	5, 4, 3, 3, 3, 4

FINANCIAL/TERMS:

Cash Investment:	$80-100K
Total Investment:	$101.7-295.8K
Minimum Net Worth:	$300K
Fees: Franchise -	$25K ($12.5K through 2009)
Royalty - 6%;	Ad. - 2%
Earnings Claims Statement:	Yes
Term of Contract (Years):	10/10
Avg. # of Employees:	2 FT, 12 PT
Passive Ownership:	Allowed
Encourage Conversions:	Yes
Area Develop. Agreements:	Yes
Sub-Franchising Contracts:	Yes
Expand in Territory:	Yes
Space Needs:	1,250-1,600 SF

SUPPORT & TRAINING:

Financial Assistance Provided:	Yes (D)
Site Selection Assistance:	Yes
Lease Negotiation Assistance:	Yes
Co-operative Advertising:	Yes
Franchisee Assoc./Member:	No
Size of Corporate Staff:	40
On-going Support:	NA,NA,C,D,E,NA,NA,h,I
Training:	10 days franchisee store;
	30 days training store; 3 days headquarters

SPECIFIC EXPANSION PLANS:

US:	IL, MI, MN, WI, AZ
Canada:	No
Overseas:	No

With over 33 years of excellence, Cousins Subs has been serving Eastern-Style submarine sandwiches that are 25% larger than the competition. Menu items include both hot and cold subs alongside freshly baked bread, delicious soups, and garden salads made to order.

Franchisees have the potential markets both within the restaurant and throughout the franchisee's market area via mobile sales units and catering opportunities. Bolstered by comprehensive support systems, Cousins Subs franchisees tap into a recession-resistant industry with implicit demand and a cash business with few receivables and minimal inventory.

Operating Units	12/31/2008	12/31/2009	12/31/2010
Franchised	133	131	130
% Change	--	-1.5%	-0.8%
Company-Owned	15	15	16
% Change	--	0%	6.7%
Total	148	146	146
% Change	--	-1.4%	0%
Franchised as % of Total	89.9%	89.7%	89%

Investment Required
The fee for a Cousins Subs franchise is $17,500.

Cousins Subs provides the following range of investments required to open your initial franchise. The range assumes that all items are paid for in cash. To the extent that you choose to finance any of these expense items, your front-end investment could be substantially reduced.

Item	Established Low Range	Established High Range
Franchise Fee	$17,500	$17,500
Leasehold Improvements	$20,000	$88,000
Equipment and Small Ware	$15,000	$75,000
Seating Package/Millwork	$7,500	$25,000
Initial Inventory and Supplies	$2,500	$6,500
POS System/Technology	$10,000	$15,000
Architectural Fees	$2,500	$4,500
Rent	$1,000	$4,500
Lease and Utility Security Deposits	$0	$3,800

Insurance	$700	$1,500
Training	$2,500	$5,500
Store Marketing Fee	$5,000	$5,000
Signage	$2,500	$6,500
Additional Funds (3 Months	$20,000	$30,000
Total Investment	$106,700	$288,300

On-going Expenses
Cousins Subs franchisees pay continuing service fees equal to 6% of gross receipts and an advertising and development fund contribution equal to 2% of gross receipts. Additional fees payable by the franchisee include local advertising fees.

What You Get—Training and Support
Franchisees and their designated managers spend a minimum of 21 days participating in on-the-job and classroom sessions at an approved Cousins Subs training facility. At store opening, franchisees receive ten days of assistance in training their staff by a Cousins Subs certified trainer. In addition, franchisees receive assistance with conducting on-site training sessions for hourly staff at least two days prior to opening day.

Each market area has an assigned Marketing Consultant who works with each franchisee. They will help to develop a local marketing plan for each store location. The National Advertising Fund provides the necessary point of sale merchandising materials to help promote sales within the store. Cousins Subs also provides professional brand-building execution of television, radio, billboards and coupon tactics. This is administered through participation with advertising co-op groups in the existing market area.

Territory
Cousins Subs grants exclusive territories only under its Area Development Agreement. Otherwise, Cousins Subs does not grant exclusive territories.

Denny's

203 E. Main St.
Spartanburg, SC 29319
Tel: (800) 304-0222
Fax: (713) 849-0722
Email: franchisedevelopment@dennys.com
Website: www.dennysfranchising.com
Lucy Clark, Coordinator, Franchise Administration
and Development

For almost 60 years, Denny's has been the trusted leader in family dining. Today, Denny's is a true icon, with brand awareness of almost 100%. Having grown to include almost 1,700 restaurants and system-wide sales of over $2.4 billion, Denny's is one of the largest and most recognized full-service family restaurant chains in the United States. We rank in the top 100 Chains in Food Service Sales in Nation's Restaurant News, Bond's Top 100 Franchises and are ranked #1 in category by Entrepreneur Magazine's Franchise 500®. If you are an experienced restaurateur or businessman, we invite you to contact us and learn more about growth opportunities within our great brand.

BACKGROUND:

	IFA Member
Established: 1953;	First Franchised: 1963
Franchised Units:	1482
Company-Owned Units:	198
Total Units:	1,680

Dist.:	US-1,587; CAN-60; O'seas-33
North America:	50 States, 5 Provinces
Density:	347 in CA, 166 in TX, 137 in FL
Projected New Units (12 Months):	50
Qualifications:	5, 5, 5, 3, NA, 5

FINANCIAL/TERMS:

Cash Investment:	$350-$400K
Total Investment:	$1.178-2.4M
Minimum Net Worth:	$1M
Fees: Franchise -	$40K
Royalty - 4%;	Ad. - 4%
Earnings Claims Statement:	Yes
Term of Contract (Years):20/10 or 20	
Avg. # of Employees:	50 FT, 25 PT
Passive Ownership:	Allowed, But Discouraged
Encourage Conversions:	Yes
Area Develop. Agreements:	Yes
Sub-Franchising Contracts:	No
Expand in Territory:	Yes
Space Needs:	4,200 SF

SUPPORT & TRAINING:

Financial Assistance Provided:	Yes (I)
Site Selection Assistance:	Yes
Lease Negotiation Assistance:	No
Co-operative Advertising:	Yes
Franchisee Assoc./Member:	Yes/Yes
Size of Corporate Staff:	250
On-going Support:	NA,NA,C,D,e,NA,G,NA,I
Training: 10 - 13 weeks at the nearest certified training restaurant	

SPECIFIC EXPANSION PLANS:

US:	All US
Canada:	All Canada
Overseas:	India, China, UK, Caribbean, C. America, Indonesia, Gulf Sts/ME

For more than 50 years, Denny's has provided the quintessential family dining experience with modestly priced meals. Denny's is committed to being the go-to restaurant for America's best breakfast and prides itself on continuously pursuing innovation to enhance its quality menu and service platform. In addition to its reputation for its breakfast items and late-night dining, Denny's has also seen substantial success with its updated lunch and dinner menus that include a variety of health-conscious choices.

With more than 1,600 restaurants worldwide and annual sales of more than $2 billion, Denny's boasts nearly 100% brand recognition as one of the largest full-service family restaurant chains in the United States.

Operating Units	12/31/2008	12/31/2009	12/31/2010
Franchised	1,149	1,241	1,339
% Change	--	8 %	7.9 %
Company-Owned	314	233	232
% Change	--	-25.8%	-0.4 %
Total	1,463	1,474	1,571
% Change	--	0.8 %	6.6 %
Franchised as % of Total	78.5 %	84.2 %	85.2 %

Investment Required
The fee for a Denny's franchise is $40,000.

Denny's provides the following range of investments required to open your initial franchise. The range assumes that all items are paid for in cash. To the extent that you choose to finance any of these expense items, your front-end investment could be substantially reduced.

Item	Established Low Range	Established High Range
Franchise Fee	$0	$40,000
Building and Improvements	$650,000	$1,400,000
Architectural Design	$13,000	$40,000
Equipment, Fixtures, and Furnishings	$350,000	$450,000
Signs	$15,000	$90,000

D.I.N.E. POS Systems	$20,000	$40,000
Opening Costs	$20,505.50	$51,115.50
Security Deposits	$10,000	$15,000
Insurance	$15,000	$20,000
Permits	$5,000	$100,000
Additional Funds (3 months)	$80,000	$150,000
Total Investment	$1,178,505.50	$2,396,115.50

On-going Expenses
Denny's franchisees pay royalties equal to 4% of gross sales and advertising fees equal to 3% or 4% of gross sales. Other fees payable by the franchisee include a local advertising co-op fee and semiannual menu costs.

What You Get—Training and Support
Denny's franchisees spend 10 to 13 weeks at a nearby certified training restaurant for hands-on training, with complete instruction in all aspects of restaurant operation, from management to food safety.

Denny's commitment to franchisee support extends to field-based real estate assistance, an industry-leading supply chain to deliver high-quality food, and ongoing advertising and field support. Additionally, Denny's continually seeks out new and innovative ways to make operations more efficient and help franchisees operate more effectively, including a recently implemented program designed to improve table turn in high-revenue day parts by using technology and operational systems.

Territory
Denny's grants non-exclusive territories. Denny's may grant exclusive territories only through its Market Growth Incentive Plan.

El Pollo Loco

3535 Harbor Blvd., #100
Costa Mesa, CA 92626
Tel: (800) 997-6556 (714) 599-5000
Fax: (714) 599-5650
Email: mwildman@elpolloloco.com
Website: www.elpolloloco.com
Michael Wildman, VP Franchise Sales/Development

El Pollo Loco is the nation's leading quick-service restaurant chain specializing in flame-grilled chicken. Offering a fresh, healthful alternative to traditional fast food, El Pollo Loco warm tortillas, fresh salsas and a variety of accompaniments. Fresh Mexican entrees (signature grilled burritos, Pollo Bowls, Pollo Salads, quesadillas, etc.) are also served. All feature the delicious citrus-marinated, flame-grilled chicken that put El Pollo Loco on the map. In January of 2010, El Pollo Loco expanded its flame-grilled offerings with the addition of flame-grilled, carne asada-style sirloin steak.

BACKGROUND: IFA Member
Established: 1980;   First Franchised: 1984
Franchised Units: 172
Company-Owned Units: 134
Total Units: 306

Dist.:	US-306; CAN-0; O'seas-0
North America:	0 States
Density:	19 in NV, 348 in CA, 21 in AZ
Projected New Units (12 Months):	5
Qualifications:	5, 5, 5, 3, 3, 5

FINANCIAL/TERMS:
Cash Investment:	$250K
Total Investment:	$502K-1.1M
Minimum Net Worth:	$1.5M
Fees: Franchise -	$40K
Royalty - 4%;	Ad. - 5%
Earnings Claims Statement:	Yes
Term of Contract (Years):	20
Avg. # of Employees:	8 FT, 17 PT
Passive Ownership:	Allowed, But Discouraged
Encourage Conversions:	Yes
Area Develop. Agreements:	Yes
Sub-Franchising Contracts:	No
Expand in Territory:	Yes
Space Needs:	2,400 SF

SUPPORT & TRAINING:
Financial Assistance Provided:	No
Site Selection Assistance:	Yes
Lease Negotiation Assistance:	No
Co-operative Advertising:	No
Franchisee Assoc./Member:	Yes/Yes
Size of Corporate Staff:	142
On-going Support:	A,NA,C,D,E,F,G,H,I
Training:	7 weeks southern CA

SPECIFIC EXPANSION PLANS:
US:	All US
Canada:	No
Overseas:	No

From its beginnings as a roadside chicken stand to its present 400 company- and franchise-owned restaurants, El Pollo Loco continues to bring dishes to consumers who desire flavorful food that complements today's active lifestyles. El Pollo Loco's signature dish features an authentic family recipe of fresh chicken marinated in special herbs, spices, and citrus juices that is flame-grilled to perfection. Through the years, El Pollo Loco has demonstrated a strong commitment to menu innovation, introducing a wide variety of fresh flavorful entrées inspired by the kitchens of Mexico.

El Pollo Loco has broad and deep consumer acceptance across a wide span of demographic and socioeconomic sectors and is a healthier alternative to traditional fast food.

Operating Units	12/31/2008	12/31/2009	12/31/2010
Franchised	248	243	241
% Change	--	-2%	-0.8%
Company-Owned	165	172	171
% Change	--	4.2 %	-0.6%
Total	413	415	412
% Change	--	0.5 %	-0.7 %
Franchised as % of Total	60.1 %	58.6 %	58.5 %

Investment Required

The fee for an El Pollo Loco franchise is $40,000.

El Pollo Loco provides the following range of investments required to open your initial franchise. The range assumes that all items are paid for in cash. To the extent that you choose to finance any of these expense items, your front-end investment could be substantially reduced.

Item	Established Low Range	Established High Range
Franchise Fee	$40,000	$40,000
Lease Payment	$3,350	$13,350
Architectural Design	$15,000	$65,000
Equipment, Fixtures and Furnishings	$275,000	$425,000
POS Equipment	$20,000	$40,000
Signage	$6,000	$50,000
Expenses While Training	$10,000	$20,000

Opening Inventory and Supplies	$20,000	$25,000
Lease Security Deposits	$5,000	$10,000
Insurance	$3,000	$6,000
Grand Opening Fee	$5,000	$5,000
Additional Funds (3 months)	$25,000	$100,000
Site Selection Costs	$500	$3,000
Total Investment	$427,850	$802,350

On-going Expenses
El Pollo Loco franchisees pay royalty fees equal to 4% of monthly gross sales and advertising fees ranging from 5% to 6% of monthly gross sales. Additional fees payable by the franchisee include training fees.

What You Get—Training and Support
Along with training materials, franchisees and their teams attend training sessions on El Pollo Loco's System that, based on each team member's position, ranges from 10-40 days. Working with seasoned veterans, franchisees gain hands-on training in restaurant operations and management. Additionally, expert real estate teams work with El Pollo Loco franchisees in market planning and site selection to determine the best possible locations for new restaurants.

El Pollo Loco provides their franchisees with first-class marketing support with a team of experienced executives and management. El Pollo Loco's marketing and advertising programs include innovative campaigns, bilingual promotional strategies, product innovation to fuel sustained growth, support for grand openings and marketing plans tailored to each market's needs.

Territory
El Pollo Loco grants non-exclusive territories.

Famous Famiglia

199 Main St., 8th Fl.
White Plains, NY 10601
Tel: (914) 328-4444
Fax: (914) 328-4479
Email: giorgio@famousfamiglia.com
Website: www.famousfamiglia.com
Giorgio Kolaj, Executive Vice President/Co-Founder

Famous Famiglia is an award-winning international pizza brand with leading sales in the pizza segment. Operating worldwide, Famous Famiglia has earned several leading industry awards for its unsurpassed product quality and customer service. Expansion plans include high-profile markets and locations such as leading airports, shopping plazas, universities, casinos, military bases, cinemas, etc. With a successful franchise program in place, a number of high-caliber locations internationally are available.

BACKGROUND: IFA Member
Established: 1986; First Franchised: 2001
Franchised Units: 72
Company-Owned Units: 23
Total Units: 95
Dist.: US-90; CAN-0; O'seas-5
  North America: 26 States

Density:	14 in PA, 39 in NY, 15 in NJ
Projected New Units (12 Months):	32
Qualifications:	4, 4, 3, 1, 4, 5

FINANCIAL/TERMS:

Cash Investment:	$200K
Total Investment:	$250-550K
Minimum Net Worth:	$1M
Fees: Franchise -	$35K
Royalty - 6%;	Ad. - 1%
Earnings Claims Statement:	No
Term of Contract (Years):	10/5-10
Avg. # of Employees:	4 FT, 8 PT
Passive Ownership:	Allowed, But Discouraged
Encourage Conversions:	Yes
Area Develop. Agreements:	Yes
Sub-Franchising Contracts:	Yes
Expand in Territory:	Yes
Space Needs:	600-1,200 SF

SUPPORT & TRAINING:

Financial Assistance Provided:	No
Site Selection Assistance:	Yes
Lease Negotiation Assistance:	Yes
Co-operative Advertising:	Yes
Franchisee Assoc./Member:	No
Size of Corporate Staff:	18
On-going Support:	A,B,C,D,E,F,G,H,I
Training: 2-4 weeks corporate headquarters, NY	

SPECIFIC EXPANSION PLANS:

US:	All US
Canada:	All Canada
Overseas:	All Countries

Famous Famiglia, established in New York City in 1986, is an award-winning national pizza brand with leading sales in the QSR pizza segment. Dubbed "New York's Favorite Pizza,"™ the pizzeria has earned several leading industry awards that herald its unsurpassed product quality and customer service. Famous Famiglia serves a wide variety of pizzas, pastas, calzones, strombolis, salads and desserts.

Famous Famiglia's expansion program revolves around building strong and meaningful partnerships with market-leading operators and landlords. Currently the company is focusing on expanding to high-profile markets and locations, such as leading theme parks, airports, universities, travel plazas, shopping centers, sporting stadiums, casinos, arenas and more. Additionally, Famous Famiglia makes a point of giving back to the community which it serves; the franchisor is engaged in various charitable programs and projects, e.g. donating funds to local children's charities.

Operating Units	12/31/2008	12/31/2009	12/31/2010
Franchised	31	36	36
% Change	--	16.1%	0%
Company-Owned	24	18	19
% Change	--	-25%	5.6%
Total	55	54	55
% Change	--	-1.8%	1.9%
Franchised as % of Total	56.4%	66.7%	65.5%

Investment Required
The fee for a Famous Famiglia franchise is $35,000 for a Standard Unit (e.g. a restaurant with 700-2,500 square feet) and $10,000 for an Express Unit (e.g. a restaurant with 200-600 square feet and a limited menu).

Famous Famiglia provides the following range of investments required to open your initial franchise. The range assumes that all items are paid for in cash. To the extent that you choose to finance any of these expense items, your front-end investment could be substantially reduced.

	Standard Unit		Express Unit	
Item	High Range	Low Range	High Range	Low Range
Franchise Fee	$35,000	$35,000	$10,000	$10,000
Leasehold Improvements	$100,000	$250,000	$25,000	$75,000

Rent	$5,000	$20,000	$0	$3,000
Equipment, Furniture and Fixture	$60,000	$85,000	$30,000	$60,000
Signage	$5,000	$15,000	$2,500	$5,000
Initial Inventory	$5,000	$12,500	$5,000	$8,000
Architectural/ Engineering	$10,000	$25,000	$2,500	$12,000
Computer & POS System	$10,000	$18,500	$5,000	$12,000
Expenses While Training	$2,500	$5,000	$2,500	$5,000
Office Supplies	$1,500	$2,500	$1,500	$2,500
Business Licenses and Permits	$250	$1,000	$250	$1,000
Delivery or Catering	$0	$3,800	$0	$3,800
Insurance (for 1st year)	$1,500	$2,500	$1,500	$2,500
Opening Advertising	$5,000	$5,000	$5,000	$5,000
Additional Funds (6 months)	$25,000	$50,000	$10,000	$30,000
Total Investment	$265,750	$530,800	$100,750	$234,800

On-going Expenses

Famous Famiglia franchisees pay royalty fees equal to 6% of gross sales for the first 5 restaurants, 5% for each additional restaurant, an advertising fee equal to 0-2% of gross sales, and a cooperate advertising fee equal to 0-2% of gross sales.

What You Get—Training and Support

A franchisee, a general manager, and two employees are required to attend a 2-4 week initial training session conducted at the Famous Famiglia corporate headquarters and a designated company-owned restaurant in White Plains, NY. Training programs cover topics on restaurant operation, management, marketing and accounting, and are offered 5-6 times a year beginning on Monday mornings. Supplementary training sessions are offered throughout the year.

Territory

Famous Famiglia does not grant exclusive territories, except for the assigned area (i.e. airport, university, shopping mall) in which each restaurant is located.

Great Wraps

The NEW American Sandwich™

4 Executive Park E., # 315
Atlanta, GA 30329
Tel: (888) 489-7277 (404) 248-9900 x16
Fax: (404) 248-0180
Email: franchise@greatwraps.com
Website: www.greatwraps.com
Mark Kaplan, President

Great Wraps is the #1 hot wrapped sandwich & grilled cheesesteak franchise, and is experiencing rapid growth. That's because we offer a franchise opportunity that is unique and proven, and provides tremendous growth potential. We feature a powerful menu that is fresher and tastier than traditional fast food, and our Great Wraps Spice Bar lets customers custom-flavor their fries. No one else offers this level of choice. Our operation is extremely efficient, and is so simple to learn, you don't even need prior food experience.

BACKGROUND:	IFA Member
Established: 1978;	First Franchised: 1981
Franchised Units:	98
Company-Owned Units:	1
Total Units:	99
Dist.:	US-99; CAN-0; O'seas-0
North America:	20 States
Density:	8 in TX, 19 in GA, 8 in FL
Projected New Units (12 Months):	15
Qualifications:	5, 3, 3, 3, 4, 4

FINANCIAL/TERMS:	
Cash Investment:	$100K
Total Investment:	$225-350K
Minimum Net Worth:	$250K
Fees: Franchise -	$22.5K
Royalty - 5.5%;	Ad. - .5%
Earnings Claims Statement:	Yes
Term of Contract (Years):	15/10
Avg. # of Employees:	5 FT, 6 PT
Passive Ownership:	Allowed, But Discouraged
Encourage Conversions:	Yes
Area Develop. Agreements:	No
Sub-Franchising Contracts:	Yes

Expand in Territory:	Yes	Size of Corporate Staff:	8
Space Needs:	600-2,000 SF	On-going Support:	NA,NA,C,D,E,NA,G,H,NA
		Training:	2 weeks Atlanta, GA
SUPPORT & TRAINING:			
Financial Assistance Provided:	Yes (I)	**SPECIFIC EXPANSION PLANS:**	
Site Selection Assistance:	Yes	US:	NE, SE, SW, MW
Lease Negotiation Assistance:	Yes	Canada:	No
Co-operative Advertising:	Yes	Overseas:	No
Franchisee Assoc./Member:	Yes/Yes		

Over the years, Great Wraps has built a loyal following with its revolutionary quick-serve food. Great Wraps's explosive growth accompanies a fresh approach: a better sandwich with less bread. Each sandwich is filled with unique, hot combinations, meat, real melted cheese, fresh produce, and special sauces that customers can customize to be indulgent or healthy, according to their preferences. Customers can enjoy the fully stocked Great Wraps spice bar where they can make the perfect sandwich/wrap creation to their personal tastes.

Great Wraps franchisees offer a tasty and unique product that customers recognize as better and healthier than many other fast food and generic sub sandwich restaurants. In addition to serving individual customers, franchisees have the opportunity to expand revenue through catering services.

Operating Units	12/31/2008	12/31/2009	12/31/2010
Franchised	70	68	67
	--	-2.9 %	-1.5%
Company-Owned	2	1	1
% Change	--	-50 %	0 %
Total	72	69	68
% Change	--	-4.2 %	-1.4 %
Franchised as % of Total	97.2%	98.6%	98.5%

Investment Required
The franchise fee for a Great Wraps franchise is $11,250.

Great Wraps provides the following range of investments required to open your initial franchise. The range assumes that all items are paid for in cash. To the extent that you choose to finance any of these expense items, your front-end investment could be substantially reduced.

Item	Established Low Range	Established High Range
Franchise Fee	$11,250	$11,250
Equipment & Furniture	$65,000	$75,000
Construction and Lease-hold Improvements	$120,000	$186,000
Signage, Menu Board	$6,000	$9,000
Cash Registers	$6,200	$6,200
Architectural Fees	$6,000	$8,000
Opening Inventory	$4,000	$6,000
Insurance	$4,500	$4,500
Security Deposit	$8,500	$12,500
Expenses While Training	$2,000	$3,000
Professional Fees	$1,000	$3,500
Additional Funds (3 months)	$75,000	$75,000
Total Investment	$309,450	$399,950

On-going Expenses

Great Wraps franchisees pay continuing franchise fees equal to 5.5% of net sales, plus a brand development royalty fee equal to 0.5% of net sales and subject to increase up to 3%.

What You Get—Training and Support

Franchisees undergo a 10-day training that prepares them for a simple, efficient and complete business operation. Great Wraps assists franchisees in contacting a local broker for site selection and helps negotiate store leases.

The Store Development Team guides franchisees through the design, permitting, bidding and construction process.

On-going training and support includes access to new sandwich recipes that are constantly in development. Strong marketing support is provided for franchisees both for Grand Opening and on an ongoing basis to support franchisee success. Additionally, Great Wraps Business Consultants make periodic visits to help franchisees implement new programs.

Territory
Great Wraps does not grant exclusive territories.

Little Caesars

2211 Woodward Ave., Fox Office Center
Detroit, MI 48201
Tel: (800) 553-5776 (313) 471-6409
Fax: (313) 983-6435
Email: usdevelopment@lcecorp.com
Website: www.littlecaesars.com
Dan Ducharme, Director of Franchise Development

After 50 years in business, Little Caesars is the fastest growing pizza chain in the United States, with consistent growth for many years. The efficient operating system enables franchisees build-out costs to remain modest while keeping the high quality standards our strong brand requires. Prime markets are available, and franchisee candidates are offered an opportunity for independence with a proven system. Visit littlecaesars.com to see why we are "The Best Kept Secret!"

BACKGROUND: IFA Member
Established: 1959; First Franchised: 1962

Unfortunately, Little Caesars does not permit the publication of any detail about the number of operating units it has.

Qualifications: 4, 2, 2, 2, 4, 5

FINANCIAL/TERMS:
Cash Investment:	$50K
Total Investment:	$194.25 - 622.5K
Minimum Net Worth:	$150K
Fees: Franchise -	$15-20K
Royalty - 6%;	Ad. - 3%
Earnings Claims Statement:	No
Term of Contract (Years):	10/10
Avg. # of Employees:	1 FT, 30 PT
Passive Ownership:	Not Allowed
Encourage Conversions:	Yes
Area Develop. Agreements:	Yes
Sub-Franchising Contracts:	No
Expand in Territory:	Yes
Space Needs:	1,400 SF

SUPPORT & TRAINING:		Training:	6 weeks Detroit, MI
Financial Assistance Provided:	Yes (I)		
Site Selection Assistance:	Yes	**SPECIFIC EXPANSION PLANS:**	
Lease Negotiation Assistance:	Yes	US:	All US
Co-operative Advertising:	Yes	Canada:	All Provinces
Franchisee Assoc./Member:	Yes/No	Overseas:	China, India, Mexico, Australia, S.
Size of Corporate Staff:	300		Korea, Europe, Caribbean
On-going Support:	NA,B,C,D,E,F,G,H,I		

Founded in 1959 and with a franchising history dating back to 1962, Little Caesars has become the fastest growing pizza chain in America. Business is still booming with Little Caesars having added more restaurants to its chain in 2009 than any other pizza brand in the world. Little Caesars pizza is made with fresh, high-quality ingredients: dough made daily in stores, fresh, never-frozen cheese, and a sauce made of vine-ripened tomatoes and a secret spice blend. The pizzeria is also known for innovation in its products, offering its Crazy Bread®, Pizza Pizza®, and Hot-N-Ready® products.

Little Caesars was named "Best Value in America" among all quick service restaurants for four consecutive years in Sandelman & Associates' Quick-Track® research study, one of the largest food industry studies. Little Caesars is also devoted to giving back to the community. Established in 1985, the company's pizza restaurant on wheels, "Love Kitchen," has been serving more than two million people in need and the homeless.

Unfortunately, Little Caesars does not permit the publication of any detail about the number of operating units it has.

Investment Required
The fee for a Little Caesars franchise is $20,000, with a $5,000 reduction for existing franchisees and for veterans (service-disabled veterans do not have to pay the fee).

Little Caesars provides the following range of investments required to open your initial franchise. The range assumes that all items are paid for in cash. To the extent that you choose to finance any of these expense items, your front-end investment could be substantially reduced.

Item	Established Low Range	Established High Range
Franchise Fee	$0 - 15,000	$20,000
Rent	$1,500	$6,000
Leasehold Improvements	$50,000	$300,000
Fixtures, Equipment, and Signage	$80,000	$170,000
Grand Opening Advertising	$11,000	$20,000
Expenses While Training	$7,000	$9,000
Start-up Inventory and Supplies	$25,000	$35,000
Insurance	$500	$1,500
Utility Expenses	$1,000	$5,000
Licenses and Permits	$50	$6,000
Additional Funds (3 months)	$17,000	$47,000
Total Investment	$193,050	$619,500

On-going Expenses

Little Caesars franchisees pay royalty fees equal to 6% of gross sales.

What You Get—Training and Support

Little Caesars has a strong belief in supporting its franchisees. Initial training, a comprehensive program lasting six weeks at corporate headquarters and company-owned restaurants in Detroit, Michigan, covers topics such as store operations, cash management, human resources, customer service, marketing and quality assurance. A two-day real estate/architecture/equipment training program is completed before franchisees continue the rest of the training.

Little Caesars supports franchisees with the tools of a proven system, including ongoing training, architectural services to help with design and construction, preferred lenders to assist with financing, ongoing research and development of new products, and continuing, effective marketing programs and support.

Territory
Little Caesars grants protected territories with a radius equal to one mile, except under certain circumstances (e.g. in highly populated urban areas).

Manhattan Bagel Company

555 Zang St., # 300
Lakewood, CO 80228
Tel: (800) BAGEL ME
Fax: (609) 737-2485
Email: kkruse@einsteinnoah.com
Website: www.manhattanbagel.com
Kevin Kruse, VP of Franchise Development

Manhattan Bagel Company franchises fast casual bagel cafes which serve over 15 varieties of authentic New York bagels, as well as gourmet coffees and deli items, and a full breakfast and lunch menu. Our franchising program includes assistance with site selection, construction, and operations training. Our comprehensive training includes a detailed operations manual and continuing assistance in baking and food preparation and service, marketing, and merchandising. We typically close each evening by 5pm, promoting a better quality of life for management and staff. Contact us to learn more about this established and growing opportunity!

BACKGROUND:	IFA Member
Established: 1987;	First Franchised: 1991
Franchised Units:	68
Company-Owned Units:	1
Total Units:	69
Dist.:	US-69; CAN-0; O'seas-0

North America:	9 States
Density:	22 in PA, 7 in NY, 29 in NJ
Projected New Units (12 Months):	6
Qualifications:	4, 4, 5, 3, 1, 5

FINANCIAL/TERMS:

Cash Investment:	$225K
Total Investment:	$482-848K
Minimum Net Worth:	$450K
Fees: Franchise -	$25K
Royalty - 5%;	Ad. - Up to 5%
Earnings Claims Statement:	Yes
Term of Contract (Years):	10/10
Avg. # of Employees:	3 FT, 9 PT
Passive Ownership:	Allowed, But Discouraged
Encourage Conversions:	Yes
Area Develop. Agreements:	Yes
Sub-Franchising Contracts:	No
Expand in Territory:	Yes
Space Needs:	1,800-2,200 SF

SUPPORT & TRAINING:

Financial Assistance Provided:	No
Site Selection Assistance:	Yes
Lease Negotiation Assistance:	Yes
Co-operative Advertising:	Yes
Franchisee Assoc./Member:	Yes/Yes
Size of Corporate Staff:	200
On-going Support:	NA,B,C,D,E,F,NA,H,NA
Training:	1 week corporate office; 2 weeks store

SPECIFIC EXPANSION PLANS:

US:	All US
Canada:	No
Overseas:	No

Manhattan Bagel is about authentic food for real people, served in a way that suggests each customer is a treasured neighbor. Its bakery menu features over twenty varieties of its award winning bagels and freshly baked pesto focaccia bread. Manhattan Bagel believes in the importance of fresh, delicious food, baking their bagels and breads fresh, making every sandwich to order, and using only authentically grilled real eggs and bacon in their sandwiches.

Manhattan Bagel is a vibrant, quick, casual bagel concept with over 65 restaurants located primarily in their core geographical area of brand strength along the East Coast. Franchisees with a background in business and the restaurant industry are enthusiastically welcomed, and their individual success will help bring Manhattan Bagel's nationally recognized brand to the next level.

Operating Units	12/31/2008	12/31/2009	12/31/2010
Franchised	68	70	72
% Change	--	2.9%	2.9%
Company-Owned	1	1	1
% Change	--	0%	0%
Total	69	71	73
% Change	--	2.9%	2.8%
Franchised as % of Total	98.6%	98.6%	98.6%

Investment Required
The fee for a Manhattan Bagel franchise is $25,000. For a previous franchisee opening up additional restaurant locations, the fee is $15,000. Manhattan Bagel also allows for an Area Developer and participates in the VetFran Program.

Manhattan Bagel provides the following range of investments required to open your initial franchise. The range assumes that all items are paid for in cash. To the extent that you choose to finance any of these expense items, your front-end investment could be substantially reduced.

Item	Established Low Range	Established High Range
Franchise Fee	$25,000	$25,000
Real Estate Leasing	$16,000	$35,000
Construction/Leasehold Improvements	$164,601	$200,000
Kitchen/Computer Equipment & Lighting	$112,003	$130,000
Furniture, Fixtures & Millwork	$28,940	$35,000
Signage and Graphics	$10,918	$30,000
Professional Fees	$18,800	$30,000
Opening Inventory, Smallwares and Supplies	$10,000	$20,000
Grand Opening Advertising	$7,500	$10,000
Insurance	$4,000	$7,500
Expenses While Training	$1,000	$14,000
Legal, Accounting & Licenses	$1,500	$8,000
Security Deposits	$4,000	$10,000
ServSafe Food Safety Training Program	$300	$600
Additional Funds (3 Months)	$12,000	$50,000
Total Investment	$416,562	$605,100

On-going Expenses
Manhattan Bagel franchisees pay a weekly royalty fee of 5% of gross sales

and a weekly advertising contribution of up to 5% of gross sales. Other fees include systems support fee and a quality control evaluation program fee.

What You Get—Training and Support
Manhattan Bagel has developed a strong system of support, made up of both an existing franchisee field support structure and a senior management of industry veterans. The Manhattan Bagel training program, consisting of 24 hours of classroom training and 170 hours of on-the-job training, extends to day-to-day operations in each individual store, from topical training to supplying the right manuals for thorough field support.

Manhattan Bagel also maintains an in-house culinary department that ranks with the best in the industry. Their culinary researchers and seasoned chefs are in a constant quest for the next "next thing." As a result, Manhattan Bagel franchisees get to showcase that cutting edge culinary prowess in their markets.

Territory
Manhattan Bagel grants exclusive territories.

Maui Wowi Hawaiian Coffees and Smoothies

5445 DTC Pkwy., # 1050
Greenwood Village, CO 80111
Tel: (877) 849-6992 x130 (303) 781-7800
Fax: (303) 781-2438
Email: info@mauiwowi.com
Website: www.mauiwowi.com
Michael Haith, CEO

Ranked as # 175 in Inc 500, with over 350 locations, Maui Wowi Hawaiian is the #1 largest smoothie/coffee franchise in the world. With 24/7 support and extensive training, Maui Wowi Hawaiian offers a simple, profitable and flexible business business model. Maui Wowi Hawaiian has thousands of locations and events throughout the country, waiting for a Maui Wowi Hawaiian franchise owner. Because of our flexibility, low investment and variety of business models, Maui Wowi Hawaiian is the fastest-growing franchise.

BACKGROUND:		Encourage Conversions:	Yes
Established: 1983;	IFA Member	Area Develop. Agreements:	Yes
Franchised Units:	First Franchised: 1997	Sub-Franchising Contracts:	No
Company-Owned Units:	500	Expand in Territory:	Yes
Total Units:	1	Space Needs:	100 SF
Dist.:	501		
North America:	US-501; CAN-0; O'seas-0	**SUPPORT & TRAINING:**	
Density:	47 States	Financial Assistance Provided:	Yes (I)
Projected New Units (12 Months):	NR	Site Selection Assistance:	Yes
Qualifications:	250-300	Lease Negotiation Assistance:	Yes
	2, 2, 1, 1, 1, 5	Co-operative Advertising:	Yes
		Franchisee Assoc./Member:	No
FINANCIAL/TERMS:		Size of Corporate Staff:	150
Cash Investment:	$50K+	On-going Support:	NA,NA,C,D,E,F,G,H,I
Total Investment:	$65-395K	Training:	5 days Denver, CO
Minimum Net Worth:	$250K		
Fees: Franchise -	$29.5-59.5K		
Royalty - 0%;	Ad. - 12%		
Earnings Claims Statement:	Yes	**SPECIFIC EXPANSION PLANS:**	
Term of Contract (Years):	10	US:	All US
Avg. # of Employees:	2 FT, 0 PT	Canada:	All Canada
Passive Ownership:	Allowed	Overseas:	All Countries

In 1983, Jeff and Jill Summerhays started Maui Wowi Hawaiian to provide their 'Ohana (family) a healthy alternative to sugar and fat-laden foods. Maui Wowi Hawaiian is famous for their line of proprietary all-natural smoothies made by blending exotic fruit juices, fruit purees, all-natural flavorings, and their own non-fat yogurt, as well as their exclusive line of Kona espresso and cappuccino drinks and a gourmet line of blended coffees. Maui Wowi Hawaiian prides themselves on providing not only world-class coffee and fresh fruit smoothies, but also an inviting store environment and Aloha customer service.

Maui Wowi offers a simple business, allowing franchisees to build their own businesses promoting healthy, quality products under the wildly successful Maui Wowi Hawaiian brand umbrella. Franchisees also benefit from the flexibility of a wide variety of business models from shopping mall kiosks to drive-through retail stores.

Operating Units	12/31/2008	12/31/2009	12/31/2010
Franchised	308	256	206

% Change	--	-16.9%	-19.5%
Company-Owned	0	0	0
% Change	--	--	--
Total	308	256	206
% Change	--	-16.9%	-19.5%
Franchised as % of Total	100%	100%	100%

Investment Required

The fee for a Maui Wowi franchise ranges from $27,500 to $59,500.

Maui Wowi provides the following range of investments required to open a Fixed Operating Unit. The range assumes that all items are paid for in cash. To the extent that you choose to finance any of these expense items, your front-end investment could be substantially reduced.

Item	Established Low Range	Established High Range
Franchise Fee	$27,500	$59,500
Expenses While Training	$650	$3,550
Real Estate Lease	$1,200	$30,000
Fixed Kiosk	$0	$90,000
Equipment/Décor	$7,500	$25,000
Construction	$10,000	$140,000
Launch Fee	$10,000	$10,000
Architect's Fees	$4,000	$12,000
Opening Inventory	$2,000	$8,000
Signage	$3,500	$12,000
POS System	$5,000	$12,000
Misc. Opening Costs	$3,000	$8,000

Additional Funds (3 Months)	$0	$40,000
Total Initial Investment	$74,350	$450,050

On-going Expenses
Maui Wowi franchisees pay a monthly royalty fee of 6% of gross revenue, plus 12% of purchase price of Maui Wowi products, supplies, and equipment.

What You Get—Training and Support
Maui Wowi franchisees undergo initial training at the Maui Wowi headquarters in Denver, CO. This covers everything from day-to-day operations such as coffee and smoothie training to accounting, leadership, and employee management training. Additionally, Maui Wowi provides franchisees with access to a library of operating manuals which includes training workbooks, store design guidebooks, and event workbooks.

Territory
Maui Wowi does not grant exclusive territories.

Papa Murphy's

Papa Murphy's produces a great pizza made from top-quality ingredients. Letting customers bake it themselves is smart business. Put the two together and you get the largest, fastest-growing Take 'N' Bake franchise in the world. Papa Murphy's now has 1,300 stores with another 100 stores expected to open in 2012.

8000 N.E. Parkway Dr., # 350
Vancouver, WA 98662
Tel: (800) 257-7272 (360) 260-7272
Fax: (360) 260-0500
Email: rhondam@papamurphys.com
Website: www.papamurphys.com
Rhonda McGrew, Manager Franchise Development

BACKGROUND:	IFA Member
Established: 1981;	First Franchised: 1982
Franchised Units:	1,250
Company-Owned Units:	51

Total Units:	1,301	Sub-Franchising Contracts:	
Dist.:	US-1,283; CAN-18; O'seas-0	Expand in Territory:	Yes
North America:	37 States, 2 Provinces	Space Needs:	1,200-1,400 SF
Density:	150 in CA, 140 in WA, 95 in OR		
Projected New Units (12 Months):	100	**SUPPORT & TRAINING:**	
Qualifications:	4, 3, 2, 3, 2, 5	Financial Assistance Provided:	Yes (I)
		Site Selection Assistance:	Yes
FINANCIAL/TERMS:		Lease Negotiation Assistance:	Yes
Cash Investment:	$80K	Co-operative Advertising:	Yes
Total Investment:	$180-275K	Franchisee Assoc./Member:	Yes/Yes
Minimum Net Worth:	$250K	Size of Corporate Staff:	150
Fees: Franchise -	$25K	On-going Support:	NA,NA,C,D,E,NA,G,H,I
Royalty - 5%;	Ad. - 2%	Training:	5 days corporate office;
Earnings Claims Statement:	Yes	20 days store;3 days/30 hours closest training store	
Term of Contract (Years):	10/5		
Avg. # of Employees:	2 FT, 8-10 PT	**SPECIFIC EXPANSION PLANS:**	
Passive Ownership:	Not Allowed	US:	Midwest, Central, South
Encourage Conversions:	Yes	Canada:	Yes
Area Develop. Agreements:	Yes	Overseas:	No

Since its inception in 1981, Papa Murphy's popular Take 'N' Bake concept has exploded into the pizza industry, and Papa Murphy's has consistently been voted as the "Best Pizza Chain in America" for years running. Today, Papa Murphy's is the largest Take 'N' Bake pizza company in the world and the fifth largest pizza company in the United States, operating over 1,300 stores in 37 states. Papa Murphy's three core values are the foundation of its success: great quality, great value, and great customer service. With its commitment to superior products and services, Papa Murphy's is proud to offer a pizza experience that is second to none.

With its domination of the Take 'N' Bake industry and its leading popularity in the American pizza industry, Papa Murphy's presents an excellent business opportunity for franchisees. Owning a Papa Murphy's requires lower initial investment than most pizza chains, as there are no ovens, delivery services, or dine-in services, making operating a Papa Murphy's franchise much easier than owning any other chain in the industry.

Operating Units	12/31/2008	12/31/2009	12/31/2010
Franchised	1,056	1,136	1,206
% Change	--	7.6%	6.2%

Company-Owned	63	35	33
% Change	--	-44.4%	-5.7%
Total	1,119	1,171	1,239
% Change	--	4.6%	5.8%
Franchised as % of Total	94.4%	97.1%	97.3%

Investment Required

The fee for a Papa Murphy's franchise is $25,000, with reduced subsequent franchise fees for additional franchised locations and/or upon signing an Area Development Agreement.

Papa Murphy's provides the following range of investments required to open your initial franchise. The range assumes that all items are paid for in cash. To the extent that you choose to finance any of these expense items, your front-end investment could be substantially reduced.

Item	Established Low Range	Established High Range
Franchise Fee	$15,000	$25,000
Lease, Utilities, Deposits & Payments	$2,500	$6,000
Leasehold Improvements	$46,200	$115,500
Signs	$5,000	$10,000
Stamped Architectural Drawings	$2,500	$4,200
Equipment, Supplies, Décor, POS System, & Smallwares	$85,000	$135,000
Inventory	$5,000	$7,000
Initial Advertising (6 Months)	$30,000	$35,000
Premises Rent (3 Months)	$3,975	$14,985

Materials and Supplies	$500	$2,000
Expenses While Training	$1,280	$17,750
Employee Training	$500	$1,500
Insurance (3 Months)	$375	$1,175
Book-keeping/Payroll Service (3 Months)	$1,500	$1,600
Additional Funds (3 Months)	$10,000	$20,000
Total Investment	$209,330	$396,710

On-going Expenses

Papa Murphy's franchisees pay royalty fees equal to 5% of weekly net sales, advertising fees equal to a maximum of 2% of weekly net sales, and mandatory local/regional co-op advertising and promotional expenditures equal to the greater of 5% of net sales or $1,500 for each four-week period. Additional ongoing expenses include monthly customer relations management fees, bookkeeping service fees and broadband fees, as well as annual software maintenance fees and hosting fees.

What You Get—Training and Support

Papa Murphy's provides considerable training and support to franchisees to ensure a positive franchise partnership and to guarantee franchisee success. Papa Murphy's assists franchisees in choosing and assessing a site location, analyzing the franchised location in relation to the market area to determine site feasibility and market potential. Franchisees participate in a comprehensive training program that consists of intensive on-site training at a designated Papa Murphy's store as well as a five-day training course held at corporate headquarters in Vancouver, WA. Training covers topics including recipes, product preparation and presentation, employee guidelines, customer relations, general business operation, retail sales practices, franchise systems management, bookkeeping and financial management, inventory control and purchasing, and marketing.

After the successful opening of a franchised location, franchisees benefit from ongoing assistance in training, advertising, sales assistance and operations. Papa Murphy's offers periodic refresher training courses, seminars and regional conferences, as well as an annual franchise convention. Furthermore, Papa Murphy's administers an advertising program and formulates and conducts national, regional and local promotional programs.

Territory
Papa Murphy's does not grant exclusive territories.

Rita's Italian Ice

1210 N. Brook Dr., # 310
Trevose, PA 19053
Tel: (800) 677-7482 (215) 876-9300
Fax: (866) 449-0974
Email: franchise_sales@ritascorp.com
Website: www.ritasice.com
Lauriena Borstein, Director of Franchise Development

Rita's is the largest Italian ice chain in the nation. With a 25-year proven business model, Rita's offers a variety of frozen treats including its famous Italian Ice, Old Fashioned Frozen Custard, and layered Gelati as well as its signature Misto and Blendini creations.

BACKGROUND:	IFA Member
Established: 1984;	First Franchised: 1989
Franchised Units:	550
Company-Owned Units:	1
Total Units:	551
Dist.:	US-551; CAN-0; O'seas-0
North America:	23 States
Density:	228 in PA, 108 in NJ, 80 in MD

Projected New Units (12 Months):	30
Qualifications:	3, 3, 3, 3, 3, 5

FINANCIAL/TERMS:	
Cash Investment:	$75K
Total Investment:	$199.4-378.4K
Minimum Net Worth:	$250K
Fees: Franchise -	$35K
Royalty - 6.5%;	Ad. - 2.5%
Earnings Claims Statement:	Yes
Term of Contract (Years):	10/10
Avg. # of Employees:	2 FT, 15 PT
Passive Ownership:	Allowed, But Discouraged
Encourage Conversions:	No
Area Develop. Agreements:	No
Sub-Franchising Contracts:	No
Expand in Territory:	Yes
Space Needs:	1,000-1,200 SF

SUPPORT & TRAINING:	
Financial Assistance Provided:	Yes (I)
Site Selection Assistance:	Yes
Lease Negotiation Assistance:	Yes
Co-operative Advertising:	Yes
Franchisee Assoc./Member:	No
Size of Corporate Staff:	80
On-going Support:	NA,NA,C,D,E,F,G,H,I
Training:	4 days on-site; 10 days corporate office

SPECIFIC EXPANSION PLANS:	
US:	East of Mississippi
Canada:	No
Overseas:	No

Since 1984, when Bob Tumolo and his mother Elizabeth began experimenting with Italian ice recipes made with chunks of real fresh fruit, Rita's Italian Ice has experienced enormous growth. Today, the Italian Ice franchise has more than 500 stores in 17 states, serving guests with one of the best-tasting, highest-quality Italian Ice around—made with real fruit, available in more than 30 flavors.

With its adherence to the "RITA" values (Respect, Integrity, Trust and Accountability), Rita's has received top rankings by highly regarded industry publications, such as *Entrepreneur Magazine* and *The Wall Street Journal*'s startupjournal.com.

Operating Units	12/31/2008	12/31/2009	12/31/2010
Franchised	546	560	552
% Change	--	2.6%	-1.4%
Company-Owned	6	2	1
% Change	--	-66.7%	-50%
Total	552	562	553
% Change	--	1.8%	-1.6%
Franchised as % of Total	98.9%	99.6%	99.8%

Investment Required
The fee for a Rita's Italian Ice franchise is $35,000. A development agreement is available for franchisees interested in purchasing two or more shops. Rita's Italian Ice participates in a minority program sponsored by the IFA and the IFA's Veterans Transition Franchise Initiative.

Rita's provides the following range of investments required to open your initial franchise. The range assumes that all items are paid for in cash. To the extent that you choose to finance any of these expense items, your front-end investment could be substantially reduced. The costs listed below are for an inline store; for a free standing store, the total initial investment ranges from $256,300 to $561,400.

Item	Established Low Range	Established High Range
Franchise Fee	$35,000	$35,000
Development Fee	$0	$66,500
Lease Deposit	$1,000	$10,000
Leasehold Improvements	$50,000	$150,000
Equipment	$60,000	$80,000
Computer	$500	$1,000
Permits & Licenses	$100	$2,000
Signs & Awnings	$5,000	$15,000
Prepaid Insurance Premium	$1,500	$1,500
Initial Order	$14,000	$18,000
Grand Opening Advertising	$2,500	$3,500
Advertising Fee and Local Advertising	$800	$800
Expenses While Training	$500	$5,000
Utility Costs and Deposits	$1,000	$1,600
Architect and Attorney Fees	$2,500	$15,000
Additional Funds (3 Months)	$25,000	$40,000
Total Investment	$199,400	$444,900

On-going Expenses

Rita's Italian Ice franchisees pay a royalty fee equal to 6.5% of estimated and/or gross sales, an advertising fee equal to 2.5% of estimated and/or gross sales, and minimum weekly advertising expenditures equal to 2% of gross sales.

What You Get—Training and Support

Training takes place at Rita's Cool University in Bensalem, PA, where franchisees learn how to successfully operate their store through a series of intensive workshops. A dedicated team of Rita's Education Specialists teaches franchisees how to make Rita's famous treats, as well as how to uphold company standards, program registers, train staff and other essential operating procedures. Following this workshop, franchisees train at specially designated Rita's locations, working alongside seasoned franchisees to gain hands-on experience in a store environment.

Rita's assists with store setup, staff development and grand opening marketing. Following store opening, franchisees have access to support via the "Cool Support Center," Rita's corporate headquarters that is home to 80 staff members dedicated to supporting franchisees, ensuring the best quality products and building the Rita's brand. Rita's online support website, the "CoolNet," provides franchisees easy access to all resources and information that is required to operate their Rita's Store.

Franchisees continue to benefit from one-on-one field support and ongoing local marketing support throughout their relationship with Rita's.

Territory

Rita's Italian Ice grants exclusive territories.

Schlotzky's Deli

200 Glenridge Point Pkwy., #200
Atlanta, GA 30342
Tel: (404) 255-3250 (404) 705-4412
Fax: (404) 257-7073
Email: spando@schlotzkys.com
Website: www.schlotzkys.com
D'Wayne Tanner, VP Franchise Sales

Since 1971, Schlotzsky's® has been the home of The Original® toasted sandwich. The menu has evolved with customers' tastes to include the highest quality sandwiches, pizzas, salads, and soups available today. With approximately 365 locations worldwide, Schlotzsky's is the fast-casual choice for a quick, healthful, and fresh dining experience.

BACKGROUND: IFA Member
Established: 1971;   First Franchised: 1977
Franchised Units: 331
Company-Owned Units: 27
Total Units: 358
Dist.:   US-341; CAN-0; O'seas-17
  North America: 35 States
  Density:
Projected New Units (12 Months):
Qualifications: 5, 5, 4, 3, 3, 5

FINANCIAL/TERMS:
Cash Investment: $650K (3 store minimum)
Total Investment: $473.6-715.3K
Minimum Net Worth: $2.2M (3 store minimum)
Fees: Franchise - $30K
  Royalty - 6%;   Ad. - 4%

Earnings Claims Statement: Yes
Term of Contract (Years):   20/10
Avg. # of Employees: 5 FT, 20 PT
Passive Ownership: Allowed, But Discouraged
Encourage Conversions: Yes
Area Develop. Agreements: No
Sub-Franchising Contracts: No
Expand in Territory: Yes
Space Needs: 2,800 +/- SF

SUPPORT & TRAINING:
Financial Assistance Provided: No
Site Selection Assistance: Yes
Lease Negotiation Assistance: Yes
Co-operative Advertising: Yes
Franchisee Assoc./Member: Yes/No
Size of Corporate Staff: 0
On-going Support: NA,NA,C,D,E,F,G,H,I
Training: 3 weeks Austin, TX

SPECIFIC EXPANSION PLANS:
US: Yes
Canada: No
Overseas: No

Founded in 1971, Schlotzsky's is a pioneer in the fast casual restaurant category, priding itself on its fun, unique, and quirky atmosphere. Schlotzsky's has created a passionate following amongst customers with over 350 locations in 35 states and four foreign countries. With features including the Lotz Better Table Service unique to this market segment, and new Lotz Better restaurant design, Schlotzsky's is primed for aggressive, responsible growth.

Schlotzksy's franchisees have the opportunity to create lasting memories for their guests, as well as becoming an integral part of the community in which they serve. Franchise opportunities are available for individuals and groups with experience in restaurant management and an interest in multi-restaurant ownership of three stores or more.

Operating Units	12/31/2008	12/12/2009	12/31/2010
Franchised	323	315	305
% Change	--	-2.5%	-3.2%
Company-Owned	22	27	29
% Change	--	22.7%	7.4%
Total	345	342	334
% Change	--	-0.9%	-2.3%
Franchised as % of Total	93.6%	92.1%	91.3%

Investment Required
The fee for a Schlotzsky's franchise is $30,000.
Schlotzsky's provides the following range of investments required to open your initial franchise. The range assumes that all items are paid for in cash. To the extent that you choose to finance any of these expense items, your front-end investment could be substantially reduced.

Item	Established Low Range	Established High Range
Franchise Fee	$30,000	$30,000
Leasehold Improvements	$182,700	$308,200
Furniture, Equipment, Graphics and POS	$134,400	$226,000
Exterior Signage	$6,000	$33,817
Licenses and Permits	$600	$2,000
Lease Acquisition / Professional Fees	$10,000	$25,000
Supplies and Inventory	$10,000	$20,000
Insurance	$15,000	$24,000
Deposits	$2,000	$10,000
Expenses While Training	$17,000	$32,000

Grand Opening Advertising and Promotions Expenditure	$15,000	$15,000
Additional Funds (3 months)	$39,000	$48,000
Total Investment	$461,700	$774,017

On-going Expenses

Schlotzsky's franchisees pay a monthly royalty fee of 6% of net sales as well as an advertising contribution fee of 4% of net sales. Additional fees include promotions and additional local advertising and promotions.

What You Get—Training and Support

Comprehensive assistance is provided to franchisees in site selection using Strategic Integrated Mapping and Modeling Systems specifically designed for Schlotzsky's. Assistance is also given with restaurant design and layout.

Schlotzsky's comprehensive training program includes continuing corporate training and on-site restaurant training, online access to Franchise Partner training tools and development support, and an in-depth operations manual. The initial management training is followed up with ongoing business consultation including business review and performance analysis by the corporate management team and up to four regular consultation visits per year.

Schlotzsky's helps franchisees stay competitive with provided marketing campaigns and continuing product development. Their innovative, targeted local and national marketing plans are designed to increase customer frequency.

Territory

Schlotzsky's grants exclusive territories.

Sonic Drive-In

America's Drive-In ®

300 Johnny Bench Dr.
Oklahoma City, OK 73104
Tel: (800) 569-6656 (405) 225-5000
Fax: (405) 225-5963
Email: lcoffman@sonicdrivein.com
Website: www.sonicdrivein.com
Cliff Hudson, President/CEO

Sonic Drive-Ins offer made-to-order hamburgers and other sandwiches, and feature signature items, such as extra-long cheese coneys, hand-breaded onion rings, tater tots, fountain favorites, including cherry limeades, slushes and a full ice-cream dessert menu.

BACKGROUND: IFA Member
Established: 1953; First Franchised: 1959
Franchised Units: 3,104
Company-Owned Units: 451
Total Units: 3,555
Dist.: US-3,555; CAN-0; O'seas-0
North America: 37 States
Density: 962 in TX, 226 in TN, 270 in OK
Projected New Units (12 Months): 40

Qualifications:	5, 5, 5, 2, 2, 4
FINANCIAL/TERMS:	
Cash Investment:	$434-545K
Total Investment:	$1,100-3,046K
Minimum Net Worth:	$2M
Fees: Franchise -	$45K
Royalty - 1-5%;	Ad. - 2% (National); 3 % (Local)
Earnings Claims Statement:	Yes
Term of Contract (Years):	20/10
Avg. # of Employees:	35 FT, 0 PT
Passive Ownership:	Not Allowed
Encourage Conversions:	Yes
Area Develop. Agreements:	Yes
Sub-Franchising Contracts:	No
Expand in Territory:	Yes
Space Needs:	1,450 SF
SUPPORT & TRAINING:	
Financial Assistance Provided:	Yes (I)
Site Selection Assistance:	Yes
Lease Negotiation Assistance:	Yes
Co-operative Advertising:	Yes
Franchisee Assoc./Member:	Yes/Yes
Size of Corporate Staff:	210
On-going Support:	NA,NA,C,D,E,F,G,H,I
Training:	11 weeks local market; 1 week Oklahoma City, OK
SPECIFIC EXPANSION PLANS:	
US:	SW, SE, West, Midwest
Canada:	No
Overseas:	No

For more than 50 years, Sonic has built a dominant position in the drive-in restaurant business and today has over 3,500 drive-ins. Sonic prides itself in sticking to what made drive-ins so popular in the first place: made-to-order American classics, signature menu items, and speedy service from friendly Carhops. Sonic's ever-growing menu is full of options to satisfy every taste, with frequent additions such as real Fruit Smoothies. Most of Sonic's new menu creations are pioneered by entrepreneurial franchisees, as was the case with the highly successful Frozen Favorites dessert menu expansion in 1996.

Today, Sonic is the largest chain of drive-in restaurants in America. As a business it continues to thrive, maintaining strong sales growth, industry-leading customer frequency and high returns for stockholders. Sonic franchisees enjoy one of the most successful businesses, with average unit sales increasing each year since 1987 and one of the lowest turnover ratios in the quick-service restaurant franchise industry, with unparalleled opportunities for personal success.

Operating Units	12/31/2008	12/31/2009	12/31/2010
Franchised	2,791	3,069	3,117
% Change	--	10%	1.6%
Company-Owned	684	475	455
% Change	--	-30.6%	-4.2%
Total	3,475	3,544	3,572
% Change	--	2%	0.8%
Franchised as % of Total	80.3%	86.6%	87.3%

Investment Required
The initial investment fee for a Sonic franchise is $45,000. SONIC also offers a Development Agreement program.

Sonic provides the following range of investments required to open your initial franchise. The range assumes that all items are paid for in cash. To the extent that you choose to finance any of these expense items, your front-end investment could be substantially reduced.

Item	Established Low Range	Established High Range
Franchise Fee	$45,000	$45,000
Payroll	$72,600	$97,900
Expenses While Training	$57,000	$106,000

Advertising Funds	$7,500	$24,000
Beginning Inventory	$32,600	$103,000
Prepaid Expenses Including Security and Utility Deposits, and Business License	$10,000	$12,000
Insurance Premiums	$8,000	$35,000
Land	$75,000	$1,200,000
Building and Site Work	$555,000	$998,000
Equipment	$140,000	$210,000
POS System	$58,600	$103,800
Sonic Sign	$9,000	$46,000
LED Electronic Message Center	$25,000	$38,000
Additional Funds (3 Months)	$7,000	$28,000
Total Initial Investment	$1,102,300	$3,046,700

On-going Expenses

Sonic franchise owners pay a monthly royalty fee equal to 5% of gross sales and a monthly advertising cooperative fee of 3.25% of gross sales. Additional fees include a monthly brand fee of 0.9% of gross sales.

What You Get—Training and Support

Sonic provides an 11-week training program that consists of eight weeks of restaurant training, three weeks at new store openings, and one week of classroom training. Classroom instruction covers leadership development, restaurant management skills, food safety, and overall business development. Sonic also has real estate professionals who help evaluate a new site and review the demographic and population mix, as well as provide architectural, construction and engineering assistance.

Sonic has a national purchasing program to help franchisees maximize economy, efficiency and profitability, as well as a research and development team working to create products customers want. Marketing assistance is provided in the form of regional and national cable advertising as well as materials such as radio and TV commercials, newspaper ads, direct mail, coupon books, promotional posters and signage that can be customized for each franchise. Furthermore, Sonic provides ongoing support from experienced operations and marketing professionals.

Territory
Sonic grants exclusive territories.

Tasti D-Lite

tasti D·lite™
dessert your guilt.

341 Cool Springs Blvd., # 100
Franklin, TN 37067
Tel: (866) 424-4640 (615) 550-3012
Fax: (615) 550-3154
Email: franchise@tastidlite.com
Website: www.tastidlite.com
Nikki Sells, VP Franchise Development

Now more than ever, people need a little Tasti D-Lite. Check out this fast-growing, good-for-you frozen dessert concept. Simple and fun to operate, featuring a low-cal, low-fat, low-carb product that's been the talk of New York for more than 20 years. Unlike other light concepts, it has a rich texture and a creamy delicious taste. So healthy, it becomes a daily habit! The world's leading guilt-free food franchise. The right opportunity. At the right time.

BACKGROUND:	
	IFA Member
Established: 1987;	First Franchised: 2008
Franchised Units:	50
Company-Owned Units:	2
Total Units:	52
Dist.:	US-50; CAN-0; O'seas-2
North America:	5 States
Density:	56 in NY, 4 in NJ
Projected New Units (12 Months):	52
Qualifications:	2, 2, 1, 3, 1, 2

FINANCIAL/TERMS:	
Cash Investment:	$70K
Total Investment:	$240-425K
Minimum Net Worth:	$250K
Fees: Franchise -	$30K
Royalty - 5%;	Ad. - 2%
Earnings Claims Statement:	No
Term of Contract (Years):	10/10
Avg. # of Employees:	2 FT, 4 PT

Passive Ownership: Allowed, But Discouraged	
Encourage Conversions: Yes	
Area Develop. Agreements: Yes	
Sub-Franchising Contracts: No	
Expand in Territory: No	
Space Needs: 1,000 SF	

Franchisee Assoc./Member: No	
Size of Corporate Staff: 28	
On-going Support: NA,NA,C,D,e,NA,NA,h,I	
Training: 1 week New York, NY; 1 week Nash-ville, TN	

SUPPORT & TRAINING:
Financial Assistance Provided: Yes (I)
Site Selection Assistance: Yes
Lease Negotiation Assistance: Yes
Co-operative Advertising: Yes

SPECIFIC EXPANSION PLANS:
US: All US
Canada: All Canada
Overseas: All Countries

Since its first store debuted in New York in 1987, Tasti D-Lite has been serving frozen desserts made of real dairy, natural ingredients and no artificial sweeteners. Tasti D-Lite's great-tasting, guilt-free treats and snacks provide people with more of what they want—creamy, delicious taste available in more than 100 flavors—and less of what they don't need—fat and calories. The frozen dessert franchise constantly seeks service and product improvement, flavor innovation and customer involvement. It has recently expanded its menu to include smoothies, cakes, and pies.

Appearing in highly rated TV shows like Sex & the City, The Apprentice, 30 Rock, The Tyra Banks Show, and The Today Show, Tasti D-Lite's popularity has grown across the globe and the frozen dessert store has built a large and loyal customer base. With the unprecedented trend of more people joining a healthy and active lifestyle, Tasti D-Lite makes for a lucrative franchise opportunity.

Operating Units	12/31/2008	12/31/2009	12/31/2010
Franchised	35	41	42
% Change	--	17.1%	2.4%
Company-Owned	3	2	2
% Change	--	-33.3%	0%
Total	38	43	44
% Change	--	13.2%	2.3%
Franchised as % of Total	92.1%	95.4%	95.5%

Investment Required

The fee for a Tasti D-Lite franchise is $30,000 with discounts available for purchasing additional franchises. Area developer agreements are also available.

Tasti D-Lite provides the following range of investments required to open your initial franchise. The range assumes that all items are paid for in cash. To the extent that you choose to finance any of these expense items, your front-end investment could be substantially reduced.

Item	Established Low Range	Established High Range
Franchise Fee	$30,000	$30,000
Opening Logistics, Training and Software Management Systems Fee	$15,000	$15,000
Grand Opening Contribution	$5,000	$5,000
Office Equipment & Supplies	$500	$1,000
Computer System	$3,100	$7,000
Hosted POS Webportal	$960	$960
Support Package	$600	$900
Radio, Voice and Data Circuits and Installation	$300	$1,950
Furnishings, Fixtures and Equipment and Installation	$73,000	$99,000
Soft Serve Equipment	$15,500	$32,000
Freight	$4,600	$11,000
Initial Inventory Order	$9,000	$11,000
Rent and Security Deposit	$10,000	$22,000

Leasehold Improvements	$51,000	$89,000
Architect and Design	$5,000	$12,000
Utility Deposits	$1,000	$2,000
Brand Wall Display Equipment and Installation	$900	$2,900
Security System and Installation	$200	$5,060
Expenses While Training	$1,100	$3,900
Professional Fees	$0	$4,000
Business Licenses, Permits	$1,000	$4,000
Insurance	$2,000	$5,000
Additional Funds (3 Months)	$10,000	$30,000
Total Initial Investment	$239,760	$394,670

On-going Expenses
Tasti D-Lite franchisees pay a royalty fee equal to 5% of gross sales and a national marketing fund contribution equal to 2% of gross sales. Other costs include a POS webportal fee of $480 per year.

What You Get—Training and Support
Tasti D-Lite provides assistance with site-selection, building design, and décor. The initial training program is provided for the franchise owner and a key employee, including five days of classroom instruction at corporate headquarters in Franklin, TN and five days of in-store training at a designated Tasti D-Lite Learning Center. The training program covers areas in business concepts, franchising, business planning, center opening, store operations, product knowledge, handling, equipment, and machinery, inventory, POS use, marketing, human resources, and financial management. Refresher courses, additional training, and conferences are held occasionally.

Tasti D-Lite also provides ongoing support in advertising, assist in maintaining a website and provide access to the Tasti D-Lite Hosted Webportal, which allows remote access to POS-related data, including consolidated reporting and system management.

Territory
Tasti D-Lite grants protected territories.

Togo's Eatery

18 N. San Pedro St.
San Jose, CA 95110-2413
Tel: (408) 280-6585 (714) 582-2236
Fax: (408) 280-5067
Email: franchisesales@togos.com
Website: www.togosfranchise.com
Lidia Larson, Franchise Development Manager

Togo's was opened in Northern California in the early 1970s by a guy who didn't have a business plan. He just made reasonably priced sandwiches the way he liked them - made to order in a deli-style format and stuffed with fresh, wholesome ingredients. Soon there were lines out the door and Togo's was well on its way to becoming California's most loved sandwich shop. Now, nearly 40 years later, Togo's is still crafting the best sandwiches, on the West Coast, with over 240 franchise restaurants serving over a million guests per month. Our bread is baked every day, especially for us, and we've added our own selection of hearty soups, fresh salads and specialty wraps worthy of the Togo's name.

BACKGROUND:

	IFA Member
Established: 1968;	First Franchised: 1977
Franchised Units:	245
Company-Owned Units:	1
Total Units:	246
Dist.:	US-246; CAN-0; O'seas-0
North America:	0 States
Density:	239 in CA
Projected New Units (12 Months):	10
Qualifications:	5, 5, 4, 4, 4, 5

FINANCIAL/TERMS:

Cash Investment:	$150K
Total Investment:	$257-417K
Minimum Net Worth:	$300K
Fees: Franchise - $40K for 20 yr, $25K for 10 yr	
Royalty - 5%; Ad. - 2% currently, but can go up to 5%	
Earnings Claims Statement:	Yes
Term of Contract (Years):	20
Avg. # of Employees:	5 FT, 8 PT
Passive Ownership:	Allowed, But Discouraged
Encourage Conversions:	No
Area Develop. Agreements:	Yes
Sub-Franchising Contracts:	No
Expand in Territory:	Yes
Space Needs:	1,200-1,500 SF

SUPPORT & TRAINING:

Financial Assistance Provided:	No

Site Selection Assistance:	Yes	Training:	3 weeks CA
Lease Negotiation Assistance:	Yes		
Co-operative Advertising:	Yes	**SPECIFIC EXPANSION PLANS:**	
Franchisee Assoc./Member:	Yes/Yes	US:	CA, WA, OR, NV, AZ
Size of Corporate Staff:	24	Canada:	No
On-going Support:	NA,NA,C,D,E,F,G,H,I	Overseas:	No

A West Coast Original, Togo's has grown into a network of over 240 restaurants since a young college student opened its first store in San Jose, CA 40 years ago. Today, Togo's restaurants are serving over a million guests each month with some of the best sandwiches on the west coast–reasonably priced, deli-style sandwiches made to order and stuffed with fresh, wholesome ingredients. The deli sandwich franchise company has also expanded its menu to include a selection of fresh salads, soups, and specialty wraps.

A Togo's franchise requires low investment and a small footprint, while it offers best-in-class operational field support and its restaurants generate one of the highest average unit volumes in the sandwich restaurant category. Franchisees also benefit from the strong brand loyalty Togo's has developed with a stable and large customer base. In this on-the-go world, Togo's highly portable products appeal to many, and the deli-style service offers guests that extra, personal touch of interacting directly with the sandwich-maker.

Operating Units	12/31/2008	12/31/2009	12/31/2010
Franchised	237	239	239
% Change	--	0.8%	0-%
Company-Owned	6	3	2
% Change	--	-50%	-33.3%
Total	243	242	241
% Change	--	-0.4%	-0.4%
Franchised as % of Total	97.5%	98.8%	99.2%

Investment Required

The initial fee for a Togo's franchise is $30,000, with a discount for veterans.

Togo's provides the following range of investments required to open your initial franchise. The range assumes that all items are paid for in cash. To the extent that you choose to finance any of these expense items, your front-end investment could be substantially reduced.

Item	Established Low Range	Established High Range
Franchise Fee	$21,000	$30,000
Leasehold Improvements	$100,000	$165,000
Real Estate/Rental Deposit	$2,500	$6,000
Equipment, Fixtures and Furniture	$57,113	$76,996
Signage	$6,300	$13,500
Architectural Fee	$5,000	$10,000
POS System	$10,000	$11,500
Opening Inventory	$8,000	$11,500
Misc. Opening Costs	$16,500	$29,000
Uniforms	$400	$800
Insurance	$4,500	$10,000
Expenses While Training	$1,500	$10,500
Grand Opening Marketing Fee	$5,000	$5,000
Additional Funds (3 Months)	$20,000	$40,000
Total Initial Investment	$257,813	$419,796

On-going Expenses
Togo's franchisees pay ongoing royalty fees equal to 5% of gross sales and a continuing marketing fee ranging from 2% to 5% of gross sales.

What You Get—Training and Support
Togo's provides a solid foundation for franchisees, with support that is unmatched in the industry. Togo's executive management team has over 150 years of restaurant experience, and Togo's CEO is constantly in the field interacting with loyal customers and franchisees. Togo's provides five weeks of management training at an approved training restaurant, followed by on-site training in advance of store opening. Prior to restaurant opening, Togo's also assists franchisees with site selection and comprehensive restaurant design specifications, and provides a list of approved general contractors, equipment vendors and architectural services.

Franchisees are assigned a Franchise Service Manager, who acts as a liaison between the franchisee and Togo's, as well as consults, coaches and assists franchisees and team members in all facets of their business. Togo's provides a variety of marketing materials and support, including local restaurant marketing strategies and materials, and an email marketing club. Franchisees also benefit from Togo's creative development of marketing materials for system-wide promotions, focus on public relations, product development and menu management.

Territory
Togo's grants exclusive territories.

Lodging 4

Choice Hotels - Comfort Inn

10750 Columbia Pike
Silver Spring, MD 20901-4427
Tel: (866) 560-9871 (301) 592-5000
Fax: (301) 592-5058
Email: emerging_markets@choicehotels.com
Website: www.choicehotelsfranchise.com
Brian Parker, VP Emerging Markets

Choice Hotels® is a leading hotel franchisor with over 65 years experience in developing brand concepts and services that are designed to optimize hotel performance. Our single focus is on the return on investment for our owners and growing our brands strategically. Brand concepts include Comfort Inn®, Comfort Suites®, Quality®, Sleep Inn®, Clarion®, MainStay Suites®, Suburban Extended Stay Hotel®, EconoLodge®, Rodeway Inn® and our new hotel membership program, Ascend Collection®. We offer brands for conversion and new build opportunities.

BACKGROUND: IFA Member
Established: 1941;   1st Franchised: 1941
Franchised Units: 6,032
Company-Owned Units: 3
Total Units: 6,035
Dist.:   US-4,908; CAN-280; O'seas-847

North America:	50 States, 10 Provinces
Density:	395 in TX, 370 in CA, 257 in FL
Projected New Units (12 Months):	NR
Qualifications:	4, 4, 4, 2, 1, 1

FINANCIAL/TERMS:

Cash Investment:	20-30% Costs
Total Investment:	$2.3-14.6M
Minimum Net Worth:	Varies
Fees: Franchise -	$10-60K
Royalty - 4.25-5.65%;	Ad. - 2.5-3.85%
Earnings Claims Statement:	Yes
Term of Contract (Years):	20/NA
Avg. # Of Employees:	Varies
Passive Ownership:	Allowed
Encourage Conversions:	Yes
Area Develop. Agreements:	No
Sub-Franchising Contracts:	No
Expand In Territory:	No
Space Needs:	Varies

SUPPORT & TRAINING:

Financial Assistance Provided:	Yes (I)
Site Selection Assistance:	Yes
Lease Negotiation Assistance:	Yes
Co-Operative Advertising:	Yes
Franchisee Assoc./Member:	Yes/Yes
Size Of Corporate Staff:	1,556
On-Going Support:	A,B,C,D,NA,F,G,h,I

SPECIFIC EXPANSION PLANS:

US:	All United States
Canada:	All Canada
Overseas:	All Countries

Comfort Inn is a member of Choice Hotels, one of the largest lodging franchisors in the world. With such sweeping brand recognition and over 2,000 locations worldwide, Comfort Inn has established itself as a leader in providing a warm atmosphere, helpful service, and high operational standards. Customers enjoy complimentary high-speed internet access as well as a complimentary hot breakfast and newspaper. As a member of Choice Hotels International, Comfort Inn franchisees have access to a support system and business model that has withstood over 20 years in the lodging industry. Comfort Inn franchisees can take pride in the established name of Choice Hotels and the value-driven service it provides for all its customers.

Operating Units	12/31/2008	12/31/2009	12/31/2010
Franchised	1,998	2,050	2,053
% Change	--	2.6%	0.1%
Company-Owned	0	0	0
% Change	--	--	--
Total	1,998	2,050	2,053
% Change	--	2.6%	0.1%
Franchised as % of Total	100%	100%	100%

Investment Required
The initial fee for a Comfort Inn franchise is $500 per room with a $50,000 minimum.

Comfort Inn provides the following range of investments required to open your initial franchise. The range assumes that all items are paid for in cash. To the extent that you choose to finance any of these expense items, your front-end investment could be substantially reduced.

Item	Established Low Range	Established High Range
Franchise Fee	$500/room, min $50,000	$500/ room, min $50,000
Architectural Plans & Inspections	$90,000	$150,000
Soil Tests	$3,000	$12,000
Legal Fees	$10,000	$45,000
Environmental Impact Study	$0	$16,000
Market Study	$10,000	$15,000
Travel	$0	$25,000
Construction	$55,000/room	$65,000/room
Insurance, Construction	$10,000	$15,000
Salaries	$50,000	$120,000
Pre-Opening Advertising	$5,000	$60,000
Professional Online Hotel Photography	$450 minimum	$450 minimum
Furniture, Fixtures and Equipment	$5,500/room	$7,500/room
choiceADVANTAGE Systems	$15,050	$20,750
Insurance, General Liability	$1,000	$40,000
Insurance, Workers Compensation	$1,000	$30,000
Opening Inventories of Supplies	$700/room	$1,400/room
TLC Orientation Fee	$1,350	$1,350
(HOST) Training Fee	$999	$999

Educational Resources Program	$200	$200
High Speed Internet Access	$10,000	$20,000
Mandatory On-Premise Signs	$20,000	$80,000
Working Capital Required Before Operations Begin	$95,000	$165,000
Additional Funds (3 Months)	$70,000	$100,000
Total Initial Investment	$6,744,449	$8,414,149

On-going Expenses

Comfort Inn franchisees pay ongoing royalty fees equal to 5.65% of the preceding month's gross room revenues, plus an annual marketing cooperative fee ranging from $400 to $2,400.

What You Get—Training and Support

The Opening Service department aids the franchisee in all pre-opening aspects of business, from architectural and property improvement plan reviews to marketing programs and training course coordination. Additionally, Opening Services Consultants help franchisees to ensure that they meet brand standards and have the knowledge and tools to assist the franchisee in passing the hotel's first Quality Assurance Review.

Franchisees undergo an initial training at the Choice Hotels headquarters in Silver Spring, Maryland. The training covers global sales, franchise services support, brand management, marketing, and much more.

Additional support includes an advance reservation system, marketing, and advertising via direct sales, online media, newspapers, and television campaigns.

Territory

Comfort Inn does not grant exclusive territories.

Hilton

HILTON
WORLDWIDE

7930 Jones Branch Drive
McLean, VA 22102
Tel: (800) 286-0645 (703) 883-1000
Fax: (703) 442-3110
Email: craig.mance@hilton.com
Website: www.hiltonfranchise.com
Craig Mance, SVP Franchise Development

One of the most recognized names in the industry, Hilton Hotels & Resorts stands as the stylish, forward thinking global leader in hospitality. From inaugural balls and Hollywood award galas to business events and days to remember, Hilton is where the world makes history, closes the deal, toasts special occasions and gets away from it all. The flagship brand of Hilton Worldwide continues to build upon its legacy of innovation by developing products and services to meet the needs of tomorrow's savvy global travelers while more than 144,000 Team Members shape experiences in which every guest feels cared for, valued and respected. Today, the brand includes more than 540 hotels in 78 countries and remains synonymous with "hotel." The brand is part of Hilton Worldwide, the leading global hospitality company that has been offering business and leisure travelers the finest in accommodations, service, amenities and value for 93 years. The company is dedicated to continuing its tradition of providing exceptional guest experiences across its global brands. Its brands are comprised of more than 3,750 hotels and timeshare properties, with 615,000 rooms in 85 countries.

BACKGROUND: IFA Member
Established: 1919;   First Franchised: 1969

Franchised Units:	231
Company-Owned Units:	293
Total Units:	524
Dist.:	US-469; CAN-14; O'seas-262
North America:	41 States, 4 Provinces
Density:	26 in TX, 29 in FL, 36 in CA
Projected New Units (12 Months):	
Qualifications:	5, 5, 5, 3, 1, 3

FINANCIAL/TERMS:

Cash Investment:	$85K minimum
Total Investment:	$53.4-90.1M
Minimum Net Worth:	$70K/Rm.
Fees: Franchise -	$85K Min.
Royalty - 5% Gross Rm. Rev;	Ad. - 4% GrRmRev
Earnings Claims Statement:	No
Term of Contract (Years):	22/10-20
Avg. # of Employees:	150 FT, 0 PT
Passive Ownership:	Allowed
Encourage Conversions:	Yes
Area Develop. Agreements:	No
Sub-Franchising Contracts:	No
Expand in Territory:	Yes
Space Needs:	135,000 SF

SUPPORT & TRAINING:

Financial Assistance Provided:	Yes (D)
Site Selection Assistance:	NA
Lease Negotiation Assistance:	No
Co-operative Advertising:	Yes
Franchisee Assoc./Member:	No
Size of Corporate Staff:	2,332
On-going Support:	NA,NA,C,D,E,NA,G,H,I
Training:	3 days Beverly Hills, CA;
	4 days Dallas, TX; 3 days regional office

SPECIFIC EXPANSION PLANS:

US:	All US
Canada:	All Canada
Overseas:	Mexico, Latin America, Europe, Asia, All Countries

One of the most recognized names in the industry, Hilton Hotels & Resorts stands as the stylish, forward-thinking global leader in hospitality. From inaugural balls and Hollywood award galas to business events and days to remember, Hilton is where the world makes history, closes the deal, toasts special occasions, and gets away from it all. The flagship brand of Hilton Worldwide continues to build upon its legacy of innovation by developing products and services to meet the needs of tomorrow's savvy global travelers, while more than 144,000 Team Members shape experiences in which every guest feels cared for, valued, and respected. Today, the Hilton Hotels & Resorts portfolio includes more than 540 hotels in 78 countries, and the brand remains synonymous with "hotel."

The Hilton Hotels & Resorts brand is part of Hilton Worldwide, the leading global hospitality company, spanning the lodging sector from luxurious full-service hotels and resorts to extended-stay suites and mid-priced hotels. For 93 years, Hilton Worldwide has been offering business and leisure travelers the finest in accommodations, service, amenities, and value. The company is dedicated to continuing its tradition of providing exceptional guest experiences across its global brands. Its brands are comprised of more than 3,750 hotels and timeshare properties, with 615,000 rooms in 85 countries and include Waldorf Astoria Hotels & Resorts, Conrad Hotels & Resorts, Hilton Hotels & Resorts, DoubleTree by Hilton, Embassy Suites Hotels, Hilton Garden Inn, Hampton Hotels, Homewood Suites by Hilton, Home2 Suites by Hilton, and Hilton Grand Vacations. The company also manages the world-class guest reward program Hilton HHonors®.

Operating Units	12/31/2008	12/31/2009	12/31/2010
Franchised	196	203	202
% Change	--	3.6%	-0.5%
Company-Owned	20	21	22
% Change	--	5%	4.8%
Total	216	224	224

% Change	--	3.7%	0%
Franchised as % of Total	90.7%	90.6%	90.2%

Investment Required

The fee for a Hilton franchise (development services fee) is $85,000 for the first 275 guest rooms or suites, plus $300 for each additional room or suite.

Hilton provides the following range of investments required to open your initial franchise. The range assumes that all items are paid for in cash. To the extent that you choose to finance any of these expense items, your front-end investment could be substantially reduced. The following figures refer to a new hotel with 300 rooms.

Item	Established Low Range	Established High Range
Development Services Fee	$92,500	$92,500
Product Improvement Plan	$7,500	$7,500
Phase 1 Environmental Assessment	$0	$10,000
Construction and Leasehold Improvements	$40,000,000	$65,000,000
Designer and Engineering Fees	$500,000	$2,000,000
Furniture, Fixtures and Equipment (includes telephone systems)	$8,000,000	$12,000,000
Inventory and Operating Equipment	$1,500,000	$3,000,000
Signs	$50,000	$150,000
Computer Software	$58,000	$173,800

HAS Stay Connected High Speed Internet	$86,000	$110,200
Required Pre-Opening Training	$15,000	$30,000
ADA Consultant Fee	$2,500	$10,000
Construction/Renovation Extension Fee	$10,000	$10,000
SPA Consultant Fee	$75,000	$75,000
Organizational Expense	$50,000	$200,000
Permits and Licenses	$100,000	$500,000
Miscellaneous Pre-Opening and Project Management Expenses	$1,000,000	$3,000,000
Contingencies	$1,540,000	$2,800,000
Additional Funds (3 Months)	$400,000	$1,000,000
Total Investment	$53,486,500	$90,169,000

On-going Expenses
Hilton franchisees pay monthly royalty fees equal to 5% of gross rooms revenues and 3% of gross food and beverage revenues, a monthly program fee equal to 4% of gross rooms revenues, and monthly OnQ® (business software) fees equal to 0.75% of gross rooms revenues. Other fees payable by the franchisee include additional OnQ®-related fees and TPCP (Travel Planner Centralized Payment Program) fees.

What You Get—Training and Support
Hilton conducts a four-day initial training program in a major market which provides hotel general managers with the skills they need to run a Hilton hotel, including Hilton service, standards, marketing and sales, training, human resources, and Hilton technology. Staff is also trained on-site in OnQ®, Hilton's proprietary computerized business system.

Hilton provides a superior level of support to franchisees prior to, during, and after opening, including site review and design consulting, a friendly and dedicated corporate staff and a business model backed by management and franchising expertise. Franchisees enjoy a large customer base fueled by the Hilton Honors guest reward program and referrals from other Hilton Family hotels through cross-selling. Franchisees also benefit from marketing and sales support provided by Hilton, including national and regional efforts, public relations and ready access to promotional materials. OnQ®, the lodging industry's first totally integrated information technology platform, helps franchisees manage inventory, efficiently run hotels and assists in profitable decision-making.

Territory
Hilton does not grant exclusive territories.

InterContinental Hotels Group (IHG®)

3 Ravinia Dr., # 100
Atlanta, GA 30346-2149
Tel: (866) 933-8356 (770) 604-2166
Fax: (770) 604-2107
Email: americas.development@ihg.com
Website: www.ihg.com
Kirk Kinsell, SVP Franchising/Bus. Development

IHG is the world's largest hotel company by number of rooms. The company operates or franchises more than 4,500 hotels and 666,000 guest rooms in nearly 100 countries. IHG offers franchises with the following brands: InterContinental Hotels & Resorts, Crowne Plaza, Hotel Indigo, Holiday Inn Hotels and Resorts, Holiday Inn Express, Staybridge Suites and Candlewood Suites. Notes: Operating Units chart represents all IHG hotel brands. Geographic Distribution chart is as of March 31, 2009 and represents all IHG hotel brands. Fees listed are for a 100 room Holiday Inn; please contact IHG directly for fee information on our other brands, www.ihg.com/development. Financial requirements chart represents fees for a typical Holiday Inn brand hotel. Training chart represents all IHG hotel brands. Expansion Plans chart represents all IHG hotel brands.

BACKGROUND:	IFA Member
Established: 1946;	First Franchised: 1954
Franchised Units:	4508
Company-Owned Units:	12
Total Units:	4,520
Dist.:	US-3,156; CAN-159; O'seas-1,205

North America:	50 States, 1 Province	Expand in Territory:	No
Density:	NR	Space Needs:	Varies per brand
Projected New Units (12 Months):	NR		
Qualifications:	5, 4, 4, NA, NA	**SUPPORT & TRAINING:**	
		Financial Assistance Provided:	No
FINANCIAL/TERMS:		Site Selection Assistance:	Yes
Cash Investment:	Varies	Lease Negotiation Assistance:	No
Total Investment:	$2-20M	Co-operative Advertising:	Yes
Minimum Net Worth:	NA	Franchisee Assoc./Member:	Yes/Yes
Fees: Franchise -	$50K Min.	Size of Corporate Staff:	1,000
Royalty - 5%;	Ad. - 2.5%	On-going Support:	NA,NA,C,D,E,NA,NA,H,I
Earnings Claims Statement:	Yes	Training:	4-5 days regional; 4 -5 days Atlanta
Term of Contract (Years):	Varies, Avg. 10/10		
Avg. # of Employees:	Varies per brand FT, 0 PT	**SPECIFIC EXPANSION PLANS:**	
Passive Ownership:	Allowed	US:	All US
Encourage Conversions:	Yes	Canada:	All Canada
Area Develop. Agreements:	No	Overseas:	All Countries
Sub-Franchising Contracts:	No		

With seven hotel brands, over 130 million stays every year, more than 666,000 rooms, and over 4,500 hotels across 100 countries, InterContinental Hotels Group is the world's largest hotel company (by number of rooms). The highly recognized brands in the IHG family are: InterContinental® Hotels & Resorts, Crowne Plaza®, Hotel Indigo®, Holiday Inn® Hotels and Resorts, Holiday Inn Express®, Staybridge Suites®, and Candlewood Suites®. The international hotel company is committed to create "Great Hotels Guests Love" by providing outstanding services.

IHG's portfolio covers everything from luxurious and upscale to reliable and economy hotels, fulfilling the needs of different market segments. This diverse portfolio allows for flexibility in responding to most types of hotel development opportunities The company's Global Development Team is there to help franchisees choose the right hotel brand and maximize the potential of a particular site. IHG manages the world's largest hotel loyalty program, Priority Club® Rewards, with 61 million members. The global lodging company offers hotel owners a competitive advantage through their brand affiliation for its ability to drive consumer demand and provide extensive operations support.

Operating Units	12/31/2008	12/31/2009	12/31/2010
Franchised	2,603	2,750	2,923
% Change	--	5.6%	6.3%
Company-Owned	9	9	10

% Change	--	0%	11.1%
Total	2,612	2,759	2,933
% Change	--	5.6%	6.3%
Franchised as % of Total	99.66%	99.67%	99.66%

*Chart represents all IHG hotel brands.

Investment Required

The application fee for a Holiday Inn franchise is $500 per room with a $50,000 minimum. The minimum will vary depending on the IHG brand franchised. Franchise Agreements are entered into with Holiday Hospitality Franchising, Inc., a member of the InterContinental Hotels Group.

IHG provides the following range of investments required to open a Holiday Inn franchise. The Holiday Inn brand has the largest representation in terms of units of franchises among all IHG hotel brands. The range assumes that all items are paid for in cash. To the extent that you choose to finance any of these expense items, your front-end investment could be substantially reduced. The following figures refer to a 100-room, 4-story Holiday Inn hotel.

Item	Established Low Range	Established High Range
Franchise Fee	$50,000	$50,000
Property Improvement Plan (PIP) Fee	$2,500	$5,000
Building	$5,300,000	$7,600,000
Furniture, Fixtures and Equipment	$1,100,000	$1,550,000
Initial Inventory	$100,000	$200,000
Signage	$50,000	$250,000
PMS Equipment, Software, Installation and Training	$60,000	$75,000
Market Feasibility Study	$15,000	$30,000
New Hotel Opening Services and Training	$5,000	$5,000

Initial Certification Training Program	$1,095	$7,500
Merlin Communication Set-up	$25	$35
Licenses and Permits, Prepaid Expenses	$2,500	$15,000
Professional Fees	$100,000	$250,000
Security Deposits	$2,500	$15,000
Insurance	$75,000	$100,000
Kem's Restaurant Training	$5,000	$5,000
Best-4-Breakfast Program	$900	$900
Additional Funds and Prepaid Expenses (3 months)	$150,000	$275,000
Total Investment	$7,036,270	$10,453,935

On-going Expenses

IHG franchisees pay a royalty fee equal to 5% of Gross Rooms Revenues (6% for Holiday Inn Express) and a services fee ranging from 2.5-3.5% of the preceding month's GRR. Other on-going fees include special marketing contributions for the frequency program, capital reserve charges and a monthly technology fee per room.

What You Get—Training and Support

IHG offers continual support to help maximize revenues through efficient operations for all brands. IHG consistently addresses owners' needs while adding bottom-line value.

• Pre-Opening Training: Initial training for hotel general managers and other personnel is held at your hotel, IHG's headquarters in Atlanta, Georgia, or a designated metropolitan location. General managers receive training on hotel operation that is unique to the IHG system.

• Hotel Opening Process: IHG supports franchisees every step of the way. From planning to grand opening, the IHG OnBoard™ Program assists owners and franchisees through the entire hotel opening process.

• Technical Assistance: IHG recognizes the importance of superior asset management in maximizing hotel returns, including the comfort and safety of guests and employees. To address this, IHG leverages the collective experience of a global team of architects, designers, engineers, and technology experts to ensure that hotels set the benchmarks for the industry.

• Training: IHG offers training and retention programs to assist IHG hotels in attracting loyal employees whose individual drive and talents take customer service to the next level.

• Revenue Maximization: With IHG's advanced reservations system and efficient revenue optimization programs, each hotel is fully equipped to maximize profitability. Since hotels no longer need a full reservations team, owners can use staff for other duties. This keeps hotel staff numbers down while owners (and customers!) still enjoy a 24-hour reservations system.

• Driving Consumer Demand: IHG drives consumer demand through an integrated system that markets each brand individually through a myriad of channels. IHG global resources and proprietary services can be leveraged into unmatched value and flexibility delivering customizable management services and cutting-edge competitive strategies to deliver more reservations to each hotel.

• IAHI, The Owners' Association: IAHI is the most established and influential franchisee association in the industry. As the unified voice of IHG owners worldwide, IAHI helps keep ownership concerns at the forefront of your business.

Territory
IHG does not grant exclusive territories.

7-Eleven

P.O. Box 711
Dallas, TX 75221
Tel: (800) 255-0711 (972) 828-7011
Fax: (972) 828-8997
Email: timothy.lankford@7-11.com
Website: www.franchise.7-eleven.com
Timothy Lankford, Franchise Marketing and Recruiting Manager

7-Eleven stores were born from the simple concept of giving people 'what they want, when and where they want it.' This idea gave rise to the entire convenience store industry. While this formula still works today, customers' needs are changing at an accelerating pace. We are meeting this challenge with an infrastructure of daily distribution of fresh perishables, regional production of fresh foods and pastries, and an information system that greatly improves ordering and merchandising decisions.

BACKGROUND: IFA Member
Established: 1927; First Franchised: 1964
Franchised Units: 39,603
Company-Owned Units: 465
Total Units: 40,068
Dist.: US-6,723; CAN-465; O'seas-32,880
  North America: 32 States, 5 Provinces

Density:	1,587 in CA, 855 in FL, 727 in VA
Projected New Units (12 Months):	400
Qualifications:	4, 4, 4, 3, 5, 5

FINANCIAL/TERMS:
Cash Investment:	Varies by Store
Total Investment:	Varies
Minimum Net Worth:	$15K
Fees: Franchise -	Varies by Store
Royalty - Gross Profit Split;	Ad. - NR
Earnings Claims Statement:	Yes
Term of Contract (Years):	10/10
Avg. # of Employees:	8 FT, 5 PT
Passive Ownership:	Not Allowed
Encourage Conversions:	Yes
Area Develop. Agreements:	No
Sub-Franchising Contracts:	No
Expand in Territory:	Yes
Space Needs:	2,400 SF

SUPPORT & TRAINING:
Financial Assistance Provided:	Yes (D)
Site Selection Assistance:	NA
Lease Negotiation Assistance:	NA
Co-operative Advertising:	No
Franchisee Assoc./Member:	Yes/Yes
Size of Corporate Staff:	1,000
On-going Support:	A,B,C,D,E,F,G,H,I
Training:	1 week Dallas, TX; 5-8 weeks various training stores throughout US

SPECIFIC EXPANSION PLANS:
US:	Yes, NW,SW,MW,NE, Great Lakes, Southeast
Canada:	All Canada
Overseas:	All Countries

For 84 years, 7-Eleven has been both a leader and an innovator in the convenience store industry. Today, as the world's largest convenience retailer with a widely recognized brand name, 7-Eleven continues to thrive. 7-Eleven operates, franchises and licenses more than 40,000 stores in 17 countries. This exposure has made 7-Eleven an industry giant and an unshakable statue of fast, reliable and convenient service while its focus on community and people has preserved its reputation as "the friendly little store that's just around the corner."

7-Eleven has a multi-faceted relationship with franchisees: it serves as landlord, financing source, and record-keeper. 7-Eleven takes an active role in the franchisee's business, investing directly in their success in an effort to ensure a profitable and beneficial relationship between the franchisee and 7-Eleven.

Operating Units	12/31/2008	12/31/2009	12/31/2010
Franchised	4,330	4,685	5,047
% Change	--	8.2%	7.7%
Company-Owned	1,387	1,185	1,075
% Change	--	-14.6%	-9.3%
Total	5,717	5,870	6,122
% Change	--	2.7%	4.3%
Franchised as % of Total	75.7%	79.8%	82.4%

Investment Required
The franchise fee for a 7-Eleven store depends on the franchised store's gross profits for the past year; i.e. the fee is higher for locations that generate more revenue. Fees for brand-new store locations are determined by the average combined gross profits of nearby locations. The fee can be reduced or waived depending on a franchisee's experience. Financing is available. Veterans receive a 10% discount on the franchise fee for their first 7-Eleven store.

7-Eleven provides the following range of investments required to open your initial franchise. The range assumes that all items are paid for in cash. The below fees vary based upon the store selected.

Item	Established Low Range	Established High Range
Franchise Fee	$0	$441,400
Initial Gas Fee	$0	$40,000
Expenses While Training	$0	$9,000
Opening Inventory	$30,350	$75,700
Cash Register Fund	$100	$10,000
Store Supplies	$250	$2,000
Licenses and Permits	$100	$3,000
Additional Funds (3 Months)	$0	$30,000
Total Initial Investment	$30,800	$611,100

On-Going Expenses
7-Eleven franchisees pay ongoing fees which are the monthly 7-Eleven charge. The amount is a variable percentage of the store's gross profit for the month. There is also an advertising fee ranging from 0.5% to 1.5% that varies based on total gross profit.

What You Get—Training and Support
Prior to store opening, franchisees undergo six weeks of initial training with one week in the 7-Eleven Store Support Center in Dallas TX, and five weeks in a designated 7-Eleven Training Store. The initial training covers the 7-Eleven concept, basic store operations, computer-based training, POS training, and store changeover support training. 7-Eleven also provides ongoing training opportunities, including in-store, computer-based training programs for employees.

7-Eleven continues to support franchisees after store opening with a field consultant who meets with the franchisee on a regular basis to help maximize store performance and profitability. 7-Eleven provides exceptional support services to its franchisees, including record keeping, bill paying, payroll services for store operations, as well as financing for all normal store operating expenses.

Territory
7-Eleven does not grant exclusive territories.

Fast-Fix Jewelry and Watch Repairs

FAST-FIX
JEWELRY AND
WATCH REPAIRS

1300 N. W. 17th Ave., # 170
Delray Beach, FL 33445-2554
Tel: (800) 359-0407 (561) 330-6060
Fax: (561) 330-6062
Email: franchise@fastfix.com
Website: www.fastfixfranchise.com
George Lambro, Director of Franchise Development

With a 27-year track record, Fast-Fix Jewelry And Watch Repairs is the #1 national chain of dedicated jewelry and watch repair stores with more than 160 franchised locations operating in the United States and Canada. Fast-Fix stores operate only in major regional malls that afford customers "while-they-shop" jewelry and watch repair service. Prior jewelry experience is not necessary. Our full training program at Fast-Fix University along with our support system that includes national conventions and regional marketing meetings will motivate you and prepare you to operate your Fast-Fix store.

BACKGROUND:		IFA Member
Established: 1984;	First Franchised:	1987
Franchised Units:		163
Company-Owned Units:		3
Total Units:		166
Dist.:	US-161; CAN-2; O'seas-3	
North America:	27 States, 2 Provinces	
Density:	39 in CA, 24 in FL, 17 in TX	
Projected New Units (12 Months):		15
Qualifications:		4, 5, 2, 2, 2, 5
FINANCIAL/TERMS:		
Cash Investment:		$100K
Total Investment:		$188.8-381.8K
Minimum Net Worth:		$250K
Fees: Franchise -		$40K
Royalty - 6%;		Ad. - 2%
Earnings Claims Statement:		Yes
Term of Contract (Years):		10/10
Avg. # of Employees:		3 FT, 2 PT
Passive Ownership:	Allowed, But Discouraged	
Encourage Conversions:		No
Area Develop. Agreements:		Yes
Sub-Franchising Contracts:		Yes
Expand in Territory:		Yes
Space Needs:		250-850 SF

SUPPORT & TRAINING:		Training:	5 days on-site; 10 days national training center in Delray Beach, FL
Financial Assistance Provided:	Yes (I)		
Site Selection Assistance:	Yes		
Lease Negotiation Assistance:	Yes	**SPECIFIC EXPANSION PLANS:**	
Co-operative Advertising:	No	US:	All US
Franchisee Assoc./Member:	Yes/Yes	Canada:	All Canada
Size of Corporate Staff:	18	Overseas:	All Countries
On-going Support:	NA,NA,C,D,E,NA,G,H,I		

Fast-Fix Jewelry And Watch Repairs began in 1984 with one location in Pittsburgh, PA. Today, Fast-Fix is the world's largest franchisor of dedicated jewelry and watch repair services and operates more than 160 stores worldwide. Fast-Fix kiosks and in-line stores are located in regional malls where high visibility and high traffic combine to create a proven sales-generating atmosphere.

Jewelry and watch repair is a year-round, multi-billion dollar business, but most jewelry stores primarily engage in retail sales, meaning customers may wait a week a more for repairs. Fast-Fix is the only international chain of stores dedicated to eliminating this wait by offering quick same-day service and even completing many repairs in front of the customer within minutes. This unparalleled convenience and the professional quality of repairs has made Fast-Fix an exceptionally strong brand.

Operating Units	12/31/2008	12/31/2009	12/31/2010
Franchised	150	150	150
% Change	--	0%	0%
Company-Owned	2	1	1
% Change	--	-50%	0%
Total	152	151	151
% Change	--	-0.7%	0%
Franchised as % of Total	98.7%	99.3%	99.3%

Investment Required

The fee for a Fast-Fix franchise is $40,000.

Fast-Fix provides the following range of investments required to open your initial franchise. The range assumes that all items are paid for in cash. To the extent that you choose to finance any of these expense items, your front-end investment could be substantially reduced.

Item	Established Low Range	Established High Range
Franchise Fee	$40,000	$40,000
Administrative Processing Fee	$250	$250
In-Line Store Construction	$148,500	$208,500
Equipment, Inventory, and Trade Fixtures	$57,800	$62,800
Initial Promotional and Advertising Expenses	$6,200	$6,200
Sub-Lease Security Deposit	$10,000	$10,000
Initial Sublease Payments	$5,000	$10,000
Security and Utility Deposits	$350	$350
Licensing	$300	$300
Insurance	$350	$350
Expenses While Training	$0	$3,000
Additional Funds (3 Months)	$20,000	$40,000
Total Initial Investment	$166,325	$202,325

On-Going Expenses

Fast-Fix franchisees pay royalty fees equal to 6% of monthly gross sales and advertising fees equal to 2% of monthly gross sales.

What You Get—Training and Support
New franchisee orientation and training takes place for 10 days at the Fast-Fix University School, located in South Florida. The training program covers every aspect of the business including hiring, training, marketing and merchandising. The multi-tiered classroom and on-site approach to training ensures that franchise owners with absolutely no experience in the jewelry industry can succeed under the Fast-Fix business model.

Fast-Fix supports franchisees in every facet of building. The Fast-Fix training team accompanies the franchisee prior to and during the opening of a new store to ensure a smooth start, and the franchisee has access to the 24/7 Fast-Fix support center for any questions that arise post-opening.

Territory
Fast-Fix grants exclusive territories within enclosed malls.

Floor Coverings International

FLOOR COVERINGS
international
200 Technology Ct., S.E., # 1200
Smyrna, GA 30082
Tel: (800) 955-4324 (770) 874-7600
Fax: (770) 874-7605

Email: djames@floorcoveringsinternational.com
Website: www.floorcoveringsinternational.com
Denise James, Franchise Administrator

Floor Coverings International is the 'Flooring Store at your Door.' FCI is the first and leading mobile 'shop at home' flooring store. Customers can select from over 3,000 styles and colors of flooring right in their own home! All the right ingredients are there to simplify a buying decision. We offer all the brand names you and your customers will be familiar with. We carry all types of flooring, as well as window blinds.

BACKGROUND:			
Established: 1988;			IFA Member
Franchised Units:			First Franchised: 1989
Company-Owned Units:			72
Total Units:			0
Dist.:			72
			US-60; CAN-3; O'seas-9

BACKGROUND: IFA Member
Established: 1988;   First Franchised: 1989
Franchised Units: 72
Company-Owned Units: 0
Total Units: 72
Dist.:   US-60; CAN-3; O'seas-9
   North America: 43 States, 5 Provinces
   Density: 15 in PA, 11 in OH, 9 in IL
Projected New Units (12 Months):   45
Qualifications: 5, 5, 4, 3, 4, 4

FINANCIAL/TERMS:
Cash Investment: $150K
Total Investment: $150K
Minimum Net Worth: $50K
Fees: Franchise - $16K
   Royalty - 5%/$325/Mo.;   Ad. - 2%/$130/Mo.
Earnings Claims Statement: No
Term of Contract (Years):   10/10
Avg. # of Employees: 1 FT, 1 PT
Passive Ownership: Allowed, But Discouraged

Encourage Conversions: Yes
Area Develop. Agreements: Yes
Sub-Franchising Contracts: No
Expand in Territory: Yes
Space Needs: NA

SUPPORT & TRAINING:
Financial Assistance Provided: Yes (D)
Site Selection Assistance: Yes
Lease Negotiation Assistance: NA
Co-operative Advertising: No
Franchisee Assoc./Member: Yes/Yes
Size of Corporate Staff: 15
On-going Support: A,B,C,D,E,NA,G,H,I
Training: 2 weeks home study; 2 weeks Atlanta, GA

SPECIFIC EXPANSION PLANS:
US: All US
Canada: All Canada
Overseas: U.K.

Floor Coverings International delivers a vast array of top-brand flooring options that come from all over the world. Franchisees alongside their design associates and project coordinators provide a custom boutique to customers looking for unique flooring solutions. From consultation to finish, Floor Coverings International covers the entire flooring process.

Floor Coverings International is the leader in the mobile flooring industry. With a powerful business model in an enormous marketplace, estimated to be $65 billion and growing, Floor Coverings International is an outstanding opportunity for entrepreneurs to build a large business that can maximize their potential.

Operating Units	12/31/2008	12/31/2009	7/31/2010
Franchised	81	83	92
% Change	--	2.5%	10.8%
Company-Owned	0	0	0

% Change	--	--	--
Total	81	83	92
% Change	--	2.5%	10.8%
Franchised as % of Total	100%	100%	100%

Investment Required

The franchise fee for a Floor Coverings International franchise is $45,000 plus $0.25 for each single family dwelling over 125,000 in the franchisee's Designated Marketing Area.

Floor Coverings International provides the following range of investments required to open your initial franchise. The range assumes that all items are paid for in cash. To the extent that you choose to finance any of these expense items, your front-end investment could be substantially reduced.

Item	Established Low Range	Established High Range
Franchise Fee	$45,000	$45,000
Inspirenet Software	$5,000	$5,000
Expenses While Training	$5,000	$7,500
Opening Package	$20,000	$45,000
Personnel/Staffing	$0	$24,000
Initial Advertising Expenses	$40,000	$60,000
Insurance (per year)	$1,500	$6,000
Misc. Opening Costs	$2,000	$15,000
FCI Vehicle	$0	$38,000
Office Equipment	$2,000	$10,000
Real Estate & Improvements	$5,000	$30,000

Additional Funds (3 Months)	$7,500	$20,000
Total Initial Investment	$133,000	$305,500

On-Going Expenses

Floor Coverings International franchisees pay royalty fees equal to 5% of gross sales or $750 in the first 12 months of operation or $2,000 per month thereafter. Additional fees payable by the franchisee include a brand fund contribution equal to 3% of gross sales and a local advertising fee equal to a minimum of 6% of gross sales.

What You Get—Training and Support

In addition to the comprehensive training that franchisees receive at the launch of their ventures, Floor Coverings International provides franchisees and their employees with continual professional development opportunities including financial and management training, relevant topic-specific seminars, sales and design training, production coordinator training, and in-field visits.

Floor Coverings International provides a customized marketing system for each and every franchisee that provides a consistency of revenue and new business. Additional brand-wide marketing efforts include internet and search engine marketing, web-based banner ad programs, highly targeted mailing programs, and social media.

Territory

Floor Coverings International grants exclusive territories.

Foot Solutions

FOOT SOLUTIONS.
Rejuvenate Your Sole™

2359 Windy Hill Rd., # 400
Marietta, GA 30067
Tel: (866) 338-2597 (770) 955-0099
Fax: (770) 953-6270
Email: fscorp@footsolutions.com
Website: www.footsolutionsfranchise.com
Alison James, Franchise Sales

Foot Solutions is the world's largest pedorthic footwear retail/mobile network, focusing on health and wellness, the baby boomer marketplace, and lifestyle shoes and inserts to change the way people live and feel. We focus on cause-related marketing including affiliations with Susan G. Komen for the Cure, Arthritis Foundation, American Diabetes Association, International Council on Active Aging, to name a few.

BACKGROUND: IFA Member
Established: 2000; First Franchised: 2000
Franchised Units: 193
Company-Owned Units: 1
Total Units: 194
Dist.: US-146; CAN-20; O'seas-28
North America: 40 States, 5 Provinces
Density: 14 in TX, 13 in FL, 20 in CA
Projected New Units (12 Months): 50
Qualifications: 3, 3, 1, 2, 3, 4

FINANCIAL/TERMS:
Cash Investment: $Store Front - $40K; Mobile Unit - $25
Total Investment: $225-250K
Minimum Net Worth: $Store Front - $300K; Mobile Unit - $150K
Fees: Franchise - $Store Front - $32.5K; Mobile Unit - $29.5K
Royalty - 5%; Ad. - 2%
Earnings Claims Statement: Yes
Term of Contract (Years): 15/5/5
Avg. # of Employees: 2-3; 1-2 (Mobile Unit) FT, 0 PT
Passive Ownership: Allowed
Encourage Conversions: Yes
Area Develop. Agreements: Yes
Sub-Franchising Contracts: No
Expand in Territory: Yes
Space Needs: 1,200-2,000 SF

SUPPORT & TRAINING:
Financial Assistance Provided: Yes (I)
Site Selection Assistance: Yes
Lease Negotiation Assistance: Yes
Co-operative Advertising: Yes
Franchisee Assoc./Member: Yes/Yes
Size of Corporate Staff: 50
On-going Support: NA,NA,C,D,E,NA,G,H,I
Training: 1 week field; 2 1/2 weeks Marietta, GA

SPECIFIC EXPANSION PLANS:
US: All US
Canada: All Canada
Overseas: All Countries

Foot Solutions combines cutting edge technology with foot and gait biomechanics to fit every customer's unique foot with customized, high-quality footwear. Foot Solutions' footwear and foot care products aim to improve body alignment, movement, balance, and posture, as well as reduce, prevent, and eliminate pain and trauma in the load-bearing joints in your body.

At each store, Foot Solutions' certified pedorthics experts give every customer a 30-minute foot assessment, which includes a computerized foot scan and an individualized consultation to determine the proper shoes for the customer's needs. Although Foot Solutions' target customers are over the age of 40, there is a full line of quality shoes, arch supports and foot care accessories for all ages.

This innovative footwear franchise extends its philosophy beyond the store to contribute to the community by supporting programs related to diabetes, fitness, retirement and children's obesity.

Operating Units	12/31/2008	12/31/2009	12/31/2010
Franchised	241	223	193
% Change	--	-7.5%	-13.5%
Company-Owned	2	1	1
% Change	--	-50%	0%
Total	243	224	194
% Change	--	-7.8%	-13.5%
Franchised as % of Total	99.2%	99.6%	99.6%

Investment Required
The fee for a Foot Solutions franchise is $32,500. There is also an option for a mobile unit, with a fee of $29,500.

Foot Solutions provides the following range of investments required to open your initial franchise. The range assumes that all items are paid for in cash. To the extent that you choose to finance any of these expense items, your front-end investment could be substantially reduced. Please note that the figures below are for a regular Foot Solutions storefront center; a mobile unit is available with a Total Initial Investment of roughly $107,800.

Item	Established Low Range	Established High Range
Franchise Fee	$32,500	$32,500
Equipment	$13,500	$13,500
Opening Inventory	$68,000	$68,000
Real Estate (Leasehold Improvements)	$15,000	$15,000
Signage	$3,500	$3,500
Grand Opening Advertising	$2,000	$2,000
Fixtures	$15,000	$15,000
Expenses While Training	$2,800	$2,800
Liability Insurance	$2,000	$2,000
POS System	$8,000	$8,000
Miscellaneous Opening Costs	$4,000	$4,000
Additional Funds (3 Months)	$40,000	$40,000
Total Investment	$206,300	$206,300

On-Going Expenses
Foot Solutions franchisees pay a monthly royalty fee equal to 5% of total net sales. They also pay a monthly brand fund contribution fee of $500 for the first year, and 2% of total net sales afterwards. Local advertising expenditures equal to $2,000 per month for the first year and 4% of sales after the first year.

What You Get—Training and Support
Training and support include initial training at Foot Solutions' corporate headquarters in Marietta, Georgia, additional field training several times throughout the year, six days of field assistance with store opening, and post-opening support.

The initial training provides 120 hours of instruction on marketing and advertising, customer service, quality control, inventory control, accounting, foot scanning, biomechanics, basic pedorthics and anatomy/pathology. Training is provided on the internet, via DVDs, classroom instruction, lab work, and in a full mock-up store. The Foot Solutions training facility is certified by the Board for Certification of Pedorthics.

Foot Solutions will also assist in preparing a loan portfolio, designing and opening the store, installing and testing equipment, and advertising, as well as post-opening support on administration, human resources, accounting, and marketing.

Territory
Foot Solutions grants protected territories with a population containing approximately 100,000 people, with variation depending on the demographics of the area and other variables.

Merkinstock

World's largest selection of merkins - both natural and synthetic. Over 35 models, 15 color selections. Custom fitting in discrete environment. Also custom dyeing. Guaranteed satisfaction. 15 stores in Far East and Europe prove that concept is ripe for aggressive expansion into the U. S. market. Looking for entrepreneurs with the desire to succeed.

P. O. Box 12488
Oakland, CA 94604
Tel: (510) 839.5462
Fax: (510) 839-2104
Email: merky@earthlink.net
Website: www.merkinstock.com
Mr. Jeffrey A. Elder, President

BACKGROUND:

Established: 1992;	First Franchised: 1995
Franchised Units:	52
Company-Owned Units:	7
Total Units:	59
Dist.:	US-42; CAN-2; O'seas-15
North America:	2 States, 1 Province
Density:	2 in CA, 1 in NV

151

Projected New Units (12 Months):	10	Space Needs:		1,200 SF; FS, SC, RM
Qualifications:	3, 5, 4, 2, 3, 5	**SUPPORT & TRAINING:**		
FINANCIAL/TERMS:		Financial Assistance Provided:		Yes (D)
Cash Investment:	$90K	Site Selection Assistance:		Yes
Total Investment:	$150K	Lease Negotiation Assistance:		Yes
Minimum Net Worth:	$250K	Co-operative Advertising:		Yes
Fees: Franchise -	$20K	Franchisee Assoc./Member:		No
Royalty – 6%;	Ad. – 2%	Size of Corporate Staff:		4
Earnings Claims Statement:	Yes	On-going Support:		a,B,C,D,E,f,G,h,I
Term of Contract (Years):	15/15	Training:	3 weeks headquarters; 2 weeks on-site;	
Avg. # of Employees:	2 FT, 0 PT			on-going.
Passive Ownership:	Not Allowed			
Encourage Conversions:	Yes	**SPECIFIC EXPANSION PLANS:**		
Area Develop. Agreements:	Yes/15	US:		All US
Sub-Franchising Contracts:	Yes	Canada:		All Canada
Expand in Territory:	No	Overseas:		All Countries

Merkinstock has brought back the popular usage of merkins as a decorative form of self-expression and personality, rather than simply a physical necessity. Merkinstock currently possesses the largest variety of colors, materials and designs in the industry with styles to suit any personality and need.

The Merkinstock brand is widely associated with personal creativity and customization, allowing customers to pick and choose their own combinations of available merkin models. The company invests tremendously in customer service, providing sales representatives sensitive and discrete enough to make any customer feel comfortable.

In 1992, founders Sydney and Bob Anning invented a line of merkins that added more spunk and inspiration to the drab, conservative merkins traditionally offered. The Annings began franchising in 1995, and have led a merkin revolution in the process. Market response to this new retail segment has been astounding in Europe and Asia and American markets show promising increases in the number of operating units and revenue gross. Now, with the popularity of body piercings and tattoos waning, merkins are perched to become the next big thing in body decoration and personalization the world over.

Operating Units	12/31/2008	12/31/2009	12/31/2010
Franchised	28	43	52
% Change	--	53.57%	20.93%
Company-Owned	10	10	7
% Change	--	0.0%	0.0%
Total	38	53	59
% Change	--	39.47%	11.32%
Franchised as % of Total	73.36%	81.13%	88.13%

Investment Required
The fee for a Merkinstock franchise is $20,000.

Merkinstock provides the following range of investments required to open your initial franchise. The range assumes that all items are paid for in cash. To the extent that you choose to finance any of these expense items, your front-end investment could be substantially reduced.

Item	Established Low Range	Established High Range
Franchise Fee	$25,500	$45,000
Advertising	$6,500	$18,500
Equipment, Fixtures, Signs	$30,000	$50,000
Inventory Control System	$5,000	$8,000
Opening Costs	$24,300	$75,600
Opening Inventory	$64,000	$135,000
Real Estate, Improvements, Fees	$25,000	$65,000
Training Expenses	$6,000	$6,000
Total Investment	$186,300	$403,100

On-Going Expenses
Merkinstock franchisees pay royalties equaling 6% and advertising contributions equaling 2.9% of gross revenue.

What You Get—Training and Support
As Merkinstock values its customer service orientation, the company provides a comprehensive training program designed to familiarize you with basic business management, merkin history and the Merkinstock product line. The program is free, but all travel, lodging and meal expenses must be paid by the franchisee. The program lasts approximately three weeks. Successful completion of the program is based upon the customization of your own merkin and your ability to properly attach, adjust and clean the merkin in the presence of a trained Merkinstock employee.

Merkinstock's support system is both strong and loving. Each year, a large convention brings franchisees together in a weekend bonding event. During the convention, franchisees share their opinions on the latest merkin models as well as tips on how to better serve their customers' needs. Merkinstock also encourages franchisees to submit their ideas for new models. In addition to the annual convention, franchisees receive support and assistance from their assigned Merkinstock experts, who will periodically visit their stores to evaluate the business's performance and product quality.

The company relies primarily upon foot traffic, word-of-mouth recommendations and gossip to gain exposure and promotion. While relaxing social rules may accommodate the emergence of merkins into the conventional marketplace, Merkinstock's marketing department believes that national advertising campaigns in major media forms would upset the delicate balance between the need for and acceptance of merkins as a major retail item and the private nature of their use. Accordingly, advertising funds are focused solely on the printing of catalogues, accompanying instructions and point-of-sale and store design displays.

Territory
Merkinstock grants exclusive territories.

Miracle-Ear

5000 Cheshire Lane N.
Plymouth, MN 55446
Tel: (888) 510-0766 (763) 268-4295
Fax: (763) 268-4253
Email: charlie.bever@amplifon.com
Website: www.miracle-ear.com
Charlie Bever, Franchise Licensing Specialist

Established in 1948, Miracle-Ear, Inc. is a network of over 1,200 retail outlets that distribute hearing aids manufactured by M-E Manufacturing and Services Inc. ("MEMSI"), a subsidiary of Siemens Medical Solutions. Miracle-Ear is a subsidiary of Amplifon S.p. A, a worldwide distributor of hearing aids based in Italy.

BACKGROUND: IFA Member
Established: 1948; First Franchised: 1984
Franchised Units: 1330
Company-Owned Units: 9
Total Units: 1,339
Dist.: US-1,339; CAN-0; O'seas-0
  North America: 50 States
  Density: 35 in TX, 51 in FL, 83 in CA
Projected New Units (12 Months): 50

Qualifications:	4, 4, 3, 2, 1, 5

FINANCIAL/TERMS:

Cash Investment:	$75-50K
Total Investment:	$127.5-450K
Minimum Net Worth:	$100K
Fees: Franchise -	$20K
Royalty - $48.80/Unit;	Ad. - $26/Inquiry
Earnings Claims Statement:	No
Term of Contract (Years):	5/5
Avg. # of Employees:	2 FT, 1 PT
Passive Ownership:	Not Allowed
Encourage Conversions:	Yes
Area Develop. Agreements:	Yes
Sub-Franchising Contracts:	No
Expand in Territory:	Yes
Space Needs:	750 SF

SUPPORT & TRAINING:

Financial Assistance Provided:	Yes (D)
Site Selection Assistance:	Yes
Lease Negotiation Assistance:	Yes
Co-operative Advertising:	No
Franchisee Assoc./Member:	No
Size of Corporate Staff:	16
On-going Support:	A,NA,C,D,E,f,G,h,I
Training:	1 week corporate headquarters; 1 week in field; on-going field staff training

SPECIFIC EXPANSION PLANS:

US:	West, Midwest, SE, NE
Canada:	No
Overseas:	No

Miracle-Ear offers technological advancement that allows us to customize a hearing solution to your individual hearing loss profile with products that are more discreet and comfortable than ever. We understand how important your hearing is. Our hearing care experts are there to step you through each process. We want you to be fully satisfied with your experience and your hearing.

By building a strong national presence, we're able to be right where you are. No one matches Miracle-Ear for convenience. We can be found in over

1200 locations across the U.S., many in Sears stores. Our association with Sears means even greater access and assurance for you. In 2008, we celebrated 60 years of experience. Miracle-Ear is your trusted resource for the hearing solutions, outstanding service and convenient locations you expect from a leader.

Operating Units	12/31/2008	12/31/2009	12/31/2010
Franchised	959	908	912
% Change	--	-5.3 %	0.4 %
Company-Owned	23	39	20
% Change	--	69.6 %	-48.7%
Total	982	947	932
% Change	--	-3.6 %	-1.6 %
Franchised as % of Total	97.66 %	95.88 %	97.85 %

Investment Required
The fee for a Miracle-Ear franchise is based on the population in your exclusive territory. The minimum initial franchise fee will equal a license fee of $20,000, plus a territory fee of $4,000 per 100,000 population (prorated to a percent per year per 100,000 population) in your exclusive territory provided, however, that the minimum territory fee required will be $10,000 for any exclusive territory with a population of up to 250,000 persons.

Miracle-Ear provides the following range of investments required to open your initial franchise. The range assumes that all items are paid for in cash. To the extent that you choose to finance any of these expense items, your front-end investment could be substantially reduced.

Item	Established Low Range	Established High Range
Initial Franchise Fee	$30,000.00	$30,000.00

Prepaid Expenses	$3,500	$12,000
Expenses While Training	$1,500	$5,000
Real Property	$10,000	$85,000
Furniture, Fixtures, and Equipment	$30,000	$120,000
Computer Equipment	$6,000	$18,000
Signage	$1,500	$10,000
Inventory	$10,000	$20,000
Additional Funds (3 months)	$30,000	$270,000
Total Initial Investment	$122,500	$570,000

On-Going Expenses

Miracle-Ear franchisees pay royalty fees equal to $48.80 for each Miracle Ear® hearing aid and $30.15 for each ME200 hearing aid, monthly Sycle. net software access fees, and at least 10% of gross sales for advertising expenditures, among others.

Franchisee Satisfaction

A critical component of the due diligence process is that you, as a prospective franchisee, have a strong sense of existing franchisee satisfaction. Please review the franchisor's ratings below for this extremely important information.

World-Class Franchise®

How do you rate Miracle-Ear in terms of:	Rating*
Overall quality of franchisor	98%
Ongoing training and support supplied by Franchisor	96%
Quality of products/services received from Franchisor	99%
Opportunity provided by this franchise system	98%

* Independent Audit of Existing Franchisees Who Rated Miracle-Ear as Excellent, Very Good, or Good

What You Get—Training and Support
Upon opening, Miracle-Ear will provide franchisees with assistance in site evaluation and the initial opening of the center. Miracle-Ear also provides customized layouts and designs for the franchisee's center.

Ongoing assistance includes site evaluation assistance for additional centers, refresher product courses, business management and operational consultations, marketing materials and services, and more. Miracle-Ear franchise offers the most recognized brand name of hearing instruments, a high-profile network of more than 1,200 locations, including many in Sears stores, the industry's most aggressive national and local advertising support, comprehensive sales, technical and management training, and ongoing field support that keeps you current with the latest industry advances.

Territory
Miracle-Ear grants exclusive territories.

More Space Place

We Make Room for Living®

5040 140th Ave., N.
Clearwater, FL 33760-3735
Tel: (888) 731-3051 (727) 539-1611
Fax: (727) 524-6382
Email: mjuarez@morespaceplace.com
Website: www.morespaceplace.com
Marty Juarez, COO & Franchise Development Mgr.

One of America's Top 100 Franchise Opportunities (as listed in Bond's Top 100 Franchises, 2004, 2006 and 2009). We create beautiful living spaces for our customers. Picture an elegant home office that converts into an extra bedroom. With our professionally installed Murphy bed and custom-designed office, it can happen. With us, you can fashionably design closets, entertainment centers, utility rooms and garages and turn spare bedrooms into multi-purpose rooms. More Space Place® Franchise is actively seeking the best candidates for ownership of our More Space Place retail stores.

BACKGROUND:

Established: 1989;	First Franchised: 1993
Franchised Units:	37
Company-Owned Units:	5
Total Units:	42
Dist.:	US-42; CAN-0; O'seas-0

North America:	14 States
Density:	3 in TX, 4 in SC
Projected New Units (12 Months):	6
Qualifications:	4, 4, 1, 3, 2, 5

FINANCIAL/TERMS:

Cash Investment:	$40-60K
Total Investment:	$133-203K
Minimum Net Worth:	$150K
Fees: Franchise -	$29.5-22K
Royalty - 4.5%;	Ad. - 2.5%
Earnings Claims Statement:	No
Term of Contract (Years):	10/10
Avg. # of Employees:	3 FT, 1 PT
Passive Ownership:	Allowed, But Discouraged
Encourage Conversions:	Yes
Area Develop. Agreements:	Yes
Sub-Franchising Contracts:	No
Expand in Territory:	Yes
Space Needs:	1,000-2,000 SF

SUPPORT & TRAINING:

Financial Assistance Provided:	Yes (I)
Site Selection Assistance:	Yes
Lease Negotiation Assistance:	Yes
Co-operative Advertising:	Yes
Franchisee Assoc./Member:	No
Size of Corporate Staff:	55
On-going Support:	NA,B,C,D,E,F,G,H,I
Training:	12 days headquarters Clearwater, FL; 6 days on-site; free on-going

SPECIFIC EXPANSION PLANS:

US:	All US
Canada:	No
Overseas:	No

Since its inception over 20 years ago, More Space Place has been committed to helping individuals discover customized furniture solutions that suit a space of any size. More Space Place makes room for the way customers live with a wide selection of beautiful, stylish and smart designs that are highly adaptable to any room. With the help of store owners, customers are able to design a room that caters to their precise needs—a custom walk-in closet, an organized pantry or utility room, an individualized garage and storage space, or a deluxe entertainment center. As the nation's largest Murphy bed retailer, customers can easily transform a bedroom at their leisure so that a home office doubles as a guest room and a child's room instantly becomes a playroom.

Rather than displaying closet and cabinetry products in warehouse spaces, More Space Place constructs beautiful, efficient and practically designed showrooms that accentuate and compliment product designs. Vignette displays, samples and proprietary software packages give customers an opportunity to visualize their rooms before making a purchase. More Space Place also provides franchisees with powerful software that can be used for in-home consultation.

Operating Units	12/31/2008	12/31/2009	12/31/2010
Franchised	38	37	37
% Change	--	-2.63%	0.0%
Company-Owned	4	5	5
% Change	--	25%	0.0%
Total	42	42	42
% Change	--	0%	0%
Franchised as % of Total	90.5%	88.1%	88.1%

Investment Required
The fee for an initial More Space Place franchise is $29,500. Additional licenses are $22,000.

More Space Place provides the following range of investments required to open your initial franchise. The range assumes that all items are paid for in cash. To the extent that you choose to finance any of these expense items, your front-end investment could be substantially reduced.

Item	Established Low Range	Established High Range
Franchise Fee	$29,500	$29,500
Training Expenses	$2,500	$4,000
Real Estate Improvements	$20,000	$38,000
Office Equipment and Supplies	$2,000	$3,000
Computer Hardware and Software	$2,200	$2,400
CAD Design Software Keys	$1,800	$3,600
Pallet Lifter or Fork Lift	$600	$3,000
Van or Trailer	$1,600	$3,700
Signage and Graphic	$5,000	$12,000
Initial Inventory	$25,500	$39,000
Store Display Accessories	$3,500	$6,000
Opening Advertising	$8,000	$12,000
Architect's Fee and Engineering Costs	$0	$3,000
Miscellaneous Operating Costs	$4,000	$6,000
Insurance	$1,800	$2,800
Additional Funds and Working Capital	$25,000	$35,000
Total Investment	$133,000	$203,000

On-Going Expenses

More Space Place franchisees pay a royalty fee equal to the greater of 4.5% of gross revenue or $500 per month, and a National Advertising Program (NAP) fee equal to the greater of 2.5% of gross revenue or $250 per month. Franchisees must contribute a minimum of 2.5% or $500 of gross sales towards regional advertising, and a minimum of $2,500 or 7% of gross sales towards local advertising.

What You Get—Training and Support

More Space Place store owners are not required to have a carpentry or designer background. Owners typically assume the role of general/sales manager and employees are hired for product installation.

Franchisees receive a comprehensive start-up package that includes site-selection support, showroom design and specifications, product selection, free owner and personnel on-site training sessions, a product line with thousands of variations and free shipping on initial furniture shipment.

Additional support is provided for furniture selection, start-up, accounting setup, product knowledge, sales training, operations, advertising and marketing. More Space Place also provides on-going and additional training sessions at various times throughout the year. Franchisees further benefit from a powerful CAD system, a product ordering and inventory system, minimal standing inventory, a single-source supplier, new product development and acquisition, group purchasing power and manufacturer product guarantees.

Territory

More Space Place has a continental United States expansion plan of approximately 200 stores under the current concept. A small city and conversion program may be available. The company grants exclusive territories that cannot be changed as long as the agreed upon store quantity is maintained. Development territories may be available to those franchisees qualified to open multiple units.

RadioShack

RadioShack.

300 RadioShack Circle
Fort Worth, TX 76102
Tel: (800) 826-3905 (817) 415-9138
Fax: (817) 415-9107
Email: franchise.opportunity@radioshack.com
Website: www.franchiseradioshack.com
Kelly Wilde, Director, Domestic Franchise Development

With reasonable investment levels and hundreds of potential markets to develop, a RadioShack® franchise represents an exciting opportunity for you to associate with one of the most powerful brands in retail. The RadioShack Franchise Program is one of the best values in the entrepreneurial franchise market as it is an extension of approximately 4,670 company-operated RadioShack stores nationwide. As a franchise owner, you benefit from the buying power of a major retail network in the purchase of fixtures, in-store signage, and other necessities for starting up a new retail business. Our low startup cost represents a true value in franchising with a nationally recognized retailer.

BACKGROUND: IFA Member
Established: 1919; First Franchised: 1968
Franchised Units: 1,100
Company-Owned Units: 6,160

Total Units:	7,260
Dist.:	US-6,980; CAN-0; O'seas-280
North America:	50 States
Density:	827 in CA, 602 in TX, 420 in NY
Projected New Units (12 Months):	20
Qualifications:	4, 4, 3, 3, 2, 3

FINANCIAL/TERMS:

Cash Investment:	$150K
Total Investment:	$150K-350K
Minimum Net Worth:	$250K
Fees: Franchise -	$39.9K
Royalty - 7%;	Ad. - 3%
Earnings Claims Statement:	No
Term of Contract (Years):	10/5
Avg. # of Employees:	Varies
Passive Ownership: Allowed, But Discouraged	
Encourage Conversions:	Yes
Area Develop. Agreements:	No
Sub-Franchising Contracts:	No
Expand in Territory:	Yes
Space Needs:	1,000 SF

SUPPORT & TRAINING:

Financial Assistance Provided: No	
Site Selection Assistance:	Yes
Lease Negotiation Assistance:	No
Co-operative Advertising:	No
Franchisee Assoc./Member:	Yes/Yes
Size of Corporate Staff:	1,200
On-going Support:	NA,b,C,D,E,F,G,h,I
Training:	1 week Ft. Worth, TX

SPECIFIC EXPANSION PLANS:

US:	All
Canada:	No
Overseas:	All Countries

For over 90 years, RadioShack has been a leading national retailer of innovative technology products and services, including personal, mobile, home technology, and power supply products. Founded by entrepreneurs, RadioShack offers consumers a wide range of products and services from leading national brands, exclusive private brands, and major wireless carriers—all in a comfortable and convenient shopping environment.

The RadioShack Franchise Program is one of the most powerful brands in retail with approximately 4,680 company-operated RadioShack stores nationwide. A RadioShack franchise offers solid benefits, including brand-driven store traffic, superior brand recognition nationally and globally, national advertising and a variety of top-quality products customers need and want. Quality support and low investment levels combine to make RadioShack a great investment. Additionally, in 2010 RadioShack was listed as one of the top 30 retail brands in the country in the Most Valuable U.S. Retail Brands report, compiled by well-regarded retail brand consultants Interbrand Design Forum.

Operating Units	9/30/2008	9/30/2009	9/30/2010
Franchised	1,358	1,273	1,172
% Change	--	-6.3%	-7.9%
Company-Owned	4,453	4,464	4,473
% Change	--	0.2%	0.2%
Total	5,811	5,737	5,645
% Change	--	-1.3%	-1.6%
Franchised as % of Total	98.4%	98.9%	99.6%

Investment Required
The fee for a RadioShack franchise is $39,900. The fee decreases according to the number of stores the franchisee intends on opening. RadioShack also offers, in limited instances, a discount to US veterans and minority-owned businesses.

RadioShack provides the following range of investments required to open your initial Full-Line Store franchise. The range assumes that all items are paid for in cash. To the extent that you choose to finance any of these expense items, your front-end investment could be substantially reduced.

Item	Established Low Range	Established High Range
Franchise Fee	$39,900	$39,900
Real Estate Improvements	$3,750	$11,000
Build-out Costs	$7,000	$150,000
Furniture and Fixtures	$22,000	$50,000
Fixture Installation	$4,500	$10,000
POS Computer System	$3,000	$7,000
Equipment	$2,360	$4,490
Exterior Signage	$4,000	$30,000
Insurance	$300	$700
Opening Inventory	$30,000	$100,000
Grand Opening Advertising Campaign	$3,000	$5,000
Training Costs	$500	$500
Security and Utility Deposits	$1,950	$5,000
Business Licenses	$100	$300
Utilities (3 Months)	$2,100	$2,315
Employee Compensation (3 Months)	$23,715	$26,146
Additional Funds (3 Months)	$50,000	$100,000
Total Initial Investment	$198,175	$542,351

On-Going Expenses

RadioShack franchisees pay a monthly royalty fee of 7% of net sales and a monthly proprietary credit card program participation fee of 2% of the gross dollar amount per transaction. Additional fees include a monthly software maintenance and upgrade fee of $39.99.

What You Get—Training and Support

RadioShack offers franchisees resources and support personnel, including dedicated franchise district managers, sales and support specialists, and bookkeepers. With over 40 years of experience, RadioShack has built a best-in-class training program in which store owners and employees receive training inside their new store, in a nearby established store and in a classroom setting. In addition, a mentor store will be assigned to guide the new store, and store employees will have an orientation/product training program to complete online.

From the Grand Opening forward, RadioShack offers continued support with local workshops and annual conventions. RadioShack franchisees receive ongoing updates about new products, services and offerings to keep them on top of customers' needs. Franchisees also benefit from the buying power of a major retail network in the purchase of fixtures, signage and other necessities for starting up the business. Additionally, RadioShack has an advertising, merchandising and marketing staff that supports the brand year round with national media campaigns, including advertising in television, digital, print, PR, as well as search engine optimization and social network seeding.

Territory

RadioShack does not grant exclusive territories.

Wild Birds Unlimited

Wild Birds Unlimited

11711 N. College Ave., # 146
Carmel, IN 46032-5634
Tel: (888) 730-7108 (317) 571-7100
Fax: (317) 208-4050
Email: pickettp@wbu.com

Website: www.wbu.com
Paul Pickett, VP of Franchise Development

Wild Birds Unlimited is North America's original and largest group of retail stores catering to the backyard birdfeeding and nature enthusiast. We currently have over 280 stores in the US and Canada. Stores provide birdseed, feeders, houses, optics and nature-related gifts. Additionally, stores provide extensive educational programs regarding backyard birdfeeding. Franchisees are provided an all-inclusive support system.

BACKGROUND:		IFA Member	Encourage Conversions:	Yes
Established: 1981;	First Franchised: 1983		Area Develop. Agreements:	No
Franchised Units:		275	Sub-Franchising Contracts:	No
Company-Owned Units:		0	Expand in Territory:	Yes
Total Units:		275	Space Needs:	1,400-1,700 SF
Dist.:	US-260; CAN-15; O'seas-0			
North America:	42 States, 3 Provinces		SUPPORT & TRAINING:	
Density:	17 in MI, 16 in OH, 17 in NC		Financial Assistance Provided:	Yes (I)
Projected New Units (12 Months):		15	Site Selection Assistance:	Yes
Qualifications:	5, 5, 1, 3, 2, 5		Lease Negotiation Assistance:	Yes
			Co-operative Advertising:	No
FINANCIAL/TERMS:			Franchisee Assoc./Member:	Yes/Yes
Cash Investment:		$25-35K	Size of Corporate Staff:	39
Total Investment:		$99-157K	On-going Support:	NA,NA,C,D,E,F,G,H,I
Minimum Net Worth:		$200K	Training:	5 days Carmel, IN; 5 days store site
Fees: Franchise -		$18K		
Royalty - 4%;		Ad. - .5%	SPECIFIC EXPANSION PLANS:	
Earnings Claims Statement:		Yes	US:	All US
Term of Contract (Years):		10/5	Canada:	All Canada
Avg. # of Employees:	2 (including owner) FT, 3 PT		Overseas:	No
Passive Ownership:		Not Allowed		

Wild Birds Unlimited operates over 280 stores in North America, offering superior bird feeding/watching and nature hobby products. Wild Birds Unlimited offers a number of goods tailored to nature enthusiasts, including bird feeders, birdhouses, birdbaths, bird food, decorative lawn and garden accessories, and unique nature gifts. Wild Birds' certified bird feeding specialists help customers transform their yards into beautiful bird feeding habitats that benefit wild birds and the environment.

Backyard bird feeding and watching represents a surprisingly profitable industry: over 55.5 million people participate in backyard bird feeding, and bird feeding/watching is a $5.4 billion industry. Thus, Wild Birds Unlimited offers prospective franchisees the opportunity to combine their business ambitions with their love for nature, and gives them access to over 25 years of experience and the highest quality nature hobby products and services available.

Operating Units	12/31/2008	12/31/2009	12/31/2010
Franchised	282	272	272

167

% Change	--	-3.5%	0.0%
Company-Owned	0	0	0
% Change	--	--	--
Total	282	272	272
% Change	--	-3.5%	0.0%
Franchised as % of Total	100.0%	100.0%	100. 0%

Investment Required

The fee for a Wild Birds Unlimited franchise is $18,000. The fee for an additional store is $9,000.

Wild Birds Unlimited provides the following range of investments required to open your initial franchise. The range assumes that all items are paid for in cash. To the extent that you choose to finance any of these expense items, your front-end investment could be substantially reduced. Please note the figures below are for a first time franchisee; for an existing franchisee to open another location the Total Initial Investment is between $81,621 and $136,436.

Item	Established Low Range	Established High Range
Franchise Fee	$18,000	$18,000
Expenses While Training	$3,483	$8,164
Lease Deposit	$2,500	$4,500
First Month's Rent	$2,500	$4,500
Leasehold Improvements	$7,800	$24,555
Insurance (First Quarter)	$125	$580
Legal/Accounting	$500	$3,000
Office Equipment	$7,916	$7,996
Signs	$1,187	$7,964
Advertising	$5,050	$6,915
Retail Fixtures	$11,462	$11,859

Opening Inventory	$18,066	$20,938
Gift Card Fee	$153	$778
Misc Expenses	$4,379	$8,187
Additional Funds (3 Months)	$10,000	$20,000
Total Initial Investment	$93,121	$147,936

On-Going Expenses
Wild Birds Unlimited franchisees pay a royalty fee equal to 4% of gross sales, a minimum local advertising fee equal to 2% of gross sales, a regional/local advertising fund fee equal to 0.5% of gross sales (maximum of $2,500 a year) and an annual fee for point-of-sale software.

What You Get—Training and Support
Wild Birds Unlimited assists franchisees throughout the entirety of the franchise relationship to ensure the success of franchised locations. Prior to opening, Wild Birds assists franchisees in site selection and provides specifications and advice for layout, décor, equipment, furnishings and signs.

Before opening a franchised location, franchisees must complete a training program at Wild Birds Unlimited's corporate headquarters in Carmel, Indiana. The initial training program includes approximately 55 hours of classroom instruction and covers a number of topics, including visual merchandising, store layout, store tours, purchasing strategies, inventory management, POS system, seed strategies, product and hobby education, marketing strategies, human resources, customer services, sales skills and strategies and financial management.

Following the store opening, Wild Birds Unlimited conducts regular additional training programs on selected topics, as well as periodic evaluations to provide constructive feedback.

Territory
Wild Birds Unlimited grants exclusive territories.

Service-Based 6

AAMCO

201 Gibraltar Rd., # 150
Horsham, PA 19044
Tel: (800) 292-8500, (800) 523-0402
Fax: (215) 956-0340
Email: franchise@aamco.com
Website: www.aamco.com
Jack Bachinsky, VP Marketing

AAMCO Transmissions is the world's largest chain of transmission specialists and one of the leaders in total car care services. AAMCO has approximately 900 automotive centers throughout the United States, Canada and Puerto Rico. Established in 1962, AAMCO is proud to have served more than 35 million drivers.

BACKGROUND:

	IFA Member
Established: 1963;	First Franchised: 1963
Franchised Units:	886
Company-Owned Units:	12
Total Units:	898
Dist.:	US-838; CAN-27; O'seas-33
North America:	48 States, 4 Provinces
Density:	71 in FL, 49 in PA, 68 in TX
Projected New Units (12 Months):	40
Qualifications:	4, 4, 1, 2, 3, 3

FINANCIAL/TERMS:

Cash Investment:	$25-125K
Total Investment:	$232-299K
Minimum Net Worth:	$50-182K
Fees: Franchise -	$39.5K
Royalty - 7.5%; Ad. - Varies, $150/mo for national	
Earnings Claims Statement:	Yes
Term of Contract (Years):	15/15
Avg. # of Employees:	4 FT, 0 PT
Passive Ownership:	Not Allowed
Encourage Conversions:	Yes
Area Develop. Agreements:	Yes
Sub-Franchising Contracts:	No
Expand in Territory:	No
Space Needs:	1,212 SF

SUPPORT & TRAINING:

Financial Assistance Provided:	Yes (I)
Site Selection Assistance:	Yes
Lease Negotiation Assistance:	Yes
Co-operative Advertising:	Yes
Franchisee Assoc./Member:	Yes/Yes
Size of Corporate Staff:	120
On-going Support:	NA,NA,C,D,E,f,G,h,I
Training:	On-going regional, annual, online; 5 weeks on-site; 3 weeks Horsham, PA

SPECIFIC EXPANSION PLANS:

US:	All US
Canada:	All Canada
Overseas:	All Countries

With over 50 years of experience, AAMCO is a recognized leader in the transmission business. In the past six years, AAMCO has expanded its services into the $300 billion general automotive repair market. AAMCO offers the mostly highly skilled technicians and provides unparalleled service in the industry. Maintaining brand recognition in over 90% of the U.S. population and with almost 900 locations nationwide, AAMCO's dominance in the industry is manifest. With such well-defined prominence in the transmission industry, AAMCO is poised to become the leader in breaks, tune-ups, air conditioning and other after-market services.

AAMCO represents an exciting franchise opportunity that offers financial freedom and a rewarding lifestyle. Industry growth is estimated at 3-5% annually, and the number of older cars present on the road is predicted to continue increasing. As such, AAMCO franchisees benefit from an advantageous market and a growing industry. With its name brand recognition and successful business model, AAMCO offers one of the best franchising opportunities in the automotive repair industry. Finally, franchisees can take advantage of hundreds of established National Fleet customers who generate millions of dollars in sales annually.

Operating Units	12/31/2008	12/31/2009	12/31/2010
Franchised	865	837	829
% Change	--	-3.2%	-1.0%
Company-Owned	0	0	7
% Change	--	--	--
Total	865	837	836
% Change	--	-3.2%	-0.1%
Franchised as % of Total	100.0%	100.0%	99.2%

Investment Required
The fee for an AAMCO franchise is $39,500. A previous franchisee opening another location pays a reduced franchise fee of $17,500.

AAMCO provides the following range of investments required to open your initial franchise. The range assumes that all items are paid for in cash. To the extent that you choose to finance any of these expense items, your front-end investment could be substantially reduced.

Item	Established Low Range	Established High Range
Initial Franchise Fee	$17,500*	$39,500
Grand Opening Operations Development Program	$10,000	$10,000
Expenses While Training	$2,100	$4,000
Leasehold Improvements	$8,500	$12,000
Real Estate Deposit	$3,500	$7,000
Equipment, Tools, Supplies & Installation of Lifts	$75,000	$86,000
Interior Design Package	$4,500	$5,500
Exterior Design Package	$10,000	$19,000
Technical Reference Materials	$6,000	$6,000
Office/Shop Package	$9,000	$9,000
Grand Opening Advertising	$3,000	$5,000
Misc. Opening Costs	$20,500	$23,400
Initial Parts and Inventory	$2,500	$2,500
Security Deposit	$5,000	$5,000
Advertising Costs (3 Months)	$4,400	$15,800
Additional Funds (3 Months)	$30,000	$50,000
Total Initial Investment	$210,500*	$299,700

*This fee is for opening an additional location. The Total Initial Investment Established Low Range for a first location is $232,500.

On-going Expenses

AAMCO franchisees pay a weekly royalty fee equal to 7.5% of total gross sales, a national creative advertising fee equal to $150 per month and local advertising fees which vary by local advertising pool and average approximately $505 per week. Other fees payable by the franchisee include monthly yellow pages advertising fees and software license and maintenance fees.

What You Get—Training and Support

AAMCO provides considerable training and support throughout the entirety of the franchise process. Prior to opening, AAMCO will offer site location recommendations and assist in layout of the center and equipment. AAMCO further orchestrates a three-week intensive training for all franchisees located at the AAMCO Operator School in Horsham, Pennsylvania. The training consists of approximately 135 hours of classroom instruction and 240 hours of on-site training and covers service system procedures, customer relations, operation, technical services, recruiting, business-to-business sales, the National Fleet Accounts program, advertising, marketing, the yellow page program and management skills. Franchisees also participate in a mandatory five-week Grand Opening Operations Development (GOOD) Training aimed to ensure that the franchisee's transition to store ownership is seamless and successful.

Following the successful opening of an AAMCO franchised location, AAMCO continues to provide business information, literature and materials to continuously enhance the franchised center's performance. Additionally, AAMCO supports franchisees by providing technical consulting services, national/regional/local advertising expertise, guidance regarding customer relations and general operations advice. Franchisees are also given the opportunity to participate in the AAMCO National Fleets Accounts program that offers work for fleet account customers according to previously established terms of agreement.

Territory

AAMCO does not grant exclusive territories; however, AAMCO agrees to limit the number of AAMCO Centers to a maximum of one Center per 100,000 motor vehicle registrations within a specific metropolitan statistical area.

AdviCoach®

Business Advisers Making Your Success A Reality

900 Main St., S., Bldg. #2
Southbury, CT 06488
Tel: (203) 405-2131
Fax: (203) 264-3516
Email: fdadmin@franchisesource.com
Website: www.advicoach.com
Dawn Ingala, Franchise Development

With over 25 years of experience, our unique Advi-Coach® business model is designed to empower business owners to increase the productivity and value of their businesses. We keep our clients focused on driving results though our coaching methodology, not by selling mass market solutions. AdviCoach® franchisees help business owners increase the value of their businesses by identifying business weaknesses, educating them on business solutions, and holding them accountable to implement appropriate "Rapid Impact Strategies" through weekly coaching sessions.

BACKGROUND: IFA Member
Established: 2002; First Franchised: 2003
Franchised Units: 70
Company-Owned Units: 0
Total Units: 70
Dist.: US-70; CAN-0; O'seas-0

North America:	24 States
Density:	5 in VA, 6 in NC
Projected New Units (12 Months):	39
Qualifications:	4, 4, 1, 3, 4, 4

FINANCIAL/TERMS:
Cash Investment:	$67K
Total Investment:	$67-77K
Minimum Net Worth:	$199K
Fees: Franchise -	$45K
Royalty - 5-15%;	Ad. - $400/mo
Earnings Claims Statement:	Yes
Term of Contract (Years):	10/10
Avg. # of Employees:	1 FT, 0 PT
Passive Ownership:	Allowed
Encourage Conversions:	Yes
Area Develop. Agreements:	Yes, 2.5-8.5 years
Sub-Franchising Contracts:	No
Expand in Territory:	Yes
Space Needs:	

SUPPORT & TRAINING:
Financial Assistance Provided:	No
Site Selection Assistance:	NA
Lease Negotiation Assistance:	NA
Co-operative Advertising:	No
Franchisee Assoc./Member:	No
Size of Corporate Staff:	35
On-going Support:	NA,b,C,D,NA,NA,G,h,I
Training:	24 weeks virtual; 5 days Southbury, CT

SPECIFIC EXPANSION PLANS:
US:	All
Canada:	All
Overseas:	All Countries

Business coaching is booming. The demand for business coaching services has increased dramatically in recent years; we have enjoyed a 100% increase in business coaching in just the last three years. That translates to over 2.8 million small and mid-sized businesses using business coaching over the next year, generating in excess of 1.5 billion dollars in coaching revenue.

With over 25 years of experience, our unique Advicoach® business model is designed to empower business owners to increase the productivity and value of their businesses. We keep our clients focused on driving results through our coaching methodology, not by selling mass market solutions. AdviCoach® franchisees help business owners increase the value of their businesses by identifying business weaknesses, educating them on business solutions, and holding them accountable to implement appropriate "Rapid Impact Strategies" through weekly coaching sessions.

Our Coaching Process includes:

• Setting income, lifestyle, wealth and equity goals
• Setting annual, quarterly and weekly goals
• Implementing Rapid Impact Strategies
• Building long-term relationships with business owners

Operating Units	12/31/2008	12/31/2009	12/31/2010
Franchised	30	55	69
% Change	--	83%	25%
Company-Owned	0	0	0
% Change	--	--	--
Total	30	55	69
% Change	--	83%	25%
Franchised as % of Total	100%	100%	100%

Investment Required

The franchise fee for an AdviCoach® franchise is $45,000.

175

AdviCoach® provides the following range of investments required to open your initial franchise. The range assumes that all items are paid for in cash. To the extent that you choose to finance any of these expense items, your front-end investment could be substantially reduced.

Item	Established Low Range	Established High Range
Initial Franchise Fee	$45,000	$45,000
Tuition (per person)	$10,000	$10,000
Real Estate and Improvements (6 Months)	$4,000	$5,000
Expenses While Training	$1,500	$2,500
Equipment	$150	$3,000
Marketing Aids	$1,000	$2,000
Vehicle Lease or Usage (6 Months)	$1,200	$2,400
Call Center	$2,000	$2,000
Technology Fee	$510	$510
Additional Funds (6 Months)	$8,000	$9,800
Total Initial Investment	$73,360	$82,210

On-going Expenses

AdviCoach® franchisees pay a monthly royalty fee ranging from 5% to 15% of gross revenues depending on amount of annual gross revenue, and a monthly system-wide brand building fund contribution of $400. Other fees include an $85 per month Technology Fee and a mandatory annual conference attendance fee of $450, plus expenses.

What You Get—Training and Support

At Advicoach®, training is not a single event, but a dynamic, ongoing educational process. Our Continuing Professional Education includes a Business Launch Curriculum that starts within 48 hours of joining our team. We leverage technology to bring continuing education and resources to our team 24/7. You'll be guided by a mentor through our virtual curriculum, which prepares you for an on-site event at our Performance Enhancement Center.

Territory
AdviCoach® grants a saturation maximum—AdviCoach® will not place more than one single unit per 1,000 payrolled businesses in a given state or group of states. The rights granted within the territory are non-exclusive.

Always Best Care
Senior Services

1406 Blue Oaks Rd.
Roseville, CA 95747
Tel: (888) 430-2273 (916) 722-6233
Fax: (916) 722-8780
Email: franchisesales@abc-seniors.com
Website: www.alwaysbestcare.com
Barry Parish, Director of Franchising

Always Best Care Senior Services is the only senior care franchise system to offer three revenue streams: Assisted Living Placement, In-Home Care, and Skilled Home Health Care. We have been in business since 1996, and have contracts with communities representing more than 2,000 assisted living units.

We provide the following: an exclusive insurance program, two weeks of one-on-one training in addition to 90 days of training modules, an exclusive care provider retention and recruitment program, national contracts for our franchisees, 24/7 call center so franchisees never miss a lead, and a virtual office (all-in-one web-based software system).

BACKGROUND:	IFA Member
Established: 1996;	First Franchised: 2007
Franchised Units:	175
Company-Owned Units:	0
Total Units:	175
Dist.:	US-169; CAN-6; O'seas-0
North America:	34 States, 1 Province
Density:	3 in OH, 9 in CA
Projected New Units (12 Months):	75
Qualifications:	5, 5, 3, 2, 3, 4

FINANCIAL/TERMS:	
Cash Investment:	$39-$43K
Total Investment:	$50.7-150K

Minimum Net Worth:	$50K	Site Selection Assistance:	NA
Fees: Franchise -	$39.5K	Lease Negotiation Assistance:	NA
Royalty - 6%;	Ad. - 2%	Co-operative Advertising:	Yes
Earnings Claims Statement:	Yes	Franchisee Assoc./Member:	No
Term of Contract (Years):	10/5	Size of Corporate Staff:	17
Avg. # of Employees:	3 FT, 0 PT	On-going Support:	NA,NA,NA,D,NA,NA,G,H,I
Passive Ownership:	Allowed, But Discouraged	Training:	One-on-one with sales trainer takes
Encourage Conversions:	Yes	about 90 days per and post training modules; 1 week	
Area Develop. Agreements:	Yes	corporate; 1 week at franchise location	
Sub-Franchising Contracts:	No		
Expand in Territory:	Yes	**SPECIFIC EXPANSION PLANS:**	
Space Needs:	NA	US:	All US
		Canada:	Yes, NA
SUPPORT & TRAINING:		Overseas:	Germany, UK, Chile, Australia
Financial Assistance Provided:	Yes (I)		

With the senior population projected to double in the next 30 years, the demand for quality healthcare for seniors is increasing at an exponential rate. Since 1996, Always Best Care has helped families with non-medical in-home care and assisted living placement services. We're now adding skilled home health care in select markets. With comprehensive training and ongoing support, Always Best Care has created a revenue model that remains stable throughout both difficult and strong economic times.

Between in-home care, assisted living placement, and skilled home health care, franchisees tap into three sectors of the healthcare industry that serve seniors in the community by providing trusted care, compassionate support, and professional advice, and have the same basic sources of business.

Operating Units	12/31/2008	12/31/2009	12/31/2010
Franchised	24	58	124
% Change	--	141.7%	113.8%
Company-Owned	1	1	0
% Change	--	0.0%	-100.0%
Total	25	59	124
% Change	--	136.0%	110.2%
Franchised as % of Total	96%	98.3%	100%

Investment Required

The fee for an Always Best Care franchise is $39,500.

Always Best Care provides the following range of investments required to open your initial franchise. The range assumes that all items are paid for in cash. To the extent that you choose to finance any of these expense items, your front-end investment could be substantially reduced.

Item	Established Low Range	Established High Range
Initial Franchise Fee	$39,500	$39,500
Expenses While Training	$1,000	$3,000
Rent (3 months)	$0	$3,000
Office Furniture & Fixtures	$1,000	$7,500
Signage	$0	$200
Insurance Premium (1 Year)	$3,000	$6,500
Opening Costs	$300	$1,500
Advertising	$1,500	$1,500
Computer Equipment, Software and Printer	$1,000	$5,000
Permits/Licenses	$125	$15,000
Professional Fees	$2,500	$5,000
Additional Funds (3 months)	$1,000	$3,000
Total Initial Investment	$50,925	$90,700

On-going Expenses

Always Best Care franchisees pay ongoing royalty fees equal to 6% of gross monthly sales plus an advertising fund contribution equal to 2% of gross monthly sales. Additional expenses include local advertising expenditures and training for additional and new employees.

What You Get—Training and Support

Always Best Care's training program includes 40 hours of classroom training and 30 hours of on-the-job training. From day-to-day operations to sales and marketing, Always Best Care's comprehensive training program equips a franchisee from any professional background to run a successful Always Best Care franchise. In addition, there is an experienced Area Representative assigned to each franchisee to provide local support.

Territory

Always Best Care grants exclusive territories.

Anytime Fitness

12181 Margo Ave. S.w
Hastings, MN 55033
Tel: (800) 704-5004 (651) 438-5000
Fax: (651) 438-5099
Email: info@anytimefitness.com
Website: www.anytimefitness.com
Mark Daly, National Media Director

Anytime Fitness is the #1 co-ed fitness club chain in the world. We've boiled our business model down to the core essentials which members expect. Our loyal family of preferred vendors supply our franchisees with quality products at the best available prices. Financial and real estate support available. More than half of our franchisees own multiple clubs. Enjoy the freedom of spending time with your friends and family - and the knowledge that you're making your community a better place to live.

BACKGROUND:	IFA Member
Established: 2002;	First Franchised: 2002
Franchised Units:	1835
Company-Owned Units:	11
Total Units:	1,846
Dist.:	US-1,635; CAN-45; O'seas-166

North America:	49 States, 4 Provinces	Expand in Territory:	Yes
Density: 101 in LA, 120 in MN, 129 in TX		Space Needs:	4,000 SF
Projected New Units (12 Months):	400		
Qualifications:	3, 2, 2, 2, 3, 4	**SUPPORT & TRAINING:**	
		Financial Assistance Provided:	Yes (D)
FINANCIAL/TERMS:		Site Selection Assistance:	Yes
Cash Investment:	$10K	Lease Negotiation Assistance:	Yes
Total Investment:	$44-300K	Co-operative Advertising:	Yes
Minimum Net Worth:	$10K	Franchisee Assoc./Member:	Yes/Yes
Fees: Franchise -	$20K	Size of Corporate Staff:	80
Royalty - $499/mo;	Ad. - $150/mo	On-going Support:	A,B,C,D,E,F,G,H,I
Earnings Claims Statement:	Yes	Training:	1 week Hastings, MN
Term of Contract (Years):	5/5		
Avg. # of Employees:	1 FT, 2 PT	**SPECIFIC EXPANSION PLANS:**	
Passive Ownership:	Allowed	US:	All 50 states
Encourage Conversions:	Yes	Canada:	All Canadian provinces
Area Develop. Agreements:	Yes	Overseas:	India, China, Japan, Australia, Europe,
Sub-Franchising Contracts:	Yes		Middle East, Latin America

As the world's largest and fastest growing, 24-hour, co-ed fitness franchise, Anytime Fitness continues to break records and receive industry accolades. With nearly a million people joining health clubs each year, pushing membership to 41.3 million people nationwide, franchisees have the opportunity to tap into Anytime Fitness's solid customer base that continues to grow.

With 30 years of business experience, founders of Anytime Fitness recognized the growing demand for 24-hour, co-ed fitness facilities. Anytime Fitness addresses a market that is rapidly growing as customers seek convenience and security in their fitness facility. With proprietary access software, security, and surveillance technology, Anytime Fitness creates safe and convenient health and fitness solutions with greatly reduced staffing needs.

Operating Units	12/31/2008	12/31/2009	12/31/2010
Franchised	942	1,185	1,378
% Change	--	25.8%	16.3%
Company-Owned	7	12	11
% Change	--	71.4%	-8.3%
Total	949	1,197	1,389

| % Change | | -- | 26.1% | 16.0% |
| Franchised as % of Total | | 99.3% | 99.0% | 99.2% |

Investment Required

The fee for an Anytime Fitness franchise is $24,999 and the fee for an Anytime Fitness Express franchise is $18,999, with a reduction for conversions, veterans, and current franchisees.

Anytime Fitness provides the following range of investments required to open your initial franchise. The range assumes that all items are paid for in cash. To the extent that you choose to finance any of these expense items, your front-end investment could be substantially reduced.

Item	Anytime Fitness		Anytime Fitness Express	
	Established Low Range	Established High Range	Established Low Range	Established High Range
Initial Franchise Fee	$12,999	$24,999	$11,999	$18,999
Expenses While Training	$1,000	$2,300	$1,000	$2,300
Real Estate and Improvements	$12,500	$165,600	$4,600	$80,700
Fitness Equipment	$10,900	$41,500	$7,500	$25,500
Tanning Equipment	$0	$1,700	$0	$900
Security System	$2,300	$12,500	$2,000	$10,000
First Aid Equipment	$1,000	$1,600	$1,000	$1,600
Signage	$4,300	$9,500	$4,300	$9,500
Opening Costs	$3,700	$8,200	$3,200	$7,500
Insurance	$1,800	$3,000	$1,200	$3,000

Supplies and Furniture	$1,000	$6,500	$1,000	$6,500
Legal and Accounting Expenses	$500	$4,500	$500	$4,500
Additional Funds (3 Months)	$8,000	$40,000	$8,000	$40,000
Total Initial Investment	$59,999	$321,899	$46,299	$210,999

On-going Expenses

Anytime Fitness franchisees pay royalty fees of $499 per month, a general advertising fee equal to the greater of $150 per month or 1% of monthly revenue, and in 40 states a local marketing fund contribution equal to the greater of $150 per month or 1% of monthly revenues. Additional fees payable by the franchisee include monthly website and software fees.

What You Get—Training and Support

Anytime Fitness provides its franchisees with support from start-up financing to marketing. Franchisees receive one week of comprehensive classroom training at the Anytime Fitness headquarters in Hasting, MN. During training, franchisees receive thorough instruction in the Anytime Franchise concept and on topics ranging from member retention to sales and marketing.

After initial training, Anytime Fitness franchisees have access to numerous lines of ongoing training and support including regional workshops, advanced managerial sessions, and an online operations manual tailored to specific phases of the franchise's business. Franchisees have the option of using Anytime Fitness's professionally developed marketing materials and business supplies, designed to heighten national branding and marketing efforts.

Territory

Anytime Fitness grants protected territories.

BONUS Building Care

BONUS ®
BUILDING CARE

P.O. Box 300
Indianola, OK 74442-0300
Tel: (800) 931-1102 (918) 823-4990
Fax: (918) 823-4994
Email: franchiseofficer@bonusbuildingcare.com
Website: www.bonusbuildingcare.com
Perry White, President

World's best investment opportunity in commercial cleaning. National rankings include: Entrepreneur Franchise 500 #20 (2008), Franchise Business Review, Franchisee Satisfaction #2 (2008), Franchise Market Magazine #5 (2008). You are offered customers, training, insurance, financing, clerical and procedural assistance as well as opportunities for expansion. Total investment, which can be partially financed by Bonus, is $9K to $41.9K

BACKGROUND: IFA Member
Established: 1996; First Franchised: 1996
Franchised Units: 1,315
Company-Owned Units: 0
Total Units: 1,315
Dist.: US-1,315; CAN-0; O'seas-0
North America: 14 States
Density: 0 in , 405 in TX, 624 in TN
Projected New Units (12 Months): 100
Qualifications: 1, 1, 2, 2, 3, 3

FINANCIAL/TERMS:

Cash Investment:	Varies
Total Investment:	$9-41.9K
Minimum Net Worth:	NA
Fees: Franchise -	$7.5K
Royalty - Support Fee 22%;	Ad. - 0%
Earnings Claims Statement:	No
Term of Contract (Years):	10/10
Avg. # of Employees:	Varies FT, 0 PT
Passive Ownership:	Allowed, But Discouraged
Encourage Conversions:	Yes
Area Develop. Agreements:	No
Sub-Franchising Contracts:	Yes
Expand in Territory:	Yes
Space Needs:	NA

SUPPORT & TRAINING:

Financial Assistance Provided:	Yes (D)
Site Selection Assistance:	NA
Lease Negotiation Assistance:	NA
Co-operative Advertising:	No
Franchisee Assoc./Member:	Yes/Yes
Size of Corporate Staff:	17
On-going Support:	NA,NA,C,D,NA,NA,G,NA,I
Training:	As needed self-study; minimum 5 hours classroom; minimum 20 hours – unlimited on-site

SPECIFIC EXPANSION PLANS:

US:	All US
Canada:	All Canada
Overseas:	All Countries

Founded in 1996, BONUS Building Care has emerged as the nationally recognized leader of the commercial cleaning franchise industry. In this recession-resistant business, franchisees take advantage of managed growth by meeting the increasing demand for professionals in the building cleaning industry.

As one of Entrepreneur magazine's Franchise 500 companies, as well as ranking among the Fastest-Growing Franchises and Low-Cost Franchises, BONUS provides franchisees with the opportunity to render a necessary service that is always in demand with training, insurance, financing, and opportunities for expansion.

184

Operating Units	12/31/2008	12/31/2009	12/31/2010
Franchised	2,297	2,573	1,711
% Change	--	12.0%	-33.5%
Company-Owned	0	0	0
% Change	--	--	--
Total	2,297	2,573	1,711
% Change	--	12.0%	-33.5%
Franchised as % of Total	100%	100%	100%

Investment Required
The fee for a BONUS Building Care franchise is $7,500. BONUS offers financing for the initial franchise fee and certain new account fees for qualifying franchisees.

BONUS Building Care provides the following range of investments required to open your initial franchise. The range assumes that all items are paid for in cash. To the extent that you choose to finance any of these expense items, your front-end investment could be substantially reduced.

Item	Established Low Range	Established High Range
Initial Franchise Fee	$7,500	$7,500
Expenses While Training	$30	$600
Equipment	$285	$2,394
Misc. Opening Costs	$525	$1,325
Insurance	$120	$1,500
Additional Funds (3 Months)	$500	$3,000
Additional Opening Accounts	$0	$25,575
Cell Phone	$60	$600
Total Initial Investment	$9,020	$41,919

On-going Expenses
BONUS Building Care franchisees pay a support fee equal to 22% of pre-tax revenue each month, as well as an insurance fee equal to 6% of gross revenue per month. Other fees payable by the franchisee include leased equipment fees, new account fees, and one-time work contract fees.

What You Get—Training and Support
BONUS provides the necessary training on a host of procedures and skills required to run a successful commercial cleaning franchise; no previous business or sales experience is needed. BONUS franchisees benefit from the initial five hours of classroom training and extended and special services training, all designed to accommodate the franchisee's schedule with flexible, mutually convenient times. Supplemental home-study sections complement and strengthen the hands-on training, allowing the franchisee to progress through the course material at a pace suited to their lifestyle.

BONUS provides marketing assistance on national, regional, and local levels in maintaining a full sales staff and telemarketers who work to obtain business for its franchisees. In addition, BONUS offers franchisees the opportunity to lease-purchase quality, commercially rated, earth-friendly janitorial equipment.

Territory
BONUS Building Care does not grant exclusive territories.

BrightStar

MAKING MORE POSSIBLE
LIFECARE | KIDCARE | STAFFING

1790 Nations Dr., # 105
Gurnee, IL 60031
Tel: (877) 689-6898 (847) 693-2029
Fax: (866) 360-0393
Email: franchise@brightstarcare.com
Website: www.brightstarfranchise.com
Bill McPherson, Senior Vice President, Global Development

Are you ready to build a business you can feel great about? At BrightStar, we are in the business of providing the full continuum of homecare, childcare, staffing and support services for individuals, families and healthcare facilities. We help keep parents and grandparents out of nursing facilities and in the comfort of their own homes, as well as assisting parents with their childcare needs. BrightStar also provides healthcare staffing solutions to businesses. We have received several awards recognizing our rapid growth, advanced systems technology and senior leadership.

BACKGROUND: IFA Member
Established: 2002;   First Franchised: 2005
Franchised Units: 231
Company-Owned Units: 1
Total Units: 232
Dist.:   US-230; CAN-2; O'seas-0
  North America: 33 States
  Density: 19 in FL, 22 in TX, 32 in CA
Projected New Units (12 Months):   100
Qualifications: 4, 4, 2, 4, 4, 5

FINANCIAL/TERMS:
Cash Investment: $100K
Total Investment: $95-162K
Minimum Net Worth: $500K

Fees: Franchise - $47.5K
  Royalty - 5%;   Ad. - 1% or $500 min
Earnings Claims Statement: Yes
Term of Contract (Years):   10/10
Avg. # of Employees: 3 FT, 2 PT
Passive Ownership: Not Allowed
Encourage Conversions: Yes
Area Develop. Agreements: Yes
Sub-Franchising Contracts: Yes
Expand in Territory: No
Space Needs: 400-800 SF

SUPPORT & TRAINING:
Financial Assistance Provided: Yes (I)
Site Selection Assistance: Yes
Lease Negotiation Assistance: Yes
Co-operative Advertising: Yes
Franchisee Assoc./Member: Yes/Yes
Size of Corporate Staff: 51
On-going Support: a,NA,C,D,E,NA,G,h,I
Training: 5 days Gurnee, IL; 3 days Gurnee, IL

SPECIFIC EXPANSION PLANS:
US: All US
Canada: British Columbia, Alberta,
                            Saskatchewan, Manitoba
Overseas: UK, Australia

With national healthcare needs on the rise, BrightStar provides the full range of LifeCare, KidCare and Staffing services. BrightStar is one of the few companies that serve multiple market segments, including care for adults and seniors in their homes, well and sick childcare, and a full range of medical staffing services. This broad range of services enables franchisees to draw from a large, established, and rapidly growing customer base. In addition to offering the full range of medical and non-medical home healthcare, BrightStar also provides medical staffing solutions to businesses and private patients, providing personnel to hospitals, nursing homes, doctors' offices, labs and patients' own homes.

Operating Units	12/31/2008	12/31/2009	12/31/2010
Franchised	79	140	198
% Change	--	77.2%	41.4%

Company-Owned	2	1	1
% Change	--	-50.0%	0.0%
Total	81	141	199
% Change	--	74.1%	41.1%
Franchised as % of Total	97.5%	99.3%	99.5%

Investment Required
The fee for a BrightStar franchise is $47,500.

BrightStar provides the following range of investments required to open your initial franchise. The range assumes that all items are paid for in cash. To the extent that you choose to finance any of these expense items, your front-end investment could be substantially reduced.

Item	Established Low Range	Established High Range
Initial Franchise Fee	$47,500	$47,500
Leased Space for Agency	$2,500	$7,000
Furnishings	$1,500	$3,000
Computer Infrastructure Package	$3,500	$5,500
Signage	$300	$1,000
Marketing Materials	$3,767	$4,887
Grand Opening Advertising	$1,500	$2,000
Utility Deposits	$100	$500
Licenses	$200	$6,439
Joint Accreditation Commission Consultants and/or Director of Nursing (Hired as Needed)	$0	$14,869
CPA to Certify Licensure Submission	$0	$750

Insurance	$2,673	$3,926
Worker's Comp Insurance	$151	$1,901
CSA Training and Certification	$1,500	$2,300
Loan Packaging Fee	$0	$2,500
Telephony	$1,000	$1,500
Expenses While Training	$3,680	$4,580
Additional Funds (3 Months)	$25,196	$52,006
Total Investment	$95,067	$162,158

On-going Expenses

BrightStar franchisees pay royalty fees equal to 5% of net billings for non-national accounts and 6% of net billings for national accounts. Reduced royalty fees are available to veterans. Additional fees payable by the franchisee include local and national advertising fees.

Franchisee Satisfaction

A critical component of the due diligence process is that you, as a prospective franchisee, have a strong sense of existing franchisee satisfaction. Please review the franchisor's ratings below for this extremely important information.

World-Class Franchise®

How do you rate BrightStar in terms of:	Rating*
Overall quality of franchisor	93%

189

Recommend to prospective franchisees	90%
Franchisor is a competent, skillful organization	92%

* Independent Audit of Existing Franchisees Who Rated BrightStar as Excellent, Very Good, or Good

What You Get—Training and Support
Training with BrightStar begins with a five-day team training session tha covers every aspect of business from how to find clients, how to answer th phones, talk to potential staff, and the Athena Business System. In addi tion to this training session, BrightStar implemented a business learnin management system and online training center in 2010 to deliver onlin learning to all franchisees and their teams to facilitate continuous learnin and improvement.

Franchisees have access to a centralized Support Center as well as a Bright Start Coach initially and a Regional Director of Field Support thereafter fo support, information, and answers to any questions.

Territory
BrightStar grants exclusive territories.

Caring Transitions

10700 Montgomery Rd., #300
Cincinnati, OH 45242
Tel: (800) 647-0766 (513) 587-4988
Fax: (513) 563-2691
Email: webinquiry@caringtransitions.net
Website: www.caringtransitions.net
Kristen Brown, Franchise Development

Ranked "Top 50 New Franchises" by Entrepreneur, 2009, this is a rewarding, home-based business helping seniors and their families transition from their homes to retirement communities. You'll work with bank trustees, Realtors®, moving companies and other professionals to help ease relocation. We provide five days of extensive, on-site training on operating and growing a successful business. With six revenue streams and the senior population expected to double by 2030, this is the next big wave in senior care.

Fees: Franchise -	$27.9K
Royalty - 6% or $300;	Ad. - $150/month
Earnings Claims Statement:	Yes
Term of Contract (Years):	10/10
Avg. # of Employees:	1 FT, 1 PT
Passive Ownership:	Allowed
Encourage Conversions:	NA
Area Develop. Agreements:	No
Sub-Franchising Contracts:	No
Expand in Territory:	No
Space Needs:	NR

BACKGROUND: IFA Member
Established: 2006; First Franchised: 2006
Franchised Units: 77
Company-Owned Units: 0
Total Units: 77
Dist.: US-77; CAN-0; O'seas-0
  North America: 30 States
  Density: 7 in VA, 7 in MO, 7 in FL
Projected New Units (12 Months): 30
Qualifications: 3, 3, 1, 2, 3, 4

SUPPORT & TRAINING:
Financial Assistance Provided: Yes (I)
Site Selection Assistance: NA
Lease Negotiation Assistance: NA
Co-operative Advertising: Yes
Franchisee Assoc./Member: No
Size of Corporate Staff: 50
On-going Support: NA,NA,C,D,NA,NA,NA,H,I
Training: 5 business days Cincinnati, OH

FINANCIAL/TERMS:
Cash Investment: $18.9K
Total Investment: $38.3-66.6K
Minimum Net Worth: $20K

SPECIFIC EXPANSION PLANS:
US: All US
Canada: All Canada
Overseas: All Countries

With its comprehensive approach to senior transitions services (senior moving, downsizing and estate sales) Caring Transitions is an industry leader in this niche market within the senior care industry. Caring Transitions is devoted to being an advocate for seniors and their families throughout transition periods, making it a trusted provider by families, attorneys, bank trustees, real estate professionals and funeral directors. Caring Transitions keeps the individual and their family's interests at heart, helping seniors to minimize stress and maximize returns throughout the transition process.

With the rapid expansion of the elderly population, more than 100 million individuals and their parents are poised to need relocation and home liquidation services. Caring Transitions dominates this industry, and thus possesses potential for significant growth in the upcoming years. Caring Transitions franchisees receive comprehensive training, ongoing support and exceptional marketing and branding programs. With over 20 years of franchise experience, Caring Transitions offers prospective franchisees a financially and personally rewarding business opportunity.

Operating Units	12/31/2008	12/31/2009	12/31/2010
Franchised	32	56	76
% Change	--	75.0%	35.7%
Company-Owned	0	0	0
% Change	--	--	--
Total	32	56	76
% Change	--	75.0%	35.7%
Franchised as % of Total	100.0%	100.0%	100.0%

Investment Required
The initial fee for a Caring Transitions franchise is $31,900 for an area with population of up to 175,000, and $37,900 with financing. For territory populations exceeding 175,000, franchisees pay an additional $300 for every 1,000 additional people.

Caring Transitions provides the following range of investments required to open your initial franchise. The range assumes that all items are paid for in cash. To the extent that you choose to finance any of these expense items, your front-end investment could be substantially reduced.

Item	Established Low Range	Established High Range
Initial Franchise Fee	$31,900	$37,900
Furniture and Equipment	$500	$1,000
Computer System	$1,000	$3,000
Expenses While Training	$750	$1,500
Initial Rent, Telephone, Bank and Other Deposits	$350	$2,000

Additional Funds (6 Months)	$4,000	$18,000
Pre-Opening Promotion	$1,000	$1,500
Technology/Software Licensing Fee & Web Hosting Fee	$700	$700.
Monthly Office Rental Payment	$200	$1,000
Insurance	$1,000	$3,000
Certified Relocation Transition Specialist Training	$500	$500
Estatesales.net	$80	$80
Total Initial Investment	$42,480	$70,680

On-going Expenses
Caring Transitions franchisees pay a monthly royalty fee equal to the greater of 6% of gross revenues or $300 and a monthly national branding fee equal to $200. Additional fees include a local cooperative advertising fee of up to 3% of monthly gross revenues.

What You Get—Training and Support
Caring Transitions is committed to ensuring franchising success and provides training and support throughout the franchise relationship. Prior to opening, Caring Transitions equips franchisees with specifications and a list of suppliers for all necessary equipment, products, services, and supplies. Caring Transitions also provides digital layouts and images for advertising, stationary, and business cards.

Franchisees complete an extensive initial training program at the Caring Transitions corporate headquarters in Cincinnati, Ohio. Topics covered in the training program include the Caring Transitions business model, marketing, services, financial management, database management, administration, marketing and promotion. Following the opening of a franchised location, Caring Transitions offers ongoing support in the form of telephone and e-mail assistance. Furthermore, Caring Transitions provides additional materials, information, training and assistance as deemed necessary.

Territory
Caring Transitions grants exclusive territories.

CMIT Solutions

Your Technology Team

500 N. Capital of TX Highway, Bldg. 6, #200
Austin, TX 78746
Tel: (800) 710-2648 (512) 879-4510
Fax: (512) 692-3711
Email: sheri@cmitsolutions.com
Website: www.cmitsolutions.com
Sheri Vandermause, VP Franchise Development
Offers IT Managed services and computer support to small businesses. Franchise can be home-based, as we service the clients remotely or at their place of business.

BACKGROUND: IFA Member
Established: 1994; First Franchised: 1997
Franchised Units: 130
Company-Owned Units: 0
Total Units: 130
Dist.: US-130; CAN-0; O'seas-0
North America: 32 States
Density:
Projected New Units (12 Months): 20
Qualifications: 2, 3, 4, 2, 4, 4

FINANCIAL/TERMS:
Cash Investment:	$45-74.2K
Total Investment:	$124-150K
Minimum Net Worth:	$300K
Fees: Franchise -	$49.5K
Royalty - 6-0%;	Ad. - 2%
Earnings Claims Statement:	Yes
Term of Contract (Years):	10/10
Avg. # of Employees:	1-2 FT, 1-2 PT
Passive Ownership:	Not Allowed
Encourage Conversions:	Yes
Area Develop. Agreements:	Yes
Sub-Franchising Contracts:	No
Expand in Territory:	No
Space Needs:	NA

SUPPORT & TRAINING:
Financial Assistance Provided:	No
Site Selection Assistance:	NA
Lease Negotiation Assistance:	NA
Co-operative Advertising:	No
Franchisee Assoc./Member:	No
Size of Corporate Staff:	17
On-going Support:	A,B,C,d,NA,NA,G,H,I
Training:	1 week Austin, TX

SPECIFIC EXPANSION PLANS:
US:	All US
Canada:	No
Overseas:	No

CMIT Solutions started as a small computer support company in Austin, Texas in 1996. Over the past decade, we have grown into a leading provider of managed services and other computer consulting services tailored to the unique needs of small business, with approximately 125 locally owned and operated locations nationwide. We're able to combine personalized local service with all the technical resources of a large national company, offering our small business clients the products, partnerships, and round-the-clock technical support that standalone locals can't always provide.

CMIT Solutions offers a broad menu of technical support and IT services that all point toward one goal: helping your small business run smoothly, profitably, and be prepared for anything. Whether you're looking for a preventative maintenance solution to keep IT costs predictable and avoid expensive computer problems, or a disaster recovery plan to get you back online quickly after an emergency, our technical support experts will meet with you to understand your business, and your IT needs, so that we can find the solution that's right for you.

Operating Units	12/31/2008	02/9/2010	12/31/2010
Franchised	See note*	121	129
% Change	--	--	6.6 %
Company-Owned	See note*	0	0
% Change	--	--	--
Total	See note*	121	129
% Change	--	--	6.6 %
Franchised as % of Total	--	100 %	100 %

*CMIT Solutions acquired the CMIT Solutions system on February 9, 2010. At this time, they became the franchisor of 121 franchisees and acquired 0 company-owned outlets.

Investment Required
The initial fee for a CMIT Solutions franchise is $49,950.

CMIT Solutions provides the following range of investments required to open your initial franchise. The range assumes that all items are paid for in cash. To the extent that you choose to finance any of these expense items, your front-end investment could be substantially reduced.

Item	Established Low Range	Established High Range
Initial Franchise Fee	$49,950	$49,950
Territory Fee	$0	$10,000
Business Licenses	$750	$1,500
Travel, Food, and Lodging while Training	$2,100	$2,500
Real Estate and Leasehold Improvements	See note*	See note*
Furniture and Equipment	$0	$4,000
Advertising and Marketing (6 months)	$14,000	$14,000
Technical Staffing (6 months)	$12,000	$12,000
Start-up Supplies	$1,000	$2,000
Additional Funds (6 months)	$45,000	$55,000
Total Initial Investment	$124,800	$150,950

*Outside office space is not required, but if you choose to do so, the costs can vary widely.

On-going Expenses
CMIT Solutions franchisees pay a royalty fee on a sliding scale of 6% to 0% of gross professional services revenue or minimum royalty, whichever is greater. There is also a marketing development fund on a sliding scale of 2% to 0% of the gross professional services revenue, or the minimum marketing development fund contribution, whichever is greater, and several other fees.

Franchisee Satisfaction

A critical component of the due diligence process is that you, as a prospective franchisee, have a strong sense of existing franchisee satisfaction. Please review the franchisor's ratings below for this extremely important information.

World-Class Franchise®

How do you rate CMIT Solutions in terms of:	Rating*
Overall quality of franchisor	100%
Initial training provided by franchisor	96%
Quality of products/services received from franchisor	100%
Opportunity provided by this franchisor	97%

* Independent Audit of Existing Franchisees Who Rated CMIT Solutions as Excellent, Very Good, or Good

What You Get—Training and Support

CMIT Solutions provides pre-opening and launch support in the following ways: a comprehensive Jump start program, initial marketing plan, and centralized execution of the marketing for each franchisee including follow-up and appointment scheduling, updated list of approved, contracted partners with pre-negotiated rates, launch support. There is also a comprehensive two-week initial training program.

Post-opening support includes one-on-one business coaching, an annual national convention, online professional development center, monthly web meetings, a centralized intranet with more than 2,000 business documents and templates, and extensive marketing and business development assistance.

Territory
CMIT Solutions grants exclusive marketing territories.

Coldwell Banker Real Estate

1 Campus Dr.
Parsippany, NJ 07054
Tel: (973) 359-5757
Fax: (973) 359-5908
Email: franchise.information@realogy.com
Website: www.coldwellbanker.com
Tim Henderson, EVP Franchise Sales

For 106 years, the Coldwell Banker™ organization has been the premiere provider of full-service real estate. With approximately 3,100 independently and company owned and operated residential real estate offices with approximately 86,000 sales associates globally, the company is an industry leader.

BACKGROUND:

	IFA Member
Established: 1906;	First Franchised: 1982
Franchised Units:	2,694
Company-Owned Units:	684
Total Units:	3,378
Dist.:	US-2,903; CAN-0; O'seas-605
North America:	50 States
Density:	148 in TX, 131 in NY, 208 in CA
Projected New Units (12 Months):	
Qualifications:	4, 4, 5, 4, 4, 4

FINANCIAL/TERMS:

Cash Investment:	
Total Investment:	$37.3-502K
Minimum Net Worth:	$25K
Fees: Franchise -	$25K
Royalty - 6%;	Ad. - 2.5%
Earnings Claims Statement:	No
Term of Contract (Years):	10/10
Avg. # of Employees:	Varies FT, 0 PT
Passive Ownership:	Not Allowed
Encourage Conversions:	Yes
Area Develop. Agreements:	No
Sub-Franchising Contracts:	No
Expand in Territory:	Yes
Space Needs:	1,000 SF

SUPPORT & TRAINING:

Financial Assistance Provided:	No
Site Selection Assistance:	No
Lease Negotiation Assistance:	No
Co-operative Advertising:	No
Franchisee Assoc./Member:	Yes/Yes
Size of Corporate Staff:	100
On-going Support:	A,NA,C,D,E,NA,G,H,I
Training:	Varied time online; 1-2 days on-site; 4 days Parsippany, NJ

SPECIFIC EXPANSION PLANS:

US:	All US
Canada:	All Canada
Overseas:	All Countries

Coldwell Banker Real Estate LLC is committed to building and maintaining relationships with its global network of affiliates by providing them with the best products and services in the industry. The Coldwell Banker brand is widely recognized as one of the world's premier real estate organizations with a presence in 51 countries and territories, where approximately 86,000 sales associates and brokers are affiliated with 3,100 offices. Coldwell Banker is the nation's oldest full-service, national real estate brand celebrating its 106th anniversary.

In addition to its legacy and global network, Coldwell Banker has a robust marketing and public relations program that has helped Coldwell Banker become the most visited national full-service real estate brand on the web, according to Nielsen and ComScore Media Metrics. Coldwell Banker University has been ranked the top real estate training program and ninth in all industries, according to *Training Magazine.*

Operating Units	12/31/2008	12/31/2009	12/31/2010
Franchised	2,173	1,997	1,864
% Change	--	-8.1%	-6.7%
Company-Owned	722	676	669
% Change	--	-6.4%	-1.0%
Total	2,895	2,673	2,533
% Change	--	-7.7%	-5.2%
Franchised as % of Total	75.1%	74.7%	73.6%

Investment Required
The initial fee for a Coldwell Banker office is $25,000.

Coldwell Banker provides the following range of investments required to open your initial franchise. The range assumes that all items are paid for in cash. To the extent that you choose to finance any of these expense items, your front-end investment could be substantially reduced.

Item	Established Low Range	Established High Range
Initial Franchise Fee	$25,000	$25,000
Building Signs	$700	$20,000
Yard Signs	$1,900	$4,600
Open House Signs	$800	$1,250
Misc. Rider Signs	$100	$200
Name Badges	$120	$300
Miscellaneous	$250	$500
Printed Materials	$5,100	$7,500
Insurance	$300	$1,000
Expenses During Orientation	$200	$2,700
Computer Equipment for Electronic Data Transfer System	$5,000	$10,000
Facility Space Planning	$1,800	$2,800
Leasehold Improvements	$20,000	$150,000
Furnishings, Computers and Communications Equipment	$40,200	$115,200
Supplies and Inventory	$5,000	$25,200
Security and Other Deposits	$7,500	$17,700
Prepaid Business Expenses	$3,000	$4,600
Grand Opening Promotion	$3,000	$5,000
Additional Funds (3 Months)	$50,000	$100,000
Total Initial Investment	$169,970	$493,550

On-going Expenses
Coldwell Banker franchisees pay ongoing royalty fees equal to 6% of gross revenue plus a national advertising fund equal to 2.5% of gross revenue, with minimums and maximums based on gross revenue monthly revenue.

What You Get—Training and Support
To ensure the continued development of Coldwell Banker-affiliated franchisees, Coldwell Banker University offers offices a wide variety of continuing education programs that can be taken in-person or online. Accessible from cbu.com, Coldwell Banker University offers a robust suite of certification, development and technology training programs.

Coldwell Banker enables franchisees to leverage and augment its national advertising efforts with targeted, local efforts by franchisees themselves. Coldwell Banker provides a wide range of pre-produced advertisements and marketing materials—from television commercials to postcards and flyers—that are customizable for local use so franchisees can distribute and broadcast them accordingly.

Territory
Coldwell Banker does not grant exclusive territories.

Color Glo International

	7111-7115 Ohms Ln.
	Minneapolis, MN 55439
	Tel: (800) 333-8523 (952) 835-1338
	Fax: (952) 835-1395
	Email: scott@colorglo.com
	Website: www.colorglo.com
	Scott L. Smith, VP of Franchise Development

Color Glo is the leader in the leather and fabric restoration and repair industry. From automotive to marine to aircraft to all-leather furniture, Color Glo leads the way with innovative products and protected application techniques. We serve all US and foreign car manufacturers.		Term of Contract (Years):	10/10
		Avg. # of Employees:	1 FT, 0 PT
		Passive Ownership:	Allowed
		Encourage Conversions:	NA
		Area Develop. Agreements:	Yes
		Sub-Franchising Contracts:	Yes
		Expand in Territory:	Yes
BACKGROUND:	IFA Member	Space Needs:	SF
Established: 1976;	First Franchised: 1983		
Franchised Units:	123	**SUPPORT & TRAINING:**	
Company-Owned Units:	0	Financial Assistance Provided:	Yes (D)
Total Units:	123	Site Selection Assistance:	Yes
Dist.:	US-90; CAN-1; O'seas-32	Lease Negotiation Assistance:	NA
North America:	30 States, 1 Province	Co-operative Advertising:	No
Density:	12 in FL, 8 in WA, 7 in OR	Franchisee Assoc./Member:	Yes/Yes
Projected New Units (12 Months):	12	Size of Corporate Staff:	15
Qualifications:	4, 4, 3, 4, 3, 3	On-going Support:	NA,B,C,D,NA,NA,G,H,I
		Training:	2 weeks headquarters, MN;
FINANCIAL/TERMS:			1 week franchisee's territory
Cash Investment:	$44.5K		
Total Investment:	$44.5-50K	**SPECIFIC EXPANSION PLANS:**	
Minimum Net Worth:	$50K	US:	All US
Fees: Franchise -	$25K	Canada:	All Canada
Royalty - 4% or $300 monthly;	Ad. - 0%	Overseas:	All Countries
Earnings Claims Statement:	Yes		

Color Glo International is the world leader in restoration and repair of leather, vinyl, velour, cloth, and hard plastics commonly found in the markets of automotive, aircraft, marine, and furniture. Formally incorporated in 1975, Color Glo began franchising in 1982. Today in hundreds of markets throughout world, Color Glo products are proven everyday to offer the correct results and best value every time they are put to the test.

Our focus is restoring and repairing common defects such as worn and faded interior components such as leather upholstery, headliners, burns, and broken plastic or composite molding. These problems are found in the interior of every automobile, RV, truck sports vehicle, plane, or boat in use today.

Operating Units	12/31/2008	12/31/2009	12/31/2010
Franchised	108	106	125
% Change	--	--	17.9%

Company-Owned	0	0	0
% Change	--	--	--
Total	108	106	125
% Change	--	--	17.9%
Franchised as % of Total	100%	100%	100%

Investment Required

The initial franchise fee for a Color Glo franchise is $25,000.

Color Glo provides the following range of investments required to open your initial franchise. The range assumes that all items are paid for in cash. To the extent that you choose to finance any of these expense items, your front-end investment could be substantially reduced.

Item	Established Low Range	Established High Range
Franchise Fee	$25,000	$25,000
Start-Up Fee	$19,500 (plus shipping)	$19,500 (plus shipping)
Travel Expenses While Training	$500	$25,000
Equipment and Supplies	$200	$300
Working Capital	$500	$1,500
Additional Funds (3 months)	$300	$1,000
Total Investment	$46,000	$49,800

On-going Expenses

Color Glo franchisees pay a maintenance fee equal to 4% of gross sales or $150.00 per month, whichever is greater, $200.00 for the second full year, or $300.00 a month following a full year of business. Other on-going fees include an annual license fee and product purchases, an audit fee, and insurance.

Franchisee Satisfaction

A critical component of the due diligence process is that you, as a prospective franchisee, have a strong sense of existing franchisee satisfaction. Please review the franchisor's ratings below for this extremely important information.

World-Class Franchise®

How do you rate Color Glo in terms of:	Rating*
Overall quality of franchisor	100%
Overall training and support supplied by the franchisor	99%
Quality of products/services received from franchisor	100%
Opportunity provided by this franchisor	100%

* Independent Audit of Existing Franchisees Who Rated Color Glo as Excellent, Very Good, or Good

What You Get—Training and Support

Color Glo will provide you with a schedule of all supplies and equipment approved by the Franchisor, provide you with an initial supply of Color Glo products, and provide one copy of Color Glo's Operating Manuals.

Color Glo also offers a comprehensive three-week training course, begun within 90 days of execution of the Franchise Agreement. CGI's classroom instructor has ten years of experience. The field training is done by a franchisee with a minimum of ten years of experience. Refresher training and additional training are conducted during regional seminars and our annual seminar in Minneapolis. Color Glo provides additional training for new products and services introduced at the annual International Seminar.

During the operation of the franchise business, Color Glo will provide certain advertising production materials, inspect your business as often as Color Glo deems necessary, protect the Marks and Business System, and provide supplements and modifications to the Operating Manuals.

Territory
Color Glo does grant exclusive territories.

ComForcare Senior Services

2510 Telegraph Rd., Ste. 100
Bloomfield Hills, MI 48302
Tel: (800) 886-4044, (248) 745-9700
Fax: (248) 745-9763
Email: info@comforcare.com
Website: www.comforcare.comfranchise.com
Phil LeBlanc, Vice President of Franchise Development

ComForcare Senior Services franchise members provide non-medical home care (assistance with the activities of daily living via companion and personal care services) and skilled nursing services to all members of the community, but primarily to the exploding market of those over the age of 65. ComForcare franchise members provide the increasingly-needed services that support individuals' independence, dignity, and quality of life.

BACKGROUND:	IFA Member
Established: 1996;	First Franchised: 2001
Franchised Units:	161
Company-Owned Units:	0
Total Units:	161
Dist.:	US-157; CAN-3; O'seas-1
North America:	29 States, 1 Province
Density:	11 in MI, 15 in NJ, 23 in CA
Projected New Units (12 Months):	40
Qualifications:	5, 5, 2, 4, 3, 5
FINANCIAL/TERMS:	
Cash Investment:	$50-75K
Total Investment:	$105-155K
Minimum Net Worth:	$300K
Fees: Franchise -	$39.5K
Royalty - 5-3%;	Ad. - 0%
Earnings Claims Statement:	Yes
Term of Contract (Years):	10/10
Avg. # of Employees:	3 FT, 18 PT
Passive Ownership:	Not Allowed
Encourage Conversions:	Yes
Area Develop. Agreements:	Yes
Sub-Franchising Contracts:	No
Expand in Territory:	Yes

Space Needs:	250-450 SF	On-going Support:	A,B,C,D,E,NA,G,H,I
		Training: 1 week at home, 1 week at franchise	
SUPPORT & TRAINING:		location, and 2 weeks Bloomfield Hills, MI	
Financial Assistance Provided:	Yes (I)		
Site Selection Assistance:	Yes	**SPECIFIC EXPANSION PLANS:**	
Lease Negotiation Assistance:	Yes	US:	All US
Co-operative Advertising:	Yes	Canada:	All
Franchisee Assoc./Member:	No	Overseas:	All Countries
Size of Corporate Staff:	22		

ComForcare Senior Services began in Bloomfield Hills, Michigan in 1996 as a company dedicated to establishing a new standard in the quality of non-medical home care. After perfecting the winning formula, ComForcare began franchising. Today, ComForcare has more than 135 franchise members operating more than 155 territories in the United States, Canada, and the U.K.

ComForcare has been ranked in the Entrepreneur Franchise 500 for the past six years, and in 2012, we received the FranSurvey's World Class Franchise Designation by the Franchise Research Institute for the fourth year in a row.

Operating Units	12/31/2008	12/31/2009	12/31/2010
Franchised	98	129	151
% Change	--	31.6 %	17.1 %
Company-Owned	1	1	1
% Change	--	--	--
Total	99	130	152
% Change	--	31.3 %	16.9 %
Franchised as % of Total	99 %	99.2 %	99.3 %

Investment Required
The initial fee for a ComForcare franchise is $39,500.

ComForcare provides the following range of investments required to open your initial franchise. The range assumes that all items are paid for in cash.

To the extent that you choose to finance any of these expense items, your front-end investment could be substantially reduced.

Item	Established Low Range	Established High Range
Initial Franchise Fee	$39,500	$39,500
Travel Expenses for Training	$2,100	$2,600
Real Estate and Expenses	$3,600	$5,400
Office Equipment, Backup, and Access Fees	$1,700	$2,900
Signs	$100	$500
Miscellaneous Opening Costs	$1,200	$5,000
Accreditation Fees	$0.00	$23,000
Insurance	$4,000.00	$7,000
Office Supplies	$1,000.00	$2,000
Local Marketing and Advertising (6 months)	$9,000.00	$15,000
Recruiting Expenses	$1,200.00	$4,000
Additional Funds (6 months)	$41,600.00	$48,100
Total Initial Investment	$105,000.00	$155,000

On-going Expenses
Franchisees pay a royalty and service fee equal to 3-5% of gross sales with a minimum royalty fee per 2-week billing period after 9 months.

Franchisee Satisfaction
A critical component of the due diligence process is that you, as a prospective franchisee, have a strong sense of existing franchisee satisfaction. Please review the franchisor's ratings below for this extremely important information.

**World-Class
Franchise®**

How do you rate ComForcare in terms of:	Rating*
Rating of the helpfulness of the franchisor's field representatives	93%
Rating of the overall quality of the franchisor	90%
Grade of the ongoing training and support provided by the franchisor	97%
Rating of the overall communication between home office personnel and franchisees	97%

* Independent Audit of Existing Franchisees Who Rated ComForcare as Excellent, Very Good, or Good

What You Get—Training and Support
ComForcare franchisees will receive support in the form of the availability of daily e-mail and telephone consultation, regular web-based conferences, annual national franchise conference, and regional meetings so franchise owners can meet and share ideas and information, a website for each franchise location (maintained by the franchise support team), access to a public relations agency that specializes in promoting franchise businesses, and weekly and monthly communications providing news, operational updates, and counsel.

ComForcare also provides the following: proprietary operational software, a time-saving software that manages all aspects of the ComForcare business including caregiver and client scheduling, billing, payroll, etc.; national strategic alliances, a long list of national strategic alliances that can create instant networking and referral possibilities for all our franchisees, offering the potential of increased revenue; and outstanding marketing materials, a variety of print and electronic materials for use in your marketing plan.

Territory
ComForcare does grant exclusive territories.

Comfort Keepers |

6640 Poe Ave., # 200
Dayton, OH 45414-2600
Tel: (888) 329-1368, (937) 264-1933
Fax: (937) 264-3103
Email: larryfrance@comfortkeepers.com
Website: www.comfortkeepersfranchise.com
Larry France, Manager, Franchise Development, Western USA

Comfort Keepers is the service leader with 95% client satisfaction. We provide non-medical, in-home care, such as companionship, meal preparation, light housekeeping, grocery and clothing shopping, grooming, and assistance with recreational activities for the elderly and others who need assistance in daily living.

BACKGROUND:

	IFA Member	
Established: 1998;	First Franchised: 1999	
Franchised Units:		712
Company-Owned Units:		0
Total Units:		712
Dist.:	US-642; CAN-39; O'seas-31	
North America:	47 States, 5 Provinces	
Density:	47 in OH, 54 in FL, 82 in CA	
Projected New Units (12 Months):		36
Qualifications:	5, 5, 2, 3, 3, 4	

FINANCIAL/TERMS:

Cash Investment:	$61.4K
Total Investment:	$61.4-88.5K
Minimum Net Worth:	$200K
Fees: Franchise -	$42K
Royalty - 5/4/3%;	Ad. - 0%
Earnings Claims Statement:	Yes
Term of Contract (Years):	10/10
Avg. # of Employees:	2 FT, 4-5 PT
Passive Ownership:	Not Allowed
Encourage Conversions:	Yes
Area Develop. Agreements:	No
Sub-Franchising Contracts:	No
Expand in Territory:	Yes
Space Needs:	400-700 SF

SUPPORT & TRAINING:

Financial Assistance Provided:	Yes (D)
Site Selection Assistance:	No
Lease Negotiation Assistance:	No
Co-operative Advertising:	Yes
Franchisee Assoc./Member:	Yes/Yes
Size of Corporate Staff:	50
On-going Support:	NA,NA,C,D,NA,NA,G,h,I
Training:	4 weeks and on-going in Dayton, OH

SPECIFIC EXPANSION PLANS:

US:	All US
Canada:	Yes
Overseas:	Yes

There are basic human needs that transcend age, the most notable being physical and mental health, companionship, independence, peace of mind, security, and–perhaps most importantly–respect and dignity. Comfort Keepers identifies such needs for the senior population, and the highly selective Comfort Keepers staff strives to make sure that these basic needs are met with love and compassion. Since its founding more than a decade ago, Comfort Keepers has been providing first-rate in-home care to thousands of seniors and is consistently recognized as a top franchise system in its field.

The senior care industry is in its infancy while the American population continues to gray: the population over age 65 is expected to exceed 86 million over the next 40 years, more than doubling the current figure. A Comfort Keepers franchise represents a golden opportunity that promises both business achievement and community contribution.

Operating Units	12/31/2008	12/31/2009	12/31/2010
Franchised	554	565	596
% Change	--	2.0%	5.5%
Company-Owned	0	0	0
% Change	--	--	--
Total	554	565	596
% Change	--	2.0%	5.5%
Franchised as % of Total	100.0%	100.0%	100.0%

Investment Required
The initial fee for a Comfort Keepers franchise is $42,000.

Comfort Keepers provides the following range of investments required to open your initial franchise. The range assumes that all items are paid for in cash. To the extent that you choose to finance any of these expense items, your front-end investment could be substantially reduced.

Item	Established Low Range	Established High Range
Initial Franchise Fee	$42,000	$42,000
Professional Fees	$600	$2,000
Business Premises	$0	$4,000
Furniture and Equipment	$1,680	$4,010
Insurance	$1,850	$3,220
Expenses While Training	$1,970	$3,140
Organizational Expenses/ Supplies/Printing	$840	$1,390
Telephone and Other Utility Deposits	$380	$400
Advertising, Marketing and Promotion	$440	$580
Licensure	$0	$2,200
Background Screening	$310	$550
Additional Funds (3 Months)	$11,840	$25,290
Total Initial Investment	$61,910	$88,780

On-going Expenses

Comfort Keepers franchisees pay a royalty fee based on monthly gross revenues (with a minimum royalty fee of $300 per month). There is a provision for descending royalty fees from 5% to as low as 3%. The base royalty is 5% of revenue; when plateau levels are achieved, royalty on incremental sales above plateaus may drop to as low as 3%. Other fees include a local advertising fee equal to a minimum of $1,000 per month.

Franchisee Satisfaction

A critical component of the due diligence process is that you, as a prospective franchisee, have a strong sense of existing franchisee satisfaction. Please review the franchisor's ratings below for this extremely important information.

**World-Class
Franchise®**

How do you rate Comfort Keepers in terms of:	Rating*
Overall quality of franchisor	97%
High standards of quality performance throughout organization	95%
Franchisor committed to positive, long-term relationship	90%
Franchisor's business versus local competition	96%

* Independent Audit of Existing Franchisees Who Rated Comfort Keepers as Excellent, Very Good, or Good

What You Get—Training and Support
Franchisees complete a comprehensive training course that helps them jump-start their business operations. Immediately following signing of the franchise agreement, the new franchisee will be assigned to a new franchisee coach who will work with the franchisee to complete the "Ready" training, which will take approximately three weeks. Upon completion of the "Ready" training, franchisees attend a five-day "Set" training class at our Franchisee Support Center. This dynamic and interactive training class is where you receive comprehensive training on the sales and networking techniques to grow your business, human resource training for successful recruitment and retention, client care instruction, sales, operations, and management of your business, and much, much more. Corporate headquarters provides ongoing support, and gives hands-on assistance to increase business growth. Franchisees can exchange ideas with one another at state, regional, and national meetings. The network of hundreds of Comfort Keep-

ers around the world produces collective knowledge and understanding among franchisees. Comfort Keepers also maintains a franchisee website, which offers a library, training resources, news, information, and online communication opportunities with other owners.

Advertising guidance and support is provided at the local and national levels, with assistance from a leading PR firm. Comfort Keepers gives franchisees a guidebook that outlines the marketing process, recruitment advertisements, and includes templates for print advertisements, ready-to-print press releases, and more.

Territory
While Comfort Keepers does not grant exclusive territories, it does grant territories with limited protection.

Compound Profit

Compound Profit® Corp

321 N. Central Expressway, Suite 355
McKinney, TX 75070
Tel: (877) 386-3716 (972) 984-1433
Fax: (888) 419-0777
Email: frandev@cprofit.com
Website: www.cprofit.com
Laura Reed, Director of Franchise Development

The company and its franchisees are dedicated to helping businesses Compound Profit® by improving their cash flow, reducing their operating costs, and increasing their bottom line. We do this through services like factoring (and other forms of alternative financing), credit collections, bill auditing, accounts receivable consulting, sales training, and more.

BACKGROUND:

Established: 2006;	First Franchised: 2006
Franchised Units:	71
Company-Owned Units:	0
Total Units:	71
Dist.:	US-71; CAN-0; O'seas-0
North America:	27 States
Density:	5 in CA, 5 in OH, 5 in FL
Projected New Units (12 Months):	24
Qualifications:	4, 4, 3, 3, 3, 4

FINANCIAL/TERMS:

Cash Investment:	$39K-92K
Total Investment:	$50K-100K
Minimum Net Worth:	$N/A
Fees: Franchise -	$34
Royalty - 8;	Ad. - 250
Earnings Claims Statement:	No
Term of Contract (Years):	10/10

Avg. # of Employees:	1 FT, 3 PT	Co-operative Advertising:	No
Passive Ownership:	Allowed	Franchisee Assoc./Member:	No
Encourage Conversions:	NA	Size of Corporate Staff:	26
Area Develop. Agreements:	Yes	On-going Support:	A,NA,C,d,NA,NA,G,h,I
Sub-Franchising Contracts:	No	Training:	5 days McKinney, TX;
Expand in Territory:	Yes		3 days pre-training (online)
Space Needs:	SF		
		SPECIFIC EXPANSION PLANS:	
SUPPORT & TRAINING:		US:	All
Financial Assistance Provided:	Yes (I)	Canada:	No
Site Selection Assistance:	NA	Overseas:	No
Lease Negotiation Assistance:	NA		

Compound Profit endorses a proven fundability system that results in businesses achieving a Business Credit Asset that will enable access to funding and credit for the life of the business. Our Business Fundability System™ offers a range of options to help increase working capital, reduce costs, and increase sales and profits. Compound Profit specializes in working with companies in the pre-banking phase, including start-ups and credit-challenged businesses.

Compound Profit works diligently to provide alternative financing solutions in these challenging economic times. They align their services to meet your specific goals and objectives. Advisors provide strategic insight, extensive experience, and practical solutions to help get the capital and tools a business needs to grow.

Operating Units	12/31/2008	12/31/2009	12/31/2010
Franchised	17	47	62
% Change	--	176.5%	31.9%
Company-Owned	0	0	0
% Change	--	--	--
Total	17	47	62
% Change	--	176.5%	31.9%
Franchised as % of Total	100%	100%	100%

Investment Required

The fee for a for a Compound Profit franchise is $34,000 for the first 15,000 businesses, plus $2.25 for each additional business.

Compound Profit provides the following range of investments required to open your initial franchise. The range assumes that all items are paid for in cash. To the extent that you choose to finance any of these expense items, your front-end investment could be substantially reduced.

Item	Established Low Range	Established High Range
Initial Franchise Fee	$34,000	$34,000
Furniture, Fixtures, Equipment, Computer System	$1,000	$3,500
Insurance	$1,000	$1,500
Executive Suite Base Rent (3 months)	$2,400	$3,000
Security Deposits, Utility Deposits, Business Licenses, and Other Prepaid Expenses	$900	$1,500
Initial Supply of Promotional Materials	$750	$1,500
Initial Training Tuition Fee	$5,000	$5,000
Travel and Living Costs While Training	$2,000	$3,000
Professional Fees	$1,500	$2,500
Additional Funds (3 months)	$15,000	$30,000
Total	$63,550	$85,500

On-going Expenses

Compound Profit franchisees pay a monthly royalty fee of 8% of gross revenue, tuition for the third and each additional person to attend initial training (not to exceed $2,500 per person), promotion and marketing fees, software license fees, and others.

Franchisee Satisfaction

A critical component of the due diligence process is that you, as a prospective franchisee, have a strong sense of existing franchisee satisfaction. Please review the franchisor's ratings below for this extremely important information.

**World-Class
Franchise®**

How do you rate Compound Profit in terms of:	Rating*
My franchisor and I are committed to a positive, long term relationship	96%
My franchisor understands that if I am successful they will be successful	96%
How would you grade the ongoing training and support supplied by your franchisor?	95%
I am able to communicate directly and effectively with senior management.	96%

* Independent Audit of Existing Franchisees Who Rated Compound Profit as Excellent, Very Good, or Good

What You Get—Training and Support

Before the franchisee opens the franchised business, Compound Profit will provide a copy of the company manual, as well as an extensive initial training program. Our advertising program for the services provided by our franchisees currently consists of online promotions, postcard distribution, letter distribution, advertisements in national publications, and promotional brochures for dissemination through networking at the local, regional, and national level. Franchise owners will be trained on all of the Compound Profit products and services and will have the support of our expert fulfillment team.

After the opening, Compound Profit will loan additions and supplements to the manual as they become available, as well as information and training with respect to each of the products and services, and general marketing and business development support .

Territory
Compound Profit does not grant exclusive territories.

Coverall Health-Based Cleaning System

Health-Based Cleaning System℠

5201 Congress Ave., # 275
Boca Raton, FL 33487
Tel: (888) 537-3371, (561) 922-2500
Fax: (561) 922-2423
Email: diane.emo@coverall.com
Website: www.coverall.com
Diane Emo, Vice President, Marketing

Take control of your future today! Own a commercial cleaning franchise that includes comprehensive training, financing, billing and collection services, and an initial customer base. With affordable franchise packages available, Coverall Health-Based Cleaning System® provides a combination of business programs and support systems that focus on meeting the needs of franchisees and their customers. Master and territory franchises are also available.

BACKGROUND:	IFA Member
Established: 1985;	First Franchised: 1985
Franchised Units:	9,361
Company-Owned Units:	0
Total Units:	9,361
Dist.:	US-8,451; CAN-280; O'seas-534
North America:	40 States, 3 Provinces
Density:	709 in CA, 772 in FL, 702 in OH
Projected New Units (12 Months):	1,176
Qualifications:	3, 3, 2, 2, 3, 5

217

FINANCIAL/TERMS:		SUPPORT & TRAINING:	
Cash Investment:	$1.1-25.6K	Financial Assistance Provided:	Yes (D)
Total Investment:	$12.6-37.1K	Site Selection Assistance:	NA
Minimum Net Worth:	$12.7K	Lease Negotiation Assistance:	NA
Fees: Franchise -	$9.1-30.6K	Co-operative Advertising:	No
Royalty - 5%;	Ad. - 0%	Franchisee Assoc./Member:	No
Earnings Claims Statement:	No	Size of Corporate Staff:	90
Term of Contract (Years):	20/20	On-going Support:	A,B,NA,D,NA,NA,G,H,I
Avg. # of Employees:	1-2 FT, 2-3 PT	Training: 32-48 hours local regional support center	
Passive Ownership:	Allowed		
Encourage Conversions:	Yes	SPECIFIC EXPANSION PLANS:	
Area Develop. Agreements:	Yes	US:	All US
Sub-Franchising Contracts:	Yes	Canada:	All Canada
Expand in Territory:	Yes	Overseas:	All Countries
Space Needs:	SF		

Interested in starting a cleaning business? Coverall Health-Based Cleaning System® has helped thousands of entrepreneurs succeed in building a commercial cleaning business. With an industry-leading approach to franchise owner training and support, together with Coverall's advanced, science-based commercial cleaning program, you gain the opportunities and skills needed to start and grow a successful cleaning business.

Coverall Health-Based Cleaning System® was founded in 1985 and is a leading franchisor in the commercial cleaning industry. Since the beginning, our mission has always been "to promote economic growth and independence for a diverse group of business owners by providing franchise ownership opportunities." Coverall Franchise Owners are trained and certified in the Coverall Health-Based Cleaning System® Program to clean and disinfect their clients' workplaces to help reduce the spread of illness-causing germs creating cleaner, healthier environments.

Coverall supports its franchisees with comprehensive training, an initial customer base, billing and collection services, financing and a global network of 90 Support Centers. The Coverall® System will work with you every step of the way to guide and support your success. When you join forces with one of the top-ranking commercial cleaning franchisors in the world, you have the competitive advantage of using a proven franchise system with over 25 years of experience and stability.

Operating Units	12/31/2008	12/31/2009	12/31/2010
Franchised	5,435	5,513	5,388
% Change	--	1.4%	-2.3%
Company-Owned	0	0	0
% Change	--	--	--
Total	5,435	5,513	5,388
% Change	--	1.4%	-2.3%
Franchised as % of Total	100.0%	100.0%	100.0%

Investment Required

The fee to purchase a Coverall franchise ranges from $9,120 to $30,643, depending on the volume of business desired by a franchisee. Coverall offers financing options that will help you obtain the capital you need to start your business, maintain a thriving franchise, and grow your company. Coverall will provide financing for the following items:

• Initial Franchise Fee
• New Equipment
• Additional Business
• Uniforms or Other Business Supply Purchases

Coverall provides the following range of investments required to open your initial franchise. The range assumes that all items are paid for in cash. To the extent that you choose to finance any of these expense items, your front-end investment could be substantially reduced.

Item	Established Low Range	Established High Range
Initial Franchise Fee	$9,120	$30,643
Initial Equipment and Supply Package	$880	$1,557

Banking, Business License, Assumed Name Filings and Permits	$37	$350
Franchise Owner On-the-Job Accident Insurance	2.4% of gross monthly billings	2.4% of gross monthly billings
Licenses and Permits	$25	$300
Office Supplies and Equipment	$0	$100
Misc. Pre-Opening Costs	$0	$100
General Liability Insurance	$72/month	$345/month
Uniforms	$0	$100
Vehicle	$225	$900
Additional Funds (4 Months)	$314	$3,400
Total Initial Investment	$10,576	$37,150

On-going Expenses

Coverall franchisees pay ongoing royalty fees equal to 5% of gross monthly billings, support fees equal to 10% of gross monthly billings, and franchise owner insurance coverage equal to 2.4% of gross monthly billings. Additional fees include optional sales and marketing fees, premium account fees and a referral fee for special one-time services such as window cleaning or floor refinishing.

What You Get—Training and Support

Coverall offers the most advanced training program in the industry with a comprehensive classroom, online and hands-on approach to training. Our franchise owners are trained and certified to become health-based cleaning professionals. The Coverall training program also includes small business ownership education, strategies for growth and further professional certification programs that can help further your expertise as an independent business owner.

With a network of 90 Support Centers, Coverall franchisees are backed by a strong team that is available to provide valuable support and advice as needed. Additional benefits include billing and collections services and a cash flow protection program to help you with your day-to-day administrative responsibilities.

Territory

Coverall's Master Franchise program offers exclusive developmental rights to operate the Coverall Health-Based Cleaning System in an entire metropolitan area.

Janitorial franchisees do not receive an exclusive territory.

CruiseOne

1201 W. Cypress Creek Rd., #100
Ft. Lauderdale, FL 33309-1955
Tel: (800) 892-3592 (954) 958-3700
Fax: (954) 958-3697
Email: tcourtney@cruiseone.com
Website: www.cruiseonefranchise.com
Tim Courtney, Director of Franchise Development

CruiseOne is a nationwide, home-based cruise & travel franchise company representing all major cruise lines and tour operators. Franchisees are professionally trained in a 6-day comprehensive program. CruiseOne provides a heritage of excellence, unrivaled buying power, industry-leading technology solutions, pride of true business ownership, and access to a large corporate support team to help you grow. CruiseOne is a member of the International Franchise Association (IFA) and participates in the VetFran and MinorityFran initiatives offering incentives and rebates to encourage business ownership.

BACKGROUND:	
Established: 1991;	IFA Member First Franchised: 1992
Franchised Units:	624
Company-Owned Units:	0
Total Units:	624
Dist.:	US-624; CAN-0; O'seas-0
North America:	45 States
Density:	40 in TX, 101 in FL, 63 in CA
Projected New Units (12 Months):	70
Qualifications:	3, 4, 2, 3, 5, 4

FINANCIAL/TERMS:	
Cash Investment:	$9.8K
Total Investment:	$7.8-9.8K
Minimum Net Worth:	NR
Fees: Franchise -	$9.8K
Royalty - 3%;	Ad. - .25%
Earnings Claims Statement:	No
Term of Contract (Years):	5
Avg. # of Employees:	1 FT, 0 PT
Passive Ownership:	Not Allowed
Encourage Conversions:	NA
Area Develop. Agreements:	No
Sub-Franchising Contracts:	No
Expand in Territory:	Yes

221

Space Needs:	NR	On-going Support:	A,B,C,D,NA,F,NA,h,I
		Training:	6 days Ft. Lauderdale, FL
SUPPORT & TRAINING:			
Financial Assistance Provided:	Yes (D)	**SPECIFIC EXPANSION PLANS:**	
Site Selection Assistance:	NA	US:	All US
Lease Negotiation Assistance:	NA	Canada:	10
Co-operative Advertising:	Yes	Overseas:	2
Franchisee Assoc./Member:	No		
Size of Corporate Staff:	80		

Founded in 1992, CruiseOne's Franchise Model has revolutionized the cruise industry. Today, CruiseOne is part of World Travel Holdings (WTH), making us the world's largest distributor of cruise vacations with unrivaled buying power. Together, we create excellent cruise line relationships, innovative marketing programs, and a superior support model that provides our Franchise Owners with a set of tools unmatched by any other in the industry. Our Franchise Owners come from many different social and professional backgrounds, but they all have one thing in common - a passion for travel and a commitment to succeed! Each year, CruiseOne launches new marketing programs and enhances our proprietary technologies, while maintaining the personal service coveted by our Franchise Owners. Whether it's planning a family reunion cruise or a corporate meeting at sea, our Franchise Owners continue to set the pace by delivering our hallmark "high tech with high touch" service. CruiseOne is large enough to lead the industry, while small enough to care about each and every franchise owner.

Operating Units	12/31/2008	12/31/2009	12/31/2010
Franchised	541	571	664
% Change	--	5.5%	16.3%
Company-Owned	0	0	0
% Change	--	--	--
Total	541	571	664
% Change	--	5.5%	16.3%
Franchised as % of Total	100%	100%	100%

Investment Required

The initial fee for a CruiseOne franchise can be $9,800, $3,195, or $495 depending on what level you have been designated (level will be noted on Schedule 3.1 of Franchise Agreement).

CruiseOne provides the following range of investments required to open your initial franchise. The range assumes that all items are paid for in cash. To the extent that you choose to finance any of these expense items, your front-end investment could be substantially reduced.

Item	Established Low Range	Established High Range
Initial Franchise Fee	$495	$9,800
Training Expenses	$200	$250
Mandatory Training Cruise	$0	$425
Additional Signatories/ Associates Training and Travel	$0	$1,245
Office Equipment and Furniture	$0	$1,500
Initial Office Supplies	$230	$545
Computer Hardware/ Software	$0	$2,500
Insurance, Legal, and Accounting	$100	$1,000
Permits, Franchises, Bonds, and Memberships	$150	$650
Initial Promotions and Advertising	$2,400	$3,600
Criminal and Civil Background Check	$0	$100

Additional Funds (3 Months)	$1,000	$5,000
Designated Credit Card	$0	$75
Total Initial Investment	$4,575	$26,690

On-going Expenses

Franchisees pay ongoing royalty fees equal to 1.5-3% of commissionable gross sales plus a travel insurance royalty fee of 3% of all annual commissionable gross sales, among others.

Franchisee Satisfaction

A critical component of the due diligence process is that you, as a prospective franchisee, have a strong sense of existing franchisee satisfaction. Please review the franchisor's ratings below for this extremely important information.

World-Class Franchise®

How do you rate CruiseOne in terms of:	Rating*
Overall quality of franchisor	97%
Franchisor and franchisee are committed to a positive, long-term relationship	96%
Franchisor understands that if I am successful, they will be successful	96%
Franchisor is a competent, skillful organization that I can rely on for help	97%

* Independent Audit of Existing Franchisees Who Rated CruiseOne as Excellent, Very Good, or Good

What You Get—Training and Support

As part of your franchise purchase, our expert training team with over 40 years of experience educates you on the core components of the cruise and travel industries while focusing on specific business building and operation skills to ensure your success. Not only do you get to meet with our corporate team, you'll also meet many cruise line representatives who introduce their product and personnel to you. You immediately learn vital product knowledge and find out who to contact for your local cruise line reps who offer additional support and assistance once you are home and in operation. Included with the training program are several tours of cruise ships, allowing you to experience firsthand some of the industry's largest and newest ships; giving you an up close and personal look at the staterooms and public areas. This provides you with a greater knowledge of the products and will allow you to hit the ground running.

Unlike other organizations, we follow up with each of our classes within their first week home as part of our Quick-Start program, which was developed by our Business Development Team. Your Business Development Liaison will guide you through those pivotal first steps from office setup to business planning and all the way through marketing and selling cruise vacations. We will even provide one-on-one training by appointment as needed for any owner/partner needing that extra attention. Your Business Development Liaison can be reached six days a week by phone or email between normal business hours.

Territory

CruiseOne does not grant exclusive territories.

Decor&You

DECOR&YOU®

LOVE THE SPACE YOU'RE IN®

900 Main St. S., Bldg. #2
Southbury, CT 06488
Tel: (203) 405-2131
Fax: (203) 264-5095
Email: fdadmin@franchisesource.com
Website: www.decorandyou.com
Dawn Ingala, Franchise Development

Decor&You® offers exciting opportunities in the growing $200 billion dollar home furnishings industry. We are primarily looking for managing partners to develop decorating firms staffed by teams of certified professional decorators who provide interior decorating services to clients. Our decorators have the advantage of our proven DecorPlan System, quality vendor manufacturer partnerships, and CIDI certified Professional Education Programs. In addition, our state of the art computerized sampling and presentation system, window treatment design tools, and more save decorators' time.

BACKGROUND:	
Established: 1994;	IFA Member
	First Franchised: 1998
Franchised Units:	70
Company-Owned Units:	0
Total Units:	70
Dist.:	US-70; CAN-0; O'seas-0
North America:	29 States
Density:	12 in CO, 8 in NJ, 2 in VA

Projected New Units (12 Months):	50
Qualifications:	4, 4, 2, 2, 4, 4

FINANCIAL/TERMS:

Cash Investment:	$30K
Total Investment:	$54-62K
Minimum Net Worth:	$100K
Fees: Franchise -	$25K
Royalty - 10%;	Ad. - 3%
Earnings Claims Statement:	No
Term of Contract (Years):	10/10
Avg. # of Employees:	2 FT, 0 PT
Passive Ownership:	Not Allowed
Encourage Conversions:	NA
Area Develop. Agreements:	Yes, 2.5-8.5 years
Sub-Franchising Contracts:	No
Expand in Territory:	Yes
Space Needs:	0 SF

SUPPORT & TRAINING:

Financial Assistance Provided:	No
Site Selection Assistance:	No
Lease Negotiation Assistance:	No
Co-operative Advertising:	Yes
Franchisee Assoc./Member:	Yes/Yes
Size of Corporate Staff:	8
On-going Support:	NA,NA,C,D,NA,NA,G,H,I
Training:	6 weeks + home-based/home office;

5 days Southbury, CT DPEC Center; 3 days (grad semester II) and advanced training course Southbury, CT DPECCenter

SPECIFIC EXPANSION PLANS:

US:	All
Canada:	No
Overseas:	No

The decorating industry is booming. Being a Decor&You® franchisee is all about having a passion for building a team, motivating and helping others to achieve success. Decor&You offers the opportunity for you to apply your skills building a decorating firm in the $200 billion dollar home furnishings industry.

At Decor&You®, we work to simplify how people achieve comfort, style and value in their homes and businesses. Clients open their doors to our DecorPlan™ that leads to a uniquely individual environment. Our commercial clients love the benefits of occupying interior spaces that emphasize brand personality and character. Our decorators capture and reflect brand values in each DecorPlan we create for the offices, restaurants, waiting rooms, and hotel rooms our commercial clients own or lease.

Like our clients, Decor&You® franchise owners are attracted to this business searching for a space they love, too – in this case, a rewarding profession and an empowering life. They discover the DecorPlan System: a successful, proven business model for achieving beautiful, fully decorated interiors. They learn the business in our dynamic Professional Education Program. They find a culture of performance enhancement thru our system tools designed for a quick ramp up. They can also look forward to "hands-on" management, which comes with a high level of attentive service that is increasingly rare in the American business landscape.

Operating Units	12/31/2008	12/31/2009	12/31/2010
Franchised	161	148	126
% Change	--	-8.1%	-14.9%
Company-Owned	0	0	0
% Change	--	--	--
Total	161	148	126
% Change	--	-8.1%	-14.9%
Franchised as % of Total	100.0%	100.0%	100.0%

Investment Required
The franchise fee for a Decor&You franchise is $25,000.

Decor&You provides the following range of investments required to open your initial franchise. The range assumes that all items are paid for in cash. To the extent that you choose to finance any of these expense items, your front-end investment could be substantially reduced.

Item	Established Low Range	Established High Range
Initial Franchise Fee	$25,000	$25,000
Expenses While Training (per person)	$1,500	$2,500
Start-up Support Package	$3,900	$3,900
Samples and Supplies	$7,000	$7,000
Equipment and Furnishings	$1,000	$3,000
Marketing Package	$1,000	$2,000
Local Advertising	$4,000	$4,000
Technology Fee	$510	$510
Phone Line and Yellow Pages Listing	$300	$500
Insurance Deposits	$350	$700
Decor Vehicle	$1,200	$2,000
Grand Opening	$750	$1200
Licenses and Registrations	$100	$200
Additional Funds (6 Months)	$8,000	$9,800
Total Initial Investment	$54,610	$62,310

On-going Expenses

Decor&You® franchisees pay continuing service fees equal to the greater of 10% of gross revenue from decorating services, 33% of gross revenues from consulting services only, or the minimum. Additional fees payable by the franchisee include system-wide brand building contributions and local advertising fees as well as an $85 per month Technology Fee.

What You Get—Training and Support

Decor&You® provides continuing professional education beginning with the business launch curriculum and culminating in National Professional Certification granted by Certified Interior Decorators International. On-site education is facilitated in Southbury, CT and at the franchisee's location and covers media planning, marketing, sales, decorator recruiting, ramp up and retention, design style and theory, product knowledge, business management, and certification preparation.

All Decor&You® franchisees are also provided with a Start-up Support Package of services, including a public relations program, set-up of DecorMail Intranet, Decor&You microsite, CRM, vendor partnerships, and email marketing program set-up. Additionally, Decor&You provides ongoing assistance with marketing materials, technical support and periodic support visits.

Territory

Decor&You grants nonexclusive territories.

The Entrepreneur's Source®

"Your success is our only business"

900 Main St. S., Bldg. # 2
Southbury, CT 06488
Tel: (203) 405-2131
Fax: (203) 264-3516
Email: fdadmin@franchisesource.com
Website: www.theentrepreneurssource.com
Dawn Ingala, Franchise Development

The Entrepreneur's Source® is an all-inclusive, one-source resource for entrepreneurship. With over 25 years of experience and 33% of the market, E-Source dominates the coaching industry. E-Source Coaches provide education, coaching, and resources to individuals who desire to achieve their dreams of becoming self-sufficient through business ownership. This allows our clients to explore alternate career options that meet their goals' needs and expectations, utilizing our Possibilities Passport Discovery process. Our coaches also work with existing franchise business owners to help them grow revenues and increase the value of their business.

BACKGROUND:	IFA Member	Passive Ownership:	Allowed
Established: 1984;	First Franchised: 1997	Encourage Conversions:	Yes
Franchised Units:	215	Area Develop. Agreements:	Yes, 2.5-8.5 years
Company-Owned Units:	0	Sub-Franchising Contracts:	No
Total Units:	215	Expand in Territory:	Yes
Dist.:	US-210; CAN-5; O'seas-0	Space Needs:	NA
North America:	40 States, 1 Province		
Density:	17 in NC, 17 in MI, 33 in CA	**SUPPORT & TRAINING:**	
Projected New Units (12 Months):	30	Financial Assistance Provided:	No
Qualifications:	4, 4, 1, 1, 2, 5	Site Selection Assistance:	NA
		Lease Negotiation Assistance:	NA
FINANCIAL/TERMS:		Co-operative Advertising:	No
Cash Investment:	$67K	Franchisee Assoc./Member:	Yes/Yes
Total Investment:	$67-77K	Size of Corporate Staff:	35
Minimum Net Worth:	$199K	On-going Support:	NA,NA,NA,D,NA,NA,NA,H,I
Fees: Franchise -	$45K	Training:	24 weeks virtual; 5 days Southbury, CT
Royalty - 5-15%;	Ad. - $750/Mo.	**SPECIFIC EXPANSION PLANS:**	
Earnings Claims Statement:	Yes	US:	All US
Term of Contract (Years):	10/10	Canada:	All Canada
Avg. # of Employees:	1 FT, 0 PT	Overseas:	Most Countries

The job market has changed permanently. It will no longer provide the security and stability that it once did for millions of people. The days of people working their entire career with a single large company are over. For over 25 years, E-Source Coaches have provided coaching to those seeking to own a franchise and those seeking to improve their franchise investment. Our proven coaching model combined with our education tools help our clients discover their ideal business opportunities.

As an Entrepreneur's Source Coach, your two primary services and revenue streams are Placement Coaching and Franchise Business Coaching. By utilizing The Entrepreneur's Source's exclusive systems crafted over a 25-year period, along with tools and technologies which allow our Coaches to achieve peak productivity, you will be positioned to reach a vast number of people who want to change their current career situation.

As an Entrepreneur's Source Coach, you will be uniquely qualified to help people understand what's possible, what options they have, and allow them to tap into their lifestyle dreams. Armed with the tools of empowerment that you provide, your clients will find vehicles in franchising that they had not known existed to achieve the income, lifestyle, wealth, and equity they have always dreamed of: employment to empowerment.

Operating Units	12/31/2008	12/31/2009	12/31/2010
Franchised	291	281	267
% Change	--	-3.4%	-5.0%
Company-Owned	0	0	0
% Change	--	--	--
Total	291	281	267
% Change	--	-3.4%	-5.0%
Franchised as % of Total	100.0%	100.0%	100.0%

Investment Required

The fee for a The Entrepreneur's Source franchise is $45,000. The Entrepreneur's Source also has an Area Development program that a franchisee can participate in.

The Entrepreneur's Source provides the following range of investments required to open your initial franchise. The range assumes that all items are paid for in cash. To the extent that you choose to finance any of these expense items, your front-end investment could be substantially reduced.

Item	Established Low Range	Established High Range
Initial Franchise Fee	$45,000	$45,000
Tuition (per person)	$10,000	$10,000
Real Estate and Improvements (6 Months)	$4,000	$5,000
Expenses While Training (per person)	$1,500	$2,500
Equipment	$150	$3,000
Marketing Aids	$1,000	$2,000

Vehicle Lease or Usage (6 Months)	$1,200	$2,400
Call Center	$2,000	$2,000
Technology Fee (6 Months)	$510	$510
Additional Funds (6 Months)	$8,000	$9,800
Total Initial Investment	$73,360	$82,210

On-going Expenses

The Entrepreneur's Source franchisees pay a monthly royalty fee ranging from 5% to 15% of gross revenues depending on amount of annual gross revenue, and a monthly system-wide brand building fund contribution of $750. Other fees include an annual E-Myth co-branded access fee of $350, an $85 per month Technology Fee, and a mandatory annual conference attendance fee of $450 plus expenses.

What You Get—Training and Support

At The Entrepreneur's Source®, training is not a single event, but a dynamic, ongoing educational process. Our Continuing Professional Education includes a Business Launch Curriculum that starts within 48 hours of joining our team. We leverage technology to bring continuing education and resources to our team 24/7. You'll be guided by a mentor through our virtual curriculum which prepares you for an on-site event at our Performance Enhancement Center.

Territory

The Entrepreneur's Source® grants a saturation maximum—TES will not place more than one single unit per 1,000 pay rolled businesses in a given state or group of states. The rights granted within the territory are non-exclusive.

ERA Franchise Systems

ERA
REAL ESTATE

1 Campus Dr.
Parsippany, NJ 07054
Tel: (800) 869-1260 (973) 407-7642
Fax: (973) 496-7354
Email: franchise.information@realogy.com
Website: www.era.com
Tim Henderson, EVP Franchise Sales

ERA Real Estate is an innovative franchising leader in the residential real estate industry with 40 years of experience in developing consumer-oriented products and services. The ERA® network includes approximately 30,000 brokers and sales associates and approximately 2,500 offices throughout the United States and 34 countries and territories. Founded in 1971 as Electronic Realty Associates, the company was the first to leverage the emerging technology of the FAX machine to build the business and the brand. Today, that spirit of innovation continues and is reflected in ERA Real Estate's custom approaches to affiliate relationships and relevant programs and tools that serve to distinguish ERA brokers and sales associates in the marketplace.

Total Units:	6,588
Dist.:	US-925; CAN-0; O'seas-1,837
North America:	50 States
Density:	64 in NY, 100 in FL, 95 in CA
Projected New Units (12 Months):	
Qualifications:	4, 4, 5, 4, 4, 4

FINANCIAL/TERMS:

Cash Investment:	Varies
Total Investment:	$47-210K
Minimum Net Worth:	$75K
Fees: Franchise -	$25K
Royalty - NR;	Ad. - 2%
Earnings Claims Statement:	No
Term of Contract (Years):	10
Avg. # of Employees:	Varies FT, 0 PT
Passive Ownership:	Not Allowed
Encourage Conversions:	Yes
Area Develop. Agreements:	No
Sub-Franchising Contracts:	No
Expand in Territory:	Yes
Space Needs:	1,000 SF

SUPPORT & TRAINING:

Financial Assistance Provided:	No
Site Selection Assistance:	No
Lease Negotiation Assistance:	No
Co-operative Advertising:	No
Franchisee Assoc./Member:	Yes/Yes
Size of Corporate Staff:	52
On-going Support:	A,NA,C,D,E,NA,G,H,I
Training:	2-3 days on-site; 1 week Parsippany, NJ

BACKGROUND: IFA Member
Established: 1971; First Franchised: 1972
Franchised Units: 6,588
Company-Owned Units: 0

SPECIFIC EXPANSION PLANS:

US:	All US
Canada:	All Canada
Overseas:	All Countries

ERA Real Estate is an innovative franchising leader in the residential real estate industry with 40 years of experience in developing consumer-oriented products and services. The ERA® network includes approximately 30,000 brokers and sales associates, and approximately 2,500 offices throughout the United States and 34 countries and territories.

Founded in 1971 as Electronic Realty Associates, the company was the

233

first to leverage the emerging technology of the fax machine to build the business and the brand. Today, that spirit of innovation continues and is reflected in ERA Real Estate's custom approaches to affiliate relationships and relevant programs and tools that serve to distinguish ERA brokers and sales associates in the marketplace.

Operating Units	12/31/2008	12/31/2009	12/31/2010
Franchised	925	828	661
% Change	--	-10.5%	-20.2%
Company-Owned	28	11	11
% Change	--	-60.7%	0.0%
Total	953	839	672
% Change	--	-12.0%	-19.9%
Franchised as % of Total	97.1%	98.7%	98.4%

Investment Required
The initial fee for an ERA franchise is $25,000 for a standard market.

ERA provides the following range of investments required to open your initial franchise. The range assumes that all items are paid for in cash. To the extent that you choose to finance any of these expense items, your front-end investment could be substantially reduced.

Item	Established Low Range	Established High Range
Initial Franchise Fee	$25,000	$25,000
Signs and Other Supplies	$5,000	$30,000
Furniture and Equipment	$500	$25,000
Insurance Deposits and Premiums	$200	$5,000
Expenses While Training	$500	$3,000

Legal Expenses	$0	$2,000
Accounting Fees	$300	$600
Multiple Listing Service (MLS) Dues	$150	$600
Advertising/Public Relations	$1,500	$20,000
Taxes	$50	$1,200
Misc. Opening Costs	$2,500	$7,500
Additional Funds (3 Months)	$12,000	$90,000
Total Initial Investment	$47,700	$209,900

On-going Expenses
ERA franchisees pay ongoing royalty fees equal to 6% of gross revenues, plus a National Marketing Fund contribution equal to 2% of monthly gross revenue subject to a monthly minimum of $362 and monthly maximum of $1,259.

What You Get—Training and Support
ERA Real Estate training programs are designed to continue franchisees' real estate employees and sales associates' education, as well as the franchisee's own education. The majority of ERA's courses are conveniently hosted online and are available at either no additional cost or are deeply discounted for ERA Real Estate affiliates. From accelerated training programs for new sales associates to improving brokers' sales skills, ERA offers a wide variety of training courses to meet franchisees' and their brokers' needs.

Territory
ERA does not grant exclusive territories.

Estrella Insurance

3750 W. Flagler St.
Miami, FL 33134
Tel: (888) 511-7722 (305) 443-2829
Fax: (305) 444-2933
Email: franchise@estrellainsurance.com
Website: www.estrellainsurance.com
Jose Merille, President

Since 1980, Estrella Insurance has built its foundation on values and excellent customer service. By continuing to exceed our customers' expectations with outstanding service and competitive rates, Estrella Insurance continues to be the #1 choice for all insurance needs. We offer auto, homeowners, and commercial insurance. We can also insure your business, boat, motorcycle, or recreational vehicle. Our loyal customers keep recommending Estrella Insurance to friends and other family members so that they, too, can receive the same friendly dedication and expertise they've come to expect from all Estrella agents.

BACKGROUND: IFA Member
Established: 1980; First Franchised: 2008
Franchised Units: 52
Company-Owned Units: 0

Total Units:	52
Dist.:	US-52; CAN-0; O'seas-0
North America:	1 State
Density:	52 in FL
Projected New Units (12 Months):	10
Qualifications:	5, 4, 4, 3, 3, 5

FINANCIAL/TERMS:

Cash Investment:	$50K
Total Investment:	$50-80K
Minimum Net Worth:	$100K
Fees: Franchise -	$25K
Royalty - 1-1.5;	Ad. - .50-.75
Earnings Claims Statement:	Yes
Term of Contract (Years):	10/10
Avg. # of Employees:	2 FT, 1 PT
Passive Ownership:	Not Allowed
Encourage Conversions:	Yes
Area Develop. Agreements:	No
Sub-Franchising Contracts:	No
Expand in Territory:	Yes
Space Needs:	

SUPPORT & TRAINING:

Financial Assistance Provided:	No
Site Selection Assistance:	Yes
Lease Negotiation Assistance:	Yes
Co-operative Advertising:	No
Franchisee Assoc./Member:	No
Size of Corporate Staff:	6
On-going Support:	a,B,C,D,E,NA,G,H,I
Training:	8 weeks at designated franchise

SPECIFIC EXPANSION PLANS:

US:	Florida and Texas
Canada:	No
Overseas:	No

Since 1980, Estrella Insurance has built its foundation on values and excellent customer service. By continuing to exceed customers' expectations with outstanding service and competitive rates, Estrella Insurance continues to be the #1 choice for all insurance needs. Estrella Insurance offers a wide variety of coverage, including auto, homeowners, commercial, business, boat, motorcycle, or recreational vehicle.

Estrella Insurance is proud of their excellence in both customer and franchisee support; they strive to maintain friendly dedication and expertise to their loyal customers and provide an environment where franchisees and employees can experience a high degree of job satisfaction and personal involvement.

Operating Units	12/31/2008	12/31/2009	12/31/2010
Franchised	15	22	45
% Change	--	46.7%	104.5%
Company-Owned	30	22	0
% Change	--	-26.7%	-100%
Total	45	44	45
% Change	--	-2.2%	2.3%
Franchised as % of Total	33.3%	50%	100%

Investment Required
The fee for an Estrella Insurance franchise is $25,000.

Estrella Insurance provides the following range of investments required to open your initial franchise. The range assumes that all items are paid for in cash. To the extent that you choose to finance any of these expense items, your front-end investment could be substantially reduced.

Item	Established Low Range	Established High Range
Initial Franchise Fee	$25,000	$25,000
Construction Leasehold, Improvements, Remodeling and Decorating Costs	$4,000	$12,000
Office Supplies	$500	$1,000
Equipment, Furnishings, Fixtures & Other Fixed Assets	$4,000	$6,000
Computer	$3,000	$6,000

Signage	$2,200	$4,500
Insurance	$3,000	$5,000
Expenses While Training	$500	$2,500
Security Deposits, Utility Deposits, Business Licenses and Other Pre-paid Expenses	$1,500	$4,000
New Agency Package	$250	$500
Fictitious Name Registration and/or Incorporation and Legal Review	$500	$1,000
Miscellaneous	$500	$1,500
Additional Funds (3 Months)	$5,000	$15,000
Total Initial Investment	$49,950	$84,000

On-going Expenses
Estrella Insurance franchisees pay a monthly royalty fee of 10% of net commissions and a monthly marketing fund fee of 5% of net commissions.

What You Get—Training and Support
Estrella Insurance initial training includes 80 hours of classroom training in corporate offices in Miami, Florida on topics including introduction to insurance, agency management, customer service, sales, human resources, operations, and "hands-on" service to customers. The classroom training is followed by 264 hours of on-the-job training at the franchisee's facility and assistance with pre-opening publicity. Facility set-up is assisted with detailed design plans for office layout and interior decoration, exterior sign design, and training with the accounting system and operations of the on-line computer terminal.

Estrella Insurance has ongoing support for franchisees in important areas such as assistance with local advertising and participation in regional advertising. Estrella conducts regular inspections and evaluations on standards of quality, service, merchandising, and advertising in order to provide advice, consultation, or training and enhance uniformity and quality control. Ongoing assistance is always available for franchisees via telephone.

Territory
Estrella Insurance grants exclusive territories.

Express Employment Professionals

8516 NW Expressway
Oklahoma City, OK 73162-5145
Tel: (877) 652-6400 (405) 840-5000
Fax: (405) 717-5665
Email: franchising@expresspros.com
Website: www.expressfranchising.com
Diane Carter, Dir. of Franchise Compliance & Admin.

Express Employment Professionals is a growing franchise within the $97 billion staffing industry. The average Express Employment Professionals franchise generated on average $3.5 million in sales in 2010. Also in 2010, Express grew 46%, setting 23 new weekly sales records. For the first half of 2011 Express has grown 32%. Express offers new franchise owners the unique chance to build income and equity while helping people grow their careers and impacting the local community.

BACKGROUND: IFA Member
Established: 1983; First Franchised: 1985
Franchised Units: 564
Company-Owned Units: 1
Total Units: 565
Dist.: US-523; CAN-27; O'seas-15
North America: 49 States, 3 Provinces
Density: 49 in CA, 34 in OK, 55 in TX

Projected New Units (12 Months): 50
Qualifications: 4, 4, 3, 4, 4, 4

FINANCIAL/TERMS:
Cash Investment: $50K
Total Investment: $95.5-134.5K
Minimum Net Worth: $200K
Fees: Franchise - $35K
 Royalty - 8-9%; Ad. - 0.6%
Earnings Claims Statement: Yes
Term of Contract (Years): 5/5
Avg. # of Employees: 3 FT, 0 PT
Passive Ownership: Not Allowed
Encourage Conversions: Yes
Area Develop. Agreements: Yes
Sub-Franchising Contracts: No
Expand in Territory: Yes
Space Needs: 1,000-1,200 SF

SUPPORT & TRAINING:
Financial Assistance Provided: No
Site Selection Assistance: Yes
Lease Negotiation Assistance: Yes
Co-operative Advertising: Yes
Franchisee Assoc./Member: No
Size of Corporate Staff: 200
On-going Support: A,NA,C,D,E,NA,G,H,I
Training: 1 week certified training office (in field);
 2 weeks Oklahoma City, OK

SPECIFIC EXPANSION PLANS:
US: All US
Canada: All Except Quebec
Overseas: South Africa and Australia

Express Employment Professionals is a growing franchise within the $97 billion staffing industry. The average Express Employment Professionals franchise generated on average $3.5 million in sales in 2010. Also in 2010, Express grew 46%, setting 23 new weekly sales records. For the first half of 2011, Express has grown 32%. Express offers new franchise owners the unique chance to build income and equity while helping people grow their careers and impacting the local community.

Operating Units	12/31/2008	12/31/2009	12/31/2010
Franchised	550	519	509
% Change	--	-5.6%	-1.9%
Company-Owned	4	2	1
% Change	--	-50.0%	-50.0%
Total	554	521	510
% Change	--	-6.0%	-2.1%
Franchised as % of Total	99.3%	99.6%	99.8%

Investment Required
The fee for an Express Employment Professionals franchise is $35,000.

Express Employment Professionals provides the following range of investments required to open your initial franchise. The range assumes that all items are paid for in cash. To the extent that you choose to finance any of these expense items, your front-end investment could be substantially reduced.

Item	Established Low Range	Established High Range
Initial Franchise Fee	$35,000	$35,000
Lease and Deposit	$2,100	$2,700
Leasehold Improvements	$4,000	$5,000
Utility Deposits	$200	$600

Expenses While Training	$3,300	$6,500
Office Equipment	$6,500	$6,900
Computer System and Software	$14,000	$18,500
Furniture and Fixture	$8,000	$8,600
Signs	$3,000	$4,000
Insurance	$400	$700
Professional Service Fees	$1,000	$2,000
Additional Funds (3 Months)	$18,000	$44,000
Total Initial Investment	$95,500	$134,500

On-going Expenses

The franchisee keeps 60% of the monthly gross margin, and Express Employment Professionals keeps the rest and takes care of the following ongoing expenses: payroll processing, client invoicing and collections, risk-management administration and worker compensation. Franchisees also pay an advertising/marketing fee equal to 0.6% of the monthly gross margin.

Franchisee Satisfaction

A critical component of the due diligence process is that you, as a prospective franchisee, have a strong sense of existing franchisee satisfaction. Please review the franchisor's ratings below for this extremely important information.

**World-Class
Franchise®**

How do you rate Express Employment Pros in terms of:	Rating*
Overall quality of franchisor	94%
Initial Training Supplied by Franchisor	99%
My Franchisor understands that if I am successful, they will be successful.	93%

* Independent Audit of Existing Franchisees Who Rated Express Employment Professionals as Excellent, Very Good, or Good

What You Get—Training and Support
Express offers comprehensive initial training, with two weeks at Express University in Oklahoma City, OK and one week in a certified field training office. The training programs cover the subjects of financial controls, sales and telemarketing techniques, maintenance of quality standards, merchandising, advertising, and administration. Franchisees and their staff have ongoing learning opportunities available through online courses, development tracks, training calls and tools available through Express University Online. In addition, Express hosts two live training events annually at the regional SALES Summit as well as an international live training event through the International Leadership Conference.

Express offers layers of support and tools, including a developer who visits each franchise location, a toll-free assistance center and technical support open weekdays from 7 AM - 7 PM CST. Franchisees have at their disposal 200 support professionals offering specialized advice at Express international headquarters, along with 70 representatives in the field, a proprietary handbook and manuals. Franchisees receive collateral sales and recruiting materials at no charge and have access to knowledge-based marketing programs unique to Express. Franchisees are equipped for success through Express' sales support programs and marketing and media relations tools.

Territory
Express Employment Professionals grants exclusive territories.

Express Oil Change

1880 Southpark Dr.
Birmingham, AL 35244
Tel: (888) 945-1771 (205) 945-1771
Fax: (205) 943-5779
Email: dlarose@expressoil.com
Website: www.expressoil.com
Don LaRose, SVP Franchise Development

We are among the top ten fast oil change chains in the world. Per unit, sales out-pace our competitors by over 40%. Attractive, state-of-the-art facilities offer expanded, highly profitable services in addition to our ten minute oil change. We also provide transmission service, air conditioning service, brake repair, tire rotation and balancing and miscellaneous light repairs. Most extensive training and franchise support in the industry.

BACKGROUND: IFA Member
Established: 1979;
First Franchised: 1984
Franchised Units: 110
Company-Owned Units: 75
Total Units: 185
Dist.: US-185; CAN-0; O'seas-0
North America: 11 States
Density: 90 in AL, 35 in GA, 20 in TN

Projected New Units (12 Months): 12
Qualifications: 5, 5, 1, 3, 3, 5

FINANCIAL/TERMS:
Cash Investment: $275-350K
Total Investment: $950-1,600K
Minimum Net Worth: $450K
Fees: Franchise - $35K
Royalty - 5%; Ad. - 0
Earnings Claims Statement: Yes
Term of Contract (Years): 10/10
Avg. # of Employees: 7 FT, 0 PT
Passive Ownership: Not Allowed
Encourage Conversions: Yes
Area Develop. Agreements: Yes
Sub-Franchising Contracts: No
Expand in Territory: Yes
Space Needs: 22,000 SF

SUPPORT & TRAINING:
Financial Assistance Provided: Yes (I)
Site Selection Assistance: Yes
Lease Negotiation Assistance: Yes
Co-operative Advertising: Yes
Franchisee Assoc./Member: Yes/Yes
Size of Corporate Staff: 44
On-going Support: A,B,C,D,E,F,G,H,I
Training: Post-opening training; continuous training; on-site; Birmingham, AL; closest training center

SPECIFIC EXPANSION PLANS:
US: South
Canada: No
Overseas: No

Founded 30 years ago in Birmingham, AL and now with more than 180 locations across 11 states, Express Oil Change & Service Center is a leading automotive service center in the South.

Express Oil Change, with its honed oil change process and a total-car-care mechanical department, is committed to giving customers the quickest oil change without sacrificing the highest-quality service. The convenience of a

243

quick oil change is expected to continue to draw customers away from long waits at automotive dealerships and mechanic shops, ensuring your franchise a secure spot in today's competitive market. Moreover, with the rising costs of vehicles, automobile owners are even more conscious of proper car maintenance to protect their investment. This trend is even more prevalent during economic downturns and makes the quick lube industry resilient even during recessionary periods.

Express Oil Change & Service Center stands on a firm foundation in a growing industry with a proven formula for success. To share its success, Express Oil Change seeks franchisees who possess the drive to succeed by delivering outstanding quality and service, proven business acumen and the willingness and ability to invest.

Operating Units	12/31/2008	12/31/2009	12/31/2010
Franchised	99	100	100
% Change	--	1.0%	0.0%
Company-Owned	69	72	74
% Change	--	4.3%	2.8%
Total	168	172	174
% Change	--	2.4%	1.2%
Franchised as % of Total	58.9%	58.1%	57.5%

Investment Required
The franchise fee for an Express Oil Change store is $35,000 for the first unit and $17,500 for each additional unit.

Express Oil Change provides the following range of investments required to open your initial franchise. The range assumes that all items are paid for in cash. To the extent that you choose to finance any of these expense items, your front-end investment could be substantially reduced.

Item	Established Low Range	Established High Range
Initial Franchise Fee	$35,000 for first unit, $17,500 for each addl.	
Expenses While Training	$2,000	$5,000
Inventory	$25,000	$30,000
Organization, Loan Origination and Professional Fees	$35,000	$70,000
Opening Advertising	$10,000	$10,000
Additional Funds (3 Months)	$60,000	$110,000
Total Initial Investment (not including real estate or leasehold improvements)	$167,000	$277,500

On-going Expenses

Express Oil Change franchisees pay royalty fees equal to 5% of gross sales and minimum local advertising expenditures equal to 3% of gross sales.

Franchisee Satisfaction

A critical component of the due diligence process is that you, as a prospective franchisee, have a strong sense of existing franchisee satisfaction. Please review the franchisor's ratings below for this extremely important information.

World-Class Franchise®

How do you rate Express Oil in terms of:	Rating*
Quality of products/services received from franchisor	96%
Rate the opportunity provided by the franchise system	96%
Franchisor's business versus local competition	96%

* Independent Audit of Existing Franchisees Who Rated Express Oil Change as Excellent, Very Good, or Good

What You Get—Training and Support
Express Oil Change provides comprehensive training to franchisees, managers, and crew members. The initial classroom and field training includes an eight-week program for the franchisee or a designated manager, and two weeks for crew members at a store training center in Alabama. The program for franchisees and managers covers oil change procedures, mechanical training, store operation, inventory control, management, marketing, accounting and human resources, while the training for crew members focuses on operational procedures. Trainings are conducted by highly experienced support officers with an average of 5-10 years in the industry. Additional or periodic training programs are also available. A certified trainer spends time at the franchisee's location during the first year and as needed.

Express Oil Change franchisees also benefit from ExpressTrack©, a proprietary management system which allows owners to easily track key indicators in their business, giving them real-time access to the elements in the operation that make the business work. Express Oil Change's business model has proven itself; exemplified by a 99% survival rate of all stores built over the last 10 years—a rare accomplishment in the franchise industry.

Territory
Express Oil Change grants protected areas.

Fantastic Sams

𝑭𝒂𝒏𝒕𝒂𝒔𝒕𝒊𝒄 𝑺𝒂𝒎𝒔®
HAIR SALONS

50 Dunham Rd., 3rd Fl.
Beverly, MA 01915
Tel: (877) 383-3831 (978) 232-5600
Fax: (888) 315-4437
Email: cgaudette@fantasticsams.com
Website: www.fantasticsamsfranchises.com
Cindy Gaudette, Project Manager, Sales & Marketing

Fantastic Sams is one of the world's largest full-service hair care franchises, with over 1,200 salons in North America. Our full service salons offer quality hair care services for the entire family, including cuts, textures, and color. When you join the Fantastic Sams family of franchisees, you'll receive both local and national support through on-going management training, educational programs, and national conferences, as well as advertising and other benefits. No hair care experience required.

BACKGROUND: IFA Member
Established: 1974; First Franchised: 1976
Franchised Units: 1,100
Company-Owned Units: 1,18
Total Units: 1,218
Dist.: US-1,209; CAN-9; O'seas-0
North America: 46 States, 1 Province
Density: 206 in CA, 108 in MN, 107 in FL

Projected New Units (12 Months):	40
Qualifications:	5, 5, 1, 4, 1, 5
FINANCIAL/TERMS:	
Cash Investment:	$75K
Total Investment:	$115-228.6K
Minimum Net Worth:	$300K
Fees: Franchise -	$25-40K
Royalty - Fixed Fee;	Ad. - $131.28
Earnings Claims Statement:	No
Term of Contract (Years):	10/10
Avg. # of Employees:	8 FT, 0 PT
Passive Ownership:	Allowed
Encourage Conversions:	Yes
Area Develop. Agreements:	No
Sub-Franchising Contracts:	
Expand in Territory:	Yes
Space Needs:	1,200 SF
SUPPORT & TRAINING:	
Financial Assistance Provided:	Yes (I)
Site Selection Assistance:	Yes
Lease Negotiation Assistance:	Yes
Co-operative Advertising:	No
Franchisee Assoc./Member:	No
Size of Corporate Staff:	53
On-going Support:	NA,NA,C,D,E,NA,G,H,NA
Training:	5 days salon fundamentals class; on-going region
SPECIFIC EXPANSION PLANS:	
US:	All US
Canada:	All Canada
Overseas:	No

Fantastic Sams has firmly established itself in the booming multibillion-dollar hair care industry with the belief that every customer should be greeted with "honesty, integrity, and responsiveness." The one-stop shop for women, men, and children of all ages provides a wide range of quality services—haircuts and styles, up-dos, straightening, coloring, highlights, texturizing, beard and mustache trims, facial waxing, and hair treatments—at affordable prices and without the need for appointments. In addition,

247

Fantastic Sams offers its own high-quality proprietary line of shampoos, conditioners, and styling aides.

Fantastic Sams serves over half a million guests per week in more than 1,200 salons in North America. With nearly 40 years of business and franchising experience, it is one of the most recognized names in the hair care industry today.

Operating Units	12/31/2008	12/31/2009	12/31/2010
Franchised	1,231	1,210	1,171
% Change	--	-1.7%	-3.2%
Company-Owned	138	116	108
% Change	--	-15.9%	-6.9%
Total	1,369	1,326	1,279
% Change	--	-3.12%	-3.5%
Franchised as % of Total	89.9%	91.3%	91.6%

Investment Required
The fee for a Fantastic Sams franchise is $30,000.

Fantastic Sams provides the following range of investments required to open your initial franchise. The range assumes that all items are paid for in cash. To the extent that you choose to finance any of these expense items, your front-end investment could be substantially reduced.

Item	Established Low Range	Established High Range
Initial Franchise Fee	$30,000	$30,000
New Owner/SFC Training Fee	$0	$2,600
Expenses While Training	$1,500	$3,000
Leasehold Improvements	$20,000	$80,000

Rent and Utility Deposit	$3,000	$7,000
Initial Hair Care Product Inventory	$8,000	$12,000
Salon Equipment	$20,500	$28,500
Other Equipment, Fixtures and Furnishings	$3,000	$7,000
Salon Identity and Graphics Kit	$500	$1,500
Insurance	$1,000	$2,000
Advertising	$7,500	$15,000
Additional Funds (3 Months)	$20,000	$40,000
Total Initial Investment	$115,000	$228,600

On-going Expenses

Fantastic Sams franchisees pay a weekly license fee equal to $325.21 and a national advertising fee equal to $130.32. Additional fees include a regional/local advertising fund fee, when applicable.

NOTE: The fees noted above are for corporate-owned regions. Fees in other regions may differ, so please consult the specific FDD for the territory you are interested in.

What You Get—Training and Support

Owner and manager classes consist of a minimum of five days of training and are held three times a year in Massachusetts. Hairstylist classes are held throughout the year at designated facilities. The owner and manager training covers the history of the Fantastic Sams system, salon operations, accounting system, inventory control, financial management, human resources, product knowledge, customer and employee relations, advertising/marketing, and more. The hairstylist training includes hairstyling techniques, the Fantastic Sams system and sales training. Regional seminars are also provided periodically.

A staff of over 50 professional instructors offers ongoing support in operations, products, and promotions. National conferences play a key role in motivating franchisees, allowing them to network and gain more training. The Fantastic Sams name is given fresh exposure annually through coordinated efforts in national and regional advertising campaigns.

Territory
Fantastic Sams grants a protected area within a half-mile radius of the salon location.

FASTSIGNS

FASTSIGNS®
More than fast. More than signs.™

2542 Highlander Wy.
Carrollton, TX 75006
Tel: (214) 346-5679
Fax: (866) 422-4927
Email: mark.jameson@fastsigns.com
Website: www.fastsigns.com
Mark L. Jameson, Senior Vice President, Franchise Support & Development

Signage has never been more important. Right now, businesses are looking for new and better ways to compete. Industries are revamping to meet compliance standards. And advertisers are expanding their reach into new media, like digital signage, QR codes, and mobile websites. Join the franchise that's leading the next generation of business communication. Now more than ever, businesses look to FastSigns® for innovative ways to connect with customers in a highly competitive marketplace.

Our high standards for quality and customer service have made FASTSIGNS® the most recognized brand in the industry, driving significantly more traffic to the web than any other sign company. We also lead in these important areas: #1 Sign Franchise in Entrepreneur magazine Franchise 500, 2011; Franchise Business Review Best in Category 2006-2010; World Class Franchisee Satisfaction Recognition, 2011 Franchise Research Institute; Franchisees' Choice Designation, 2011 Canadian Franchise Association. FASTSIGNS is one of only a handful of franchises approved for the Franchise America Finance Program, with 6 million dollars in financing for approved franchise owners.

BACKGROUND:	IFA Member
Established: 1985;	First Franchised: 1986
Franchised Units:	529
Company-Owned Units:	0
Total Units:	529
Dist.:	US-451; CAN-22; O'seas-56
North America:	45 States, 6 Provinces
Density:	58 in TX, 35 in FL, 45 in CA
Projected New Units (12 Months):	25
Qualifications:	5, 5, 1, 3, 4, 5

FINANCIAL/TERMS:	
Cash Investment:	$75K
Total Investment:	$169.7K
Minimum Net Worth:	$250K
Fees: Franchise -	$34.5K
Royalty - 6%;	Ad. - 2%
Earnings Claims Statement:	Yes

Term of Contract (Years):	20/10	Lease Negotiation Assistance:	Yes
Avg. # of Employees:	2-3 FT, 0 PT	Co-operative Advertising:	No
Passive Ownership:	Allowed	Franchisee Assoc./Member:	Yes/Yes
Encourage Conversions:	Yes	Size of Corporate Staff:	100+
Area Develop. Agreements:	Yes	On-going Support:	NA,NA,C,D,E,NA,G,H,I
Sub-Franchising Contracts:	No	Training:	2 weeks Dallas, TX; 1 week on-site
Expand in Territory:	Yes		
Space Needs:	1,200-1,500 SF	**SPECIFIC EXPANSION PLANS:**	
		US:	All US
SUPPORT & TRAINING:		Canada:	All Canada except Quebec
Financial Assistance Provided:	Yes (I)	Overseas:	UK, New Zealand, Australia
Site Selection Assistance:	Yes		

FASTSIGNS is a pioneer and leader in the signs and graphics industry, combining advanced technology with innovative ideas to design and produce signs for businesses and organizations of all types and sizes. FastSigns offers consulting, design, production, file transfer, delivery, and installation for a full range of sign and graphic products. Since 1985, the company has grown to a network spanning across the globe. FastSigns has been ranked among the top in Entrepreneur's Annual 500 for over 15 years and has been named #1 in the Business Services Category by Franchise Business Review for five years in a row.

Operating Units	12/31/2008	12/31/2009	12/31/2010
Franchised	460	453	452
% Change	--	-1.5%	-0.2%
Company-Owned	0	0	0
% Change	--	--	--
Total	460	453	452
% Change	--	-1.5%	-0.2%
Franchised as % of Total	100%	100%	100%

Investment Required
The fee for a FASTSIGNS franchise is $34,500. If you establish an additional franchise, the initial fee is $17,500.

251

FASTSIGNS provides the following range of investments required to open your initial franchise. The range assumes that all items are paid for in cash. To the extent that you choose to finance any of these expense items, your front-end investment could be substantially reduced.

Item	Established Low Range	Established High Range
Initial Franchise Fee	$34,500	$34,500
Leasehold Improvements	$8,264	$58,000
Furniture, Fixtures, Signage	$8,517	$13,166
Lease/Utility Deposits	$3,500	$9,000
Store Graphics	$4,456	$4,556
Tools and Saw	$5,659	$6,792
Output Devices	$30,359	$30,828
POS Computer	$5,659	$6,809
Signage	$2,800	$5,300
Initial Inventory	$3,722	$4,078
Architectural and Engineering Costs	$0	$2,500
Initial Advertising	$12,500	$12,500
Expenses While Training	$11,380	$14,844
Administrative Supplies	$1,880	$2,030
Licenses and Permits	$500	$1,000
Insurance (3 Months)	$646	$1,000
Professional Fees	$2,117	$4,617
Sample Kit	$2,899	$2,899
Bancorp Participation Fee	$0	$2,000
Working Capital	$30,000	$60,000
Total Initial Investment	$169,668	$276,419

On-going Expenses

FASTSIGNS franchisees pay a royalty fee equal to 6% of gross sales and a National Advertising Council fee equal to 2% of gross sales. Other fees include a possible advertising cooperative fee equal to a maximum of 2% of gross sales and the cost of various advertising, promotional materials and sales training.

Franchisee Satisfaction

A critical component of the due diligence process is that you, as a prospective franchisee, have a strong sense of existing franchisee satisfaction. Please review the franchisor's ratings below for this extremely important information.

World-Class Franchise®

How do you rate FASTSIGNS in terms of:	Rating*
Overall quality of franchisor	99%
Initial training supplied by franchisor	97%
High standards of quality performance throughout organization	95%
Franchisor's business versus local competition	100%

* Independent Audit of Existing Franchisees Who Rated FASTSIGNS as Excellent, Very Good, or Good

What You Get—Training and Support

The new franchise owner, a computer graphics designer, and a customer service representative are provided with an initial training program, which includes two weeks of classroom instruction for up to nine hours a day in Carrollton, Texas as well as at least 32 hours of in-store training. For the owner, the training includes topics on sales, marketing, and administrative and financial management; for the computer graphics designer and customer service representative, training topics include sales, product knowledge, POS, product fulfillment and other related subjects. FASTSIGNS also offers site-selection assistance, construction consulting, operation manuals, and grand opening support to ensure each franchisee's success.

Ongoing support for FASTSIGNS franchisees includes support from a FASTSIGNS Franchise Business Consultant and optional additional managing and operations advisory assistance by means of written materials, toll free telephone service, electronic communication, or at the FASTSIGNS office. FASTSIGNS also holds regular franchise conventions.

Territory
FASTSIGNS grants protected territories encompassing a minimum of 4,000 businesses divided by zip code boundaries.

Fibrenew

The Experts in Leather & Plastic Restoration

Box 33, Site 16, RR. 8
Calgary, AB T2J 2T9 Canada
Tel: (800) 345-2951 (403) 278-7818
Fax: (402) 278-1434
Email: info@fibrenew.com
Website: www.fibrenew.com
Denele Shelby, VP Franchising

Fibrenew is a "niche market" business refurbishing and re-dyeing all leather and plastic, offering clients a "green" environmental and cost-saving alternative to replacing or recovering damaged pieces. Fibrenew supports men and women worldwide into owning and operating a successful home-based mobile service business. Fibrenew accomplishes this by encouraging cooperation between our franchises to share their knowledge and experience. We promote education through seminars, workshops and self-directed business, and personal studies. Fibrenew strives to be environmentally responsible. Our services prevent thousands of tons of used leathers, plastics, and vinyl from filling our landfills annually.

BACKGROUND:		Encourage Conversions:	NA
Established: 1985;	First Franchised: 1987	Area Develop. Agreements:	No
Franchised Units:	198	Sub-Franchising Contracts:	No
Company-Owned Units:	0	Expand in Territory:	Yes
Total Units:	198	Space Needs:	NA
Dist.:	US-105; CAN-72; O'seas-21		
North America:	32 States, 10 Provinces	**SUPPORT & TRAINING:**	
Density:		Financial Assistance Provided:	Yes (I)
Projected New Units (12 Months):	20	Site Selection Assistance:	NA
Qualifications:	5, 3, 1, 1, 2, 3	Lease Negotiation Assistance:	NA
		Co-operative Advertising:	No
FINANCIAL/TERMS:		Franchisee Assoc./Member:	No
Cash Investment:	$70K	Size of Corporate Staff:	7
Total Investment:	$82K-105K	On-going Support:	NA,B,C,D,NA,NA,G,h,I
Minimum Net Worth:	$150K	Training:	2 weeks Calgary, AB Canada
Fees: Franchise -	$67K		
Royalty - $550/mo. starting;	Ad. - NA	**SPECIFIC EXPANSION PLANS:**	
Earnings Claims Statement:	Yes	US:	ALL except ND, SD, and HI
Term of Contract (Years):	7/7	Canada:	BC, AB, SK, ON, QC, NS
Avg. # of Employees:	1 FT, PT	Overseas:	Australia
Passive Ownership:	Not Allowed		

Fibrenew specializes in the repair, restoration, and renewal of leather, plastics, vinyl, fabric and upholstery servicing five major markets: automotive, aviation, commercial, marine, and residential. There are many reasons why repairing cracked vinyl and plastic or damaged leather in a car, boat, airplane, home or office is good for the environment. Fibrenew technicians have the equipment and expertise to make cracks, stains, scratches, holes, rips and fades in leather, plastic, vinyl, fabric, and upholstery look new again. Restoration is an environmentally-friendly and cost-effective alternative to replacement.

Since 1987, Fibrenew has been the industry leader with the development of exceptional leather and vinyl repair products and restoration techniques. The combined knowledge and experience of our 200+ franchisees around the world is unparalleled. Since 1987, we have expanded our global presence to include franchise units in the United States, Canada, Mexico, New Zealand, Australia, and Ecuador.

Operating Units	12/31/2008	12/31/2009	12/31/2010
Franchised	54	69	97

255

% Change	--	27.8 %	40.6 %
Company-Owned	0	0	0
% Change	--	--	--
Total	54	69	97
% Change	--	27.8 %	40.6 %
Franchised as % of Total	100 %	100%	100 %

Investment Required

The initial franchise fee for a Fibrenew franchise is $65,000.

Fibrenew provides the following range of investments required to open your initial franchise. The range assumes that all items are paid for in cash. To the extent that you choose to finance any of these expense items, your front-end investment could be substantially reduced.

Item	Established Low Range	Established High Range
Initial Franchise Fee	$40,000	$80,000
Start-up Fee	$25,000	$25,000
Insurance – 1 year	$700	$2,000
Organizational Expenses	$200	$2,000
Training Expenses	$2,400	$2,800
Shipping Cost of Start-up Kit	$450	$625
Office Equipment	$0	$1,000
Work Vehicle – 3 months	$175	$1,509
Vehicle Signs	$750	$1,500
Internet Access (3 months)	$150	$300
Business Licenses/ Permits	$50	$200

Office or Storage Area	Unable to predict	Unable to predict
Additional Funds	$600	$1,000
Total	$70,475	$117,934

On-going Expenses

Fibrenew franchisees pay a monthly technical assistance fee of $550, a minimum of $3,000 per year on proprietary products, a fee for training additional people, and other fees.

Franchisee Satisfaction

A critical component of the due diligence process is that you, as a prospective franchisee, have a strong sense of existing franchisee satisfaction. Please review the franchisor's ratings below for this extremely important information.

World-Class Franchise®

How do you rate Fibrenew in terms of:	Rating*
Overall quality of franchisor	100%
Initial training supplied by franchisor	99%
Rating of the quality of products and/or services received from franchisor	100%
General rating of opportunity provided by franchise system	100%

* Independent Audit of Existing Franchisees Who Rated Fibrenew as Excellent, Very Good, or Good

What You Get—Training and Support
When you are awarded a Fibrenew franchise, you receive an exclusive protected territory; use of trade name and trademark; access to proprietary products and methods and manuals; a comprehensive training program; complete inventory and equipment; business cards, invoices, statements, envelopes and brochures; ongoing technical support via phone and internet; access to our technical library, continuous education; and support via seminars, workshops, and conferences.

Fibrenew's ongoing support comes in the form of newsletters, meetings, toll-free phone lines, internet, field operations/evaluations, and more.

Territory
Fibrenew does grant exclusive territories, but no specific location is designated for the premises of the franchised business.

Fiesta Auto Insurance and Tax Service

16162 Beach Blvd., # 100
Huntington Beach, CA 92647
Tel: (877) 905-3437 (714) 842-5420
Fax: (714) 842-5401
Email: franchising@fiestainsurance.com
Website: www.fiestafranchise.com
Glen Wielandt, Franchise Business Development

Fiesta Insurance Franchise Corporation is an authorized franchisor rapidly growing throughout the US. With a Fiesta Auto Insurance & Tax Service franchise, you gain immediate access to many personal lines insurance programs and the ability to process every kind of income tax return, as well as offer bank products. Additional revenue from services such as accounting and bookkeeping, travel, money transfers, motor vehicle registrations and notary public are available in some states. Fiesta Insurance Franchise Corporation will provide you with the necessary structure and training to run a successful insurance and tax preparation business.

BACKGROUND:	
Established: 1999;	First Franchised: 2007
Franchised Units:	150
Company-Owned Units:	3
Total Units:	153
Dist.:	US-153; CAN-0; O'seas-0
North America:	13 States
Density:	50 in CA, 22 in TX, 13 in NY
Projected New Units (12 Months):	150
Qualifications:	4, 4, 1, 3, 3, 5

FINANCIAL/TERMS:	
Cash Investment:	$25-35K
Total Investment:	$35-55K
Minimum Net Worth:	NR
Fees: Franchise -	$10K
Royalty - 10-25%;	Ad. - 0%
Earnings Claims Statement:	Yes
Term of Contract (Years):	5/5
Avg. # of Employees:	1 FT, 1 PT

Passive Ownership:	Allowed, But Discouraged
Encourage Conversions:	Yes
Area Develop. Agreements:	Yes
Sub-Franchising Contracts:	No
Expand in Territory:	Yes
Space Needs:	700-1,200 SF

SUPPORT & TRAINING:	
Financial Assistance Provided:	Yes (I)
Site Selection Assistance:	Yes
Lease Negotiation Assistance:	Yes
Co-operative Advertising:	Yes
Franchisee Assoc./Member:	No
Size of Corporate Staff:	25
On-going Support:	A,B,C,D,E,NA,G,H,I
Training:	1 week Huntington Beach, CA

SPECIFIC EXPANSION PLANS:	
US:	All US
Canada:	No
Overseas:	No

In 2006, Fiesta Auto Insurance and Tax Services began its franchise operations and since then has given customers access to many top insurance carriers—at the very best prices available. Fiesta's team of professionals offer insurance coverage for auto, home, commercial, rental property, boat, motorcycle, and anything else that might need to be insured. All Fiesta Auto Insurance offices also offer income tax preparation services. The Fiesta team accurately determines tax liability, identifies all deductions, and works to get customers the biggest refunds or least tax liability.

Fiesta Auto Insurance offers franchisees an attractive opportunity in a stable recession proof industry with consistent growth every year. Both insurance, which people are often legally required to obtain, and taxes are considered necessary services. Regardless of whether the economy is enjoying good times or not, these two essential services are a successful combination.

Operating Units	12/31/2008	12/31/2009	12/31/2010
Franchised	30	54	78
% Change	--	80.0%	44.4%

Company-Owned	1	2	0
% Change	--	100.0%	-100.0%
Total	31	56	78
% Change	--	80.6%	39.3%
Franchised as % of Total	96.8%	96.4%	100.0%

Investment Required

The franchise fee for a Fiesta Auto Insurance franchise is $10,000. Options are available for a retail tax office/kiosk-based business for a fee of $5,000. An Area Development program (three for the price of two territories), and our Master Developer program are also available.

Fiesta Auto Insurance provides the following range of investments required to open your initial franchise. The range assumes that all items are paid for in cash. To the extent that you choose to finance any of these expense items, your front-end investment could be substantially reduced. The following figures are for opening a new standard franchise; the estimated initial investment for a retail office/kiosk-based business is $12,875 – $80,900.

Item	Established Low Range	Established High Range
Initial Franchise Fee	$5,000	$10,000
Expenses While Training	$0	$1,500
Real Estate & Improvements	$2,000	$36,000
Equipment	$1,600	$9,000
Signs	$200	$6,000
Miscellaneous Opening Costs	$0	$1,000
Insurance Coverage	$1,000	$3,000
Software & Licensing Fees	$575	$900

Marketing Package	$2,500	$3,500
Additional Funds (3 Months)	$0	$10,000
Total Initial Investment	$12,875	$80,900

On-going Expenses
Fiesta Auto Insurance franchisees pay a monthly royalty fee equal to the greater of between 10% to 25% of total insurance commissions (depending on the type of franchise) or $250. Additional fees include a policy manager software licensing fee of $150 a month and an insurance ratings software licensing fee of $125 to $250 a month. There is an annual licensing fee for the tax software.

What You Get—Training and Support
Fiesta Auto Insurance provides plenty of support both in training and preparation of the day-to-day business. Training starts with one week at the corporate office and is followed by continuous education via Fiesta University and weekly webinars.

In terms of day-to-day business, Fiesta Auto Insurance provides the added support from the corporate office and a sophisticated Agency Information Management System (Policy Manager) that reaches into the franchisee's office on the insurance side, and easy-to-understand and user-friendly tax software (MaxTax) for the tax side. Fiesta Auto Insurance also offers all franchisees professional and highly effective marketing communication material through an automated ordering system.

Territory
Fiesta Insurance grants exclusive territories.

Furniture Medic

 FURNITURE MEDIC®

3839 Forest Hill-Irene Rd.
Memphis, TN 38125-2502
Tel: (800) 230-2360 (901) 597-8600
Fax: (901) 597-8660
Email: fmfranchiseinfo@furnituremedic.com
Website: www.furnituremedicfranchise.com
David Messenger, Vice President

Furniture Medic is a division of The ServiceMaster Company. It is the largest furniture and wood repair and restoration company in the world with over 300 franchises. Furniture Medic has unique products and processes which enable much of the work to be done on-site, reducing costs and saving time for its residential and commercial customers. Financing is provided for the initial franchise fees, start-up equipment and vehicles to qualified candidates through ServiceMaster Acceptance Company.

BACKGROUND: IFA Member
Established: 1990; First Franchised: 1992
Franchised Units: 361
Company-Owned Units: 0
Total Units: 361
Dist.: US-230; CAN-51; O'seas-80
North America: 47 States
Density: 21 in VA, 38 in FL, 18 in IL
Projected New Units (12 Months): 30

Qualifications:	4, 4, 2, 3, 3, 5
FINANCIAL/TERMS:	
Cash Investment:	$20-25K
Total Investment:	$51-66K
Minimum Net Worth:	$75K
Fees: Franchise -	$29.9K
Royalty - 7%/$250 Min.;	Ad. - 1%/$50 Min.
Earnings Claims Statement:	No
Term of Contract (Years):	5/5
Avg. # of Employees:	1 FT, 1 PT
Passive Ownership:	Not Allowed
Encourage Conversions:	Yes
Area Develop. Agreements:	No
Sub-Franchising Contracts:	No
Expand in Territory:	Yes
Space Needs:	NA
SUPPORT & TRAINING:	
Financial Assistance Provided:	Yes (D)
Site Selection Assistance:	NA
Lease Negotiation Assistance:	No
Co-operative Advertising:	Yes
Franchisee Assoc./Member:	Yes/Yes
Size of Corporate Staff:	21
On-going Support:	A,B,NA,NA,NA,NA,G,h,I
Training:	3 weeks Memphis, TN
SPECIFIC EXPANSION PLANS:	
US:	Most metropolitan markets in US
Canada:	All Canada
Overseas:	All Countries

As the world's largest on-site wood and furniture repair and restoration companies, Furniture Medic owes its success to its commitment to providing customers with unsurpassed, quality service. Utilizing advanced technology, Furniture Medic specializes in enhancement, refinishing and restoration for antiques, specialty items, millwork, paneling, doors and banisters, cabinetry and mantels, hardwood floors and upholstery for both residential and commercial customers. Since 1992, it has grown to a network of more than 250 franchises throughout North America and Europe. The company has been named as the #1 furniture repair and restoration franchise by the

Entrepreneur magazine for 10 years running.

Furniture Medic—along with ServiceMaster Clean, Amerispec, Merry Maids, Terminix, American Home Shield and Trugreen—is part of the ServiceMaster family, providing a wide array of home maintenance, commercial cleaning and restoration services.

Operating Units	12/31/2008	12/31/2009	12/31/2010
Franchised	264	258	234
% Change	--	-2.3%	-9.3%
Company-Owned	0	0	0
% Change	--	--	--
Total	264	258	234
% Change	--	-2.3%	-9.3%
Franchised as % of Total	100.0%	100.0%	100.0%

Investment Required

The fee for a Furniture Medic franchise is $29,900. Furniture Medic may offer discounts to existing franchisees, ServiceMaster affiliates and employees, women, minorities and to those who have served in the military.

Furniture Medic provides the following range of investments required to open your initial franchise. The range assumes that all items are paid for in cash. To the extent that you choose to finance any of these expense items, your front-end investment could be substantially reduced. Furniture Medic's affiliate, SMAC, offers financing for the initial franchise fee and opening product equipment package.

Item	Established Low Range	Established High Range
Initial Franchise Fee	$29,900	$29,900
Expenses While Training	$1,065	$3,125

Opening Package	$13,000	$13,000
Insurance Liability/Vehicle	$2,500	$4,500
Internet Connection	$45	$150
Fax Machine	$200	$200
Misc. Opening Costs	$200	$1,500
Service Vehicle	$2,000	$25,000
Van Detail Package	$260	$644
Advertising Fund	$150	$150
Initial Marketing	$100	$3,000
Additional Funds (3 Months)	$2,000	$6,000
Total Initial Investment	$51,420	$87,169

On-going Expenses
Furniture Medic franchisees pay royalty fees equal to the greater of $250 per month or 7% gross sales, a national advertising fund fee equal to the greater of $50 per month or 1% of gross sales, and a monthly software fee equal to $30 after the first year.

What You Get—Training and Support
The initial training consists of a Pre-Academy program of roughly 40 hours, a two-week, hands-on training session at the FM training center in Memphis, TN and a one-week Post-Academy training which takes place 90-120 days after graduation from the Academy. The program covers topics on business plans, marketing, record keeping, technical skills and more.

After graduation from the Academy, franchisees may opt to participate in a mentoring program that pairs experienced franchisees with new owners in the same general service area. The purpose of the mentoring program is to press new skill sets into use while developing finesse in customer acquisition.

Franchisees also benefit from around-the-clock telephone support and comprehensive marketing strategies that target brand awareness.

Territory
Furniture Medic does not grant exclusive territories. A protected area containing at least 100,000 people will be granted.

Goddard School

THE
Goddard School®
FOR EARLY CHILDHOOD DEVELOPMENT

1016 Ninth Ave.
King of Prussia, PA 19406
Tel: (800) 272-4901 (610) 265-7128
Fax: (610) 265-7194
Email: jtravitz@goddardsystems.com
Website: www.goddardsystems.com
Jeff Travitz, Director of Franchise Sales

The Goddard School, franchised by Goddard Systems, Inc. (GSI), is recognized as the "#1 Franchise Preschool Chain in the U.S." (Entrepreneur, 01/08) and is ranked in the "Top 200 Franchises," (Franchise Times, 10/07). GSI has 290+ schools licensed in 37 states, and is expanding the network throughout the United States and Canada. GSI has achieved its initial goal as the acknowledged leader in franchised childcare and now has its sights on the next level - recognition as the premier childcare provider.

BACKGROUND:	IFA Member
Established: 1988;	First Franchised: 1988
Franchised Units:	371
Company-Owned Units:	0
Total Units:	371
Dist.:	US-280; CAN-0; O'seas-0

North America:	37 States
Density:	57 in NJ, 41 in OH, 34 in PA
Projected New Units (12 Months):	50
Qualifications:	5, 4, 2, 3, 1, 5

FINANCIAL/TERMS:

Cash Investment:	$130K
Total Investment:	$550K
Minimum Net Worth:	$600K
Fees: Franchise -	$135K
Royalty - 7%;	Ad. - 4% or $2,000
Earnings Claims Statement:	Yes
Term of Contract (Years):	15/5
Avg. # of Employees:	15+ FT, 10+ PT
Passive Ownership:	Not Allowed
Encourage Conversions:	NA
Area Develop. Agreements:	No
Sub-Franchising Contracts:	No
Expand in Territory:	No
Space Needs:	NA

SUPPORT & TRAINING:

Financial Assistance Provided:	No
Site Selection Assistance:	Yes
Lease Negotiation Assistance:	Yes
Co-operative Advertising:	No
Franchisee Assoc./Member:	No
Size of Corporate Staff:	105
On-going Support:	A,NA,C,D,E,F,G,H,I
Training:	3 weeks King of Prussia, PA

SPECIFIC EXPANSION PLANS:

US:	All US
Canada:	All Canada
Overseas:	No

Goddard Systems, Inc. (GSI) is expanding The Goddard School® network of accredited childcare centers throughout the United States. Headquartered in King of Prussia, PA, Goddard Systems currently licenses over 360 franchised schools in 37 states for children aged between 6 weeks to 6 years old. Goddard School uses a dual management system: while the owner is on-site to oversee day-to-day management and operations, the education director focuses on curriculum and programming.

Goddard Systems is committed to providing an unsurpassed level of quality in the childcare industry. With a successful system in place and dedicated franchisees, GSI is an acknowledged leader in franchised childcare – with its sights set on becoming the premier childcare provider in the United States.

Operating Units	12/31/2008	12/31/2009	12/31/2010
Franchised	278	320	357
% Change	--	15.1%	11.6%
Company-Owned	0	0	0
% Change	--	0.0%	0.0%
Total	278	320	357
% Change	--	15.1%	11.6%
Franchised as % of Total	100.00%	100.00%	100.00%

Investment Required
The fee for a Goddard School franchise is $135,000.

The Goddard School provides the following range of investments required to open your initial franchise. The range assumes that all items are paid for in cash. To the extent that you choose to finance any of these expense items, your front-end investment could be substantially reduced.

Item	Established Low Range	Established High Range
Franchise Fee	$135,000	$135,000
Initial Training and Opening Assistance Fee	$35,000	$35,000
Initial Advertising Contribution	$35,000	$35,000
Real Estate Assistance and Support Fee	$30,000	$30,000
Background Check	$2,500	$2,500
Furniture, Fixtures, and Equipment Package	$135,000	$149,000
Stationery, Forms, Curriculum and Frames	$11,000	$11,000
Sign Package	$8,500	$8,500
Computer Software Package, Computer Hardware, Telephone and Digital Signage Package	$13,200	$13,200
Initial Promotional Package	$3,000	$3,000
Security System Package	$11,000	$11,000
Rent—Three Months	$30,000	$45,000
Miscellaneous Opening Cost	$71,000	$71,000
Advertising Contributions—Three Months	$6,000	$6,000
Additional Funds—Three Months	$22,510	$91,600
Total Investment (does not include applicable taxes or shipping costs)	$548,710	$646,800

On-going Expenses

Goddard School franchisees pay royalty fees equal to 7% of gross receipts—royalty fees are reduced during the first year of operation, ranging from 2-6%, depending on how long the franchisee has been in business. Franchisees also pay a monthly advertising contribution equal to the greater of 4% of gross receipts or $2,000, and other fees including telephone service charges, directory advertising and convention registration fees and expenses.

Franchisee Satisfaction

A critical component of the due diligence process is that you, as a prospective franchisee, have a strong sense of existing franchisee satisfaction. Please review the franchisor's ratings below for this extremely important information.

**World-Class
Franchise®**

How do you rate The Goddard School in terms of:	Rating*
Overall Quality of Franchisor	94%
Recommended to Prospective Franchisees	92%
Franchisor Understands that if I am Successful, They Will be Successful.	87%

* Independent Audit of Existing Franchisees Who Rated Goddard School as Excellent, Very Good, or Good

What You Get—Training and Support

Goddard School franchisees complete a 12-day, comprehensive training program covering all aspects of operation, marketing, customer service, staff hiring and training, and management of a school. Goddard School owners attend annual conferences and meetings to enhance the initial training with current research.

Goddard Systems provides on-going support in all aspects of managing and marketing a Goddard School. Franchisees receive support before their school opens in the form of site selection, demographic analysis, lease negotiation, construction management and equipment and furniture installation. Goddard Systems continues to support franchisees after the opening of the school with on-going professional development for teachers; guidance with sales, marketing and advertising; and help with budget and expense control.

Territory
The Goddard School does not grant exclusive territories, but controls the density of schools so that it does not exceed 1 per 10,000 households in the county in which the school is located.

Granite Transformations

10360 USA Today Way
Miramar, FL 33025
Tel: (800) 685-5300 (954) 435-5538
Fax: (954) 435-5579
Email: info@granitetransformations.com
Website: www.granitetransformations.com
Carl Griffenkranz, VP Marketing

Granite Transformations is a franchise organization that provides an important and compelling service to homeowners allowing them to transform kitchen and baths with our gorgeous Trend Stone, Trend Glass, and Trend Mosaic surfaces. Trend Stone is engineered to outperform ordinary granite! It's heat, scratch, and stain resistant, and we're the only surface engineered to fit right over existing countertop surfaces. That means no costly demolition, no mess, and fast and easy installation, usually in about a day!

BACKGROUND:	IFA Member
Established: 1995;	First Franchised: 1995
Franchised Units:	160
Company-Owned Units:	0
Total Units:	0
Dist.:	US-80; CAN-10; O'seas-80
North America:	32 States, 3 Provinces
Density:	7 in ON, 6 in FL, 11 in CA
Projected New Units (12 Months):	12
Qualifications:	4, 5, 2, 2, 4, 5

FINANCIAL/TERMS:	
Cash Investment:	$50-100K
Total Investment:	$131.5K- 346K
Minimum Net Worth:	$100K
Fees: Franchise -	$25-75K

269

Royalty - 2%;	Ad. - 1%	Site Selection Assistance:	Yes
Earnings Claims Statement:	Yes	Lease Negotiation Assistance:	No
Term of Contract (Years):	10/10	Co-operative Advertising:	No
Avg. # of Employees:	7 FT, 2 PT	Franchisee Assoc./Member:	No
Passive Ownership:	Not Allowed	Size of Corporate Staff:	15
Encourage Conversions:	NA	On-going Support:	NA,NA,C,D,E,F,G,h,I
Area Develop. Agreements:	No	Training:	5 days corporate office;
Sub-Franchising Contracts:	No		10 days franchise site
Expand in Territory:	No		
Space Needs:		**SPECIFIC EXPANSION PLANS:**	
		US:	All
SUPPORT & TRAINING:		Canada:	All
Financial Assistance Provided:	No	Overseas:	UK

Granite Transformations is a franchise organization that provides an important and compelling service to homeowners, builders, commercial building owners, and more to literally transform their kitchen, baths, bars, or other areas with TREND STONE, TREND GLASS and TREND MOSAIC surfaces. Each surface is made in the USA, and is created to bring a designer feel and impact to every room. Many franchisees offer cabinet refacing, an additional service to our customers, and another way for our franchisee team to generate revenue and create fans.

Granite Transformations core product is an engineered stone that outperforms ordinary granite. It is heat, scratch, and stain resistant, and adds a dramatic, gorgeous look to kitchens, bathrooms and more. We are the only surface engineered to fit right over existing countertop surfaces. That means no costly demolition, no mess, and fast and easy installation, usually in one day. The Trend Stone, Trend Glass, and Trend Mosaics are manufactured from the finest stones, granites, quartz, and recycled glass available. The products are fabricated in Sebring, Florida and are used in homes and commercial buildings worldwide.

Operating Units	12/31/2008	12/31/2009	12/31/2010
Franchised	78	82	79
% Change	--	5.1 %	-3.7 %
Company-Owned	0	0	0

% Change	--	0 %	0 %
Total	78	82	79
% Change	--	5.1 %	-3.7 %
Franchised as % of Total	100 %	100%	100%

Investment Required

The initial fee for a Granite Transformations franchise will range between $25,000 ($100,000 housing units) to $75,000 (300,000 housing units) depending on the number of housing units in the territory of your choice.

Granite Transformations provides the following range of investments required to open your initial franchise. The range assumes that all items are paid for in cash. To the extent that you choose to finance any of these expense items, your front-end investment could be substantially reduced.

Item	Established Low Range	Established High Range
Initial Franchise Fee	$25,000	$75,000
Travel and Living Expenses	$500	$2,000
Grand Opening Advertising	$5,000	$30,000
Personal Car or Light Truck	$0	$25,000
Working Truck and Fork Lift	$0	$15,000
Rent (first 3 months)	$2,000	$8,000
Business Licenses, Permits, and Contractors License	$0	$7,000
Leasehold Improvements	$5,000	$15,000

Equipment, Furniture, and Fixtures	$5,000	$21,000
Signage	$2,000	$8,000
Tools	$10,000	$20,000
Initial Granite Inventory and Supplies	$35,000	$45,000
Insurance	$10,000	$20,000
Misc. Costs	$2,000	$5,000
Additional Funds (3 Months)	$30,000	$50,000
Total Initial Investment (Excluding Real Estate)	$131,500	$346,000

On-going Expenses
Franchisees pay ongoing royalty fees equal to 2% of gross sales per month plus a local advertising fee of a minimum of 3% of monthly gross sales, and a national/regional advertising fee of 1% of monthly gross sales, not to exceed 2%.

What You Get—Training and Support
As a new franchisee, you will be trained in all the key areas of the business so that you can kick off your new business with confidence. You'll learn how to work with the product, even if that's not the aspect of the business you plan to be routinely involved in. Our training programs provide both initial and ongoing support in areas such as showroom design, generating sales, operations management, personnel development, accounting procedures, and building referral business. Your installation teams will be certified through our rigorous process so that you can be secure in the quality of the finished work your customers will have in their homes.

Since marketing is the lifeblood of this business, we spend a lot of time, energy and money on developing tools for your local use – magazine and newspaper campaigns, television and radio spots, direct mail and door hangers, home show flyers, even a specialized program of graphics for your vehicles. Building brand recognition in a new city is always a challenge, but this package of materials takes a lot of expensive guesswork out of the process.

Territory
Granite Transformations does not grant exclusive territories.

Great Clips

Great Clips®

7700 France Ave. S., # 425
Minneapolis, MN 55435-5847
Tel: (800) 947-1143 (952) 893-9088
Fax: (952) 844-3443
Email: franchise@greatclips.com
Website: www.greatclipsfranchise.com
Rob Goggins, VP Franchise Development

High-volume haircutting salon, specializing in haircuts for the entire family. What really makes this business concept unique is the fact that it's recession resistant, simple, and has steady growth; you will be hard pressed to find a better business that meets all three. Strong, local support to franchisees, excellent training programs.

BACKGROUND: IFA Member
Established: 1982; First Franchised: 1983
Franchised Units: 2800
Company-Owned Units: 1
Total Units: 2,801
Dist.: US-2,740; CAN-61; O'seas-0
　North America: 42 States, 3 Provinces
　Density: 220 in OH, 174 in IL, 176 in CA
Projected New Units (12 Months): 200
Qualifications: 5, 4, 1, 3, 3, 5

FINANCIAL/TERMS:
Cash Investment: $25K
Total Investment: $109.4-202.5K
Minimum Net Worth: $300K
Fees: Franchise - $20K
　Royalty - 6%; Ad. - 5%
Earnings Claims Statement: Yes
Term of Contract (Years): 10/10
Avg. # of Employees: 3 FT, 5 PT
Passive Ownership: Allowed
Encourage Conversions: No
Area Develop. Agreements: Yes
Sub-Franchising Contracts: No
Expand in Territory: Yes
Space Needs: 900-1,200 SF

SUPPORT & TRAINING:
Financial Assistance Provided: Yes (I)
Site Selection Assistance: Yes
Lease Negotiation Assistance: Yes
Co-operative Advertising: Yes
Franchisee Assoc./Member: Yes/Yes
Size of Corporate Staff: 200
On-going Support: A,B,C,D,E,f,G,H,I
Training: 2.5 weeks local market;
4 days Minneapolis, MN

SPECIFIC EXPANSION PLANS:
US: All US
Canada: Western Canada, Toronto

273

Established in 1982, Great Clips is the largest brand in the $55 billion hair care industry, with approximately 2,800 outlets. Great Clips salons are conveniently located in strip malls in more than 130 markets throughout the U.S. and Canada. No appointments are necessary for men, women and children to get quality haircuts and perms at competitive prices. With an extensive support system, Great Clips will undoubtedly continue to capture significant market share in the value haircut segment of the hair care industry.

Great Clips satisfies a built-in demand that is stable and immune to recessions. Serious franchisees are allowed to purchase multiple units to increase their market penetration—on average, a franchisee owns five to six salons after five years of operation. Great Clips is efficiently run as a cash business with no receivables and little inventory. Salons can be operated by managers and franchisees can maintain their corporate positions while opening multiple units.

Operating Units	12/31/2008	12/31/2009	12/31/2010
Franchised	2,646	2,738	2,794
% Change	--	3.5%	2.0%
Company-Owned	1	0	1
% Change	--	-100.0%	--
Total	2,647	2,738 2,795	
% Change	--	3.4%	2.1%
Franchised as % of Total	99.9%	100.0%	99.9%

Investment Required
The franchise fee for a Great Clips franchise is $20,000.

Great Clips provides the following range of investments required to open your initial franchise. The range assumes that all items are paid for in cash. To the extent that you choose to finance any of these expense items, your front-end investment could be substantially reduced.

Item	Established Low Range	Established High Range
Initial Franchise Fee	$20,000	$20,000
Initial Advertising Contribution to the Market Development Ad Fund	$5,000	$5,000
Expenses While Training (per person)	$1,500	$2,500
Architecture Fees	$500	$3,000
Leasehold Improvements	$20,000	$50,000
Rent and Security Deposits	$1,000	$8,000
Fixtures, Signage and Furnishings	$30,000	$40,000
Freight	$1,200	$2,200
Sales Tax on Fixtures, Signage and Furnishings	$0	$1,500
Opening Inventory and Supplies	$4,700	$6,400
Grand Opening Advertising	$10,000	$12,000
Insurance	$1,500	$2,400
Lease Liability Fee	$0	$3,000
Lease Review Fee	$850	$2,000
Additional Funds (6 - 12 Months)	$12,000	$45,000
Total Initial Investment	$108,250	$203,000

On-going Expenses

Great Clips franchisees pay continuing franchise fees equal to 6% of gross sales plus continuing advertising contributions to the North American

Advertising Fund equal to 5% of gross sales.

What You Get—Training and Support

Great Clips provides comprehensive training to the franchisee, salon manger and stylists. Franchisees and managers (recommended) receive the New Franchisee Orientation and Training both online and in-person. The classroom training is two days long and is held at the training site in Minneapolis, MN. The program covers topics on establishing and operating a Great Clips Salon. Marketing training and ongoing support are offered at area training centers, through email and online courses. Professional Stylist Training and employee training are also given at area training centers, reducing costs. Great Clips focuses on recruitment and provides a range of custom recruiting tools to gain quality staff.

In addition to constantly updated operating manuals, forms, brochures, tools and handbooks that assist in everyday operations, Great Clips provides an informative newsletter for franchisees, management staff and stylists. Annual meetings, conventions and leadership conferences provide further educational opportunities and allow for the exchange of news and ideas. Great Clips promotes the Great Clips brand in print, radio and television. Great Clips devotes itself to consumers' needs, and assists franchisees in maintaining local public relations, community relations and marketing and advertising efforts.

Territory

Great Clips grants protected areas with a radius ranging from 0.1 to 0.75 of a mile depending on population density and geographical areas.

Griswold Home Care

Griswold
HOME CARE
Exceptional Service for Over 30 Years

717 Bethlehem Pk., # 300
Erdenheim, PA 19038
Tel: (215) 402-0200 x116
Fax: (215) 402-0202
Email: joe@griswoldhomecare.com
Website: www.griswoldhomecare.com
Joe Ross, Franchise Development

Griswold Home Care is dedicated to providing extraordinary home care at affordable rates. We refer caregivers for older adults, people recovering from illness or surgery, and people with long-term disabilities. Caregiver services include personal care, homemaking, companionship, incidental transportation and other services to clients wishing to remain safe and independent. We operate a model that is completely unique in the industry. We also offer the largest protected territories and lowest on-going fees.

BACKGROUND: IFA Member
Established: 1982; First Franchised: 1984
Franchised Units: 153
Company-Owned Units: 11
Total Units: 164
Dist.: US-164; CAN-0; O'seas-0
North America: 26 States
Density: 17 in NJ, 10 in OH, 20 in PA
Projected New Units (12 Months): NR

Qualifications:	5, 4, 2, 3, 4, 5
FINANCIAL/TERMS:	
Cash Investment:	$33-60K
Total Investment:	$75-95K
Minimum Net Worth:	$250K
Fees: Franchise -	$39.5K
Royalty - 3-5%; Ad. - $200 gross billings mo*NTE	
Earnings Claims Statement:	Yes
Term of Contract (Years):	10/5
Avg. # of Employees:	3-5 (in office) FT, PT
Passive Ownership:	Allowed
Encourage Conversions:	No
Area Develop. Agreements:	No
Sub-Franchising Contracts:	No
Expand in Territory:	Yes
Space Needs:	Minimum 150 SF
SUPPORT & TRAINING:	
Financial Assistance Provided:	No
Site Selection Assistance:	Yes
Lease Negotiation Assistance:	NA
Co-operative Advertising:	Yes
Franchisee Assoc./Member:	No
Size of Corporate Staff:	23
On-going Support:	NA,NA,C,D,NA,NA,G,H,I
Training:	7 days corporate office;
	1-2 days franchisee's location;
SPECIFIC EXPANSION PLANS:	
US:	45 offices
Canada:	NA
Overseas:	No

Experience the benefits of business ownership for you and your family while making a difference in your community. Griswold Home Care is dedicated to providing "Extraordinary Home Care at Affordable Rates". We refer Caregivers for older adults, people recovering from illness or surgery, and people with long-term disabilities. Caregiver services include personal care, homemaking, companionship, incidental transportation and other services to Clients wishing to remain safe and independent. Griswold Home Care strives to achieve this balance of superior quality and affordability,

277

and the company is recognized as the world's oldest, non-medical home care company. Our winning business model cuts overhead costs, allowing franchisees to:

1. Keep rates low to attract more clients.
2. Insure highest industry wages to attract the best caregivers.

Operating Units	12/31/2008	12/31/2009	12/31/2010
Franchised	87	102	114
% Change	--	17.2%	11.8%
Company-Owned	14	9	11
% Change	--	-35.7%	22.2%
Total	101	111	125
% Change	--	9.9%	12.6%
Franchised as % of Total	86.1%	91.9%	91.2%

Investment Required

The fee for a Griswold Home Care franchise is $39,500, and larger territories can be purchased for a higher fee.

Griswold Home Care provides the following range of investments required to open your initial franchise. The range assumes that all items are paid for in cash. To the extent that you choose to finance any of these expense items, your front-end investment could be substantially reduced.

Item	Established Low Range	Established High Range
Initial Franchise Fee	$39,500	$39,500
Expenses While Training	$1,000	$2,500
Local Lift-Off Program	$7,500	$7,500
Office Lease	$0	$5,000
Office Equipment	$2,000	$3,500
*accela*care Usage Fee	$1,200	$1,200

Signage	$0	$1,000
Opening Office Supplies and Inventory	$0	$1,000
Insurance	$1,125	$1,800
Printed Materials and Shipping	$0	$300
License, permit registration or certificate costs	$0	$2,000
Additional Funds (6 - 18 Months)	$20,000	$30,000
Total Initial Investment	$72,325	$95,600
Lease Review Fee	$850	$2,000
Additional Funds (6 - 12 Months)	$12,000	$45,000
Total Initial Investment	$108,250	$203,000

On-going Expenses

Griswold Home Care has the lowest royalty fees in the industry (effective range of 3.5%+/-) and general marketing fund contributions of 0.5%.

What You Get—Training and Support

Griswold Home Care provides training that is unparalleled in the industry: three weeks of pre-training preparation, seven full days at our Homecare Academy in suburban Philadelphia, PA, eight-week post training Quick-Start program, annual conference, regional conferences, ongoing webinars and workshops, and more. We operate company units, so we really understand the business.

Territory

Griswold Home Care has choice territories available nationwide, protected territory of up to 300,000 people, ability to increase to 400,000, and multi-unit opportunities.

The Growth Coach

THE
GROWTH
COACH®

Driving Success. Balancing Life.™

10700 Montgomery Rd., # 300
Cincinnati, OH 45242
Tel: (888) 292-7992 (513) 563-0570
Fax: (513) 563-2691
Email: webinquiry@thegrowthcoach.com
Website: www.thegrowthcoach.com
Kristen Brown, Franchise Development

The Growth Coach, ranked in the "Top 10 New Franchises" by Entrepreneur Magazine, is the leader in business coaching. Small business owners and self-employed professionals will invest in themselves to achieve success. Our coaches utilize a proven coaching process to help their clients transform their businesses and balance their lives.

BACKGROUND: IFA Member
Established: 2002; First Franchised: 2002
Franchised Units: 136
Company-Owned Units: 0
Total Units: 136
Dist.: US-126; CAN-8; O'seas-0
  North America: 40 States, 2 Provinces
  Density: 11 in TX, 15 in OH, 12 in FL
Projected New Units (12 Months): 60

Qualifications: 3, 3, 1, 3, 3, 4

FINANCIAL/TERMS:
Cash Investment: $7-36.9K
Total Investment: $47.2-76.4K
Minimum Net Worth: $22.9K
Fees: Franchise - $36.9K
  Royalty - Varied based on annual resources;
  Ad. - $ 200/Mo.
Earnings Claims Statement: No
Term of Contract (Years): 10/10/10
Avg. # of Employees: 1 FT, 0 PT
Passive Ownership: Not Allowed
Encourage Conversions: Yes
Area Develop. Agreements: Yes
Sub-Franchising Contracts: No
Expand in Territory: Yes
Space Needs: NR

SUPPORT & TRAINING:
Financial Assistance Provided: Yes (D)
Site Selection Assistance: NA
Lease Negotiation Assistance: NA
Co-operative Advertising: No
Franchisee Assoc./Member: No
Size of Corporate Staff: 50
On-going Support: NA,NA,C,D,E,NA,G,H,I
Training: 5 Business days Cincinnati, OH

SPECIFIC EXPANSION PLANS:
US: All US
Canada: All Canada
Overseas: All Countries

The Growth Coach is a leading provider of business coaching in North America, serving small business owners, franchisees, self-employed professionals, high-end sales and financial services professionals and managers from businesses of all sizes. The company's goal is to help clients gain greater focus and leverage so they can work less, earn more and enjoy richer, more fulfilling lives. All Growth Coach client solutions are driven by a unique, strategy-focused process—a proven, systematic and structured method for clients to think, plan, monitor and achieve greater results in their businesses and lives. In the end, clients have greater clarity about where they want to go, possess a strategic and focused plan to get there, and receive ongoing accountability to make critical adjustments to stay on track.

The Growth Coach has been recognized by countless national publications, including Entrepreneur magazine, which named it as one of the "Top 50 Rising Stars" and "Top Home-Based Franchises" in 2009. The Growth Coach is a great opportunity to become a part of the booming business-coaching industry.

Operating Units	12/31/2008	12/31/2009	12/31/2010
Franchised	137	140	133
% Change	--	2.2%	-5.0%
Company-Owned	0	0	0
% Change	--	--	--
Total	137	140	133
% Change	--	2.2%	-5.0%
Franchised as % of Total	100.0%	100.0%	100.0%

Investment Required

The initial fee for a Growth Coach franchise ranges from $39,900 to $45,900 depending on financing and territory size.

Growth Coach provides the following range of investments required to open your initial franchise. The range assumes that all items are paid for in cash. To the extent that you choose to finance any of these expense items, your front-end investment could be substantially reduced.

Item	Established Low Range	Established High Range
Initial Franchise Fee	$39,900	$45,900
Furniture and Equipment	$500	$1,000

Computer System	$1,000	$3,000
Expenses While Training	$750	$1,500
Initial Rent, Telephone, Bank, Licensing Fees and Other Deposits	$350	$2,000
Grand-Opening Promotion	$1,000	$4,500
Lead Generation Program	$3,000	$3,000
Insurance	$500	$2,000
Monthly Office Rental Payment	$0	$1,000
Additional Funds (3 Months)	$5,000	$18,000
Total Initial Investment	$52,000	$81,900

On-going Expenses

The Growth Coach franchisees pay flat-fee royalties based on monthly gross revenues with a minimum of $500 per month. Other fees include a national branding fee of $250 per month and a local advertising contribution equal to 3% of gross revenues.

What You Get—Training and Support

A five-day initial training program is provided for up to two employees at corporate headquarters in Cincinnati, OH. Training covers the areas of database management, the Growth Coach business model, coaching strategies, sales, financial management and marketing.

Additionally, The Growth Coach maintains a website, provides assistance with finding suppliers, and offers ongoing assistance with marketing and promotional materials. The Growth Coach also holds national franchise meetings to discuss sales techniques and proven strategies as well as introduce new management tools and marketing programs.

Territory
The Growth Coach grants protected territories.

The HomeTeam Inspection Service

HomeTeam
INSPECTION SERVICE
SM

575 Chamber Dr.
Milford, OH 45150
Tel: (800) 598-5297 (513) 831-1300
Fax: (513) 831-6010
Email: salesleads@hometeaminspection.com
Website: www.hometeaminspection.com
Dennis Malik, Franchise Development

The opportunities to succeed with the HomeTeam franchise are better today then ever before. When buying a home, it has become standard practice to have a home inspection before the sale closes. You've definitely found the right franchise category and in HomeTeam, you've found the right franchise partner. Why are we so confident about that? As with all successful businesses, the key is in the business model.If you have a superior business model, you'll realize success. Invest in a so-so business model, and no matter how hard you work, you'll struggle. The team approach to Inspections is unique in the industry and will enable you to immediately differentiate yourself from the competition and carve your niche out of the home inspection marketplace. But it doesn't stop there; clients and real estate professionals alike also appreciate our timely, narrative reports and our unique approach to the walk through.

BACKGROUND: IFA Member
Established: 1991; First Franchised: 1992
Franchised Units: 201
Company-Owned Units: 0
Total Units: 201

Dist.:	US-193; CAN-8; O'seas-0
North America:	48 States, 2 Provinces
Density:	16 in TX, 32 in FL, 16 in CA
Projected New Units (12 Months):	5
Qualifications:	5, 4, 1, 2, 4, 5

FINANCIAL/TERMS:
Cash Investment:	$35K+
Total Investment:	$40-80K
Minimum Net Worth:	NA
Fees: Franchise -	$27.9-39.8K
Royalty - 6%;	Ad. - 3%
Earnings Claims Statement:	No
Term of Contract (Years):	10/10/10
Avg. # of Employees:	1 FT, 1 PT
Passive Ownership:	Allowed, But Discouraged
Encourage Conversions:	NA
Area Develop. Agreements:	No
Sub-Franchising Contracts:	No
Expand in Territory:	Yes
Space Needs:	NR

SUPPORT & TRAINING:
Financial Assistance Provided:	No
Site Selection Assistance:	NA
Lease Negotiation Assistance:	NA
Co-operative Advertising:	No
Franchisee Assoc./Member:	Yes/Yes
Size of Corporate Staff:	20
On-going Support:	A,B,C,D,NA,NA,G,H,I
Training:	2 weeks corporate headquarters, Cincinnati, OH

SPECIFIC EXPANSION PLANS:
US:	All US
Canada:	All Canada
Overseas:	No

When buying a home, it has become standard practice to have a home inspection before the sale closes. In fact, the number of real estate home inspections performed each year is on the rise; almost 90 percent of all homes sold are inspected. Also, many mortgage companies now require a home inspection as a financing requirement.

HomeTeam home inspection franchise has set the standard of professionalism in the industry. Throughout the growth of the HomeTeam franchise network, its primary focus has remained the same: to offer top-quality home inspections, while running an effective and efficient operation to help control costs. This high-value, low-cost combination is the bedrock of HomeTeam's operating philosophy.

Operating Units	12/31/2008	12/31/2009	12/31/2010
Franchised	220	195	182
% Change	--	-11.4%	-6.7%
Company-Owned	0	0	0
% Change	--	--	--
Total	220	195	182
% Change	--	-11.4%	-6.7%
Franchised as % of Total	100.0%	100.0%	100.0%

Investment Required
The initial fee for a HomeTeam franchise is $9,800, plus a territory fee that ranges from $12,000 to $30,000.

HomeTeam Home Inspection provides the following range of investments required to open your initial franchise. The range assumes that all items are paid for in cash. To the extent that you choose to finance any of these expense items, your front-end investment could be substantially reduced.

Item	Established Low Range	Established High Range
Initial Franchise Fee	$9,800	$9,800
Territory Fee	$12,000	$30,000
Start-Up Package Fee	$9,200	$9,200
Vehicle	$1,000	$4,000
Furniture and Equipment	$500	$1,000
Telephone, Bank and Other Deposits	$500	$1,000
Expenses While Training	$1,000	$2,000
Insurance	$1,800	$4,000
Permits, Licenses & Professional Memberships	$500	$2,000
Additional Funds (3 Months)	$3,000	$7,500
Total Initial Investment	$39,300	$70,500

On-going Expenses

HomeTeam franchisees pay ongoing royalty fees equal to 6% of gross sales, plus an annual minimum royalty equal to 6% of gross sales. Additional fees payable by franchisees include an advertising contribution equal to 3% and a local advertising fee equal to $2,500 for half of the calendar year and then 4% of gross sales.

What You Get—Training and Support

HomeTeam franchisees undergo a comprehensive two-week training course, where certified instructors teach successful home inspection operations and business practices. In addition to extensive classroom training, franchisees gain actual hands-on experience. During training, franchisees perform home inspections, first as observers, then as home inspectors. HomeTeam also gives instruction that covers entire marketing system, including how to make compelling presentations to referral sources in addition to powerful programs designed for the real estate professional and homebuyer.

HomeTeam franchisees also learn the ins and outs of the TeamWorks© proprietary computer and pocket PC software used during the home inspection to aid in gathering information used in completing professional home inspection reports. Ongoing regional and international meetings help franchisees stay on top of their inspection business. These meetings allow great networking opportunities with other HomeTeam Inspection Service franchise owners.

Territory
HomeTeam grants exclusive territories.

Huntington Learning Center

496 Kinderkamack Rd.
Oradell, NJ 07649-1512
Tel: (800) 653-8400 (201) 261-8400
Fax: (800) 361-9728
Email: franchise@hlcmail.com
Website: www.huntingtonfranchise.com
Eric O'Connor, VP Franchise Sales

Offers tutoring to 5-19-year-olds in reading, writing, language development study skills and mathematics, as well as programs to prepare for standardized entrance exams. Instruction is offered in a tutorial setting and is predominately remedial in nature.

BACKGROUND:

	IFA Member
Established: 1977;	First Franchised: 1985
Franchised Units:	249
Company-Owned Units:	30
Total Units:	279
Dist.:	US-383; CAN-0; O'seas-0
North America:	41 States
Density:	30 in CA, 26 in FL, 26 in NY
Projected New Units (12 Months):	60
Qualifications:	5, 3, 1, 3, 1, 5

FINANCIAL/TERMS:

Cash Investment:	$60K
Total Investment:	$162-258K
Minimum Net Worth:	$250K
Fees: Franchise -	$24K
Royalty - 9%/$1.8K Min.;	Ad. - 2%/$500 Min
Earnings Claims Statement:	Yes
Term of Contract (Years):	10/10
Avg. # of Employees:	2-4 FT, 12-20 PT

Passive Ownership:	Not Allowed	Lease Negotiation Assistance:	Yes
Encourage Conversions:	Yes	Co-operative Advertising:	Yes
Area Develop. Agreements:	Yes	Franchisee Assoc./Member:	No
Sub-Franchising Contracts:	No	Size of Corporate Staff:	100
Expand in Territory:	No	On-going Support:	NA,NA,C,D,E,F,G,h,I
Space Needs:	1,200-1,400 SF	Training:	On-going regional; 1 week Oradell, NJ (corporate headquarters); 2 weeks online
SUPPORT & TRAINING:			
Financial Assistance Provided:	Yes (I)	**SPECIFIC EXPANSION PLANS:**	
Site Selection Assistance:	Yes	US:	Contiguous US

With nearly 300 centers nationwide, Huntington Learning Center is the premier leader in the $6 billion parent-pay tutoring industry. Through its commitment to empowering children with a lasting education, Huntington has garnered an established reputation for excellence. Huntington offers an innovative, individualized approach to learning; providing K-12 tutoring in reading, writing, math, phonics, spelling, study skills and test preparation (i.e. SAT and ACT). Huntington builds a personalized learning program for each child, working one-on-one with skilled teachers, based on individual strengths and personal pace and needs as determined by a comprehensive diagnostic evaluation.

Huntington Learning Center offers franchisees the chance to fulfill their aspirations of becoming successful business owners and to make a positive difference in the lives of thousands of children. With its 30 years of experience, an established reputation for excellence, and a proven business model, Huntington dominates the tutoring industry within the exploding education market, representing a timely and tremendous business opportunity. Advice from Huntington is available to franchisees 24/7 to ensure the highest level of franchisee success.

Operating Units	12/31/2008	12/31/2009	12/31/2010
Franchised	336	293	251
% Change	--	-12.8%	-14.3%
Company-Owned	36	33	32
% Change	--	-8.3%	-3.0%

Total	372	326	283
% Change	--	-12.4%	-13.2%
Franchised as % of Total	90.3%	89.9%	88.7%

Investment Required

The initial franchise fee for a Huntington Learning Center franchise is $24,000 for a standard franchise and $43,000 for an expanded franchise.

Huntington Learning Center provides the following range of investments required to open your initial franchise. The range assumes that all items are paid for in cash. To the extent that you choose to finance any of these expense items, your front-end investment could be substantially reduced.

Item	Established Low Range	Established High Range
Initial Franchise Fee	$24,000	$24,000
Development Fee	$0	$0
Turn Key Management Fee	$0	$17,200
Expenses While Training	$200	$2,000
Curricula	$29,600	$29,600
Furniture, Computers, Equipment	$27,200	$27,200
Start-up Supplies	$8,700	$8,700
Opening Advertising	$10,000	$10,000
Software License Fee	$14,000	$14,000
Software Maintenance Fee	$0	$4,250
Phone Number License Fee	$500	$500
Call Center Set-up Fee	$500	$500

Conference Center Set-up Fee	$500	$500
Architect Design	$2,000	$4,000
Security and Utility Deposits; License Fees	$2,000	$5,000
Real Estate & Improvements	$12,000	$100,700
Signage	$2,800	$2,800
Center Graphics	$1,500	$1,500
Professional Fees	$900	$3,500
Insurance	$400	$4,300
Additional Funds (3 Months)	$25,000	$35,000
Total Initial Investment	$161,800	$295,250

On-going Expenses

Huntington Learning Center franchisees pay a monthly royalty fee equal to the greater of 9% of gross revenue or $1,800 for a standard franchise, and the greater of 8% of gross revenue or $1,600 for an expanded franchise. Franchisees also pay a monthly advertising fee equal to the greater of 2% of gross revenue or $400, and an annual local advertising investment equal to a minimum of $57,000. Franchisees may also be subject to a cooperative advertising fee of approximately $2,000 to $3,000 per month as determined by the Advertising Cooperative Association. Other expenses include annual software support and maintenance fees, white and yellow pages fees, a phone number monthly access fee, call center licensing fees and conference services licensing fees.

What You Get—Training and Support

Huntington Learning Center devotes itself to the success of its franchisees, and as such, franchisees receive considerable ongoing training and support throughout the franchise relationship. Prior to opening, Huntington provides franchisees design specifications for the prototypical Huntington Learning

Center layout as well as a list of required products and services. Franchisees attend a 12-day initial training program at corporate headquarters in Oradell, NJ that consists of 80 hours of classroom instruction, 40 hours of on-site training and 15 hours of online courses. The training program covers topics such as school marketing, business planning, center operation and analysis, diagnostic testing, exam preparation, hiring staff, initial teacher training, software, facilities and procedures. After opening, franchisees participate in ongoing occasional trainings, meetings, workshops and an annual convention.

Territory
Huntington Learning Center grants exclusive territories.

i9 Sports

1723 S. Kings Ave.
Brandon, FL 33511
Tel: (800) 975-2937 (813) 662-6773
Fax: (813) 662-9114
Email: sales@i9sportsfranchise.com
Website: www.i9sportsfranchise.com
Kevin Brandt, Franchise Development Manager

i9 Sports is the world's first complete amateur sports franchise for the 42 million youth athletes nationwide. i9 Sports offers franchise opportunities for people to own and operate local amateur sports leagues, tournaments, camps, clinics, special events and child development programs for kids of all ages. i9 Sports provides a low-investment, low-overhead, fully-computerized business that you can run from home. Turn your love of amateur sports into a rewarding home-based business.

BACKGROUND:	IFA Member
Established: 1995;	First Franchised: 2003
Franchised Units:	140
Company-Owned Units:	2
Total Units:	142
Dist.:	US-142; CAN-0; O'seas-0
North America:	30 States
Density:	10 in NY, 16 in FL, 9 in CA
Projected New Units (12 Months):	50
Qualifications:	4, 4, 4, 4, 4, 4

FINANCIAL/TERMS:	
Cash Investment:	$40-80K
Total Investment:	$44.9-69.9K
Minimum Net Worth:	$100K

Fees: Franchise -	$28.4-39.9K	Site Selection Assistance:	Yes
Royalty - 7.5%;	Ad. - 1%	Lease Negotiation Assistance:	NA
Earnings Claims Statement:	Yes	Co-operative Advertising:	Yes
Term of Contract (Years):	10/10	Franchisee Assoc./Member:	Yes/Yes
Avg. # of Employees:	0-1 FT, 0-1 PT	Size of Corporate Staff:	10
Passive Ownership:	Not Allowed	On-going Support:	A,B,C,D,E,F,G,H,I
Encourage Conversions:	No	Training:	2 days Territory field visit;
Area Develop. Agreements:	Yes		5 days Tampa, FL
Sub-Franchising Contracts:	No		
Expand in Territory:	Yes	**SPECIFIC EXPANSION PLANS:**	
Space Needs:	NR	US:	All US
		Canada:	All Canada
		Overseas:	No
SUPPORT & TRAINING:			
Financial Assistance Provided:	Yes (I)		

In 2003 i9 Sports became the first franchise company to specialize in both youth sports leagues and camps. Since that time, i9 Sports has grown to over 130 franchise locations servicing 400,000 members nationwide and is on track to open its 200th location in the United States by the end of 2012. i9 Sports offers franchise opportunities for people to own and operate local amateur sports leagues, tournaments, camps, clinics, special events and child development programs for kids of all ages. i9 Sports provides a low-investment, low-overhead, fully-computerized business that franchisees can run from home.

i9 Sports has received numerous awards for industry leadership, rapid growth, and overall excellence in supporting its franchise owners from Fox Business News, CNN, HBO Real Sports, ESPN Radio, and The Wall Street Journal. Most recently, i9 Sports Corporation was named the #1 Child Fitness Franchise in 2011 by Entrepreneur magazine.

Operating Units	12/31/2008	12/31/2009	12/31/2010
Franchised	109	126	124
% Change	--	15.6%	-1.6%
Company-Owned	0	2	2
% Change	--	--	0.0%
Regional Directors	4	2	1

Total	113	130	127
% Change	--	15.0%	-2.3%
Franchised as % of Total	96.5%	96.9%	97.6%

Investment Required

The fee for an i9 Sports franchise is $19,900.

i9 Sports provides the following range of investments required to open your initial franchise. The range assumes that all items are paid for in cash. To the extent that you choose to finance any of these expense items, your front-end investment could be substantially reduced.

Item	Established Low Range	Established High Range
Initial Franchise Fee	$19,900	$19,900
Territory Fee	$5,000	$20,000
Grand Opening Advertising	$5,000	$10,000
Insurance	$1,000	$1,500
Legal & Accounting Services	$800	$1,500
Furniture, Equipment, Inventory, and Supplies	$2,000	$3,000
Expenses While Training	$1,200	$2,000
Additional Funds (3 Months)	$10,000	$15,000
Total Initial Investment	$44,900	$72,900

On-going Expenses

i9 Sports franchisees pay a royalty fee of 7.5% of network revenues or a minimum of $375 to $450 depending on territory level and a local advertising fee of up to 2% of network revenues. Other fees include a customer service center fee of 2.5% or a minimum of $375 to $450 depending on the territory level, and a national brand fund contribution of $275 per month.

What You Get—Training and Support
i9 Sports holds a five-day training session for franchisees in i9 headquarters in Tampa, FL. A free custom website complete with Search Engine Optimization (SEO) and ad campaigns with Google and Yahoo is launched quickly and easily during this training session, and some franchise owners have customer registrations before leaving training.

In addition to providing a website, i9 Sports provides a customer calling center, both for parents calling to register their kids, or for a franchisee calling with any questions. Ongoing support is provided by an assigned franchise business coach and team of marketing, purchasing, finance, and IT professionals. Their support includes monthly huddle calls, continuous training, and regional/national conferences on the latest trends and new ways to grow a business.

Territory
i9 Sports grants exclusive territories.

The Interface Financial Group

THE
INTERFACE
FINANCIAL
GROUP

7910 Woodmont Avenue Suite 1430
Bethesda, MD 20814
Tel: (800) 387-0860 (905) 475-5701
Fax: (866) 475-8688
Email: ifg@interfacefinancial.com
Website: www.interfacefinancial.com
Marvin Franklin, President

Franchise buys quality accounts receivables from client companies at a discount to provide short-term working capital to expanding businesses.	Avg. # of Employees: NR
	Passive Ownership: Not Allowed
	Encourage Conversions: NA
	Area Develop. Agreements: No
BACKGROUND: IFA Member	Sub-Franchising Contracts: No
Established: 1972; First Franchised: 1990	Expand in Territory: Yes
Franchised Units: 192	Space Needs: NA
Company-Owned Units: 0	
Total Units: 192	**SUPPORT & TRAINING:**
Dist.: US-137; CAN-16; O'seas-39	Financial Assistance Provided: No
North America: 34 States, 6 Provinces	Site Selection Assistance: NA
Density: 26 in TX, 7 in BC	Lease Negotiation Assistance: NA
Projected New Units (12 Months): 24	Co-operative Advertising: No
Qualifications: 1, 5, 2, 3, 1, 1	Franchisee Assoc./Member: Yes/Yes
	Size of Corporate Staff: 13
FINANCIAL/TERMS:	On-going Support: NA,NA,NA,D,NA,NA,G,NA,NA
Cash Investment: $100K+	Training: 6 days total (2 days on-site)
Total Investment: $88.3-139.3K	
Minimum Net Worth: $150K	**SPECIFIC EXPANSION PLANS:**
Fees: Franchise - $39K	US: All US
Royalty - 8%; Ad. - NR	Canada: All Canada
Earnings Claims Statement: No	Overseas: All Countries
Term of Contract (Years): 10/5	

Founded in 1972, The Interface Financial Group enjoyed almost immediate success and began offering franchises in 1990 to meet the growing demand for Interface's unique invoice discounting system. Interface now has over 150 franchised offices throughout the United States, Canada, Australia, New Zealand, Singapore, the United Kingdom and the Republic of Ireland.

Our international headquarters are located in Markham, Ontario, and our United States headquarters are located in Bethesda, Maryland. Entrepreneur Magazine, the recognized leader for franchise information, reviews and analyzes the 5000+ North American franchises on an annual basis, and then rates the Top 500 by category. For the past 7 years Interface has been in the Franchise 500 ranking. In 2010 Interface was in the Top 101 Homebased franchises ranking. Interface is also a World Class Franchise as classified by the Franchise Research Institute.

Operating Units	12/31/2008	12/31/2009	12/31/2010
Franchised	129	137	137

% Change	--	6.2%	0%
Company-Owned	0	0	0
% Change	--	--	--
Total	129	137	137
% Change	--	6.2%	0%
Franchised as % of Total	100%	100%	100%

Investment Required
The initial franchise fee for an Interface Financial franchise is $39,000.

Interface Financial provides the following range of investments required to open your initial franchise. The range assumes that all items are paid for in cash. To the extent that you choose to finance any of these expense items, your front-end investment could be substantially reduced.

Item	Established Low Range	Established High Range
Franchise Fee	$39,000	$39,000
Living and Travel Expenses for Training	$500	$1,000
Equipment	$800	$13,000
Initial Promotion	$1,000	$1,000
Additional Funds (3 months)	$50,000	$100,000
Total Investment	$91,300	$142,300

On-going Expenses
Interface Financial franchisees pay a royalty fee equal to 8% of gross profits.

Other on-going fees include a monthly maintenance fee, a training fee for transferees, and audits.

Franchisee Satisfaction
A critical component of the due diligence process is that you, as a prospective franchisee, have a strong sense of existing franchisee satisfaction. Please review the franchisor's ratings below for this extremely important information.

**World-Class
Franchise®**

How do you rate Interface Financial in terms of:	Rating*
Overall quality of franchisor	100%
Initial training supplied by franchisor	100%
Quality of products and/or services received from franchisor	100%
Long term growth potential for franchise	98%

* Independent Audit of Existing Franchisees Who Rated Interface Financial as Excellent, Very Good, or Good

What You Get—Training and Support
Interface Financial will loan a copy of the operating manual, and provide up to six days of training. Other key advantages include:

- No staff to hire, fire, or manage
- No storefront to own, lease, or maintain
- No Inventory or stock to purchase
- No extensive travel because IFG franchisees do business locally

- Business-to-Business, professional environment with regular business hours of operations
- Flexibility to relocate for part of the year or permanently and continue doing business

Territory
Interface Financial does not grant exclusive territories.

Jani-King International

16885 Dallas Pkwy.
Addison, TX 75001-5215
Tel: (800) 552-5264 (972) 991-0900
Fax: (972) 239-7706
Email: tlooney@janiking.com
Website: www.janiking.com
Ted Looney, Vice President

Jani-King International is the world's largest commercial cleaning franchisor, with locations in 19 countries and over 125 regions in the US and abroad. Our franchise opportunity includes initial customer contracts, training, continuous local support, admin-istrative and accounting assistance, an equipment leasing program, and national advertising. If you are searching for a flexible business opportunity, look no further.

BACKGROUND:	IFA Member
Established: 1969;	First Franchised: 1974
Franchised Units:	13,000
Company-Owned Units:	22
Total Units:	13,022
Dist.:	US-12,153; CAN-351; O'seas-528
North America:	39 States, 7 Provinces
Density:	880 in TX, 307 in FL, 737 in CA
Projected New Units (12 Months):	1,000
Qualifications:	2, 2, 1, 2, 2, 3

FINANCIAL/TERMS:	
Cash Investment:	$2.9-33K
Total Investment:	$8-74K
Minimum Net Worth:	$2.9-33K

297

Fees: Franchise -	$8-33K	Site Selection Assistance:	NA
Royalty - 10%;	Ad. - 1%	Lease Negotiation Assistance:	NA
Earnings Claims Statement:	No	Co-operative Advertising:	No
Term of Contract (Years):	20/20	Franchisee Assoc./Member:	Yes/Yes
Avg. # of Employees:	FT, 0 PT	Size of Corporate Staff:	65
Passive Ownership:	Allowed	On-going Support:	A,B,C,D,NA,NA,G,H,I
Encourage Conversions:	NA	Training:	2 weeks local regional office
Area Develop. Agreements:	Yes		
Sub-Franchising Contracts:	Yes	**SPECIFIC EXPANSION PLANS:**	
Expand in Territory:	Yes	US:	All US
Space Needs:	NA	Canada:	All Canada
		Overseas:	All Countries
SUPPORT & TRAINING:			
Financial Assistance Provided:	No		

Jani-King is one of the world's leading commercial cleaning franchise companies with more than 12,000 authorized franchise owners worldwide. Through a network of more than 115 regional offices, Jani-King contracts commercial cleaning services, while the work is performed by franchisees who own and operate their own business. Since 1974, Jani-King has been a leader in franchising. Entrepreneur magazine recognizes Jani-King as one of the Top 10 Franchise companies, ranking it as the #3 Commercial Cleaning Franchise for 2010 and the #2 Low-Cost Franchise for 2010.

Jani-King's top rankings are a direct reflection of the opportunity and support provided by Jani-King International and Jani-King regional offices around the world. A Jani-King franchise offers aspiring new business owners the chance to begin their business with an initial client base to service, and a well-organized support system that helps new franchisees achieve a desired level of success.

Operating Units	12/31/2008	12/31/2009	12/31/2010
Franchised	9,713	9,377	9,224
% Change	--	-3.5%	-1.6%
Company-Owned	21	21	21
% Change	--	0.0%	0.0%
Total	9,734	9,398	9,245

% Change	--	-3.5%	-1.6%
Franchised as % of Total	99.8%	99.8%	99.8%

Investment Required

The fee for a Jani-King franchise ranges from $16,250 to $142,750, including an initial finder's fee. The fee may be higher depending on the plan chosen.

Jani-King provides the following range of investments required to open your initial franchise. The range assumes that all items are paid for in cash. To the extent that you choose to finance any of these expense items, your front-end investment could be substantially reduced.

Item	Established Low Range	Established High Range
Initial Franchise Fee	$16,250	$142,750
Real Estate	$0	$5,000
Supplies	$600	$800
Equipment	$1,819	$5,181
Security Deposits	$100	$1,000
Business Entity Establishment Fees	$100	$1,000
Additional Funds (3 Months)	$800	$8,500
Total Initial Investment	$19,669	$164,231

On-going Expenses

Jani-King franchisees pay royalty fees equal to 10% of monthly gross revenue (subject to monthly minimums), an accounting fee equal to 5% of monthly gross revenue and an advertising fee equal to 1% of monthly gross revenues.

What You Get—Training and Support

Jani-King offers a level of training, business development and administrative support that is unparalleled in the cleaning industry. Jani-King's local regional offices provide franchisees with initial training in the operation of a franchise business. The program provides training in Jani-King's methods and practices of professional cleaning services, management and industry-specific training. Training also includes classroom lectures and discussions, actual demonstrations, printed manuals, video presentations, formal instruction and practical hands-on training. Home study materials, additional training seminars and refresher courses are available to help keep franchisees informed of the latest trends and technology in the industry.

Jani-King supports franchisees on an ongoing basis by providing advice, business development support and technical support through its regional offices. Each office has a marketing staff whose goal is to provide new business to Jani-King franchisees and ensure the satisfaction of clients. The regional offices also provide franchisees with complete customer invoicing and other administrative support. Local operations teams are available 24 hours a day and perform routine inspections of each account. Jani-King franchisees have a vested interest in the work they perform because satisfaction is what drives their business.

Territory
Jani-King does not grant exclusive territories.

Jan-Pro Cleaning Systems

Measurable Cleaning. Guaranteed Results.®

2520 Northwinds Pkwy., # 375
Alpharetta, GA 30009
Tel: (866) 355-1064 (678) 336-1780
Fax: (678) 336-1782
Email: brad.smith@jan-pro.com
Website: www.jan-pro.com
Bradford M. Smith, VP of Franchise Licensing

Jan-Pro provides one of today's exceptional business opportunities, allowing you to enter one of the fastest-growing industries by safely becoming your own boss through the guidance and support of an established franchise organization.

BACKGROUND:

	IFA Member
Established: 1991;	First Franchised: 1992
Franchised Units:	10,090
Company-Owned Units:	2
Total Units:	10,092
Dist.:	US-9,235; CAN-793; O'seas-64
North America:	39 States, 2 Provinces
Density:	858 in GA, 695 in FL, 1,316 in CA
Projected New Units (12 Months):	12 masters and over 2,000 units
Qualifications:	3, 2, 1, 1, 1, 1

FINANCIAL/TERMS:

Cash Investment:	$1-30K
Total Investment:	$125-1500K
Minimum Net Worth:	$50K
Fees: Franchise -	$1-30K
Royalty - 10%;	Ad. - 0%

Earnings Claims Statement:	No
Term of Contract (Years):	5/5
Avg. # of Employees:	0 FT, 0 PT
Passive Ownership:	Allowed, But Discouraged
Encourage Conversions:	Yes
Area Develop. Agreements:	Yes
Sub-Franchising Contracts:	Yes
Expand in Territory:	Yes
Space Needs:	0 SF

SUPPORT & TRAINING:

Financial Assistance Provided:	Yes (D)
Site Selection Assistance:	Yes
Lease Negotiation Assistance:	Yes
Co-operative Advertising:	No
Franchisee Assoc./Member:	Yes/No
Size of Corporate Staff:	15
On-going Support:	A,B,C,D,E,F,G,H,I
Training:	5 weeks regional and local

SPECIFIC EXPANSION PLANS:

US:	All US
Canada:	All Canada
Overseas:	All Countries except England and Ireland

Jan-Pro offers high quality and professional cleaning services at the best possible prices and using the latest technology in the industry. The commercial cleaning franchise company utilizes a decentralized management structure, which is one of the underlying factors for the company's success and robust growth. While unit franchise owners are responsible for serving clients, master franchise owners act as regional managers who award and manage unit franchises and bring in new clients. Jan-Pro provides comprehensive training and support, leaving master and unit franchisees free to manage and clean effectively.

With over $175 million in sales and more than 10,000 franchisees nationwide, Jan-Pro is a major force in the nearly $150 billion commercial cleaning industry.

301

Regional Master Franchise Operating Units	12/31/2008	12/31/2009	12/31/2010
Franchised	86	86	93
% Change	--	0.0%	8.1%
Company-Owned	3	3	0
% Change	--	0.0%	-100.0%
Total	89	89	93
% Change	--	0.0%	4.5%
Franchised as % of Total	96.6%	96.6%	100.0%

Investment Required
The fee for a Jan-Pro Cleaning Systems franchise ranges from $75,000-$600,000 depending on the population of the franchisee's territory.

Jan-Pro Cleaning Systems provides the following range of investments required to open your initial franchise. The range assumes that all items are paid for in cash. To the extent that you choose to finance any of these expense items, your front-end investment could be substantially reduced.

Item	Established Low Range	Established High Range
Initial Franchise Fee	$75,000	$600,000
Real Estate	$800	$2,000
Initial Supplies	$1,500	$2,000
Equipment and Office Furniture	$7,500	$14,000
Licenses, Permits, Deposits and Other Prepaid Expenses	$1,000	$3,000
Insurance	$1,000	$3,000
Expenses While Training	$3,000	$5,000

Legal Fees and Registration Expenses	$1,500	$2,000
Computer Hardware and Software	$2,750	$5,000
Initial Advertising Expenses	$1,500	$2,250
Additional Funds (3 Months)	$50,000	$70,000
Total Initial Investment	$145,550	$708,250

On-going Expenses

Jan-Pro Regional Master franchisees pay contract services fees equal to 4% of gross monthly revenue, monthly advertising fees equal to $150 (an amount which can increase up to 2% of gross monthly revenue) and sales royalty fees equal to 10% of total initial franchise fees. Account upgrade fees and financing charges are paid by unit franchisees. Additional fees payable by the franchisee include a monthly software license fee, computer-related service fees and national accounts management fees equal to 2% of national accounts revenues.

What You Get—Training and Support

Initial training for master franchisees is located at Jan-Pro headquarters in Alpharetta, GA, and consists of four weeks of classroom and on-the-job training. Topics include franchise sales, recruiting, office management and procedures, contract sales, and cleaning methods and procedures. Jan-Pro's tried and true support system continues after initial training, with ongoing regional support and meetings. Jan-Pro also provides assistance with site selection, as well as regularly updated training manuals, videos and presentations.

Territory

Jan-Pro grants exclusive territories to Regional Master Franchisees containing a minimum of 350,000 people.

Kiddie Academy

Community Begins Here.®

CHILD CARE LEARNING CENTERS

3415 Box Hill Corporate Center Dr.
Abington, MD 21009
Tel: (800) 554-3343 (410) 515-0788
Fax: (410) 569-2729
Email: sales@kiddieacademy.com
Website: www.kiddieacademy.com
Sue Hilger, VP Franchise Development

We offer comprehensive training and support without additional cost. Kiddie Academy's step-by-step program assists with staff recruitment, training, accounting support, site selection, marketing, advertising and curriculum. A true turn-key opportunity that provides on-going support so you can focus on running a successful business.

BACKGROUND: IFA Member
Established: 1981; First Franchised: 1992
Franchised Units: 96
Company-Owned Units: 2
Total Units: 98
Dist.: US-98; CAN-0; O'seas-0
North America: 24 States
Density: 13 in NJ, 15 in NY, 13 in PA
Projected New Units (12 Months): 25

Qualifications:	4, 4, 2, 3, 2, 4
FINANCIAL/TERMS:	
Cash Investment:	$150K
Total Investment:	$351.7-620K
Minimum Net Worth:	$450K
Fees: Franchise -	$20K
Royalty - 7%;	Ad. - 2%
Earnings Claims Statement:	Yes
Term of Contract (Years):	15/15
Avg. # of Employees:	10-12 FT, 10-12 PT
Passive Ownership:	Allowed, But Discouraged
Encourage Conversions:	Yes
Area Develop. Agreements:	No
Sub-Franchising Contracts:	No
Expand in Territory:	Yes
Space Needs:	7,000-10,000 SF

SUPPORT & TRAINING:	
Financial Assistance Provided:	Yes (D)
Site Selection Assistance:	Yes
Lease Negotiation Assistance:	Yes
Co-operative Advertising:	Yes
Franchisee Assoc./Member:	Yes/No
Size of Corporate Staff:	50
On-going Support:	a,B,C,D,E,NA,G,H,I
Training:	2 weeks staff training;
1 week director training, corporate headquarters;	
2 weeks owner training, corporate headquarters	

SPECIFIC EXPANSION PLANS:	
US:	All US
Canada:	No
Overseas:	No

Since its launch more than 30 years ago, Kiddie Academy has become a leader in early child education with locations coast to coast. At the center of Kiddie Academy's educational philosophy is an age-appropriate curriculum based on the individual needs of each child. Kiddie Academy's Life Essentials program emphasizes taking advantage of learning opportunities throughout a child's normal daily routine, a learning approach that sets Kiddie Academy apart from ordinary nursery schools. Along with healthy eating habits and character development, Kiddie Academy provides well-rounded, enriching, and educationally focused care that parents everywhere constantly seek.

Operating Units	12/31/2008	12/31/2009	12/31/2010
Franchised	90	99	98
% Change	--	10.0%	-1.0%
Company-Owned	5	5	2
% Change	--	0.0%	-60.0%
Total	95	104	109
% Change	--	9.5%	-3.8%
Franchised as % of Total	94.7%	95.2%	98%

Investment Required
The franchise fee for a Kiddie Academy franchise is $120,000.

Kiddie Academy provides the following range of investments required to open your initial franchise. The range assumes that all items are paid for in cash. To the extent that you choose to finance any of these expense items, your front-end investment could be substantially reduced.

Item	Established Low Range	Established High Range
Initial Fees	$120,000	$120,000
Lease Deposit	$20,000	$70,000
Professional Fees and Loan Fees	$5,000	$30,000
Kitchen Equipment	$10,000	$18,000
Supplies/Equipment for Inside of Academy, Playground and Online Training Component	$80,000	$100,000
Outdoor Fixed Playground Equipment	$30,000	$85,000
Computer Hardware and Software	$10,000	$15,000
Office Equipment	$10,000	$20,000

Signage	$8,000	$16,000
Expenses While Training	$1,000	$5,000
Transportation Vehicles and Equipment	$0	$5,000
Insurance and Utility Deposits	$2,500	$5,000
Business Licenses	$200	$1,000
Start-Up Advertising and Marketing Investment	$30,000	$30,000
Additional Funds (3 Months)	$25,000	$100,000
Total Initial Investment	$351,700	$620,000

On-going Expenses
Kiddie Academy franchisees pay a royalty fee equal to 7% of gross revenue and a marketing fund contribution equal to 2% of gross revenue.

What You Get—Training and Support
Kiddie Academy assists with site-selection and building design, including providing the franchisee with standard plans and specifications for interior/exterior design and appearance, equipment, signage and furnishings. Additionally, Kiddie Academy provides on-site support visits. Assistance with obtaining all childcare facility licenses required by local governmental agencies and purchasing necessary children's learning and play equipment is also provided.

Kiddie Academy offers an initial eight-day owner training program and five-day director training held at corporate headquarters near Baltimore, MD prior to opening. Additional on-site training, covering day-to-day management and operations is provided for the employees. Kiddie Academy also provides ongoing assistance with educational materials and marketing of the academy.

Territory
Kiddie Academy grants exclusive territories.

Kinderdance International

Education Through Dance

INTERNATIONAL
"Established in 1979"

1333 Gateway Dr., # 1003
Melbourne, FL 32901
Tel: (800) 554-2334 (321) 984-4448
Fax: (321) 984-4490
Email: leads@kinderdance.com
Website: www.kinderdance.com
Richard Maltese, Vice President Franchise Development

Kinderdance® is the original developmental dance, motor Skills, gymnastics, music and fitness program, blended with academics, specifically designed for boys and girls age 2 to 12. Kinderdance® franchisees are trained to teach 5 developmentally unique "Education Through Dance and Motor Development" programs: Kinderdance®, Kindergym®, Kindertots®), Kindercombo®, as well as Kindermotion®, which are designed for boys and girls ages 2-12. Children learn the basics of ballet, tap, gymnastics, motor development and creative dance, as well as learning numbers, colors, shapes and songs. No studio or dance experience required. Franchisees teach at child care centers and other viable locations.

BACKGROUND: IFA Member
Established: 1979; First Franchised: 1985
Franchised Units: 125

Company-Owned Units:	2
Total Units:	127
Dist.:	US-121; CAN-2; O'seas-4
North America:	38 States, 1 Province
Density:	8 in TX, 14 in FL, 12 in CA
Projected New Units (12 Months):	20
Qualifications:	2, 2, 1, 2, 2, 5

FINANCIAL/TERMS:

Cash Investment:	$12-40K
Total Investment:	$15-46K
Minimum Net Worth:	NA
Fees: Franchise -	$12-40K
Royalty - 6-15%;	Ad. - 3%
Earnings Claims Statement:	Yes
Term of Contract (Years):	5/5
Avg. # of Employees:	2 FT, 1-2+ PT
Passive Ownership:	Allowed, But Discouraged
Encourage Conversions:	Yes
Area Develop. Agreements:	Yes
Sub-Franchising Contracts:	No
Expand in Territory:	Yes
Space Needs:	NA

SUPPORT & TRAINING:

Financial Assistance Provided:	Yes (D)
Site Selection Assistance:	NA
Lease Negotiation Assistance:	NA
Co-operative Advertising:	Yes
Franchisee Assoc./Member:	Yes/Yes
Size of Corporate Staff:	8
On-going Support:	A,B,C,D,E,F,G,H,I
Training:	6 days plus on-site Melbourne, FL

SPECIFIC EXPANSION PLANS:

US:	All US
Canada:	All Canada
Overseas:	Europe, Asia, New Zealand, S. America, Mexico, Australia

307

Kinderdance makes a positive difference in the lives of young children by blending dance, gymnastics, physical education and academics into an innovative learning program. Through Kinderdance programs, children learn creative movement, ballet, tap, gymnastics and modern dance skills, in addition to colors, numbers, shapes, words and songs. They develop imagination and learn physical, verbal and social skills—an early foundation for higher education. Along with the standard Kinderdance program for pre-schoolers, there are four other specialized programs focusing on classes specifically for two-year-olds, for beginning dance techniques, for gymnastics, and for athletic/fitness pursuits.

Franchisees can teach all five of the Kinderdance programs themselves or complete training to manage a team of instructors. Franchisees work out of their own home and take their services straight to the day-care centers, preschools, YMCAs, churches and community centers where Kinderdance programs are most in demand.

Operating Units	12/31/2008	12/31/2009	12/31/2010
Franchised	118	120	125
% Change	--	1.7%	4.2%
Company-Owned	1	2	2
% Change	--	100.0%	0.0%
Total	119	122	127
% Change	--	2.5%	4.1%
Franchised as % of Total	99.2%	98.4%	98.4%

Investment Required

A Kinderdance franchise is available for purchase at three different levels, with different restrictions as regards to territory and number of employees. A Bronze Kinderdance franchise is has an initial fee of $12,000, a Silver franchise as an initial fee of $20,000 and a Gold franchise has an initial fee of $30,000.

Kinderdance International provides the following range of investments required to open your initial franchise. The range assumes that all items are paid for in cash. To the extent that you choose to finance any of these expense items, your front-end investment could be substantially reduced.

Item	Established Low Range	Established High Range
Initial Franchise Fee*	$12,000	$12,000
Initial Inventory*	$100	$100
Expenses While Training	$450	$1,000
Insurance	$400	$600
Additional Funds	$2,000	$4,000
Total Bronze Level Investment	$14,950	$17,700
Total Silver Level Investment	$23,100	$25,850
Total Gold Level Investment	$33,350	$36,100

*Fees marked with an asterisk vary for the Bronze, Silver and Gold level franchises. Numbers listed are for a Bronze level franchise, and Total Investment is listed for all three. In addition to a different Franchise Fee and Initial Inventory, the Gold level franchise also has an Area Representative Fee, which is included in calculations for the Total Gold Level Investment.

On-going Expenses

Kinderdance franchisees pay variable ongoing royalty fees depending on the level of their franchise. A Bronze level franchise has a royalty fee of the greater of 12% of gross monthly sales or $100 per month minimum, a Silver level has a royalty fee of the greater of 7% to 10% of gross monthly sales or $200 per month minimum, and Gold level has a royalty fee of the greater of 6% to 7% of gross monthly sales or $300.00 per month minimum. All franchises pay an advertising contribution of 3% of gross monthly sales.

What You Get—Training and Support

Kinderdance provides franchisees with "no-extra-cost" start-up packages valued anywhere from $850 to $2,000, as well as "no cost 'quick start'" on-site visits from corporate to aid in initial marketing efforts. Franchisees receive initial training on the basic Kinderdance programs and the operation of a Kinderdance business, conducted over a six-day period at corporate headquarters in Melbourne, FL.

Ongoing support includes annual continuing education conferences, local PR, a quarterly newsletter and a free webpage maintained and administered by Kinderdance.

Territory

A Kinderdance Gold level franchise is granted exclusive territories with unlimited locations within that territory. Silver and Bronze level franchises are granted non-exclusive territories, and are limited in number of locations—Silver is allowed up to 20 locations and Bronze is allowed up to 10 locations.

Kumon North America

MATH. READING. SUCCESS.

300 Frank W. Burr Blvd., #6
Teaneck, NJ 07666
Tel: (866) 633-0740 (201) 928-0444
Fax: (201) 692-3130
Email: tkuczek@kumon.com
Website: www.kumonfranchise.com
Thomas Kuczek, Franchise Recruitment Manager

Premiere supplemental education franchise where you'll find success, one child at a time.

BACKGROUND:	IFA Member
Established: 1958;	First Franchised: 1958
Franchised Units:	25,169
Company-Owned Units:	30
Total Units:	25,199
Dist.:	US-1,288; CAN-331; O'seas-23,580
North America:	50 States, 9 Provinces
Density:	110 in TX, 93 in NY, 241 in CA
Projected New Units (12 Months):	120
Qualifications:	3, 3, 3, 5, 4, 4

FINANCIAL/TERMS:		SUPPORT & TRAINING:	
Cash Investment:	$70K	Financial Assistance Provided:	NA
Total Investment:	$67.8-145.3K	Site Selection Assistance:	Yes
Minimum Net Worth:	$150K	Lease Negotiation Assistance:	No
Fees: Franchise -	$1K, Materials: $1K	Co-operative Advertising:	Yes
Royalty - $32-36/subj./mo.;	Ad. - NA	Franchisee Assoc./Member:	Yes/Yes
Earnings Claims Statement:	Yes	Size of Corporate Staff:	400
Term of Contract (Years):	3/5	On-going Support:	NA,NA,C,D,E,F,G,H,I
Avg. # of Employees:	1 FT, 1-3 PT	Training:	Kumon University Teaneck, NJ;
Passive Ownership:	Not Allowed		8-11 days total start-up
Encourage Conversions:	NA		
Area Develop. Agreements:	No	**SPECIFIC EXPANSION PLANS:**	
Sub-Franchising Contracts:	No	US:	All US
Expand in Territory:	No	Canada:	All Canada
Space Needs:	1,000 SF	Overseas:	All Countries

As a leader in the after-school enrichment programs industry, Kumon is one of the largest and most established franchises in the world. With nearly 310,000 students enrolled in over 1,500 centers in North America, Kumon tailors highly effective after-school math and reading programs specializing in individualized, self-paced learning. Services cater to both students who need extra help and advanced students who need a challenge. The individualized programs provide students a richer and more successful learning experience, fostering the confidence that is necessary to accomplish more on their own.

Kumon is looking for achievement-oriented franchisees who love to work with children. A background in education is not necessary, as Kumon provides all the training and support franchisees will need in order to run a successful business and help children with their goals in education.

Operating Units	12/31/2008	12/31/2009	12/31/2010
Franchised	1,281	1,293	1,589
% Change	--	0.9%	22.9%
Company-Owned	23	28	30
% Change	--	21.7%	7.1%
Total	1,304	1,321	1,619

% Change	--	1.3%	22.6%
Franchised as % of Total	98.2%	97.9%	98.2%

Investment Required
The fee for a Kumon franchise is $1,000.

Kumon provides the following range of investments required to open your initial franchise. The range assumes that all items are paid for in cash. To the extent that you choose to finance any of these expense items, your front-end investment could be substantially reduced.

Item	Established Low Range	Established High Range
Initial Franchise Fee	$1,000	$1,000
Training Agreement Deposit Fee	$500	$800
Expenses While Training	$3,945	$5,460
Initial Purchase of Materials	$1,000	$1,000
Architect Design	$0	$9,500
Leasehold Improvements	$30,000	$60,000
Security Deposit	$0	$4,500
Rent	$1,500	$4,500
Furniture, Signs, Personal, Equipment & Supplies	$10,000	$20,000
Notebook Computer at Kumon Center	$800	$1,500
Professional Fees	$1,000	$3,000
Liability Insurance	$400	$400
Business License, Name Registration	$100	$200

Separate Business Phone Line and Answering System	$200	$400
Grand Opening Advertising	$500	$2,000
Junior Kumon Kit	$800	$1,000
Junior Kumon Library of Books	$900	$1,500
Recommended Reading List	$0	$1,700
Fingerprinting, Criminal Background Check	$18	$60
Payroll Cost for Assistants	$3,600	$3,600
Additional Funds (3 Months)	$12,000	$24,000
Total Initial Investment	$67,763	$145,320

On-going Expenses

Kumon franchisees pay an initial enrollment fee of $15.00 for each newly enrolled student, and monthly royalty fees equal to $36.00 times the number of full-paying students enrolled and $18.00 times the number of partially exempt and/or prorated tuition students during the Temporary License Period. After completion of the Temporary License Period, franchisees pay monthly royalty fees equal to $32.00 times the number of full-paying students enrolled and $16.00 times the number of partially exempt and/or prorated tuition students. Kumon franchisees also pay insurance fees of $4.00 per math student per year.

What You Get—Training and Support

Before awarding a franchise, Kumon requires applicants to complete Start-Up Training, which consists of training in a Kumon center, online training, and study of Kumon curriculum and worksheets. Once this is completed, the franchisee will attend a comprehensive eight-day program conducted in Chicago, IL. The program, which is divided into two four-day cycles, covers the Kumon curriculum, as well as business strategies for owning and operating a Kumon franchise center. Kumon offers continuous support to franchisees both in program administration and center growth and development by providing follow-up training and monthly instructor meetings at branch offices. Kumon reviews student materials to keep learning methods updated and efficient. Kumon marketing efforts have become increasingly aggressive to support current franchisees in their efforts to reach as many potential students as possible.

Territory
Kumon does not grant exclusive territories.

Learning Express

29 Buena Vista St.
Devens, MA 01434
Tel: (800) 436-8697 (978) 889-1000
Fax: (978) 889-1010
Email: linda@learningexpress.com
Website: www.learningexpress.com
Linda Moore, Director Franchise Development

Largest franchisor of specialty toy stores in the United States, currently operating in 26 states. Average sales significantly out-performs independent operators. Comprehensive training and turn-key services by franchisor.

BACKGROUND: IFA Member
Established: 1987; First Franchised: 1989
Franchised Units: 145
Company-Owned Units: 0
Total Units: 145
Dist.: US-145; CAN-0; O'seas-0
 North America: 26 States
 Density: 14 in TX, 13 in NJ, 12 in FL
 Projected New Units (12 Months): 10-20
 Qualifications: 4, 3, 2, 3, 1, 5

FINANCIAL/TERMS:
Cash Investment: $100-150K
Total Investment: $199.5-345K
Minimum Net Worth: $300K
Fees: Franchise - $35K
 Royalty - 5%; Ad. - NR
Earnings Claims Statement: Yes
Term of Contract (Years): 10/10
Avg. # of Employees: 2 FT, 8-10 PT
Passive Ownership: Allowed, But Discouraged
Encourage Conversions: NA
Area Develop. Agreements: No
Sub-Franchising Contracts: No
Expand in Territory: Yes
Space Needs: 2,500-3,000 SF

SUPPORT & TRAINING:
Financial Assistance Provided: No
Site Selection Assistance: Yes
Lease Negotiation Assistance: Yes
Co-operative Advertising: Yes
Franchisee Assoc./Member: Yes/Yes
Size of Corporate Staff: 25
On-going Support: NA,NA,C,D,E,F,G,H,I
Training: 4 weeks on-site; 8 days home office

SPECIFIC EXPANSION PLANS:
US: All US
Canada: No
Overseas: No

314

Learning Express has more than 140 franchised stores in 26 states, which makes it the largest and most established specialty toy franchise business in America with average sales significantly out-performing independent operators. Additionally, the toy industry in general continues to be a vibrant market, generating billions of dollars in sales annually.

Learning Express offers franchisees with an entrepreneurial spirit, a love of toys and kids, and an enthusiasm for learning the opportunity to own a Learning Express store. Every Learning Express store reflects the personality of its owner. Learning Express celebrates individuality and independence because when storeowners succeed and grow, the entire franchise benefits. The company relentlessly pursues breakthrough ideas in product mix, direct marketing, and training programs so it can provide its franchisees with everything they need to accomplish their unique goals.

Operating Units	12/31/2008	12/31/2009	12/31/2010
Franchised	140	146	160
% Change	--	4.3%	9.6%
Company-Owned	0	0	0
% Change	--	--	--
Total	140	146	160
% Change	--	4.3%	9.6%
Franchised as % of Total	100%	100%	100%

Investment Required
The fee for a Learning Express franchise is $35,000.

Learning Express provides the following range of investments required to open your initial franchise. The range assumes that all items are paid for in cash. To the extent that you choose to finance any of these expense items, your front-end investment could be substantially reduced.

Item	Established Low Range	Established High Range
Initial Franchise Fee	$35,000	$35,000
Lease and Leasehold Improvements	$15,000	$65,000
POS Equipment	$17,500	$17,500
Signage, Equipment, Furniture and Fixtures	$30,000	$62,000
Organizational and Training Costs	$3,500	$7,000
Opening Inventory	$90,000	$140,000
Grand Opening Advertising	$7,500	$7,500
Insurance	$1,000	$6,000
Additional Funds (3 Months)	$10,000	$30,000
Total Initial Investment	$209,500	$370,000

On-going Expenses
Learning Express franchisees pay a royalty fee of 5% of gross revenue and an advertising fee of 1% of gross revenue when the fund begins. Other fees include gift card related expenses and an email address fee.

What You Get—Training and Support
Learning Express provides thorough starting support, including giving assistance with site location, lease negotiations, and store layout. Each franchisee works closely with an assigned advisor in New Store Operations as well as a Store Opening Coordinator/Regional Developer to help with everything from Opening Day preparation to merchandising, employee training, and management and accounting. Additionally an eight-day training program is provided at the Learning Express facility in Devens, MA which encompasses both a classroom format and a practical, hands-on approach in a store setting.

The Learning Express home office provides ongoing support for franchisees, including marketing support, training materials for employees, field visits, a Suggested Store Inventory Mix for best product recommendations, an annual Convention, the Learning Express Intranet, and email and telephone support.

Territory

Learning Express grants exclusive territories.

Liberty Tax Service

1716 Corporate Landing Pkwy.
Virginia Beach, VA 23454
Tel: (800) 790-3863 (757) 493-8855
Fax: (800) 880-6432
Email: sales@libtax.com
Website: www.libertytaxfranchise.com
David Tarr, Director of Franchise Development

Liberty Tax Service is the fastest-growing international tax service ever, and has been ranked on Entrepreneur Magazine's annual "Franchise 500" every year since 1998. Any given year, there is a ready market of taxpayers, and as the tax laws change frequently, many taxpayers are turning to professional preparers to complete that annual task. Liberty's growth is fueled by a proven operating system that has been fine-tuned by the leadership and field support staff's more than 600 total years of experience. As a result, no prior tax experience is required to put this system to work. Founder/CEO John Hewitt has worked 42 tax seasons, including 12 years with H&R Block. Accounting Today magazine has named

Hewitt one of the accounting profession's Top 100 Most Influential People - 11 times! The International Franchise Association has honored Hewitt as its "Entrepreneur of the Year."

BACKGROUND:	IFA Member
Established: 1997;	First Franchised: 1997
Franchised Units:	3,781
Company-Owned Units:	47
Total Units:	3,828
Dist.:	US-3,575; CAN-253; O'seas-0
North America:	50 States, 10 Provinces
Density:	483 in CA, 328 in TX, 233 in FL
Projected New Units (12 Months):	400-500
Qualifications:	2, 4, 2, 1, 3, 5

FINANCIAL/TERMS:	
Cash Investment:	$56.8-69.9K
Total Investment:	$56.8-69.9K
Minimum Net Worth:	NA
Fees: Franchise -	$40K
Royalty - Varies;	Ad. - 5%
Earnings Claims Statement:	No
Term of Contract (Years):	5/5
Avg. # of Employees:	4-6 FT, 2 PT
Passive Ownership:	Allowed
Encourage Conversions:	No
Area Develop. Agreements:	Yes
Sub-Franchising Contracts:	No
Expand in Territory:	Yes
Space Needs:	400+ SF

SUPPORT & TRAINING:		Training: 5 days Virginia Beach, VA - initial,
Financial Assistance Provided:	Yes (I)	intermediate, advanced; 3 days various cities - inter-
Site Selection Assistance:	Yes	mediate, advanced
Lease Negotiation Assistance:	Yes	
Co-operative Advertising:	No	**SPECIFIC EXPANSION PLANS:**
Franchisee Assoc./Member:	No	US: All US
Size of Corporate Staff:	992	Canada: Yes
On-going Support:	A,B,C,D,E,F,G,H,I	Overseas: No

Founded in 1997, Liberty Tax Service has experienced explosive growth i the past 14 years. With over 3,800 offices opened, Liberty Tax Service ha been growing more than three times faster than any other tax preparatio company. Throughout this decade, Liberty Tax Service has demonstrate significant gains in an industry formerly dominated by tax giant H&I Block and, during the 21st century, Liberty has grown by more tax returm than both Jackson Hewitt and H&R Block combined. Liberty Tax Servic is ranked as the #1 tax franchise on Entrepreneur magazine's "Franchis 500" in 2011, and is the *only* tax franchise on the Forbes "Top 20 Franchise to Start."

Liberty Tax franchise costs are significantly less than most franchises du to its seasonal work force and low inventory costs. Its proven system, com prehensive training program as well as one-on-one, ongoing assistance pro vides an excellent opportunity for people seeking a small business oppo tunity.

Operating Units	12/31/2008	12/31/2009	12/31/2010
Franchised	2,374	2,881	3,217
% Change	--	21.4%	11.7%
Company-Owned	50	43	57
% Change	--	-14.0%	32.6%
Total	2,424	2,924	3,274
% Change	--	20.6%	12%
Franchised as % of Total	97.9%	98.5%	98.3%

Investment Required

Liberty Tax® franchise costs are significantly less than most franchise

Liberty Tax offers affordable, low cost franchise opportunities, less than $69,900 (U.S.) and $54,900 (Canada) in most cases (including franchise fee required for start-up, start-up costs and comprehensive training).

Liberty Tax Service provides the following range of investments required to open your initial franchise. The range assumes that all items are paid for in cash. To the extent that you choose to finance any of these expense items, your front-end investment could be substantially reduced.

Item	Established Low Range	Established High Range
Initial or Resale Franchise Fee	$40,000	$40,000
Initial Advertising	$5,000	$7,500
Expenses While Training	$100	$2,500
Equipment and Office Furniture	$2,000	$3,000
Signs	$500	$1,000
Rent	$3,000	$6,000
Payroll	$3,000	$5,000
Insurance	$200	$400
Additional Funds (3 Months)	$3,000	$4,500
Total Initial Investment	$56,800	$69,900

Estimated Franchise Start-Up and Operating Costs for Canada
Note: Some costs are variable depending on your local area)

Item	Established Low Range	Established High Range
Initial Franchise Fee	$15,000	$25,000
Initial Advertising	$5,000	$7,500

Expenses While Training	$100	$2,500
Equipment and Office Furniture	$2,000	$3,000
Signs	$500	$1,000
Lease/Leasehold Improvements	$3,000	$6,000
Payroll	$3,000	$5,000
Insurance	$200	$400
Additional Funds (3 Months)	$3,000	$4,500
Total Initial Investment	$33,350	$54,900

* Offices that have operated previously are priced separately. Some expenses vary based upon your local market.

On-going Expenses
Liberty Tax Service franchisees pay royalty fees equal to 14% of gross receipts with the following minimums: $5,000 for first year, $8,000 for second year, and $11,000 for third year and beyond. Additional fees payable by the franchisee include kiosk rentals during tax season and marketing training sessions.

What You Get—Training and Support
Training consists of two phases. First, Liberty Tax Services provides a comprehensive, minimum five-day Effective Operations Training (EOT) course in Virginia Beach, VA that instructs franchisees on the basics of operating an income tax preparation office. Other subjects include accounting, marketing, hiring and staffing, management, customer services, budgeting and software applications. This course is followed by a one-day, hands-on training at designated franchisee locations across the country and covers topics on preparing and processing tax returns, delivering bank products, guerilla marketing and office procedures.

For one to three days every year, an advanced training session is conducted across the country or via the internet to update franchisees on new tax laws, software and marketing programs. Franchisees also benefit from a support system of employees who have a combined total of 600 years of industry experience.

Territory
Liberty Tax Service grants exclusive territories.

Liquid Capital

FINANCING SUCCESS

5525 N. MacArthur Blvd. Ste. 535
Irving, TX 75038
Tel: (877) 228-0800 (416) 342-8199
Fax: (866) 611-8886
Email: birnbaum@liquidcapitalcorp.com
Website: www.lcfranchise.com
Brian Birnbaum, President

Factoring is the funding of B2B receivables. It is a $2 trillion global industry. The Liquid Capital competitive advantage is the relationship a client enjoys with the franchisee. Typically, a franchisee has 10-15 clients, who generally will factor their receivables for 2 to 3 years. Liquid Capital is a low overhead, high return, home-based business that provides a franchisee with a great life style with high earning potential. Liquid Capital will loan its franchisees up to 6 times their investment.

BACKGROUND:	IFA Member
Established: 1999;	First Franchised: 2000
Franchised Units:	60
Company-Owned Units:	2
Total Units:	62
Dist.:	US-32; CAN-28; O'seas-0
North America:	32 States, 6 Provinces
Density:	7 in AB, 5 in FL, 3 in IL

Projected New Units (12 Months):	12
Qualifications:	5, 5, 2, 4, 2, 3

FINANCIAL/TERMS:	
Cash Investment:	$50K
Total Investment:	$150K-10M
Minimum Net Worth:	$250K
Fees: Franchise -	$50K
Royalty - 8;	Ad. - $500 monthly
Earnings Claims Statement:	Yes
Term of Contract (Years):	10/10
Avg. # of Employees:	1 FT, 0 PT
Passive Ownership:	Not Allowed
Encourage Conversions:	NA
Area Develop. Agreements:	No
Sub-Franchising Contracts:	No
Expand in Territory:	No
Space Needs:	

SUPPORT & TRAINING:	
Financial Assistance Provided:	Yes (D)
Site Selection Assistance:	NA
Lease Negotiation Assistance:	NA
Co-operative Advertising:	Yes
Franchisee Assoc./Member:	Yes/Yes
Size of Corporate Staff:	8
On-going Support:	NA,NA,NA,NA,NA,NA,NA,NA,NA
Training:	5 days Toronto, Canada

SPECIFIC EXPANSION PLANS:	
US:	All US
Canada:	All
Overseas:	No

321

Liquid Capital™ is an international commercial finance company with more offices across North America than any other factoring firm. This extensive geographic network of local offices allows them to be the only commercial finance firm able to provide clients with an unmatchable level of individual client service and satisfaction. Well-recognized for their specialty of providing clients with accounts receivable financing, Liquid Capital™ also has the ability to fund purchase orders, or provide credit and trade insurance.

For over a decade, the company has successfully combined the strengths of a top-tier finance corporation with a personalized approach to full-service funding through local professionals who know the community and understand business. Liquid Capital™ principals are consistently recognized for the prompt, friendly service and personal attention expected from financing executives who live in the communities they do business in. Liquid Capital™ regularly funds business transactions, companies who are in the process of restructuring, launches new product lines, support market expansion, or just helps businesses survive seasonal ups and downs.

US Numbers

Operating Units	12/31/2008	12/31/2009	12/31/2010
Franchised	32	31	31
% Change	--	-3.1%	0%
Company-Owned	1	1	1
% Change	--	0%	0%
Total	33	32	32
% Change	--	-3.0%	0%
Franchised as % of Total	97%	96.9%	96.9%

Canada Numbers

Operating Units	12/31/2008	12/31/2009	12/31/2010

Franchised	58	56	59
% Change	--	-3.4%	5.4%
Company-Owned	2	2	2
% Change	--	0%	0%
Total	60	58	61
% Change	--	-3.3%	5.2%
Franchised as % of Total	96.7%	96.6%	96.7%

Investment Required

The fee for a single territory Liquid Capital™ franchise is $50,000. If you qualify for the multi-territory program, the initial franchise fee is $130,000 for the first three territories and $40,000 for each additional territory.

Liquid Capital™ provides the following range of investments required to open your initial franchise. The range assumes that all items are paid for in cash. To the extent that you choose to finance any of these expense items, your front-end investment could be substantially reduced.

Item	Established Low Range	Established High Range
Initial Franchise Fee	$50,000	$50,000
Office Supplies	$500	$1,000
Lease	$0	$2,000
Furniture, Fixtures, and Equipment	$0	$12,000
Signage	$0	$2,000
Computer Hardware and Software	$2,500	$9,000
Insurance	$1,000	$1,500
Initial Training	$600	$2,600
Professional Services	$1,500	$5,000

Additional Funds (3 Months)	$2,100	$10,000
Total Initial Investment	$58,200	$95,100

On-going Expenses

Liquid Capital™ franchisees pay a continuing royalty fee equal to 8% of gross revenue.

Other ongoing fees include back office services fees, exchange fees, management fees, renewal fees, insurance fees, etc.

Franchisee Satisfaction

A critical component of the due diligence process is that you, as a prospective franchisee, have a strong sense of existing franchisee satisfaction. Please review the franchisor's ratings below for this extremely important information.

World-Class Franchise®

How do you rate Liquid Capital in terms of:	Rating*
My franchisor understands that if I am successful, they will be successful.	96%
How would you grade the initial training supplied by your franchisor?	95%
I can communicate directly and effectively with senior management.	93%

* Independent Audit of Existing Franchisees Who Rated Liquid Capital as Excellent, Very Good, or Good

What You Get—Training and Support

Liquid Capital™ provides one week of comprehensive training at its corporate headquarters in Toronto that covers all aspects of factoring, accounts receivable management, security issues and credit-related matters. It also includes 16 hours of marketing and sales training. The Liquid Capital Factoring Advisory Team, a group of highly experienced factoring specialists, also mentors principals on an ongoing basis. In addition, a strong corporate infrastructure and back-office administrative support system streamlines operations for principals while providing them with a myriad of resources.

Liquid Capital™ will direct all advertising programs, including the creative concepts, materials and media used in the programs. Franchisees also receive access to the Operations Manual. Liquid Capital™ will also assist the franchisee with the opening as far as training, etc.

Territory

Liquid Capital™ grants exclusive territories.

The Little Gym

Serious Fun.

7001 N. Scottsdale Rd., # 1050
Scottsdale, AZ 85253
Tel: (888) 228-2878 (480) 948-2878
Fax: (480) 948-2765
Email: info@thelittlegym.com
Website: www.thelittlegymfranchise.com
Ruk Adams, SVP Franchise Development and Services

The Little Gym is the world's leading children's motor-skill development franchise. Children ages 4 months to 12 years build confidence and develop an appreciation for a healthy active lifestyle through a gymnastics-based, noncompetitive curriculum. Children progress at their own pace with the support of our caring and nurturing instructors. We now set the standard for high-quality children's development programs and have been ranked #1 in Children's Fitness by Entrepreneur magazine for the 4th straight year.

BACKGROUND:	IFA Member
Established: 1976;	First Franchised: 1992
Franchised Units:	218
Company-Owned Units:	2
Total Units:	220

Dist.:	US-220; CAN-20; O'seas-39	Expand in Territory:	No
North America:	34 States, 5 Provinces	Space Needs:	2,450-3,800 SF
Density:	26 in TX, 19 in NJ, 20 in CA		
Projected New Units (12 Months):	15	**SUPPORT & TRAINING:**	
Qualifications:	4, 4, 1, 3, 4, 5	Financial Assistance Provided:	Yes (I)
		Site Selection Assistance:	Yes
FINANCIAL/TERMS:		Lease Negotiation Assistance:	Yes
Cash Investment:	$75-100K	Co-operative Advertising:	No
Total Investment:	$147.5-294K	Franchisee Assoc./Member:	No
Minimum Net Worth:	$150-200K	Size of Corporate Staff:	32
Fees: Franchise -	$39.5-69.5K	On-going Support:	NA,NA,C,D,E,NA,NA,h,NA
Royalty - 8%;	Ad. - 1%	Training:	7 days various locations;
Earnings Claims Statement:	Yes		14 days Scottsdale, AZ
Term of Contract (Years):	10/10		
Avg. # of Employees:	2-3 FT, 4-8 PT	**SPECIFIC EXPANSION PLANS:**	
Passive Ownership:	Not Allowed	US:	All US
Encourage Conversions:	NA	Canada:	All Canada
Area Develop. Agreements:	Yes	Overseas:	All Countries
Sub-Franchising Contracts:	Yes		

With more than 300 locations in 20 countries, The Little Gym is the world's premier experiential learning and physical development franchise for children ages four months through 12 years. For over 35 years, our trained instructors have nurtured happy, confident kids through a range of programs including parent/child classes, gymnastics, karate, dance and sports skills development, plus enjoyable extras like camps, Parents' Survival Nights and Awesome Birthday Bashes. Each week, progressively structured classes and a positive learning environment create opportunities for children to try new things and build self-confidence, all with a grin that stretches from ear to ear.

It is not necessary for The Little Gym franchise owners to have experience in education or physical fitness, just a passion for helping children and making a difference in their communities. The Little Gym is a recipient of the 2007, 2008, and 2009 Franchise Satisfaction Awards Top 50 Franchise from Franchise Business Review, and Ranked #1 in Category from Entrepreneur magazine in 2007, 2008, 2009, and 2010.

Operating Units	12/31/2008	12/31/2009	12/31/2010
Franchised	266	246	235

% Change	--	-7.5%	-4.5%
Company-Owned	0	0	2
% Change	--	--	--
Total	266	246	237
% Change	--	-7.5%	-3.7%
Franchised as % of Total	100%	100%	99.2%

Investment Required

The fee for a The Little Gym Standard Territory franchise is $69,500. A Small Market Territory is also offered for an initial fee of $39,500.

The Little Gym provides the following range of investments required to open your initial franchise. The range assumes that all items are paid for in cash. To the extent that you choose to finance any of these expense items, your front-end investment could be substantially reduced.

Item	Standard Territory		Small Market Territory	
	Established Low Range	Established High Range	Established Low Range	Established High Range
Initial Franchise Fee	$69,500	$69,500	$39,500	$49,500
Start-Up Equipment and Inventory Package	$59,000	$69,000	$53,000	$65,000
Signs, Fixtures, Other Fixed Assets	$7,000	$14,000	$5,000	$12,000
Furnishings, Other Equipment & Supplies	$8,000	$14,000	$6,000	$12,000
Initial Sales Promotion	$10,000	$18,000	$6,000	$13,000

Security Deposits and Prepaid Expenses	$4,000	$15,000	$3,000	$10,000
Training Related Expenses	$5,000	$10,000	$5,000	$10,000
Insurance Premiums	$2,500	$3,500	$2,000	$3,000
Misc. Expenses before start of Operations	$4,000	$11,000	$3,000	$9,000
Operating Funds for First Three Months	$35,000	$70,000	$25,000	$50,000
Total Investment	$204,000	$294,000	$147,500	$33,500

On-going Expenses

The Little Gym franchisees pay a royalty fee of 8% of gross monthly revenue subject to an annual minimum royalty requirement and a local and regional advertising fee of 4% of gross monthly revenues or $1,250 minimum on average. Additional fees include marketing fund fee and a proprietary software maintenance fee.

What You Get—Training and Support

Initial training involves a 21-day Business Startup Training Program that teaches every aspect of successful gym operation. Franchisees are taught The Little Gym's meticulously designed curriculum which allows franchisees without a background in physical education or child development to successfully own a The Little Gym franchise. Training also covers how to work with children of all ages and how to recruit and train staff.

The Little Gym assigns each franchise owner a personal New Business Consultant to help them through every step of starting up the franchise and after opening assigns an Operations Consultant for ongoing advice.

Territory

The Little Gym grants exclusive territories.

MAACO

128 S. Tryon St., Suite 900
Charlotte, NC 28202
Tel: (800) 275-5200
Fax: (704) 377-9904
Email: dave.schaefers@drivenbrands.com
Website: www.maacofranchise.com
Dave Schaefers, VP of Franchise Development

There are over 400 MAACO franchise centres in Canada, the US,. and Puerto Rico. Between them, these franchises repair and paint over 800,000 vehicles a year. Thousands of car owners as well as local and national fleet administrators rely upon their local MAACO centre to maintain their vehicles' appearance. In 2011, MAACO was ranked #1 in Automotive Appearance Services in Entrepreneur magazine's annual Franchise 500.

BACKGROUND: IFA Member
Established: 1972; First Franchised: 1972
Franchised Units: 458
Company-Owned Units: 0
Total Units: 458
Dist.: US-427; CAN-31; O'seas-0
  North America: 27 States, 6 Provinces
  Density: 19 in ON, 6 in AB, 3 in British Columbia
Projected New Units (12 Months): 30

Qualifications:	3, 4, 1, 2, 4, 5
FINANCIAL/TERMS:	
Cash Investment:	$90K
Total Investment:	$297K
Minimum Net Worth:	$250K
Fees: Franchise -	$40K
Royalty - 9%;	Ad. - $850/Wk.
Earnings Claims Statement:	Yes
Term of Contract (Years):	15/5
Avg. # of Employees:	6-10 FT, 0 PT
Passive Ownership:	Not Allowed
Encourage Conversions:	Yes
Area Develop. Agreements:	No
Sub-Franchising Contracts:	No
Expand in Territory:	Yes
Space Needs:	8,000 SF
SUPPORT & TRAINING:	
Financial Assistance Provided:	Yes (I)
Site Selection Assistance:	Yes
Lease Negotiation Assistance:	Yes
Co-operative Advertising:	No
Franchisee Assoc./Member:	Yes/Yes
Size of Corporate Staff:	100
On-going Support:	A,B,C,D,E,F,G,H,I
Training:	On-going as required in store;
3 weeks in store; 4 weeks King of Prussia, PA	
SPECIFIC EXPANSION PLANS:	
US:	
Canada:	All Canada
Overseas:	No

Poised as a leader in the colossal automotive aftercare industry, MAACO offers considerable stable and profitable entrepreneurial opportunities. Since 1972, MAACO has served communities throughout the United States and abroad, providing reliable, superior auto paint and auto body repair services to over 16.5 million vehicles throughout its history. Today, MAACO operates nearly 500 franchises that service approximately 650,000 vehicles per year. Moreover, the automotive aftercare market is one of the fastest growing industries in the U.S., representing a nearly $290 billion industry in 2010. With new car sales declining and more people choosing to retain their vehicles for longer periods of time, the automotive collision and cosmetic repair industry possesses considerable potential for explosive growth in the next few years.

Franchisees benefit from unparalleled brand recognition and the stability of a company with an impressive 45% of the U.S. market share within the industry. MAACO offers a reliable business model, complete with an exceptional, comprehensive training program. Moreover, by working with MAACO, franchisees have the chance to build a family-oriented business with comfortable operating hours and a substantial, stable income potential.

Operating Units	12/31/2009	12/31/2010	12/31/2011
Franchised	429	442	431
% Change	--	3.0%	-2.5%
Company-Owned	6	6	2
% Change	--	0.0%	-66.7%
Total	435	448	433
% Change	--	3.0%	-3.3%
Franchised as % of Total	98.6%	98.7%	99.5%

Investment Required
The initial fee for a MAACO franchise is $40,000.

MAACO provides the following range of investments required to open your initial franchise. The range assumes that all items are paid for in cash. To the extent that you choose to finance any of these expense items, your front-end investment could be substantially reduced.

Item	Established Low Range	Established High Range
Initial Franchise Fee	$20,000	$40,000
Initial Training/Opening Fee	$10,000	$23,000

Initial Advertising	$15,000	$30,000
Equipment	$2,071.43	$161,417
Opening Inventory/Supplies	$7,123	$17,000
Stationary & Promotional Materials	$337	$900
Signage	$2,102.15	$16,765.59
Miscellaneous	$20,000	$45,000
Initial Software License Fee	$5,000	$5,000
Initial Computer Hardware	$1,444.25	$4,500
Additional Funds (3 Months)	$8,600	$150,000
Total Initial Investment	$91,679.33	$493,585.59

On-going Expenses

MAACO franchisees pay royalty fees equal to 9% of gross sales, a minimum advertising contribution of $850 per week, and a national marketing fee of $50 per week.

What You Get—Training and Support

Prior to opening, MAACO assists franchisees by providing site standards for the general location, zoning, neighborhood, parking and layout. Franchisees further benefit from specifications for inventory, supplies, equipment and exterior/interior signage, as well as grand opening promotional materials and initial advertising provided by MAACO.

Franchisees attend a mandatory four-week intensive training program conducted at the MAACO headquarters in King of Prussia, Pennsylvania, or another designated training location. The training focuses on management methods and techniques, including local advertising, marketing, POS system, merchandising, paints/solvents/thinners, painting equipment and

331

maintenance, safety regulations, personnel management customer relations, sales, national and local fleet accounts, accounting, budgeting, insurance and facilities maintenance. Following this initial training, MAACO offers additional on-site assistance for approximately four to five weeks throughout the grand opening process.

Continuing assistance and support includes marketing, with MAACO supplying advertising programs and promotional materials. MAACO conducts occasional inspections and evaluations of the franchise center regarding operational success and efficiency, and offers feedback and guidance accordingly. Franchisees further benefit from ongoing training programs, meetings and conventions concerning sales, operations and advertising.

Territory
MAACO does not grant exclusive territories.

The Maids

Referred for a reason.

9394 W. Dodge Rd., Ste. 140
Omaha, NE 68114
Tel: (800) 843-6243, (402) 558-5555
Fax: (402) 558-4112
Email: rcordova@maids.com
Website: www.themaidsfranchise.com
Ronn Cordova, Vice President of Franchise Development

Distinguished as the number one residential cleaning franchise in 2007, 2008, 2009, 2011, and 2012, and the fastest growing residential cleaning franchise four years running by Entrepreneur magazine, The Maids is the quality leader in the industry. The Maids was founded in 1979 and began franchising in 1980. We currently have 165 franchise partners operating over 1,000 territories in the US and Canada. Franchise partners benefit from a time-tested cleaning system and business model based on leading-edge technology. The Maids provides the most comprehensive package of training, support, and exclusive territory in the industry. We provide extensive training, including seven weeks of pre-training and nine days of classroom and field training. We are in touch and involved with the new franchisee a minimum of 195 days within the first year. With The Maids, you can build a great business and achieve the lifestyle you desire, all with nights, weekends, and holidays off. The Maids is looking for individuals to join its franchise system. We are looking for people who want an executive experience. With The Maids you are working on the business, not in the business. Our franchise partners are not cleaning homes, and are building their business Monday through Friday - no nights, no weekends, and no holidays. The Maids ideal franchise candidate will have good management and business skills, and most importantly, great people skills.

BACKGROUND:	IFA Member	Area Develop. Agreements:	No
Established: 1979;	First Franchised: 1980	Sub-Franchising Contracts:	No
Franchised Units:	1094	Expand in Territory:	Yes
Company-Owned Units:	26	Space Needs:	1,000 - 1,200 SF
Total Units:	1,120		
Dist.:	US-1,090; CAN-30; O'seas-0	**SUPPORT & TRAINING:**	
North America:	39 States, 4 Provinces	Financial Assistance Provided:	Yes (I)
Density:	78 in TX, 77 in MA, 107 in CA	Site Selection Assistance:	Yes
Projected New Units (12 Months):	80	Lease Negotiation Assistance:	No
Qualifications:	5, 5, 1, 2, 1, 5	Co-operative Advertising:	Yes
		Franchisee Assoc./Member:	No
FINANCIAL/TERMS:		Size of Corporate Staff:	35
Cash Investment:	$60-100K	On-going Support:	A,B,C,D,E,F,G,h,I
Total Investment:	$93,545-$121,295	Training:	9 days Corporate training - Omaha, NE;
Minimum Net Worth:	$250K		2-3 days power training - franchisee location;
Fees: Franchise -	$10K + $.95 per QHH		7 weeks foundation training (pre-training) done
Royalty - 3.9-6.9%;	Ad. - 2%		from France
Earnings Claims Statement:	Yes		
Term of Contract (Years):	20/20	**SPECIFIC EXPANSION PLANS:**	
Avg. # of Employees:	2 FT, 6 to start (maids) PT	US:	All US
Passive Ownership:	Allowed, But Discouraged	Canada:	All except Saskatchewan and Quebec
Encourage Conversions:	Yes	Overseas:	No

The multi-billion dollar home services industry is booming due to busy dual-career families, increased corporate demands and long commutes. In this climate, maid service is no longer a luxury; it is a time management tool for leisure-starved households. A leader in its field, The Maids has been recognized as the fastest growing residential cleaning franchise by Entrepreneur magazine for the past four years.

Offering the broadest service package and the highest quality cleaning services, The Maids enjoys excellent customer loyalty that draws from primarily affluent families with high disposable income. In allowing ownership of large markets, The Maids franchise system offers franchisees the greatest opportunity in the home services industry.

Operating Units	12/31/2008	12/31/2009	12/31/2010
Franchised	1,033	1,060	1,068
% Change	--	2.6%	0.8%
Company-Owned	26	26	26

% Change	--	0.0%	0.0%
Total	1,059	1,086	1,094
% Change	--	2.5%	0.7%
Franchised as % of Total	97.5%	97.6%	97.6%

Investment Required
The fee for a Maids franchise is $10,000, plus an initial territory fee of $0.95 for each potential customer in the Designated Market Area. The Maids may offer financing to qualified prospective franchisees for up to 75% of the Initial Franchise Fee.

The Maids provides the following range of investments required to open your initial franchise. The range assumes that all items are paid for in cash. To the extent that you choose to finance any of these expense items, your front-end investment could be substantially reduced.

Item	Established Low Range	Established High Range
Initial Franchise Fee	$10,000	$10,000
Territory Fee	$28,500	$28,500
Initial Equipment and Supply Package	$15,100	$16,100
Initial Software License	$2,895	$4,895
Office Security Deposit	$700	$1,000
Computer Hardware	$3,000	$5,000
Office Fixtures, Decorations and Furniture	$2,500	$3,500
Auto Painting	$750	$1,500
Telephone Deposit	$100	$200
Insurance Deposit	$1,500	$2,500
Signage	$500	$1,000

Washer and Dryer	$800	$1,000
Start Up Professional Services	$500	$1,500
Expenses During Corporate Training	$4,900	$8,050
Operating Expenses (3 Months)	$20,800	$35,550
Total Investment	$92,545	$120,295

On-going Expenses

The Maids franchisees pay royalty fees ranging from 3.9% to 6.9% of gross revenues (2.4% to 6.9% for conversions), advertising fees equal to 2% of gross revenues (0.5% to 2% for conversions) and required local advertising expenditures equal to $1.20 per potential customer, per year. Additional fees payable by the franchise include a national convention registration fee and an annual software membership fee.

What You Get—Training and Support

The Maids training is one of the most intensive and advanced in the franchise community. Training includes an initial program to help ensure a successful opening, comprehensive corporate training, site visits by trainers and business coaches to streamline operations and a post-training program designed to help franchisees focus on business goals.

The Maids' marketing staff and business coaches provide comprehensive marketing support throughout opening and operations. The Maids helps franchisees build an initial marketing plan and provides ongoing consulting, ad design, public relations and direct mail support. The Maids also assigns a franchise business coach to provide franchisees with one-on-one counsel and support in all facets of business growth and management.

Territory

The Maids grants exclusive territories.

Meineke

128 S. Tryon St., # 900
Charlotte, NC 28202
Tel: (800) 275-5200
Fax: (704) 377-9904
Email: dave.schaefers@meineke.com
Website: www.meinekefranchise.com
Dave Schaefers, VP Driven Brands Franchise Development

Meineke has been offering superior automotive repair services at discount prices for over 30 years. We are a nationally-recognized brand with a proven system. Brand recognition, comprehensive training, and on-going technical and operational support are some of the benefits enjoyed by Meineke franchisees.

BACKGROUND: IFA Member
Established: 1972; First Franchised: 1972
Franchised Units: 927
Company-Owned Units: 17
Total Units: 944
Dist.: US-867; CAN-34; O'seas-43
  North America: 27 States, 6 Provinces
  Density: 19 in ON, 6 in AB, 3 in British Columbia
Projected New Units (12 Months): 45

Qualifications:	4, 4, 1, 2, 3, 4
FINANCIAL/TERMS:	
Cash Investment:	$75K
Total Investment:	$149-416K
Minimum Net Worth:	$250K
Fees: Franchise -	$30K
Royalty - 9%;	Ad. - 8%
Earnings Claims Statement:	Yes
Term of Contract (Years):	15/15
Avg. # of Employees:	6-10 FT, 0 PT
Passive Ownership:	Not Allowed
Encourage Conversions:	Yes
Area Develop. Agreements:	Yes
Sub-Franchising Contracts:	
Expand in Territory:	Yes
Space Needs:	8,000 SF
SUPPORT & TRAINING:	
Financial Assistance Provided:	Yes (I)
Site Selection Assistance:	Yes
Lease Negotiation Assistance:	Yes
Co-operative Advertising:	No
Franchisee Assoc./Member:	Yes/Yes
Size of Corporate Staff:	110
On-going Support:	A,B,C,D,E,NA,G,H,I
Training:	4 weeks Charlotte, NC
SPECIFIC EXPANSION PLANS:	
US:	All US
Canada:	All Canada
Overseas:	All Countries

Nearly four decades ago, Sam Meineke began his first store in Houston, TX with a single product line and a simple concept: provide quality products and workmanship at a fair price. That concept, along with the application of new technology and strategies, has made Meineke Car Care Centers one of the most recognized and trusted automotive franchise brands in North America. Today, the automotive franchise has over 900 centers worldwide and has successfully evolved into a one-stop automotive business that consumers are looking for.

The Meineke franchise represents a great opportunity as more people are holding on to older cars longer, driving the demands for professional repair and maintenance services. The U.S. automotive aftermarket repair and service business is approaching $200 billion in annual sales.

Operating Units	12/31/2009	12/31/2010	12/31/2011
Franchised	847	837	844
% Change	--	-1.2%	0.8%
Company-Owned	7	8	7
% Change	--	14.3%	-12.5%
Total	854	845	851
% Change	--	-1.1%	0.7%
Franchised as % of Total	99.2%	99.1%	99.2%

Investment Required
The fee for a Meineke franchise is $30,000.

Meineke provides the following range of investments required to open your initial franchise. The range assumes that all items are paid for in cash. To the extent that you choose to finance any of these expense items, your front-end investment could be substantially reduced. Please note the figures below represent expenses for a 4 Bay Location. Franchisees can also purchase a 5 Bay Location, with a Total Initial Investment of $149,432.81 – $344,802.55, and a 6 Bay Location with a Total Initial Investment of $163,132.90 – $415,833.47.

Item	Established Low Range	Established High Range
Initial Franchise Fee	$15,000	$30,000
Expenses While Training	$1,875	$2,700
Rent, Security Deposits and Utility Deposits	$3,200	$9,620
Opening Inventory	$1,000	$30,000

Equipment, Signs, Tools, etc.	$79,206.29	$106,349.53
Freight	$1,500	$2,500
POS Software, Computer Hardware	$4,995	$7,729
Center Supplies	$10,672.16	$10,672.16
Insurance	$1,000	$2,000
Initial Marketing	$1,200	$5,000
Legal/Accounting Expenses	$1,000	$6,000
Pre-Paid Expenses	$300	$25,000
Additional Funds (3 Months)	$30,000	$60,000
Total Initial Investment	$150,948.45	$297,570.86

On-going Expenses

Meineke franchisees pay a royalty fee equal to the greater of an annual minimum of $20,800 or a fee ranging from 3-7% of gross revenue, depending on the types of services or products provided. Other fees include an advertising fund contribution equal to 1.5% of gross revenue generated from tire sales, towing services and inspections, and 8% of all other gross revenue.

What You Get—Training and Support

An initial training program is conducted every month at the Meineke University in Charlotte, NC and lasts a maximum of 25 days–the length for each trainee depends on the trainee's job function(s). During week one, training covers the areas of advertising/marketing strategies, human resources, computer software, selling and pricing, telephone/drive-in procedures and management of finances. Week two training focuses on inventory management, customer relations/complaint handling, the warranty and intershop program, the commercial selling process, technical issues, safety procedures, undercar inspections and hands on repairs. During week three, franchisees are introduced to the hydraulic theory and similar principles, selling brakes, basic brake theory and corresponding principles, brake cataloging, shocks and struts, constant velocity joints, coil and leaf springs, and the rack and pinion/conventional steering system. The final week of training (week four) familiarizes franchisees with front-end parts, batteries, universal joints, motor and transmission mounts, trailer hitches, belts, the cooling system service and oil and filter changes.

Ongoing support with advertising and training is also provided.

Territory
Meineke grants protected territories.

Mighty Distributing System of America

650 Engineering Dr.
Norcross, GA 30092-2821
Tel: (800) 829-3900 (770) 448-3900
Fax: (770) 446-8627
Email: franchising@mightyautoparts.com
Website: www.mightyfranchise.com
Barry Teagle, Vice President Franchising

Wholesale distribution of original equipment-quality, Mighty-branded auto parts. Franchisees operate in exclusive territories, supplying automotive maintenance and repair facilities with under-car and under-hood products, such as filters, belts, tune-up, and brake parts.

BACKGROUND: IFA Member

Established: 1963;	First Franchised: 1970
Franchised Units:	103
Company-Owned Units:	4
Total Units:	107
Dist.:	US-107; CAN-0; O'seas-0
North America:	38 States
Density:	9 in TX, 7 in FL, 7 in CA
Projected New Units (12 Months):	10
Qualifications:	5, 4, 3, 3, 3, 4

FINANCIAL/TERMS:

Cash Investment:	$70-80K
Total Investment:	$150-250K
Minimum Net Worth:	$500K
Fees: Franchise -	$5K+ $.035/Vcl
Royalty - 5%;	Ad. - 0.5%
Earnings Claims Statement:	Yes
Term of Contract (Years):	10/1
Avg. # of Employees:	4 FT, 2 PT
Passive Ownership:	Not Allowed
Encourage Conversions:	Yes
Area Develop. Agreements:	No
Sub-Franchising Contracts:	No

Expand in Territory:	Yes	Size of Corporate Staff:	50
Space Needs:	3,000 SF	On-going Support: NA,NA,NA,D,NA,NA,NA,NA,NA	
		Training: 1 week on-the-job training;	
SUPPORT & TRAINING:		1 week home office	
Financial Assistance Provided:	No		
Site Selection Assistance:	No	**SPECIFIC EXPANSION PLANS:**	
Lease Negotiation Assistance:	No	US:	All US
Co-operative Advertising:	Yes	Canada:	All Canada
Franchisee Assoc./Member:	Yes/Yes	Overseas:	No

Mighty Auto Parts has offered franchise opportunities to individual entrepreneurs since 1970. Mighty Auto Parts enjoys a strong reputation within the automotive aftermarket - a key blueprint for success for qualified investors.

Mighty sources the finest quality auto parts from the world's leading manufacturers both in the United States and abroad, serving as the connection between manufacturers and professional technicians throughout the country. Mighty prides itself on its organizational culture that makes personal service a priority of the company and does whatever it takes to enhance the success of its customer-partners. This company culture is articulated in the Mighty slogan: "Partners to the Automotive Professional."

Operating Units	12/31/2007	12/31/2008	12/31/2009
Franchised	106	107	102
% Change	--	0.09%	-4.7%
Company-Owned	5	4	4
% Change	--	-20.0%	0.0%
Total	111	111	106
% Change	--	0.0%	-4.5%
Franchised as % of Total	95.5%	96.4%	96.2%

Investment Required
The fee for a Mighty franchise ranges between $12,875-$34,750.

Mighty Distributing provides the following range of investments required to open your initial franchise. The range assumes that all items are paid for in cash. To the extent that you choose to finance any of these expense items, your front-end investment could be substantially reduced.

Item	Established Low Range	Established High Range
Franchise Fee	$12,875	$34,750
Office Equipment	$1,500	$2,000
Warehouse Equipment	$2,000	$7,500
Stationery and Supplies	$250	$250
Initial Training Travel Expense	$1,200	$1,800
Professional Fees	$500	$1,000
Opening Inventory	$50,000	$60,000
Vehicles	$10,000	$30,000
Computer Equipment	$22,000	$27,000
Initial Promotions	$3,000	$5,000
Required Insurance	$2,500	$2,500
Deposits, Licenses	$500	$500
Additional Funds (3 months)	$30,000	$50,000
Total Investment*	$139,300	$210,400

On-going Expenses
Mighty franchisees pay a monthly royalty fee equal to 5% of total gross sales, and an advertising fee equal to 0.5% of total gross sales per month. Other fees payable by the franchisee include a one-time Franchisees Association fee of $250 and Franchisees Association dues of $100 per year.

What You Get—Training and Support
Mighty Distributing provides the franchisee and/or the designated manager

with approximately 5-10 days of training in the operation of the Franchised Business, including classroom business and sales training, and field sales and operations training. The franchisee receives various written instructions, buying guides and confidential manuals, including Mighty's online "Buying Guide" and "Operations Manual," which are amended periodically.

Franchisees are also provided with pre-opening or opening assistance in the initial operation of the franchised business. They are informed of sources for signs, equipment, fixtures, furnishings, improvements and other available products and services for the operation of the Mighty Franchise.

Territory
Mighty Distributing grants exclusive territories.

Mosquito Squad

2924 Emerywood Parkway, Ste. 101
Richmond, VA 23294
Tel: (800) 722-4668 (804) 353-6999
Fax: (804) 358-1878
Email: dbuchel@outdoorlivingbrands.com
Website: www.mosquitosquadfranchise.com
David Buchel, Franchising Recruitment Coordinator

Mosquito Squad is North America's fastest growing outdoor living franchise concept with an incredible, high-margin recurring revenue stream. Since joining the Outdoor Living Brands' franchise lineup in 2009, Mosquito Squad has been experiencing explosive franchise unit and consumer sales growth. Clients want to take back their backyards by combating annoying insect bites and protecting their families and pets from the dangerous diseases such as Lyme disease, encephalitis, and west nile virus.

BACKGROUND:	IFA Member
Established: 2004;	First Franchised: 2005
Franchised Units:	97
Company-Owned Units:	0
Total Units:	97
Dist.:	US-97; CAN-0; O'seas-0
North America:	26 States
Density:	9 in IL, 9 in VA, 8 in NC
Projected New Units (12 Months):	30
Qualifications:	5, 5, 1, 3, 3, 4

FINANCIAL/TERMS:

Cash Investment:	$35K
Total Investment:	$30-60K
Minimum Net Worth:	$75K
Fees: Franchise -	$22.5K

Royalty - $400-1,900 monthly; Ad. - $100-400/mo.		Site Selection Assistance:	NA
Earnings Claims Statement:	Yes	Lease Negotiation Assistance:	NA
Term of Contract (Years):	7/7	Co-operative Advertising:	No
Avg. # of Employees:	1 FT, 2 PT	Franchisee Assoc./Member:	No
Passive Ownership:	Allowed	Size of Corporate Staff:	30
Encourage Conversions:	Yes	On-going Support:	NA,b,C,D,E,F,G,h,I
Area Develop. Agreements:	Yes	Training:	4-5 days depending on class size in
Sub-Franchising Contracts:	No		Richmond, VA
Expand in Territory:	Yes		
Space Needs:	NA	**SPECIFIC EXPANSION PLANS:**	
		US:	All US
SUPPORT & TRAINING:		Canada:	All
Financial Assistance Provided:	Yes (D)	Overseas:	No

Mosquito Squad is proud to be North America's first, best, and most trusted choice to eliminate mosquitoes, ticks, and the diseases they can bring to families and communities. We are the leading national brand with the most locations, largest footprint, and largest client base in the category. No one has eliminated more mosquitoes and ticks—and it's not even close! Our founders are industry pioneers and created many of the programs utilized by the entire industry category, including our competitors.

With over 100 franchises in operation and many more on the way, Mosquito Squad has grown at an incredible rate of 496% over the last three years, as recognized by *Inc. Magazine*. And we enjoy the strongest market share in the industry, by far.

Operating Units	12/31/2008	12/31/2009	12/31/2010
Franchised	18	45	64
% Change	--	150%	42.2 %
Company-Owned	0	0	0
% Change	--	--	--
Total	18	45	64
% Change	--	--	--
Franchised as % of Total	100 %	100%	100%

Investment Required

The initial fee for a Mosquito Squad franchise is $22,500 for a standard territory, and $10,000 for a micro market territory.

Mosquito Squad provides the following range of investments required to open your initial franchise. The range assumes that all items are paid for in cash. To the extent that you choose to finance any of these expense items, your front-end investment could be substantially reduced.

Item	Established Low Range	Established High Range
Initial Franchise Fee	$1,875	$22,500
Travel and Living Expenses	$500	$1,000
Tools and Equipment	$800	$1,700
Computer Hardware and Software	$800	$2,000
Inventory	$1,200	$3,000
Trade Show Booth	$2,500	$2,500
Storage Facility for Inventory and Equipment	$0	$375
Vehicle	$0	$2,250
Vehicle Signage	$1,300	$1,800
Initial Marketing Expenses	$5,000	$10,000
Start-up Expenses and Working Capital for the First 3 Months	$2,500	$7,500
Total Initial Investment (Excluding Real Estate)	$16,475	$54,625

On-going Expenses

Mosquito Squad franchisees pay a monthly brand licensing fee that increases yearly, ranging from $400-$1,650 for standard territories and $300-$900 for micro market territories. Other fees include an individual yearly advertising fee and a monthly national branding or marketing fee.

Franchisee Satisfaction

A critical component of the due diligence process is that you, as a prospective franchisee, have a strong sense of existing franchisee satisfaction. Please review the franchisor's ratings below for this extremely important information.

World-Class Franchise®

How do you rate Mosquito Squad in terms of:	Rating*
Overall quality of franchisor	96%
Rating of the opportunity provided by this franchisor	97%
Franchisor understands that their success is based on success of franchisees	93%
Recommend this franchise to a prospective franchisee?	91%

* Independent Audit of Existing Franchisees Who Rated Mosquito Squad as Excellent, Very Good, or Good

What You Get—Training and Support

Mosquito Squad franchisees will receive a 3.5 day training course, a copy of the company operations manual, letterhead, business cards, etc., and on-

345

site opening and pre-opening assistance (at our discretion and possibly for a fee).

The Mosquito Squad team is fully committed to whatever it takes to support you and your goals as our franchisee. And by being part of the Outdoor Living Brands family of franchise companies, this support system expands exponentially. You'll have access to responsive support from a smart, professional staff in all the key disciplines you'll need. This includes lead generation (a proven, well-respected track record of lead generation and business development practices shared by multiple brands), marketing support (thoughtful, impactful and proven communications tools and strategies), customer acquisition and retention (best practices to deliver world class customer service and proven CRM programs and technology), support, training and technology (a world-class training process, near-constant phone support and on-site guidance and training), and a franchise partner network.

Territory
Mosquito Squad does grant exclusive territories.

NaturaLawn of America

THE LEADER IN ORGANIC-BASED LAWN CARE®
www.nl-amer.com

1 E. Church St.
Frederick, MD 21701
Tel: (800) 989-5444 (301) 694-5440
Fax: (301) 846-0320

Email: franchise@nl-amer.com
Website: www.nl-amer.com
Randy Loeb, VP Franchise Development

NaturaLawn of America is the only nationwide lawn care franchise offering an environmentally friendly lawn care service incorporating natural, organic-based fertilizers and biological controls. Our franchise owners provide residential and commercial customers with fertilization, weed control, insect control, disease control and lawn diagnosis services using safer and healthier products, eliminating the need for harsh chemicals and pesticides.

BACKGROUND:			
Established: 1987;	First Franchised: 1989		
Franchised Units:	64		
Company-Owned Units:	4		
Total Units:	68		
Dist.:	US-68; CAN-0; O'seas-0		
North America:	27 States		
Density:	5 in VA, 5 in PA, 6 in MD		
Projected New Units (12 Months):	10-12		
Qualifications:	4, 4, 1, 4, 3, 5		

FINANCIAL/TERMS:	
Cash Investment:	$50K
Total Investment:	$108-155K
Minimum Net Worth:	$250K
Fees: Franchise -	$29.5K
Royalty - 7-9%;	Ad. - 0%
Earnings Claims Statement:	Yes
Term of Contract (Years):	5/10
Avg. # of Employees:	1-3 FT, 0 PT
Passive Ownership:	Not Allowed

Encourage Conversions:	Yes
Area Develop. Agreements:	No
Sub-Franchising Contracts:	Yes
Expand in Territory:	Yes
Space Needs:	1,200 SF

SUPPORT & TRAINING:	
Financial Assistance Provided:	Yes (D)
Site Selection Assistance:	Yes
Lease Negotiation Assistance:	Yes
Co-operative Advertising:	No
Franchisee Assoc./Member:	No
Size of Corporate Staff:	14
On-going Support:	A,B,C,D,E,F,G,h,I
Training:	1 week home office; 1 week Field office; 1 week on-site

SPECIFIC EXPANSION PLANS:	
US:	All US
Canada:	All Canada
Overseas:	No

No other lawn care franchise opportunity offers the name brand recognition that NaturaLawn of America does. NaturaLawn carries an exclusive and proprietary line of organic-based products, opportunity to become part of the nation's most innovative and fastest growing natural, organic-based/ biological lawn care company.

NaturaLawn's marketing and public relations efforts and numerous association and consumer contacts give franchisees a leg up in the lawn care industry. NaturaLawn seeks franchisees with management or entrepreneurial experience who welcome a challenging and rewarding career path in addition to growing a rather significant green business.

Operating Units	12/31/2008	12/31/2009	12/31/2010
Franchised	61	60	59
% Change	--	-1.6%	-1.7%
Company-Owned	5	5	5
% Change	--	0.0%	0.0%

Total	66	65	64
% Change	--	-1.5%	-1.5%
Franchised as % of Total	92.4%	92.3%	92.2%

Investment Required

The fee for a NaturaLawn of America franchise is $29,500, but discounts are available for franchisees with previous business similar to NaturaLawn.

NaturaLawn of America provides the following range of investments required to open your initial franchise. The range assumes that all items are paid for in cash. To the extent that you choose to finance any of these expense items, your front-end investment could be substantially reduced.

Item	Established Low Range	Established High Range
Initial Franchise Fee	$29,500	$29,500
Opening Inventory	$0	$15,000
Lawn Care Equipment Purchases	$5,000	$10,000
Vehicle (Purchase or Lease for 6 Months)	$0	$5,000
Office Furniture & Equipment	$0	$5,000
Expenses While Training	$2,800	$3,400
Computer & Technology Expenses	$1,500	$2,000
Initial Annual Advertising and Marketing	$50,000	$50,000
Licenses	$250	$500
Professional Fees (Accounting, Legal, etc.)	$1,250	$2,000

Lease Deposits (Rent, Utilities, etc.)	$4,000	$5,000
Insurance Deposit	$3,500	$5,500
Additional Funds (6 Months or More)	$10,000	$12,000
Total Initial Investment	$107,800	$144,900

On-going Expenses

NaturaLawn of America franchisees pay a monthly royalty fee of 9% of gross sales.

What You Get—Training and Support

NaturaLawn of America provides franchisees with up to 40 hours of in-depth classroom at its headquarters in Frederick, Maryland on topics including business start-up, budget, business planning, customer service, accounting, agronomic and sales/marketing training. This is followed by up to 80 hours of on-site field training and covers additional topics such as agronomic, software, office set-up and equipment training.

Franchisees have access to a wide range of products and materials designed to help their business including proprietary natural, organic-based fertilizers, professionally created marketing and promotional materials, and national buying programs to reduce costs.

Territory

NaturaLawn of America grants exclusive territories.

Padgett Business Services

PADGETT
THE SMALL BIZ PROS

400 Blue Hill Dr., #201
Westwood, MA 02090
Tel: (877) 729-8725 (781) 251-9410
Fax: (781) 251-9520
Email: padgett@smallbizpros.com
Website: www.smallbizpros.com
Carol Clark, Franchise Development

America's top-rated and fastest-growing tax and accounting franchise serves the fastest-growing segment of the economy - America's small business owners. Includes initial training, specialized software, and on-going support.

BACKGROUND: IFA Member
Established: 1966; First Franchised: 1975
Franchised Units: 400
Company-Owned Units: 0
Total Units: 400
Dist.: US-299; CAN-101; O'seas-0
North America: 45 States, 8 Provinces
Density: 38 in QC, 67 in ON, 26 in GA
Projected New Units (12 Months): 50
Qualifications: 3, 3, 4, 4, 2, 4

FINANCIAL/TERMS:
Cash Investment:	$100K
Total Investment:	$106K
Minimum Net Worth:	$100K
Fees: Franchise -	$38K +18K Training
Royalty - 9-4.5%;	Ad. - 0%
Earnings Claims Statement:	Yes
Term of Contract (Years):	10/10
Avg. # of Employees:	1 FT, 2 PT
Passive Ownership:	Not Allowed
Encourage Conversions:	Yes
Area Develop. Agreements:	No
Sub-Franchising Contracts:	No
Expand in Territory:	Yes
Space Needs:	200-400 SF

SUPPORT & TRAINING:
Financial Assistance Provided:	No
Site Selection Assistance:	Yes
Lease Negotiation Assistance:	NA
Co-operative Advertising:	No
Franchisee Assoc./Member:	Yes/Yes
Size of Corporate Staff:	40
On-going Support:	A,NA,C,D,NA,NA,G,H,I
Training:	3 (2.5 day) site visits; 2.5 weeks Athens, GA

SPECIFIC EXPANSION PLANS:
US:	All US
Canada:	All Canada
Overseas:	No

Padgett Business Services is America's top-rated and fastest-growing tax and accounting franchise. With a network of over 400 offices in the United States and Canada, Padgett is one of the largest privately-owned small business services firms in the country, providing a wide array of financial services including tax planning and preparation, payroll services, financial reporting, business consultation and other services pertinent to small businesses. Padgett franchisees help other entrepreneurs reach their full potential by building strong relationships with clients and running their businesses more effectively and efficiently.

With plans to open 200 franchised units in the next five years, Padgett is actively recruiting new franchise owners to help build on their proven formula of success. Initial training, specialized software and ongoing support for franchisees ensure they are equipped with the tools needed to successfully branch out and reach their goals.

Operating Units	12/31/2008	12/31/2009	12/31/2010
Franchised	293	299	306
% Change	--	2.0%	2.3%
Company-Owned	0	0	0
% Change	--	--	--
Total	293	299	306
% Change	--	2.0%	2.3%
Franchised as % of Total	100.0%	100.0%	100.0%

Investment Required

The fee for a Padgett Business Services franchise is $56,000. This fee is divided into a $1,000 application fee, a $37,000 initial license fee, and a $18,000 training fee.

Padgett Business Services provides the following range of investments required to open your initial franchise. The range assumes that all items are paid for in cash. To the extent that you choose to finance any of these expense items, your front-end investment could be substantially reduced.

Item	Established Low Range	Established High Range
Application Fee	$1,000	$1,000
Initial License Fee	$37,000	$37,000
Initial Training Fee	$18,000	$18,000
Expenses While Training	$2,000	$2,000
Equipment and Fixtures	$3,500	$3,500
Marketing & Branding	$16,080	$16,080

Appointment Setting	$14,400	$14,400
Initial Software & Hardware Fee	$4,000	$4,000
Office Supplies	$2,000	$2,000
Initial Insurance	$800	$800
Rent, Telephone, Postage, etc.	$3,600	$3,600
Other Expenses	$2,375	$2,375
Additional Funds (3 Months)	$1,200	$1,200
Total Initial Investment	$105,955	$105,955

On-going Expenses
Padgett Business Services franchisees pay royalty fees equal to the greater of 9% of gross receipts or a fixed amount, ranging from $50 to $750 per month depending on how long the franchisee has been in business. Franchisees also pay advertising contributions equal to up to 2% of gross receipts.

What You Get—Training and Support
New franchisees receive training in the Padgett Marketing and Operations System before opening their own franchise, and an additional course after six months of operation. Step-by-step courses and seminars are held on all major aspects of the business. Additionally, Padgett Business Services offers franchisees free ongoing professional training several times a year where they can polish their knowledge, learn about developments in the industry and network with each other at annual tax seminars and marketing conferences.

Padgett provides its franchisees with telephone support, web support and has a franchisee-staffed Advisory Board where franchisees can voice ideas and opinions to the Padgett support team. Padgett supplies marketing plans, professionally designed programs, and ready-made sales materials that create qualified business leads. Franchisees also receive help in promoting their new business from Padgett's in-house Public Relations department. Monthly newsletters keep franchisees updated on what's happening at Padgett and ensure that owners stay in constant contact with clients. Padgett's research and development team provides timely computer updates, new methods of client development, and workable solutions to many day-to-day problems.

Territory
Padgett Business Services does not grant exclusive territories.

Pop-A-Lock

"Trusted Locksmith" ®

1018 Harding St., # 101
Lafayette, LA 70503-2400
Tel: (877) 233-6211 (337) 233-6211
Fax: (337) 233-6655
Email: michaelkleimeyer@systemforward.com
Website: www.popalock.com/franchising.php
Michael Kleimeyer, Director of Franchise Development

Pop-A-Lock is America's largest locksmith, car door unlocking, and roadside assistance service. We provide fast, professional, guaranteed service using our proprietary tools and opening techniques. We offer an outstanding community service through our industry.

BACKGROUND:	IFA Member
Established: 1991;	First Franchised: 1994
Franchised Units:	182
Company-Owned Units:	0
Total Units:	182
Dist.:	US-182; CAN-0; O'seas-0
North America:	40 States
Density:	22 in TX, 14 in LA, 17 in FL
Projected New Units (12 Months):	38

Qualifications:	4, 5, 1, 3, 3, 4

FINANCIAL/TERMS:

Cash Investment:	$30-120K
Total Investment:	$100-350K
Minimum Net Worth:	$250-400K
Fees: Franchise - $29K+$66/1000 of population	
Royalty - 6%;	Ad. - 1%
Earnings Claims Statement:	No
Term of Contract (Years):	10/10
Avg. # of Employees:	2 FT, 2 PT
Passive Ownership:	Allowed
Encourage Conversions:	NA
Area Develop. Agreements:	No
Sub-Franchising Contracts:	No
Expand in Territory:	Yes
Space Needs:	

SUPPORT & TRAINING:

Financial Assistance Provided:	Yes (I)
Site Selection Assistance:	NA
Lease Negotiation Assistance:	NA
Co-operative Advertising:	No
Franchisee Assoc./Member:	Yes/Yes
Size of Corporate Staff:	11
On-going Support:	A,b,C,D,e,F,G,h,I
Training: 10 days in Lafayette, LA, plus add'l local	

SPECIFIC EXPANSION PLANS:

US:	All US
Canada:	Toronto/GTA
Overseas:	Ireland, UK, China

353

Pop-A-Lock was established in 1991 to provide unlocking service for automobiles' doors. Now they have grown to serve a wide range of locksmith service customers from any business, home or auto. Now Pop-A-Lock is the market leader in the mobile security industry. The company started franchising in 1994 and currently has more than 4,000 service centers nationwide.

Pop-A-Lock provides mobile security services with all new modern technologies, proprietary tools and opening techniques to ensure secure access. They also provide emergency services like Emergency Car Door Unlocking (EDU) Program when human life is in danger such as a child locked inside car. This free-of-cost Pop-A-Lock service has rescued over 280,000 children from locked vehicles since the company began its journey.

Operating Units	12/31/2008	12/31/2009	12/31/2010
Franchised	133	136	136
% Change	--	2.3%	0%
Company-Owned	0	0	0
% Change	--	--	--
Total	133	136	136
% Change	--	2.3%	0%
Franchised as % of Total	100%	100%	100%

(*Franchised numbers above are by Agreement, not Franchise service areas; i.e., one Agreement could be 40 franchise territories.)

Investment Required
The initial franchise fee for a Pop-A-Lock franchise is $15,500 for an exclusive territory population of 125,000. (Multiple territories may be awarded, based on exclusive population density.)

Pop-A-Lock provides the following range of investments required to open your initial franchise. The range assumes that all items are paid for in cash. To the extent that you choose to finance any of these expense items, your front-end investment could be substantially reduced.

Item	Established Low Range	Established High Range
Franchise Fee	$15,500	$15,500
Pop-A-Lock Tool Kits	$1,600	$1,600
Printed Materials	$647	$647
CDU (Technical) Training	$1,600	$1,600
Travel and Living Expenses While Training	$3,520	$3,520
Equipment- Communication	$600	$600
Equipment- Roadside Service	$600	$600
Locksmith Service Training	$1,950	$1,950
Locksmith Service Equipment	$15,000	$20,000
Equipment- Office (Computer System)	$1,500	$1,500
Telephone Directory Display Advertisement	$250	$1,000
Initial Advertising (12 months)	$2,500	$2,500
Miscellaneous Opening Costs	$800	$1,200
Working Capital	$36,000	$41,000
Vehicle Identification	$1,500	$2,500
Mentor Program	$2,200	$2,200
Total Investment	$85,767	$97,917

On-going Expenses

Pop-A-Lock franchisees pay a royalty fee equal to 6% of monthly gross sales, an advertising and marketing fee equal to 1% of gross sales, an employee training fee, and others. Franchisee Orientation Training is included in Franchise Fee.

Franchisee Satisfaction
A critical component of the due diligence process is that you, as a prospective franchisee, have a strong sense of existing franchisee satisfaction. Please review the franchisor's ratings below for this extremely important information.

**World-Class
Franchise®**

How do you rate Pop-A-Lock in terms of:	Rating*
Initial training supplied by the franchisor	100%
Helpfulness and communication between franchisees	90%
Overall communication between home office personnel and franchisees	95%

* Independent Audit of Existing Franchisees Who Rated Pop-A-Lock as Excellent, Very Good, or Good

What You Get—Training and Support
The Pop-A-Lock Franchisee Training Program introduces the various facets of operating one of their franchises, including operations, standards, human resources, administration, accounting, and advertising and marketing. New Franchisee training is conducted at the corporate offices in Lafayette, Louisiana. This program is followed by technical training for staff. This training demonstrates how to use Pop-A-Lock's proprietary equipment and techniques to open vehicles. The course includes comprehensive, high tech locksmith instruction and is conducted at the national training facility in

Lafayette, Louisiana.

Franchise compliance specialists will periodically contact or visit each franchise location to perform a field inspection. They will solicit input and feedback, try to assist with any operational problems, and share best practices throughout the franchise system. Pop-A-Lock regularly posts updated vehicle information and lock diagrams for the Confidential Manual to a secure website for downloadable updates. The franchisee and technicians will also be able to contact a research and development specialist 24 hours a day, seven days a week in the event there is a need for technical assistance to open a vehicle in the field.

Territory
Pop-A-Lock does grant exclusive territories.

Postal Annex +

Your Home Office®

7580 Metropolitan Dr., # 200
San Diego, CA 92108-4417
Tel: (800) 456-1525 (619) 563-4800
Fax: (619) 563-9850
Email: rheine@annexbrands.com
Website: www.postalannexfranchise.com
Ryan Heine, Director of Franchising

Retail business service center, providing packaging, shipping, copying, postal, mail box rental, printing fax, notary, office supplies, and more.

BACKGROUND:	IFA Member
Established: 1985;	First Franchised: 1986
Franchised Units:	335
Company-Owned Units:	0
Total Units:	335
Dist.:	US-334; CAN-0; O'seas-1

North America:	25 States
Density:	20 in OR, 17 in MI, 130 in CA
Projected New Units (12 Months):	36
Qualifications:	5, 3, 1, 1, 3, 3

FINANCIAL/TERMS:	
Cash Investment:	$50K
Total Investment:	$138.8-200.1K
Minimum Net Worth:	$200K
Fees: Franchise -	$29.95K
Royalty - 5%;	Ad. - 2%
Earnings Claims Statement:	Yes
Term of Contract (Years):	15/15
Avg. # of Employees:	1 FT, 2 PT
Passive Ownership:	Allowed
Encourage Conversions:	Yes
Area Develop. Agreements:	Yes
Sub-Franchising Contracts:	No
Expand in Territory:	Yes
Space Needs:	1,200 SF

SUPPORT & TRAINING:	
Financial Assistance Provided:	Yes (D)

Site Selection Assistance:	Yes	Training:	2 weeks San Diego, CA; 1 week on-site
Lease Negotiation Assistance:	Yes		
Co-operative Advertising:	No	**SPECIFIC EXPANSION PLANS:**	
Franchisee Assoc./Member:	Yes/Yes	US:	All US
Size of Corporate Staff:	21	Canada:	All Canada
On-going Support:	NA,NA,c,d,E,NA,G,H,I	Overseas:	All Countries

PostalAnnex+ and its affiliates have grown to nearly 300 franchises across 22 states as a result of the demand that today's busy lifestyles creates for postal, shipping and packaging, copying, and printing services. PostalAnnex+ saves consumers time and money, an aspect of PostalAnnex+ that garners high and consistent customer retention rates. With PostalAnnex+, small and home-based business owners can take advantage of one-stop shopping for all their business needs. PostalAnnex+ offers mailbox rentals, UPS, FedEx and USPS shipping, postal services, packaging, copying, and a variety of other services.

From tested methods of site selection to ongoing advertising and support, franchisees can count on the expertise of PostalAnnex+ to help franchisees develop their own postal and shipping franchise business.

Operating Units	12/31/2008	12/31/2009	12/31/2010
Franchised	5	4	4
% Change	--	-20.0%	0.0%
Company-Owned	0	0	0
% Change	--	--	--
Total	5	4	4
% Change	--	-20.0%	0.0%
Franchised as % of Total	100%	100%	100%

Investment Required
The initial regional license fee for a PostalAnnex+ franchise ranges from $50,000 to $250,000, depending on the rate and populations of your territory.

PostalAnnex+ provides the following range of investments required to open your initial franchise. The range assumes that all items are paid for in cash. To the extent that you choose to finance any of these expense items, your front-end investment could be substantially reduced.

Item	Established Low Range	Established High Range
Regional License Fee	$50,000	$250,000
Insurance (General Liability)	$1,500	$2,500
Expenses While Training	$1,000	$3,500
Initial Advertising	$12,000	$15,000
Sales Presentation Materials	$500	$1,000
Office Supplies	$7,000	$19,000
Business Licenses, Permits	$300	$500
Additional Funds (3 Months)	$6,500	$12,000
Total Initial Investment	$78,800	$303,500

On-going Expenses
PostalAnnex+ franchisees pay ongoing non-participating advertising fees equal to $5,000, an advertising and promotion fee equal to at least $1,000. Additional fees include an area/regional licensee association fee equal to $50 quarterly.

What You Get—Training and Support
PostalAnnex's site selection team utilizes demographic and market research as well as local real estate knowledge to help franchisees identify and select advantageous packing franchise sites close to potential customers' offices, businesses, and residences. Additionally, PostalAnnex+ provides professional design and buildout of franchisees' stores.

Franchisees undergo a comprehensive training program that begins with 10 days training at the PostalAnnex+ Home Office. Instruction includes operating procedures, products and services, operating systems, business management, and marketing. PostalAnnex+ maintains a full line of ready-to-use marketing materials including flyers, posters, counter cards and direct mail pieces along with an individual store website and more. The PostalAnnex+ Marketing Communications Department ensure that franchisees reach their target customer bases and the Franchise Services Department helps franchisees solve and work through challenging issues.

Territory
PostalAnnex+ grants protected territories.

Postal Connections of America

Postal Connections™

275 East Douglas Street, Suite 115
El Cajon, CA 92020
Tel: (800) 767-8257 (619) 294-7550
Fax: (619) 294-4550
Email: deb@postalconnections.com
Website: www.postalconnections.com
Debbie Andrew, Operations and Marketing

Postal Connections of America franchises are specialty postal and copy service centers offering a variety of services, including packing, shipping, mailbox rentals, fax, money transfer & money orders and notary services. Our newer outlets also include state-of-the-art technology features, such as computer work stations with high speed Internet access, e-mail address, video conferencing and meeting rooms, truly making our locations "virtual offices."

BACKGROUND:	
	IFA Member
Established: 1985;	First Franchised: 1996
Franchised Units:	83
Company-Owned Units:	0
Total Units:	83
Dist.:	US-83; CAN-0; O'seas-0
North America:	24 States
Density:	7 in OR, 29 in CA, 12 in AZ
Projected New Units (12 Months):	36
Qualifications:	4, 3, 1, 3, 1, 4

FINANCIAL/TERMS:	
Cash Investment:	$34-49K
Total Investment:	$115.9-152.9K
Minimum Net Worth:	$100K
Fees: Franchise -	$21K
Royalty - 4%;	Ad. - 0

Earnings Claims Statement:	No
Term of Contract (Years):	10/10
Avg. # of Employees:	0 FT, 2 PT
Passive Ownership:	Allowed, But Discouraged
Encourage Conversions:	Yes
Area Develop. Agreements:	Yes
Sub-Franchising Contracts:	No
Expand in Territory:	Yes
Space Needs:	1,200 SF
SUPPORT & TRAINING:	
Financial Assistance Provided:	Yes (I)
Site Selection Assistance:	Yes

Lease Negotiation Assistance:	Yes
Co-operative Advertising:	No
Franchisee Assoc./Member:	No
Size of Corporate Staff:	12
On-going Support:	NA,NA,C,d,e,NA,NA,h,I
Training:	4 days new location; 5 days at store
SPECIFIC EXPANSION PLANS:	
US:	All US
Canada:	All Canada
Overseas:	Asia, Europe, South America, Middle East, Australia

Founded in 1985, Postal Connections of America is a growing postal, shipping, and business services franchise. Postal Connections provides households, small offices, and businesses essential postal and shipping services in a convenient, efficient environment. Postal Connections offers an assortment of goods and services including shipping, copying, printing, scanning, faxing, mail receiving and forwarding, notary, and packing and office supplies. The Postal Connections business model was developed in the 1980s to deliver a swift and agreeable postal and shipping experience, and since then, the concept has expanded worldwide.

Postal Connections offers a sizable business opportunity for prospective franchisees. Postal and shipping services represent an enormous industry, and Postal Connections is positioned to serve millions of potential customers. Franchisees benefit from a management team with years of experience and a proven business model. Furthermore, with its service alternatives, flexible options, low entry costs, and low on-going royalties, Postal Connections is designed for vigorous competition in the market. By owning a Postal Connections franchise, investors have the opportunity to pursue personal financial success while connecting communities throughout the world.

Operating Units	12/31/2007	12/31/2008	12/31/2009
Franchised	65	67	55
% Change	--	3.1%	-17.91%

361

Company-Owned	0	0	0
% Change	--	0.0%	0.0%
Total	65	67	55
% Change	--	3.1%	-17.91%
Franchised as % of Total	100%	100%	100%

Investment Required

The fee for an initial Postal Connection franchise is $24,900. The initial franchise fee for honorably discharged U.S. veterans is $21,165. The initial fee for additional franchises is $12,900 and $10,900 respectively.

Postal Connection provides the following range of investments required to open your initial franchise. The range assumes that all items are paid for in cash. To the extent that you choose to finance any of these expense items, your front-end investment could be substantially reduced.

Item	Established Low Range	Established High Range
Franchise Fee	$21,165	$24,900
Real Estate Expenses	$1,500	$5,500
Architect Fees	$0	$1,500
Store Construction and Installation	$42,450	$43,650
Store Build Out/Signage	$17,200	$17,500
Inventory and Supplies	$6,900	$7,800
Point of Sale System	$2,000	$3,500
Additional Equipment	$2,150	$15,150
Insurance	$250	$1,200
Grand Opening Advertising	$1,500	$3,000

Initial Training Expenses	$650	$1,000
Training Fee	$6,500	$6,500
Design Fee	$500	$500
Miscellaneous Operating Costs	$1,900	$3,500
Additional Funds (3 months)	$15,000	$20,000
Total Investment	$119,665	$155,200

On-going Expenses
Postal Connections franchisees pay a monthly royalty fee equal to 4% of gross volume, and a monthly local advertising and promotions fee equal to 5% of gross volume.

What You Get—Training and Support
Postal Connections franchise owners and their general managers receive training at a designated Postal Connections Store. This training consists of one day of business plan development training, 6 days of business development training (which includes business administration and advertising education), 5 days of field training, and 4 days of in-store training.

The franchisee receives a Postal Connections Training Package with a template for a business plan, a Training Preparation Handbook, a Stages of Development Handbook, and an operations manual. Postal Connections may periodically conduct an annual conference, convention or training session for franchisees.

Territory
Postal Connections offers exclusive territories in sizes varying from a radius of two city blocks in an urban area to a possible radius of 20 miles in a suburban or rural area. Postal Connections will not locate another company-owned or franchised Postal Connections Store in a franchisee's exclusive territory.

Postnet

CREATE • DUPLICATE • DELIVER

1819 Wazee St.
Denver, CO 80202
Tel: (800) 338-7401 (303) 771-7100
Fax: (303) 771-7133
Email: info@postnet.com
Website: www.postnetfranchise.com
Brian Spindel, President/COO

PostNet Centers offer graphic design, digital printing and copying, computer rental stations and much more. Consumers count on PostNet for high quality printing services, digital copy services in black and white or full color, and a host of finishing services to professionally complete any project. And, when it's time to send or receive something, PostNet offers domestic and international parcel shipping with companies like UPS, FedEx, and DHL, traditional postal services, packaging services and supplies, and private mailboxes. Create, duplicate, deliver. That's the PostNet advantage.

BACKGROUND: IFA Member
Established: 1985;   First Franchised: 1993
Franchised Units: 900
Company-Owned Units: 0
Total Units: 900
Dist.:   US-440; CAN-78; O'seas-382
  North America: 41 States, 4 Provinces
  Density: 46 in TX, 46 in CA, 37 in AZ

Projected New Units (12 Months):	50
Qualifications:	5, 3, 1, 3, 4, 5

FINANCIAL/TERMS:

Cash Investment:	$60K
Total Investment:	$172-198K
Minimum Net Worth:	$300K
Fees: Franchise -	$30K
Royalty - 5%;	Ad. - 2%
Earnings Claims Statement:	No
Term of Contract (Years):	15/15
Avg. # of Employees:	2 FT, 1 PT
Passive Ownership:	Not Allowed
Encourage Conversions:	Yes
Area Develop. Agreements:	Yes
Sub-Franchising Contracts:	No
Expand in Territory:	Yes
Space Needs:	1,200 SF

SUPPORT & TRAINING:

Financial Assistance Provided:	Yes (I)
Site Selection Assistance:	Yes
Lease Negotiation Assistance:	Yes
Co-operative Advertising:	No
Franchisee Assoc./Member:	No
Size of Corporate Staff:	30
On-going Support:	NA,NA,C,D,E,F,G,H,I
Training:	2 weeks Denver, CO;
	1 week store opening; 2-3 days follow-up

SPECIFIC EXPANSION PLANS:

US:	All US
Canada:	All Canada
Overseas: All Countries Not Currently Represented	

PostNet offers full-fledged services—digital printing and copying, scanning, graphic design, computer rental, document finishing services, packing, private mailbox rental and more—to help small businesses and busy customers get their projects done. Each PostNet location is also an authorized domestic and international shipping center for UPS, FedEx, DHL and the U.S. Postal Service, providing great convenience and efficiency.

Since 1993, PostNet has grown to a global network of nearly 800 locally owned locations. Unlike other shipping, copying, or printing franchises, PostNet's business model is based on diversification. The company is committed to an open and inclusive culture, seeking to involve franchisees in all aspects of the organization.

Operating Units	12/31/2008	12/31/2009	12/31/2010
Franchised	802	767	725
% Change	--	-4.4%	-5.5%
Company-Owned	0	0	0
% Change	--	--	--
Total	802	767	725
% Change	--	-4.4%	-5.5%
Franchised as % of Total	100%	100%	100%

Investment Required
The fee for a PostNet franchise is $29,900. PostNet also makes arrangements for an Area Representative Agreement and a Development Agreement.

PostNet provides the following range of investments required to open your initial franchise. The range assumes that all items are paid for in cash. To the extent that you choose to finance any of these expense items, your front-end investment could be substantially reduced.

Item	Established Low Range	Established High Range
Initial Franchise Fee	$29,900	$29,900
Center Development Fee	$97,900	$97,900
Fee for First Year Start-up Advertising Program	$6,500	$6,500
Lease of Center Premises	$1,375	$6,000

Equipment Lease or Rental Payments	$970	$970
Security Deposit Fees	$3,000	$8,000
Insurance	$900	$2,000
Initial Training Expenses	$1,000	$2,500
Miscellaneous Pre-Opening Expenses	$3,500	$7,500
Additional Funds (8 - 12 Months)	$30,000	$40,000
Total Initial Investment	$175,045	$201,270

On-going Expenses
PostNet franchisees pay a monthly royalty fee of 5% of gross sales as well as a monthly national advertising fund contribution fee of 2% of gross sales.

What You Get—Training and Support
PostNet's comprehensive, three-step training program includes 7-10 days of classroom training, 40 hours of on-site training, and a follow-up training visit about 60-90 days after the center's opening. PostNet's real estate department helps franchisees to identify the best location after considering more than twenty factors including demographics, traffic patterns, physical attributes, competition and more. PostNet offers franchisees a complete development package that includes construction and layout advice, interior and exterior signage, initial inventory, an equipment package, a fully integrated point-of-sale store-management system, and a customer database to assist in marketing.

After opening, PostNet offers ongoing support over the phone, field support, and an online franchisee network. Additional training is conducted through online programs and workshops at annual conventions and regional meetings.

Territory
PostNet grants exclusive territories.

PrideStaff

PRIDESTAFF®

7535 N. Palm Ave. #101
Fresno, CA 93711
Tel: (800) 774-3316 (559) 449-5805
Fax: (559) 432-4371
Email: info@pridestaff.com
Website: www.pridestaff.com
Jane Blocker, EVP/Chief Operating Officer

We specialize in supplemental staffing (temporary help), outsourcing, and full-time placement. Pridestaff fills administrative, clerical, customer service, data entry, word processing, and light industrial positions. The staffing industry is one of the fastest-growing industries in the United States.

BACKGROUND:

Established: 1974;	First Franchised: 1994
Franchised Units:	32
Company-Owned Units:	0
Total Units:	32
Dist.:	US-32; CAN-0; O'seas-0
North America:	13 States
Density:	4 in IL, 12 in CA, 4 in AZ
Projected New Units (12 Months):	NR
Qualifications:	NA

FINANCIAL/TERMS:

Cash Investment:	$75-100K
Total Investment:	$80.4-126.9K
Minimum Net Worth:	NA
Fees: Franchise -	$12.5K
Royalty - 65% Gross Margin;	Ad. - NA
Earnings Claims Statement:	No
Term of Contract (Years):	10/5/5/5
Avg. # of Employees:	2 FT, 0 PT
Passive Ownership:	Not Allowed
Encourage Conversions:	No
Area Develop. Agreements:	No
Sub-Franchising Contracts:	No
Expand in Territory:	Yes
Space Needs:	1,200 SF

SUPPORT & TRAINING:

Financial Assistance Provided:	No
Site Selection Assistance:	Yes
Lease Negotiation Assistance:	Yes
Co-operative Advertising:	No
Franchisee Assoc./Member:	No/No
Size of Corporate Staff:	16
On-going Support:	A,NA,C,D,E,NA,G,H,I
Training: 1 week Fresno, CA; 1 week branch office	

SPECIFIC EXPANSION PLANS:

US:	All US
Canada:	No
Overseas:	No

In 1978, George Rogers had a vision, a dream to create a new type of staffing organization—one that offered the resources and expertise of a national firm with the spirit, dedication and personal service of smaller, entrepreneurial firms. The result is PrideStaff, a national staffing organization delivering innovative solutions to the challenges employers face every day. Through a combination of strong leadership at the national and local level, PrideStaff has consistently delivered exceptional service to franchisees, clients, and field associates.

With businesses increasingly demanding more "just-in-time" solutions to their hiring needs, and the US Department of Labor forecasting increasing talent shortages over the next 20 years or more, the staffing industry is

367

poised for significant long-term growth. In fact, the staffing industry is forecast to produce more new jobs than any other industry through 2012. PrideStaff franchisees will be at the forefront of capitalizing on that job growth.

Operating Units	12/31/2008	12/31/2009	12/31/2010
Franchised	36	26	28
% Change	--	-27.8%	7.7%
Company-Owned	3	4	3
% Change	--	33.3%	-25.0%
Total	39	30	31
% Change	--	-23.1%	3.3%
Franchised as % of Total	92.3%	86.7%	90.3%

Investment Required
The initial fee for a Pridestaff franchise is $32,000.

Pridestaff provides the following range of investments required to open your initial franchise. The range assumes that all items are paid for in cash. To the extent that you choose to finance any of these expense items, your front-end investment could be substantially reduced.

Item	Established Low Range	Established High Range
Initial Franchise Fee	$32,000	$32,000
Business Premises	$3,600	$6,000
Leasehold Improvements	$0	$12,000
Utility Deposits	$0	$1,500
Furnishings	$3,000	$13,500
Business Equipment	$5,000	$6,000
First Year Skills Testing Software License Fee	$1,166.00	$2,000

Signage	$1,000.00	$5,000
Expenses to attend initial training	$5,000.00	$6,500
Permits, Memberships, Subscriptions	$500.00	$1,000
Business Insurance Premiums	$1,600.00	$2,000
Initial Supplies	$500.00	$1,000
Additional Funds - 3 Months	$109,100.00	$135,100
Total Investment	$162,466.00	$223,600

On-going Expenses
Pridestaff franchisees pay ongoing royalty fees equal to 35% of gross margin or 6% of net billings plus 21% of direct hire and conversion fees.

What You Get—Training and Support
PrideStaff's competitive difference is marked by specially developed business management, marketing, training and promotional programs. To ensure consistent quality, franchisees are provided with leading computerized software programs for the evaluation, training and selection of Field Associates. Franchisees tap into Pridestaff's planned approach to the recruiting process that maximizes access to passive job candidates. Franchisees have access to Pridestaff's internal applicant tracking and skill matching system, which uses state-of-the-art technology to expedite the order fulfillment process and provide flexible reporting capabilities.

PrideStaff's award-winning direct marketing system that provides a step-by-step process for attracting the attention of staffing decision makers and creating opportunities to close business, plus a quality assurance and continuous improvement process designed to guarantee client satisfaction. Through Pridestaff's corporate intranet, onsite sales and operations training, and the annual PAC conference, franchisees are provided with the most up-to-date techniques to maximize the effectiveness of their sales and servicing activities.

Territory
PrideStaff does grant exclusive territories.

Pronto Insurance

805 Media Luna, # 400
Brownsville, TX 78520
Tel: (956) 574-9787
Fax: (956) 574-9076
Email: sidney.williams@prontoinsurance.com
Website: www.prontoinsurance.com
Sidney Williams, Franchise Director

The Pronto Insurance franchise is a full-service retail office dedicated to providing low cost insurance products and income tax services. Pronto provides itself in providing fast and efficient services. "Pronto. It's our name and our promise" speaks for itself. The company has enjoyed stunning growth, more than quadrupling its size in the last three years. We have 100+ locations and our own in-house claims and underwriting departments. Through aggressive marketing, brand awareness and highly competitive pricing, we have quickly become an industry leader in Texas.

BACKGROUND:

Established: 1997;	First Franchised: 2009
Franchised Units:	34
Company-Owned Units:	97
Total Units:	131
Dist.:	US-131; CAN-0; O'seas-0
North America:	1 State
Density:	131 in TX

Projected New Units (12 Months):	40
Qualifications:	3, 5, 1, 2, 3, 5

FINANCIAL/TERMS:

Cash Investment:	$50-60K
Total Investment:	$60-100K
Minimum Net Worth:	$200K
Fees: Franchise -	$20K
Royalty - 3%;	Ad. - $1,000/Mo.
Earnings Claims Statement:	No
Term of Contract (Years):	5/5
Avg. # of Employees:	4 FT, 0 PT
Passive Ownership:	Allowed
Encourage Conversions:	Yes
Area Develop. Agreements:	Yes
Sub-Franchising Contracts:	No
Expand in Territory:	Yes
Space Needs:	1,200 SF

SUPPORT & TRAINING:

Financial Assistance Provided:	Yes (I)
Site Selection Assistance:	Yes
Lease Negotiation Assistance:	Yes
Co-operative Advertising:	No
Franchisee Assoc./Member:	No
Size of Corporate Staff:	300
On-going Support:	A,B,C,D,E,NA,G,H,I
Training:	2 weeks OR San Antonio, TX; 2 weeks OR Brownsville, TX; 2 weeks Houston, TX

SPECIFIC EXPANSION PLANS:

US:	TX; CA, FL, AZ in 2011
Canada:	No
Overseas:	No

Pronto Insurance has more than 14 years of experience operating large numbers of highly successful insurance agencies in the state of Texas. It has developed a competitive product line and an effective business model that consistently outperforms the competition. Pronto Insurance strives to provide peace of mind to the value-focused consumer through convenient insurance and financial products.

A Pronto franchisee receives the advantage of brand recognition as well as extensive training and expert support in operations, marketing, and human resources. This affordable franchise is one-of-a-kind and unique in the industry. There is no need to invest in high-cost equipment, large inventories or a large staff like the majority of franchises. Franchisees simply equip an office in a retail location, hire a few employees, and are on their way to running a Pronto Insurance Franchise.

Operating Units	12/31/2008	12/31/2009	12/31/2010
Franchised	0	2	23
% Change	--	--	1050.0%
Company-Owned	33	55	87
% Change	--	66.7%	58.2%
Total	33	57	110
% Change	--	72.7%	93.0%
Franchised as % of Total	0.0%	3.5%	20.9%

Investment Required
The franchise fee for a Pronto Insurance agency store is $20,000. Co-branded franchises or a franchise converted from an existing insurance agency has a fee of $15,000. Pronto Insurance also has an Area Development Program available.

Pronto Insurance provides the following range of investments required to open your initial franchise. The range assumes that all items are paid for in cash. To the extent that you choose to finance any of these expense items, your front-end investment could be substantially reduced.

Item	Established Low Range	Established High Range
Initial Franchise Fee	$20,000	$20,000
Business Licenses & Permits	$150	$300
Leasehold Improvements	$15,000	$25,000
Fixtures, Furnishings & Equipment	$15,500	$26,000
Computer System	$1,800	$2,400
Architect/Engineering Fees	$150	$250
Rent, Security Deposits and Utility Deposits	$2,400	$4,000
Other Professional Fees	$100	$200
Insurance Deposit	$225	$400
Initial Inventory of Operating Supplies	$250	$350
Expenses While Training	$500	$1,200
Grand Opening Advertising	$5,000	$5,000
Additional Funds (3 Months)	$10,000	$15,000
Total Initial Investment	$71,075	$100,100

On-going Expenses
Pronto Insurance collects all gross franchise revenue earned by the franchise, and pays franchisees a sales commission equal to 12% of all insurance premium revenue and 90% of all tax preparation fee revenue, with a minimum of $150 retained each month. Additional fees include an advertising obligation of up to the greater of $500 per month or 1% of gross franchise revenue and a quality control evaluation fee not to exceed $500 per year.

What You Get—Training and Support

Pronto Insurance has developed a comprehensive training program that teaches franchisees every aspect of the insurance business model. This model can be broken down into the following: selling policies, providing excellent customer service, managing employees, and bookkeeping. Pronto Insurance also assists franchisees in the site selection process, which is extremely important to the success of a business. The approval of a specific location is dependent on a vigorous demographic study, contingent upon a proven formula that incorporates a large number of factors like specific demographics, traffic counts, physical attributes and competition. Franchisees are also provided with the Pronto Insurance proprietary software needed to track and maintain a book of business.

The Managing General Agency at Pronto Insurance corporate headquarters provides the support that franchisee customers need when dealing with a claim or policy care. Local Pronto staff supports franchisees in taking care of their clients. Furthermore, two million dollars is spent by Pronto Insurance in advertising and marketing across the state to provide franchisees with a strong marketing presence.

Territory

Pronto Insurance offers area development agreements.

Re-Bath Corporation

421 W. Alameda Dr.
Tempe, AZ 85282
Tel: (800) 426-4573 (480) 844-1575
Fax: (480) 833-7199
Email: tmccarthy@rebath.com
Website: www.rebath.com
Tim McCarthy, VP Franchising

Re-Bath is the world's largest bathroom remodeler and offers bathtubs and bathtub liners, showers and shower base liners, wall surround systems, bathtub-to-shower conversions, walk-in bathtubs, vanity cabinets and tops, toilets, shower spas, faucets, mirrors, and accessories.

BACKGROUND: IFA Member
Established: 1979;   First Franchised: 1991
Franchised Units: 220
Company-Owned Units: 0
Total Units: 220
Dist.:   US-217; CAN-7; O'seas-7
    North America: 48 States, 5 Provinces
    Density: 22 in TX, 7 in NY, 14 in CA
Projected New Units (12 Months):   40+
Qualifications: 4, 4, 4, 3, 3, 5

FINANCIAL/TERMS:
Cash Investment: $6-40K
Total Investment: $62-344K
Minimum Net Worth: $75K
Fees: Franchise - $16-80K
    Royalty - Varies, average $15;   Ad. - 0%
Earnings Claims Statement: No
Term of Contract (Years):   7/7

Avg. # of Employees: 4 FT, 3 PT
Passive Ownership: Allowed
Encourage Conversions: No
Area Develop. Agreements: No
Sub-Franchising Contracts: No
Expand in Territory: Yes
Space Needs: 1,200 SF

SUPPORT & TRAINING:
Financial Assistance Provided: Yes (D)
Site Selection Assistance: Yes
Lease Negotiation Assistance: No
Co-operative Advertising: No
Franchisee Assoc./Member: Yes/Yes
Size of Corporate Staff: 50
On-going Support: NA,NA,C,D,E,F,G,h,I
Training: 5 days in field in Arden, NC or Decatur,IL;
                              5 days in field in Phoenix, AZ;
                              3 days in field in Mobile, AL

SPECIFIC EXPANSION PLANS:
US: All US
Canada: All Canada
Overseas: Europe, Mexico, Latin America,
                                      S. America, Australia

For over 30 years, Re-Bath has been the leader in bathroom remodeling with well over 1 million installations. Re-Bath offers proprietary products, the largest selection of colors and patterns, patented installation techniques, and ongoing training.

Re-Bath specializes in a wide range of services including replacement bathtubs, walk-in bathtubs, bathtub-to-shower conversions, and much more.

Operating Units	12/31/2008	12/31/2009	12/31/2010
Franchised	213	221	229
% Change	--	3.8%	-5%
Company-Owned	0	0	0
% Change	--	--	--
Total	213	221	229

% Change	--	3.8%	-5%
Franchised as % of Total	100%	100%	100%

Investment Required

The fee for a Re-Bath franchise is eight cents per person, depending on the population of the territory.

Re-Bath provides the following range of investments required to open your initial franchise. The range assumes that all items are paid for in cash. To the extent that you choose to finance any of these expense items, your front-end investment could be substantially reduced.

Item	Large Market	Small Market
Initial Franchise Fee	$60,000 - $100,000	Up to $28,000
Start-Up Package	$7,000	$4,000
Pre-Opening Salaries, Transportation for Initial Training	$1,500 - $5,000	$1,500 - $3,000
Improvements, Construction Costs (showrooms)	$3,000 - $30,000	$3,000.00 - $30,000.00
Mall Kiosk	$6,750 each	$6,750.00 each
Barricade Graphics	$400 - $800	$400.00 - $800.00
Real Estate (for mall kiosks or barricade graphics placements)	$1,500	$1,500.00
Mobile Showroom	$0 - $32,495	As arranged by you
Mobile Showroom Registration and Taxes	$200 - $6,000	$200.00 - $6,000.00
Home Show Booth	$15,000	$15,000.00
Custom In-Store Product Displays	$0 - $10,000	$0.00 - $10,000.00

Real Estate (for showroom)	$325 - $1,875	$325.00 - $1,875.00
Signage (for showrooms)	$3,000 - $5,000	$3,000 - $5,000
Vehicle Wraps	$1,000 - $4,000	$1,000 - $4,000
Opening Advertising	$13,500 - $27,000	$6,700 - $13,400
National Advertising Fund (per month)	$1, 595 - $10,000	$395 - $10,000
Insurance	$3,000 - $5,000	$3,000 - $5,000
Supplies/Office and Misc.	$2,000 - $6,000	$2,000 - $6,000
Additional Funds (3 months)	$7,500 - $60,000	$7,500 - $13,125
Permits, Certificates, and Licenses	$1,000 - $6,000	$1,000 - $6,000
Total	$149,400 - $344,550	$62,270 - $201,945

On-going Expenses

Re-Bath franchisees pay royalty fees equal to $5 for each wall panel, $14 for replacement tubs and shower bases, and $28 for each bathtub liner or shower base liner purchased from us or an approved supplier. Additional fees include $150-$249 monthly (depending on territory size) for 1-800-BATH-TUB, a transfer fee of $5,000, a document fee of $350, a renewal fee of $2,000, and others.

Franchisee Satisfaction

A critical component of the due diligence process is that you, as a prospective franchisee, have a strong sense of existing franchisee satisfaction. Please review the franchisor's ratings below for this extremely important information.

**World-Class
Franchise®**

How do you rate Re-Bath in terms of:	Rating*
Overall quality of franchisor	96%
Quality of products and/or services provided	99%
Rating of long term growth potential	94%
General rating of opportunity provided by this franchisor	95%

* Independent Audit of Existing Franchisees Who Rated Re-Bath as Excellent, Very Good, or Good

What You Get—Training and Support
As a Re-Bath franchisee you receive the following: prime exclusive territory, the industry's leading products, ongoing sales, marketing, and operational support, complete 14-day training program, proprietary products, patented and installation technology. You will also be provided with extensive advice in selecting a showroon site, and possibly the same for mall kiosks. Re-Bath holds seminars, special conferences, and advanced installation training as well.

Territory
Re-Bath grants exclusive territories.

ServiceMaster Clean

ServiceMASTER Clean ®

3839 Forest Hill-Irene Rd.
Memphis, TN 38125
Tel: (800) 255-9687 (901) 597-7500
Fax: (901) 597-7580
Email: dmessenger@smclean.com
Website: www.ownafranchise.com
David Messenger, Vice President

ServiceMaster Clean is a division of The Service-Master Company. With over 60 years of franchising experience and over 4,000 franchises, ServiceMaster Clean continues to grow each year and offers franchise opportunities in three distinct categories: 1) commercial cleaning services, 2) floor care services, and 3) disaster restoration services. Financing is provided for the initial franchise fee, start-up equipment, and vehicles to qualified candidates through Service-Master Acceptance Co.

BACKGROUND:

	IFA Member
Established: 1947;	First Franchised: 1952
Franchised Units:	4,450
Company-Owned Units:	0
Total Units:	4,450
Dist.:	US-2,914; CAN-176; O'seas-1,360
North America:	50 States, 10 Provinces

Density:	155 in CA, 200 in IL, 139 in OH
Projected New Units (12 Months):	150
Qualifications:	5, 3, 2, 2, 3, 5

FINANCIAL/TERMS:

Cash Investment:	$12K
Total Investment:	$41-104.7K
Minimum Net Worth:	$50K
Fees: Franchise -	$24.9-65K
Royalty - 4-10%;	Ad. - 0.5-1%
Earnings Claims Statement:	No
Term of Contract (Years):	5/5
Avg. # of Employees:	3 FT, 2 PT
Passive Ownership:	Allowed, But Discouraged
Encourage Conversions:	Yes
Area Develop. Agreements:	No
Sub-Franchising Contracts:	Yes
Expand in Territory:	Yes
Space Needs:	NA

SUPPORT & TRAINING:

Financial Assistance Provided:	Yes (D)
Site Selection Assistance:	No
Lease Negotiation Assistance:	No
Co-operative Advertising:	Yes
Franchisee Assoc./Member:	Yes/Yes
Size of Corporate Staff:	200
On-going Support:	A,B,C,D,NA,F,G,H,I
Training:	1 week location; 2 weeks Memphis, TN

SPECIFIC EXPANSION PLANS:

US:	All US
Canada:	All Canada
Overseas:	All Countries

ServiceMaster Clean provides cleaning services for millions of people every day. These services include disaster restoration, commercial cleaning, floor care services, and janitorial cleaning. ServiceMaster Clean's range of services also includes mold remediation and carpet and upholstery maintenance required by homes and offices.

With more than 60 years of franchising experience and over 3,000 franchises in the United States and 4,500 franchises worldwide, ServiceMaster Clean has an established reputation for excellence. It strives to remain on the cutting edge and most recently has pursued a "healthy building main-tenance" initiative that uses cleaning products that exceed current environ-mental standards. ServiceMaster Clean is part of the ServiceMaster family of brands that include Merry Maids, Furniture Medic, AmeriSpec, and Ter-minix.

Operating Units	12/31/2008	12/31/2009	12/31/2010
Franchised	3,019	3,016	3,031
% Change	--	-0.1%	0.5%
Company-Owned	0	0	0
% Change	--	--	--
Total	3,019	3,016	3,031
% Change	--	-0.1%	0.5%
Franchised as % of Total	100.0%	100.0%	100.0%

Investment Required
The fee for a ServiceMaster Clean franchise depends on the type of franchise license selected. The costs of different licenses are as follows: $59,900 to $65,000 for disaster restoration services, $24,900 for floor-care services, and $31,900 for janitorial services. Financing available for qualified appli-cants.

ServiceMaster Clean provides the following range of investments required to open your initial franchise. The range assumes that all items are paid for in cash. To the extent that you choose to finance any of these expense items, your front-end investment could be substantially reduced.

Item	Established Low Range	Established High Range
Initial Franchise Fee	$24,900	$65,000
Equipment	$21,900	$56,525
Vehicles	$3,000	$4,000

Expenses While Training	$600	$1,000
Computer Software	$3,500	$7,000
Insurance	$3,200	$15,150
Advertising (3 Months)	$600	$30,750
Misc. Opening Costs	$1,000	$7,200
Additional Funds (3 Months)	$7,500	$18,500
Total Initial Investment	$66,200	$205,125

On-going Expenses
ServiceMaster Clean franchisees pay royalty fees equal to 10% of gross monthly sales with a $250 minimum and national advertising fees ranging from 0.5% to 1% of gross monthly sales with a $20 minimum.

What You Get—Training and Support
ServiceMaster Clean franchisees complete the Pre-Academy program that involves home study, training at a designated regional office, and passing a written test. Franchisees must supplement this training in attending the Academy of Service in Memphis, TN for two to five weeks. There, franchisees receive comprehensive instruction on standard administrative, accounting, hiring, pricing, inventory control procedures, and troubleshooting ideas for operating problems and technical training.

ServiceMaster Clean provides year-round support including national advertising and marketing and business counseling.

Territory
ServiceMaster Clean grants non-exclusive territories.

SERVPRO

SERVPRO®

Fire & Water - Cleanup & Restoration™

801 Industrial Dr.
Gallatin, TN 37066
Tel: (800) 826-9586 (615) 451-0200
Fax: (615) 451-1602
Email: franchise@servpronet.com
Website: www.servpro.com
Kevin Brown, Dir. Franchise Expansion

A completely diversified cleaning and restoration business, with multiple income opportunities. The insurance restoration market (fire, smoke, and water damages) is our main focus. We also specialize in commercial and residential cleaning. SERVPRO teaches effective management, marketing, and technical skills. We are seeking qualified individuals with the desire to own their own business and become part of the SERVPRO team. If you want to be the best, join the best team. Call 1-800-826-9586.

BACKGROUND:

Established: 1967;	First Franchised: 1969	
Franchised Units:		1,571
Company-Owned Units:		0
Total Units:		1,571
Dist.:	US-1,571; CAN-1; O'seas-0	
North America:	47 States, 1 Province	
Density:	172 in CA, 101 in FL, 95 in TX	
Projected New Units (12 Months):		95

Qualifications:	3, 4, 1, 3, 4, 4

FINANCIAL/TERMS:

Cash Investment:	$60-70K
Total Investment:	$132,050-180,450
Minimum Net Worth:	$150K
Fees: Franchise -	$42K
Royalty - 3-10%;	Ad. - 3%
Earnings Claims Statement:	No
Term of Contract (Years):	5/5
Avg. # of Employees:	5-10 FT, 2-4 PT
Passive Ownership:	Not Allowed
Encourage Conversions:	Yes
Area Develop. Agreements:	Yes
Sub-Franchising Contracts:	No
Expand in Territory:	No
Space Needs:	1,500+ SF

SUPPORT & TRAINING:

Financial Assistance Provided:	Yes (D)
Site Selection Assistance:	Yes
Lease Negotiation Assistance:	No
Co-operative Advertising:	Yes
Franchisee Assoc./Member:	No
Size of Corporate Staff:	320
On-going Support:	NA,NA,C,D,E,NA,G,H,I
Training:	2.5 weeks Gallatin, TN;
	1 week franchisee's location

SPECIFIC EXPANSION PLANS:

US:	All US
Canada:	All
Overseas:	No

SERVPRO is a leading franchisor of cleanup and restoration services for fire, water, mold, and more. Founded in 1967, SERVPRO has grown to an extensive network of more than 1,500 franchises covering 48 states. Ranked #1 in the restoration services category in *Entrepreneur Magazine*'s Franchise 500, SERVPRO has established a brand name with national recognition. For the last 40 years, SERVPRO has grown rapidly with a winning business model based on services that are a necessity. Today, SERVPRO franchise owners respond to property emergencies ranging from multi-million dollar disasters to those suffered by individual businesses and homeowners.

381

Operating Units	12/31/2008	12/31/2009	12/31/2010
Franchised	1,459	1,521	1,571
% Change	--	4.2%	3.3%
Company-Owned	0	0	0
% Change	--	--	--
Total	1,459	1,521	1,571
% Change	--	4.2%	3.3%
Franchised as % of Total	100.0%	100.0%	100.0%

Investment Required

The fee for a SERVPRO franchise is $42,000 for territories with populations of approximately 50,000-80,000. SERVPRO franchisees may purchase additional territory at a cost of $462 per population of 1,000. Franchisees must also purchase a standard equipment and products package costing $56,500. SERVPRO offers financing for qualifying franchisees.

SERVPRO provides the following range of investments required to open your initial franchise. The range assumes that all items are paid for in cash. To the extent that you choose to finance any of these expense items, your front-end investment could be substantially reduced.

Item	Established Low Range	Established High Range
Initial Franchise Fee	$42,000	$42,000*
Vehicle	$600	$29,000
Equipment and Products Package	$60,250	$60,250
Supplies	$3,100.	$7,500
Insurance	$3,000	$3,750
Advertising and Promotions	$250	$1,500
Expenses While Training	$550	$1,900

Deposits, Permits and Licenses	$700	$2,550
Accounting Services, On-Line Tak Table Service and QuickBooks Pro Training	$600	$1,500
Xactimate Estimating and Pricing Software and Training	$1,000	$2,500
Real Estate	$0	$3,000
Additional Funds (3 Months)	$20,000	$25,000
Total Investment	$132,050.	$180,450*

*Plus $462.00 per 1,000 over maximum population.

On-going Expenses

SERVPRO franchisees pay royalty fees ranging from 3-10% of monthly gross volume, a fixed monthly fee ranging from $45-$115, depending on monthly gross volume, a monthly advertising fee equal to 0.5% of gross volume, and an additional advertising fee equal to 2.5% of annual gross volume.

What You Get—Training and Support

SERVPRO prides itself on its comprehensive training program, which begins with a home study program and pre-opening projects designed to help franchise owners research and prepare to open their business. Following this, franchisees visit the SERVPRO National Training Center for an extensive program which teaches the basics, demonstrates proper techniques, and includes hands-on training in each area of business operation.

After training takes place, SERVPRO assigns a Trainer to support the franchise owner throughout set-up and grand opening. Throughout the first year, the franchisee has access to the full SERVPRO support system in order to learn the business while gaining field experience. SERVPRO supports the franchisee through marketing efforts, business growth, and ongoing training sessions.

Territory
SERVPRO does not grant exclusive territories.

ShelfGenie

ShelfGenie®

Designed to Transform

1642 Powers Ferry Rd., S.E., #200
Marietta, GA 30067
Tel: (877) 434-3634 (770) 955-4377
Fax: (320) 923-8858
Email: franchise@shelfgenie.com
Website: www.shelfgenie.com
Mike Pollock, Director of Franchise Development

Want to glide into a fabulous business opportunity? We're looking for a select group of franchise owners who want to provide great products and services to customers in their own protected territories. As a franchise owner with ShelfGenie, you'll have a wealth of resources that take away many of the administrative headaches of running your business (phone calls, manufacturing, and installations) along with advanced technologies that help you make informed management decisions.

BACKGROUND:	IFA Member
Established: 2000;	First Franchised: 2008
Franchised Units:	117
Company-Owned Units:	11
Total Units:	128
Dist.:	US-128; CAN-0; O'seas-0
North America:	26 States

Density:	16 in TX, 12 in FL, 7 in CA
Projected New Units (12 Months):	25
Qualifications:	3, 3, 1, NR, 4, 5

FINANCIAL/TERMS:

Cash Investment:	$80-128K
Total Investment:	$80-128K
Minimum Net Worth:	$50K
Fees: Franchise -	$45K
Royalty - 4%;	Ad. - 2%
Earnings Claims Statement:	Yes
Term of Contract (Years):	5/5
Avg. # of Employees:	0 FT, 4 PT
Passive Ownership:	Allowed, But Discouraged
Encourage Conversions:	Yes
Area Develop. Agreements:	No
Sub-Franchising Contracts:	No
Expand in Territory:	No
Space Needs:	NA

SUPPORT & TRAINING:

Financial Assistance Provided:	Yes (I)
Site Selection Assistance:	No
Lease Negotiation Assistance:	No
Co-operative Advertising:	Yes
Franchisee Assoc./Member:	No
Size of Corporate Staff:	24
On-going Support:	NA,NA,C,D,E,F,G,H,NA
Training:	8 days Atlanta, GA

SPECIFIC EXPANSION PLANS:

US:	All US
Canada:	All Canada

ShelfGenie manufactures Glide-Out™ shelving solutions that are custom built to fit virtually any existing cabinet, pantry, or furniture. Glide-Out shelves are ideal for homeowners due to their durability, affordability, utility in their increased accessibility, as well as the fact that they are environmentally friendly and made in the USA.

ShelfGenie target customer demographics include both "Luxury Purchasers" desiring to make affordable upgrades to their homes as well as "Necessity Purchasers" who are adapting to smaller homes or desiring greater accessibility due to disability or age. This range of customers in addition to the growth that the home remodeling industry has been experiencing means that even in today's challenging economy ShelfGenie franchisees are doing exceptionally well.

Operating Units	12/31/2008	12/31/2009	12/31/2010
Franchised	7	55	85
% Change	--	685.7%	54.5%
Company/Affiliate-Owned	3	7	7
% Change	--	133.3%	0.0%
Total	10	62	92
% Change	--	520.0%	48.4%
Franchised as % of Total	70.0%	88.7%	92.4%

Investment Required
The fee for a ShelfGenie franchise is $45,000.

ShelfGenie provides the following range of investments required to open your initial franchise. The range assumes that all items are paid for in cash. To the extent that you choose to finance any of these expense items, your front-end investment could be substantially reduced.

Item	Established Low Range	Established High Range
Initial Franchise Fee	$45,000	$45,000
Leasehold Improvements	$0	$1,000
Vehicles	$0	$25,000
Furniture and Fixtures	$0	$10,000
Technology and Office Equipment/Supplies	$500	$1,000

385

Other Equipment	$1,000	$1,250
Business Licenses and Permits	$100	$1,000
Professional Fees	$2,000	$5,000
Insurance	$500	$2,500
Expenses While Training	$1,000	$3,500
Initial Marketing	$15,000	$15,000
Additional Funds (3 Months)	$5,000	$15,000
Total Initial Investment	$70,100	$125,250

On-going Expenses
ShelfGenie franchisees pay a weekly royalty fee of 4% of gross revenues (percentage may rise to 5% after October 1, 2011) as well as a weekly marketing contribution fee of 2% of gross revenues. Additional fees include a local advertising minimum spending requirement.

What You Get—Training and Support
The ShelfGenie support team provides franchisees with assistance in both opening and operation, including up to eight days of comprehensive start-up training at the home office in Marietta, GA. This initial training is followed by on-site start up assistance, periodic field visits and ongoing remote support from experienced ShelfGenie representatives. ShelfGenie also provides a confidential operations manual detailing day-to-day operations and professionally designed consumer marketing materials.

ShelfGenie franchisees are given access to the ShelfGenie Business Support Center customer calling center for assistance with customer service, as well as a proprietary web-based business management system.

Territory
ShelfGenie grants exclusive territories.

Snap-on Tools

Snap-on®

2801 80th St., P.O. Box 1410
Kenosha, WI 53141-1410
Tel: (800) 786-6600 (877) 476-2766
Fax: (262) 656-5635
Email: franchiseopportunities@snapon.com
Website: www.snaponfranchise.com
Mike Doweidt, Director of Franchising

The premier solutions provider to the vehicle service industry. Premium quality products, delivered and sold with premium service. We are proud of our heritage and are boldly addressing the future needs of our customers with improved efficiency, creating products and services from hand tools to data and management systems. Contact us today for discussion.

BACKGROUND: IFA Member
Established: 1920; First Franchised: 1991
Franchised Units: 4,520
Company-Owned Units: 246
Total Units: 4,766
Dist.: US-3,445; CAN-357; O'seas-964
North America: 50 States, 12 Provinces
Density: 363 in CA, 186 in PA, 240 in TX
Projected New Units (12 Months):
Qualifications: 3, 4, 2, 2, 3, 5

FINANCIAL/TERMS:
Cash Investment: $17.9-80K
Total Investment: $17.9-289K
Minimum Net Worth:
Fees: Franchise - $7.5-15K
 Royalty - $102/Mo.; Ad. - 0%
Earnings Claims Statement: Yes
Term of Contract (Years): 10/5
Avg. # of Employees: 1 FT, 0 PT
Passive Ownership: Not Allowed
Encourage Conversions: Yes
Area Develop. Agreements: No
Sub-Franchising Contracts: No
Expand in Territory: Yes
Space Needs: NA

SUPPORT & TRAINING:
Financial Assistance Provided: Yes (D)
Site Selection Assistance: NA
Lease Negotiation Assistance: NA
Co-operative Advertising: No
Franchisee Assoc./Member: No
Size of Corporate Staff: 0
On-going Support: A,B,C,D,E,F,G,h,I
Training: Minimum of 3 weeks on-the-job;
 6 days national training facility

SPECIFIC EXPANSION PLANS:
US: All US
Canada: All Canada
Overseas: Japan, UK, Germany, Australia, New Zealand, S. Africa

Founded in 1920, Snap-on has over 90 years of experience in the tool industry. Today it has become a $2.6 billion S&P 500 Company that is universally recognized by professionals as providing the highest quality products in the industry. As the #1 professional tool brand in the world, Snap-on produces over 22,000 products and operates more than 4,200 locations in over 130 countries. Snap-on offers a variety of products, including hand tools, tool storage solutions, diagnostic equipment, information and management systems, and "under-car" shop implements such as hydraulic lifts and tire changers. Snap-on serves the auto, marine and aviation industries, as well as the government, utilities, and industrial organizations.

Snap-on commands tremendous brand name recognition and an exemplary reputation within the industry. Snap-on is driven by a determination to provide the best quality, practical, original and innovative solutions to customers. In joining the Snap-on Tools team, franchisees enjoy this impeccable reputation, as well as benefit from selling the most demanded product in the market.

Operating Units	4/30/2006	4/30/2007	4/30/2008
Franchised	3,035	2,992	3,015
% Change	--	-1.4%	0.8%
Company-Owned	93	165	196
% Change	--	77.4%	18.8%
Gateway	227	220	181
% Change	--	-3.1%	-17.7%
Total	3,355	3,377	3,392
% Change	--	0.7%	0.4%
Franchised as % of Total	90.5%	88.6%	88.9%

Investment Required
The initial license fee for a Snap-on Tools Standard Franchise ranges from $7,500 to $15,000. In some instances, Snap-on offers a Gateway Franchise Program with a reduced required investment and a two-year term.

Snap-on provides the following range of investments required to open your initial standard franchise. The range assumes that all items are paid for in cash. To the extent that you choose to finance any of these expense items, your front-end investment could be substantially reduced.

Item	Established Low Range	Established High Range
Initial License Fee	$7,500.	$15,000

Initial Inventory	$72,000	$76,000
Technology Package	$0	$2,700
Uniforms & Supplies	$0	$800
Accounting Service Set-up Fee	$0	$220
New Franchisee Credit Marketing Program	$480	$500
Van & Van Delivery Charge	$6,190	$98,650
Van Merchandise Displays and Safety Equipment	$1,600	$4,000
Van Insurance (3 months)	$250	$1,250
License	$200	$2,400
Acquisition/Development of Revolving Accounts	$52,500	$52,500
Other Equipment, Fixtures and Expenses	$150	$350
Computer Software License Fee	$770	$770
Invoice Line of Credit Repayment	$0	$20,000
Additional Funds (3 Months)	$8,974	$13,940
Total Initial Investment	$150,614	$289,080

Ongoing Expenses

Franchise owners operating a Standard Franchise pay a monthly license fee equal to $102 and a monthly computer software maintenance fee equal to $26.

What You Get—Training and Support

Snap-on is dedicated to providing franchisees considerable training and support. Prior to opening, Snap-on provides an initial inventory of products, uniforms, and a technology package that includes a computer, applicable software, a printer and an electronic signature pad. Franchisees attend an initial training program that involves approximately 135 hours (45 hours/ week) of on-site training and 50 hours of classroom instruction at the Snap-on training facility in Ft. Worth, Texas. The classroom training covers a range of topics including selling skills, computer training, business management and product knowledge regarding hand tools, tool storage, trade-ins, diagnostics and power tools. The in-the-field training program is conducted by Snap-on personnel, including a franchise developer and a business manager or sales developer, and lasts a minimum of three weeks.

Snap-on offers ongoing training and support, including assistance with bookkeeping and operational methods, inventory control methods, product knowledge, and sales and marketing. Assistance is available to franchisees through visits from field representatives, over the phone, in meetings, and through internet communication. Snap-on conducts national advertising campaigns and may opt to administer specialized, regional advertising programs as deemed appropriate. Furthermore, Snap-on arranges and distributes promotional materials.

Territory
Snap-on does not grant exclusive territories.

Spherion

*recruiting and staffing excellence*ˢᴹ

2015 South Park Place SE
Atlanta, GA 30339
Tel: (800) 903-0082 (770) 303-6770

Fax: (678) 867-3190
Email: sandymazur@spherion.com
Website: www.spherion.com
Sandy Mazur, EVP License/Franchise Division

Spherion franchise opportunities provide individuals a chance to join an exciting and rewarding industry: temporary staffing. We placed millions of workers in flexible and full-time jobs during our nearly 60 years in business.

Continuous innovation and decades of growth have helped Spherion become an industry leader. Entrepreneur Magazine ranked Spherion "Best Staffing Service" for five straight years. Our franchisees contribute their talent, commitment and passion to building our brand.	

Term of Contract (Years):	10/5
Avg. # of Employees:	3 FT, 0 PT
Passive Ownership:	Not Allowed
Encourage Conversions:	Yes
Area Develop. Agreements:	No
Sub-Franchising Contracts:	No
Expand in Territory:	Yes
Space Needs:	1,500 SF

BACKGROUND: IFA Member
Established: 1946; First Franchised: 1956
Franchised Units: 149
Company-Owned Units: 248
Total Units: 397
Dist.: US-493; CAN-0; O'seas-0
North America: 46 States
Density: 29 in FL, 29 in CA, 27 in OH
Projected New Units (12 Months): 10
Qualifications: 5, 4, 1, 3, 4, 4

FINANCIAL/TERMS:
Cash Investment: $100-170K
Total Investment: $98-164K
Minimum Net Worth: $100K
Fees: Franchise - $25K
Royalty - 3-6%/25%; Ad. - 0.25%
Earnings Claims Statement: Yes

SUPPORT & TRAINING:
Financial Assistance Provided: No
Site Selection Assistance: Yes
Lease Negotiation Assistance: Yes
Co-operative Advertising: Yes
Franchisee Assoc./Member: No
Size of Corporate Staff: 525
On-going Support: A,B,C,D,E,NA,G,H,I
Training: Additional self-paced instruction; over 112 hours in-office instruction

SPECIFIC EXPANSION PLANS:
US: Targeted cities in US
Canada: No
Overseas: No

Spherion Staffing Services is a leading recruiting and staffing provider that specializes in placing administrative, clerical, customer service and light industrial candidates in temporary and full-time opportunities. As an industry pioneer for more than 60 years, Spherion has sourced, screened and placed millions of individuals in virtually every industry through a network of offices across the United States and Canada.

Services include temporary, permanent, and outsourced placement within Accounting & Finance, Engineering, Healthcare, Industrial, IT, Legal, Life Sciences, and Office. Other offerings include payrolling, managed services, recruitment process outsourcing and HR consulting solutions.

Operating Units	12/31/2008	12/31/2009	12/31/2010
Franchised	166	150	149
% Change	--	-9.6%	-0.7%

Company-Owned	396	264	248
% Change	--	-33.3%	-6.1%
Total	562	414	397
% Change	--	-26.3%	-4.1%
Franchised as % of Total	29.5%	36.2%	37.5%

Investment Required
The fee for a for a Spherion franchise is $25,000.

Spherion provides the following range of investments required to open your initial franchise. The range assumes that all items are paid for in cash. To the extent that you choose to finance any of these expense items, your front-end investment could be substantially reduced.

Item	Established Low Range	Established High Range
Initial Franchise Fee	$25,000	$25,000
Computer System	$3,650	$5,750
Real Property	$1,000	$3,200
Leasehold Improvements, Furniture, and Fixture	$7,500	$15,500
Equipment	$4,650	$10,500
Opening Advertisement	$1,050	$5,150
Training Expenses	$1,050	$3,100
Start-Up Supplies	$510	$1,050
Insurance	$2,100	$7,850
Utility Expenses	$160	$1,100
Professional Fees	$1,050	$5,200
Business Franchises	$160	$1,100

Hardware Installation	$720	$1,100
Additional Funds (12 months)	$51,500	$82,500
Total	$100,000	$168,000

On-going Expenses
Spherion franchisees pay a temporary sales fee, a full-time placement fee, and a computer system support fee, among others.

Franchisee Satisfaction
A critical component of the due diligence process is that you, as a prospective franchisee, have a strong sense of existing franchisee satisfaction. Please review the franchisor's ratings below for this extremely important information.

World-Class Franchise®

How do you rate Spherion in terms of:	Rating*
Overall quality of this franchisor	100%
Overall training and support supplied by franchisor	100%
Would you recommend this franchise to a prospective franchisee?	100%
General opportunity provided by this franchisor system	98%

* Independent Audit of Existing Franchisees Who Rated Spherion as Excellent, Very Good, or Good

What You Get—Training and Support

Spherion bills clients, pays employees, and provides the software applications and cutting-edge technology that connect the franchisee to the corporate network, eliminating many operating costs associated with running the business. Some of the highlights include a dedicated and experienced field support team, extensive training programs, in-depth mentoring and coaching programs, centralized recruiter tools and helpful resources, comprehensive pre-opening procedures, centralized sales and marketing tools, national sales programs, web-based technology and tools, 100% financing for temporary payroll, client invoicing, accounting support, and a call center for operations and technical help.

Once the franchisee is in business, Spherion provides the following assistance and services: standardized sales and promotional programs, campaigns and materials; prepare and pay the weekly payroll for temporary employees, including payroll taxes and other direct labor costs, prepare and deliver invoices to the customer for full-time placements and for services performed by temporary employees, and provide all other management information services and equipment previously discussed; provide advice and guidelines in handling customer collections, arrange and pay for accrued expenses relating to insurance; a mailing list of current and prospective customers, full-time placement applicants and temporary employees; match the national advertising fee paid by the franchisee.

Territory

Spherion grants exclusive territories.

Sport Clips

SportClips
(HAIRCUTS)
IT'S GOOD TO BE A GUY

P.O. Box 3000-266
Georgetown, TX 78627
Tel: (800) 872-4247 (512) 869-1201
Fax: (512) 868-4699
Email: franchise@sportclips.com
Website: www.sportclips.com
Gayle Longmore, Director of Franchise Support

Our fun, sports-themed, men's and boys' haircutting concept is so unique, it's made us the fastest-growing haircutting franchise in the country. This is a great recession-resistant business that's all cash, no receivables, and no industry experience is necessary. Better yet, you keep your current job, while building your Sport Clips business for the future.

BACKGROUND: IFA Member
Established: 1995;   First Franchised: 1995
Franchised Units: 820
Company-Owned Units: 21
Total Units: 841
Dist.:   US-820; CAN-0; O'seas-0
  North America: 38 States
  Density: 64 in CA, 57 in IL, 171 in TX
Projected New Units (12 Months):   150
Qualifications: 4, 5, 1, 1, 3, 5

FINANCIAL/TERMS:
Cash Investment: $100K
Total Investment: $153-277K
Minimum Net Worth: $300K
Fees: Franchise-$25K-1 lic., $39.5K-2 lic.,
                                       $49.5K-3 lic.
  Royalty - ;   Ad. - $300/Wk.
Earnings Claims Statement: Yes
Term of Contract (Years):   5/5
Avg. # of Employees: 6-8 FT, or PT
Passive Ownership: Allowed
Encourage Conversions: No
Area Develop. Agreements: Yes
Sub-Franchising Contracts: No
Expand in Territory: Yes
Space Needs: 1,200 SF

SUPPORT & TRAINING:
Financial Assistance Provided: Yes (D)
Site Selection Assistance: Yes
Lease Negotiation Assistance: Yes
Co-operative Advertising: Yes
Franchisee Assoc./Member: No
Size of Corporate Staff: 60
On-going Support: NA,NA,C,D,E,F,G,H,I
Training: 1 week locally for manager; 1 week
          locally; 5 days Georgetown, TX for franchisee

SPECIFIC EXPANSION PLANS:
US: All US
Canada: No
Overseas: No

The haircutting industry is worth nearly $50 billion, but the majority of hair salon franchises are tailored towards women. Sport Clips is designed to fill a niche in the hair industry by providing great haircutting experiences for men, including an exciting sports-themed environment where customers can watch sports while getting their hair cut. This innovative concept has made Sport Clips a highly successful, fast growing franchise opportunity, with more than 820 locations in 38 states.

Since 1993, the Sport Clips team of experts has refined every aspect of the franchise, and it has paid off—Sport Clips is consistently awarded

395

accolades as one of the top franchise opportunities, including *Entrepreneur Magazine*'s Top 50 fastest growing franchises and *The Wall Street Journal Start Up*'s Top 25 Performers.

Operating Units	12/31/2008	12/31/2009	12/31/2010
Franchised	610	650	729
% Change	--	6.6%	12.2%
Company-Owned	13	19	21
% Change	--	46.2%	10.5%
Total	623	669	750
% Change	--	7.4%	12.1%
Franchised as % of Total	97.9%	97.2%	97.2%

Investment Required
The initial fee for a Sport Clips franchise is $25,000.

Sports Clips provides the following range of investments required to open your initial franchise. The range assumes that all items are paid for in cash. To the extent that you choose to finance any of these expense items, your front-end investment could be substantially reduced.

Item	Established Low Range	Established High Range
Initial Franchise Fee	$25,000	$25,000
Expenses While Training	$1,000	$2,000
Opening Inventory	$4,000	$6,000
Fixtures and Equipment	$35,000	$45,000
Leasehold Improvements	$35,000	$100,000
Supplemental Services Fee	$3,000	$5,000
Professional Fees	$1,000	$5,000
Permits and Licenses	$1,000	$3,500

Lease Deposit	$0	$5,000
Signage	$4,000	$8,000
Misc. Opening Costs	$3,000	$5,000
Insurance	$1,200	$2,400
Grand Opening Advertising	$15,000	$15,000
Additional Funds (3 Months)	$25,000	$50,000
Total Investment	$153,200	$276,900

On-going Expenses
Sport Clips franchisees pay royalty fees equal to 6% of net sales, weekly advertising fees equal to the greater of 5% of net sales or $300, and a weekly local advertising co-op fee of up to $300. Other fees payable by the franchisee include a training fee equal to the greater of 1% of net sales or $55 per week, a monthly computer software maintenance fee of $30, and meeting registration fees not to exceed $1,000 during the term of the franchise agreement.

What You Get—Training and Support
Initial training begins with five days of comprehensive classroom and on-the-job instruction at corporate headquarters in Georgetown, TX, and covers all facets of running a Sport Clips business: business operations, team development, marketing, and Sport Clips standards. Franchisees also receive one week of hands-on training at their store location.

Sport Clips continues to support franchisees after store opening with ongoing training and responsive phone support. Sport Clips provides local, regional, and national advertising programs, and partners with national and local sports teams and NASCAR to promote individual store locations.

Territory
Sport Clips grants exclusive territories only for the initial five-year term of the franchise agreement.

Spring-Green Lawn Care

SPRING-GREEN®

Your Neighborhood Lawn Care Professional®

11909 Spaulding School Dr.
Plainfield, IL 60585
Tel: (800) 777-8608 (815) 436-8777
Fax: (815) 436-9056
Email: franinfo@spring-green.com
Website: www.springgreenfranchise.com
James Young, President

Spring-Green delivers lawn and tree care services nationwide. Our service is centered on the beautification of middle class and affluent neighborhoods and communities. Our customers include both residential and commercial establishments. Spring-Green services include lawn, tree, and shrub fertilization as well as disease and perimeter pest control. Spring-Green has been beautifying the environment for more than 30 years as your national lawn care team.

BACKGROUND: IFA Member
Established: 1977; First Franchised: 1980
Franchised Units: 90
Company-Owned Units: 26
Total Units: 116
Dist.: US-116; CAN-0; O'seas-0
   North America: 25 States
   Density: 15 in WI, 10 in NC, 30 in IL
Projected New Units (12 Months): 15
Qualifications: 4, 3, 1, 3, 2, 4

FINANCIAL/TERMS:
Cash Investment: $30K
Total Investment: $99-212K
Minimum Net Worth: $160K
Fees: Franchise - $30K
   Royalty - 10-8%; Ad. - 2%
Earnings Claims Statement: Yes
Term of Contract (Years): 10/10
Avg. # of Employees: NA FT, NA PT
Passive Ownership: Not Allowed
Encourage Conversions: Yes
Area Develop. Agreements: No
Sub-Franchising Contracts: No
Expand in Territory: No
Space Needs: NR

SUPPORT & TRAINING:
Financial Assistance Provided: Yes (I)
Site Selection Assistance: NA
Lease Negotiation Assistance: NA
Co-operative Advertising: No
Franchisee Assoc./Member: Yes/Yes
Size of Corporate Staff: 22
On-going Support: NA,NA,C,D,E,F,G,h,i
Training: 1 week corporate headquarters; ongoing online pre-training; minimum 2 days each, 3 annual on-site visits

SPECIFIC EXPANSION PLANS:
US: All except AK, AZ, CA, CT, NY, NV, ND, HI, MA, ME, MS, NM, RI, VT
Canada: No
Overseas: No

Founded in 1977, Plainfield, Illinois-based Spring-Green Lawn Care has been delivering both traditional and organic lawn and tree care services nationwide for 35 years. Its service is centered on the beautification of residential and commercial customers in middle-class and affluent neighborhoods and communities. Spring-Green is an attractive opportunity for candidates who do not want to be tied to a storefront operation, retail hours, or set appointments. Franchisees enjoy a lifestyle of being in an outdoor-based business with recurring revenues that allow the business to continue to scale. Spring-Green currently has 119 franchises operating in 26 states, and projections call for 10 new franchises in 2012.

Operating Units	12/31/2008	12/31/2009	12/31/2010
Franchised	92	93	93
% Change	--	1.1 %	0 %
Company-Owned	26	26	26
% Change	--	0 %	0 %
Total	118	119	119
% Change	--	0.8%	0 %
Franchised as % of Total	78 %	78.2 %	78.2 %

Investment Required
The franchise fee for Spring-Green franchise is $40,000 for a geographic territory containing 60,000 single family dwelling units.

Spring-Green provides the following range of investments required to open your initial franchise. The range assumes that all items are paid for in cash. To the extent that you choose to finance any of these expense items, your front-end investment could be substantially reduced.

Single Territory

Item	Established Low Range	Established High Range
Initial franchise Fee	$30,000	$40,000
Vehicles, Equipment, and Fixtures	$5,398	$6,798
Technology Equipment and Software	$1,864	$1,864
Opening Inventory and Supplies	$4,500	$4,500
Initial Marketing Campaign Fee	$25,000	$25,000

Training Expenses	$950	$950
3 Months Rent	N/A	N/A
Security Deposits	N/A	N/A
Miscellaneous Opening Costs	$2,000	$2,000
Additional Funds – 6 Months	$30,000	$30,000
Total	$99,712	$111,112

Multiple Territories

Item	Established Low Range	Established High Range
Initial franchise Fee	$60,000	$80,000
Vehicles, Equipment, and Fixtures	$7,132	$8,532
Technology Equipment and Software	$1,864	$1,864
Opening Inventory and Supplies	$4,500	$4,500
Initial Marketing Campaign Fee	$50,000	$50,000
Training Expenses	$950	$950
3 Months Rent	$0	$3,900
Security Deposits	$0	$850
Miscellaneous Opening Costs	$2,000	$2,000
Additional Funds – 6 Months	$60,000	$60,000
Total	$186,446	$212,596

Ongoing Expenses

Spring-Green's franchisees pay ongoing royalty fees of 8-10% of gross sales, advertising fund contributions of 2% of gross sales, regional advertising fees up to 2% of gross sales, and others.

Franchisee Satisfaction
A critical component of the due diligence process is that you, as a prospective franchisee, have a strong sense of existing franchisee satisfaction. Please review the franchisor's ratings below for this extremely important information.

World-Class Franchise®

How do you rate Spring-Green in terms of:	Rating*
Overall quality of franchisor	94%
Franchisor encourages high standards of quality performance	97%
Initial opening support provided by franchisor	92%
Helpfulness of franchisor's field representatives	96%

* Independent Audit of Existing Franchisees Who Rated Spring-Green as Excellent, Very Good, or Good

Training and Support
Spring Green's provides a dedicated startup support team. They will work on the areas that are most critical to the success of your business and they never give up. As you leave your initial training program, a member of this team will follow you home and begin your in-field training, helping with staff development, computer support, and in-field marketing support. You can expect daily communication, conference calls with your peers, and multiple field visits your first and second year.

On-going support is provided in the following areas: hiring and staff development, technology support, financial support, agronomic support, equipment, and marketing. Spring-Green believes that the collective knowledge

401

of its franchise owners can propel the franchise organization faster than anyone can accomplish individually. This means that as your franchisor, we need to be listening as much as we are teaching and coaching. Throughout the year, we will offer franchise owners the opportunity to meet with their peers and discuss relevant topics surrounding the Spring-Green business. We may facilitate these meetings, but more importantly franchise owner feedback is helping to shape our agenda.

Territory
Spring-Green grants protected areas.

TGA Premier Junior Golf

Premier Junior Golf

390 N. Sepulveda Blvd., # 1060
El Segundo, CA 90245
Tel: (310) 333-0622
Fax: (310) 607-0055
Email: info@golftga.com
Website: www.golftga.com
Steve Tanner, National Program Director/COO

TGA Premier Junior Golf is a youth development program for kids ages 3-15 to learn golf at their schools before transitioning to the golf course. TGA conducts a 5-level after-school golf enrichment program through a curriculum that includes lesson plans in character development, physical fitness and educa-

tional principles such as math, English, science and history. TGA programs are conducted indoors or out, on concrete or grass, year-round. As students matriculate through the five level enrichment program, TGA provides opportunities for them to apply the skills they've learned at their schools to a golf course through TGA camps, clinics and tournaments at partner facilities. A geographical TGA franchise provides the tools, training, and support needed to partner with schools and CBOs, make golf course relationships, find instructors, promote the program to parents, run great programs, integrate into community, and scale the business quickly. TGA receives regular PR exposure locally and nationally, has strong partnerships with golf and education organizations, has won several industry awards and has a non-profit arm called TGA Golf Foundation.

BACKGROUND:	IFA Member
Established: 2003;	First Franchised: 2006
Franchised Units:	47
Company-Owned Units:	2
Total Units:	49

Dist.:	US-49; CAN-0; O'seas-0	Sub-Franchising Contracts:	No
North America:	22 States	Expand in Territory:	No
Density:	4 in MI, 4 in FL, 12 in CA	Space Needs:	SF
Projected New Units (12 Months):	8-12		
Qualifications:	3, 4, 4, 4, 3, 4	**SUPPORT & TRAINING:**	
		Financial Assistance Provided:	No
FINANCIAL/TERMS:		Site Selection Assistance:	Yes
Cash Investment:	$5-40K	Lease Negotiation Assistance:	NA
Total Investment:	$13-57K	Co-operative Advertising:	No
Minimum Net Worth:	$50K	Franchisee Assoc./Member:	Yes/Yes
Fees: Franchise -	$5-40K	Size of Corporate Staff:	6
Royalty - 8%;	Ad. - 0	On-going Support:	A,B,C,D,NA,NA,G,H,NA
Earnings Claims Statement:	No	Training:	3-4 days in your territory
Term of Contract (Years):	5/5		
Avg. # of Employees:	1 FT, 5-15 PT	**SPECIFIC EXPANSION PLANS:**	
Passive Ownership:	Allowed, But Discouraged	US:	All US
Encourage Conversions:	NA	Canada:	No
Area Develop. Agreements:	Yes	Overseas:	No

TGA Premier Junior Golf is a youth development program for kids ages 3-15 to learn golf at their schools before transitioning to the golf course. TGA conducts a five-level, after-school golf enrichment program through a curriculum that includes lesson plans in character development, physical fitness, and academic subjects such as math and science. As students matriculate through the five level enrichment program, TGA provides opportunities for them to apply the skills they've learned at their schools to the golf course through TGA camps, clinics, and tournaments at partner facilities.

A geographical TGA franchise provides franchisees with the training and support needed to partner with schools and CBOs, make golf course relationships, find and train instructors, market the programs to parents, run fun and engaging programs promoting student retention, and integrate into the community.

Operating Units	12/31/2008	12/31/2009	12/31/2010
Franchised	34	40	44
% Change	--	17.6%	10%
Company-Owned	2	2	3

% Change	--	0.0%	50%
Total	36	42	47
% Change	--	16.7%	11.9%
Franchised as % of Total	94.4%	95.2%	93.6%

Investment Required

The franchise fee for a TGA Premier Junior Golf franchise ranges from $5,000 to $45,000.

TGA Premier Junior Golf provides the following range of investments required to open your initial franchise. The range assumes that all items are paid for in cash. To the extent that you choose to finance any of these expense items, your front-end investment could be substantially reduced.

Item	Established Low Range	Established High Range
Initial Franchise Fee	$5,000	$45,000
Office Equipment and Computer System	$0	$2,250
Initial Equipment Package	$1,500	$1,500
Insurance	$500	$1,000
Additional Training	$150	$450
Additional Initial Expenses	$1,000	$2,000
Additional Funds (3 Months)	$5,000	$10,000
Total Initial Investment	$13,150	$62,200

Ongoing Expenses

Royalty fees for Total Golf Adventures franchisees vary based on initial franchise fee. If the franchise fee is less than $10,000, franchisees pay the greater of 8% of gross revenue or $200 per month during the first year, $350 per month during the second year, or $500 per month during the third to fifth years.

If the franchise fee is more than $10,000, franchisees pay the greater of 8% of gross revenue or $300 per month during the first year, $450 per month during the second year, or $600 per month during the third to fifth years.

Training and Support

Training includes a mandatory two-day program that details TGA's strategic development, marketing strategies, and operating procedures. Franchisees learn everything necessary to run a successful TGA franchise, including staffing procedures, TGA computer and website operations, and customer relations. Training is conducted by veteran TGA franchise owners who continue to provide support to franchisees post-training.

Territory

TGA Premier Junior Golf grants exclusive territories.

Tradebank International

1000 Laval Blvd.
Lawrenceville, GA 30043-5913
Tel: (888) 568-5680 (678) 533-7119
Fax: (678) 533-7129
Email: tgerry@tradebank.com
Website: www.tradebank.com
Todd M. Gerry, President, SVP Marketing

Tradebank International is one of the world's largest trade exchanges with offices in over 70 cities across the United States, Canada and East Central Europe. Since 1987, we have completed over two million transactions, each helping our clients conserve cash and make their business more profitable. Tradebank franchise owners are responsible for new client acquisition and management throughout their protected territories. There are unlimited possibilities.

BACKGROUND:

	IFA Member
Established: 1987;	First Franchised: 1995
Franchised Units:	57
Company-Owned Units:	16
Total Units:	73
Dist.:	US-55; CAN-18; O'seas-0
North America:	15 States, 4 Provinces
Density:	7 in TN, 12 in ON, 12 in GA
Projected New Units (12 Months):	12
Qualifications:	4, 3, 5, 3, 2, 1

FINANCIAL/TERMS:

Cash Investment:	$10K
Total Investment:	$10-50K
Minimum Net Worth:	$25K
Fees: Franchise -	$35-50K

Royalty - 30-40%;	Ad. - 0%	Site Selection Assistance:	NA
Earnings Claims Statement:	No	Lease Negotiation Assistance:	NA
Term of Contract (Years):	5/5/5	Co-operative Advertising:	Yes
Avg. # of Employees:	3 FT,	Franchisee Assoc./Member:	Yes/Yes
Passive Ownership: Allowed, But Discouraged		Size of Corporate Staff:	12
Encourage Conversions:	NA	On-going Support:	A,B,C,D,E,NA,g,h,I
Area Develop. Agreements:	Yes	Training: 3 days broker; 5 days opening;	
Sub-Franchising Contracts:	Yes	5 days Atlanta, GA	
Expand in Territory:	Yes		
Space Needs:	400 SF	**SPECIFIC EXPANSION PLANS:**	
		US:	All US
SUPPORT & TRAINING:		Canada:	All Canada
Financial Assistance Provided:	Yes (D)	Overseas:	All Countries

The barter industry is a $20 billion a year industry and continues to be one of the fastest-growing, most dynamic industries in the world. Currently, 92% of Fortune 500 companies and hundreds of thousands of other businesses around the world barter. In barter's simplest form, two businesses or professionals exchange items of equivalent value. Tradebank, however, opens up a whole new dimension. Now you don't have to find someone who simultaneously needs your product or service and has what you need. Only one trader's need is required to start the process, and with the help of a trade broker, everyone comes out with something they need. Barter is a business tool that can be used by anyone who wants to conserve cash and increase profits – the market is basically limitless.

Today, barter has become a highly valued business method and Tradebank International is a world leader, with offices across the United States, Canada and East Central Europe. Tradebank International is revolutionizing the barter industry using the internet and state-of-the art proprietary technology. Since its start in 1987, Tradebank International has completed over two million transactions, each helping clients conserve cash, expose new customers to their product or service, and make their business more profitable.

Operating Units	12/31/2008	12/31/2009	12/31/2010
Franchised	30	39	44
% Change	--	30.0%	12.8%

Company-Owned	22	16	15
% Change	--	-27.3%	-6.3%
Total	52	55	59
% Change	--	5.8%	7.3%
Franchised as % of Total	57.7%	70.9%	74.6%

Investment Required

The fee for a Tradebank International franchise is $30,000 for a territory with a population of up to 500,000; there is an additional $5,000 for each 500,000 additional population.

Tradebank International provides the following range of investments required to open your initial franchise. The range assumes that all items are paid for in cash. To the extent that you choose to finance any of these expense items, your front-end investment could be substantially reduced.

Item	Established Low Range	Established High Range
Initial Franchise Fee	$30,000	$30,000
Office Rent and Deposit	$400	$1,200
Legal Fees and Accounting Fees	$600	$1,400
Business Licenses	$65	$180
Insurance	$200	$500
Utility Deposits	$200	$500
Office Supplies and Printing	$400	$1,000
Telephone System	$300	$1,000
Additional Funds (6 Months)	$9,600	$18,600
Total Initial Investment	$41,765	$54,380

Ongoing Expenses

Tradebank International franchisees pay ongoing fees including a new client retainer fee of $495 per client, a client's second account fee of $100 per client, and a quarterly accounting fee of $29.95 per client. Additional fees payable by franchisees include a brokerage fee of 12% to 14% of client purchases. Please note that the new client retainer fee, quarterly accounting fee, and brokerage fee are subject to a partial refund.

What You Get—Training and Support

Tradebank provides franchisees with a step-by-step procedure to set up their new franchise and offers ongoing, comprehensive training. Tradebank provides franchisees with five days of training in marketing and sales at Tradebank's corporate office, and five days of training in a franchisee's new territory. A professional Tradebank Broker is assigned to all new franchisees to provide the broker services until franchisees attain their first 50 clients, allowing them to concentrate their efforts on building their business. Later, additional training is provided for franchisees and their brokers in brokerage and operational concepts. Ongoing training is also offered at national and international training seminars.

The Tradebank corporate office does all "back office" bookkeeping, updating accounts on a 24/7 basis for every transaction fee charged to the clients and providing all clients with monthly statements. Marketing programs, strategies, and material including a monthly newsletter for clients are supplied. Additionally, Tradebank International provides franchisees with direct access to their proprietary internet trading system, a copy of the operations Reference Manual, and a phone system for customer assistance.

Territory

Tradebank International grants exclusive territories.

TSS Photography

TSS Photography®

2150 Boggs Rd., # 200
Duluth, GA 30096
Tel: (866) 877-4746 (678) 740-0800
Fax: (678) 740-0808
Email: tom@tssphotography.com
Website: www.tssphotographyfranchise.com
Tom Bouhan, Manager of Franchise Development

TSS Photography has been the leader in youth, sports, and school photography since 1983. We specialize in team picture days, sports photography, school photography, special events, and tournament photos. It has been said that when you do what you love, you'll never have to work another day in your life. And our franchise owners love what they do. They especially love controlling their own destiny, the flexibility of scheduling their own time, and calling their own shots. Please visit www.tssphotography.com for more information.

BACKGROUND:

	IFA Member
Established: 1983;	First Franchised: 1984
Franchised Units:	213
Company-Owned Units:	1
Total Units:	214
Dist.:	US-207; CAN-0; O'seas-7
North America:	42 States
Density:	17 in TX, 15 in FL, 16 in CA

Projected New Units (12 Months):	20
Qualifications:	3, 3, 1, 1, 3, 4

FINANCIAL/TERMS:

Cash Investment:	$9,075-22,545
Total Investment:	$30.25-75.15K
Minimum Net Worth:	
Fees: Franchise -	$11.1-39.05K
Royalty - 0;	Ad. - $60-175/month
Earnings Claims Statement:	No
Term of Contract (Years):	10/10
Avg. # of Employees:	1-2 FT, 1-2 PT
Passive Ownership:	Allowed, But Discouraged
Encourage Conversions:	Yes
Area Develop. Agreements:	Yes
Sub-Franchising Contracts:	No
Expand in Territory:	Yes
Space Needs:	100 SF

SUPPORT & TRAINING:

Financial Assistance Provided:	No
Site Selection Assistance:	NA
Lease Negotiation Assistance:	NA
Co-operative Advertising:	No
Franchisee Assoc./Member:	No
Size of Corporate Staff:	35
On-going Support:	A,B,C,D,NA,NA,G,h,I
Training:	16 hours photography (infield) - franchisee's territory;24 hours sales and marketing - franchisee's territory; 8 hours; initial photography - franchisee's territory

SPECIFIC EXPANSION PLANS:

US:	All US
Canada:	No
Overseas:	No

As an established leader in youth, school, and sports photography, TSS Photography offers many advantages to potential franchisees. For over 25 years, TSS Photography has specialized in team picture days, sports photography, school photography, special events, and tournament photos. With over 200 franchise locations, TSS Photography serves nearly two million children every year. As the industry leader throughout the U.S., TSS Photography is committed to consistently providing customers quality service, excellent products, and fresh designs every year.

A TSS Photography franchisee can expect to benefit from this impeccable track record, excellent reputation, and a time-tested, proven business model. As a home-based business with no need for a storefront, studio, or commercial office space, TSS Photography offers a low overhead cost and therefore more room for profit. Furthermore, TSS franchisees receive immediate cash flow and no royalties, meaning that franchisees retain all profits from a given photo shoot. TSS Photography offers an innovative product line, an established business model, a flexible schedule, and a chance for artistic expression in individuals searching for a reliable and exciting franchise opportunity.

Operating Units	12/31/2008	12/31/2009	12/31/2010
Franchised	229	215	211
% Change	--	-6.1%	-1.9%
Company-Owned	0	0	0
% Change	--	--	--
Total	229	215	211
% Change	--	-6.1%	-1.9%
Franchised as % of Total	100%	100%	100%

Investment Required
The fee for a TSS Photography franchise ranges from $5,000-$39,050, depending on the plan purchased. The plans are based, in part, on the population within the territory, although additional territory can be purchased during or after signing the Franchise Agreement. There is a discount for multiple franchises. Due to the current economic climate, TSS Photography has also recently created a Stimulus Package Plan that offers a reduced initial franchising fee for relatively more territory.

TSS Photography provides the following range of investments required to open your initial franchise. The range assumes that all items are paid for in cash. To the extent that you choose to finance any of these expense items, your front-end investment could be substantially reduced.

Item	Established Low Range	Established High Range
Initial Franchise Fee	$5,000	$39,050
Training expenses	$0	$2,000
Real Estate/Office	$50	$100
Office Equipment, Supplies and Furniture	$200	$3,300
Cameras and Other Photo-graphic Equipment	$13,950	$13,95
Computer Equipment	$2,000	$2,000
Initial Inventory	$2,200	$3,500
Transportation	$750	$1,500
Advertising	$0	$1,000
Misc. Opening Costs	$250	$1,250
Website Maintenance	$0	$250
Processing & Developing Fees	$500	$1,250
Additional Funds (3 Months)	$1,000	$6,000
Total Initial Investment	$30,250	$75,150

Ongoing Expenses
TSS Photography franchisees pay processing and developing fees, which are subject to a surcharge ranging from 0% to 10% depending on the plan purchased, and a monthly sales and marketing fund contribution ranging from $60 to $175, depending on the plan purchased.

Training and Support
TSS Photography provides franchisees with computer hardware and software equipment, photography equipment, a marketing starter kit, presentation materials, a photo presentation book, and initial photo samples to aid in business start-up. TSS Photography provides extensive in-field and

corporate training in sales, marketing, business development, photography, and computer systems for new franchisees. Additional trainings and classes are available to all franchisees through the TSS University.

TSS holds an annual convention where franchisees exchange ideas, attend workshops and see new products. During the year, TSS conducts mini-conferences throughout the country that assist franchisees in expanding and growing their business. In addition to ongoing trainings and conventions, TSS Photography offers franchisees an array of professional services, including a customized website, online purchasing, sales brochures, presentation materials, assistance in contacting potential customers, and advice for purchasing additional photographic equipment.

Territory
TSS Photography grants exclusive territories with populations ranging from 100,000-400,000, depending on the plan purchased.

Vanguard Cleaning Systems

Cleaning Systems

655 Mariners Island Blvd., # 303
San Mateo, CA 94404
Tel: (800) 564-6422 (650) 287-2400
Fax: (650) 591-1545
Email: mheisten@vanguardcleaning.com
Website: www.vanguardcleaning.com
Mark Heisten, VP Business Development

Vanguard Cleaning Systems has been successfully franchising in the commercial cleaning industry since 1984. Vanguard is currently seeking unit and master franchisees in the United States and Canada. Currently, Vanguard has 1,847 franchises and 51 regional offices.

BACKGROUND:	
Established: 1984;	IFA Member
	First Franchised: 1984
Franchised Units:	2,152
Company-Owned Units:	0
Total Units:	2,152
Dist.:	US-1,996; CAN-156; O'seas-0
North America:	27 States, 2 Provinces
Density:	386 in CA
Projected New Units (12 Months):	700
Qualifications:	2, 2, 3, 1, 3, 5

FINANCIAL/TERMS:	
Cash Investment:	$1.5-35K
Total Investment:	$7.5-35K
Minimum Net Worth:	$1.5-35K
Fees: Franchise -	$7-35K
Royalty - 5%;	Ad. - NR

Earnings Claims Statement:	No	Site Selection Assistance:	NA
Term of Contract (Years):	10/10	Lease Negotiation Assistance:	NA
Avg. # of Employees:	FT, 1 PT	Co-operative Advertising:	No
Passive Ownership:	Allowed, But Discouraged	Franchisee Assoc./Member:	No
Encourage Conversions:	Yes	Size of Corporate Staff:	26
Area Develop. Agreements:	No	On-going Support:	A,NA,C,D,NA,NA,G,H,I
Sub-Franchising Contracts:	Yes	Training:	2 weeks+ at local regional office
Expand in Territory:	Yes		
Space Needs:	NA	**SPECIFIC EXPANSION PLANS:**	
SUPPORT & TRAINING:		US:	All US
Financial Assistance Provided:	Yes (D)	Canada:	All Canada

Vanguard Cleaning Systems has a network of 2,000 franchisees who provide high quality janitorial services for over 10,000 commercial cleaning accounts. Founded in 1984, Vanguard's franchisees provide a wide range of specialized janitorial services—general office cleaning, carpet cleaning, hard surface floor care, window washing, power washing, and green cleaning—to many different commercial facilities including office complexes, industrial buildings, medical offices, schools, and more.

Vanguard provides its franchisees with expert training and customer service support. Vanguard franchisees can choose to grow their business at their own pace, allowing for a steady revenue base at start-up and lower risk.

Operating Units	12/31/2008	12/31/2009	12/31/2010
Franchised	1,458	1,734	1,996
% Change	--	18.9%	15.1%
Company-Owned	0	0	0
% Change	--	--	--
Total	1,458	1,734	1,996
% Change	--	18.9%	15.1%
Franchised as % of Total	100%	100%	100%

Investment Required

The fee for a Vanguard Cleaning Systems franchise ranges from $7,650 to $37,000.

Vanguard Cleaning Systems provides the following range of investments

413

required to open your initial franchise. The range assumes that all items are paid for in cash. To the extent that you choose to finance any of these expense items, your front-end investment could be substantially reduced.

Item	Established Low Range	Established High Range
Initial Franchise Fee	$7,650	$33,300
Equipment	$0	$50
Licenses and Permits	$25	$150
Insurance	$200	$600
Additional Funds (3 months)	$200	$300
Total Initial Investment	$8,075	$34,400

Ongoing Expenses
Vanguard Cleaning Systems franchisees pay ongoing royalty fees of 10%, plus business support service fees. Equipment leasing is available to select franchisees for an additional fee.

Training and Support
Vanguard provides franchisees with an initial training program that includes DVD instruction, web-based/e-learning, interactive classroom training and practical, on-site activities explaining the methods and procedures of the commercial cleaning system. During training, we strive to ensure that each franchise owner has the know-how to deliver high quality service to clients on a consistent basis.

Vanguard supports franchisees on an ongoing basis by maintaining support personnel at each office. Vanguard's staff is available for franchisees to answer any questions about customer cleaning needs or to provide technical assistance. Vanguard provides monthly billing services of client accounts, assists in customer relations and provides collections support.

Territory
Vanguard Cleaning Systems does not grant exclusive territories for its unit franchises.

Alphabetical Listing of Franchisors